CW00346149

'A most enjoyable book, with some wonder
splendid stuff. Mr Bowler is not afraid to make his points, or
to argue his case with due emphasis'   *World Soccer*

'Bowler deserves credit for doing his homework – there are
plenty of interviews here and the pages turn easily enough'
Planet Football

'Quite simply, a joy'   *Football 365*

'Dave Bowler is a biographer of some distinction in the
sporting world . . . informative and entertaining. Bowler
interviewed a whole host of players, past and present, for this
excellent piece of English footballing history. It is well worth
having a look at'   *Morning Star*

'An excellent, highly readable book'   *Sport First*

'Dave Bowler offers a timely exploration of what it means to
play for England . . . He has unearthed some fascinating
recollections from bygone days'   *Time Out*

Dave Bowler is the author of *Shanks: The Authorized Biography of Bill Shankly*; *No Surrender: A Biography of Ian Botham*; *Danny Blanchflower: A Biography of a Visionary* and *Winning Isn't Everything: A Biography of Sir Alf Ramsey*. He lives in Tamworth, Staffordshire.

THREE LIONS ON THE SHIRT

Playing for England

DAVE BOWLER

ORION

An Orion paperback
First published in Great Britain, by
Victor Gollancz in 1999
This paperback edition published in 2000 by
Orion Books Ltd,
Orion House, 5 Upper St Martin's Lane,
London WC2H 9EA

A CIP catalogue record for this book
is available from the British Library.

ISBN 0 75283 705 2

Printed and bound in Great Britain by
The Guernsey Press Ltd, Guernsey, C.I.

Contents

....

Acknowledgements

This book could never have been begun, never mind completed, without the generous assistance of several generations of England players who were good enough to submit to my questioning. I am especially grateful to the following: Viv Anderson, Jimmy Armfield, Joe Baker, Colin Bell, Paul Bracewell, Ivor Broadis, Trevor Cherry, George Cohen, Bryan Douglas, Robbie Earle, Les Ferdinand, Sir Tom Finney, Tim Flowers, Mark Hateley, Steve Hodge, Sir Geoff Hurst, Francis Lee, Gary Lineker, Rodney Marsh, Roy McFarland (congratulations on promotion!), Paul Merson, Gary Neville, Phil Neville, Maurice Norman, Peter Osgood, David Platt, Cyrille Regis (there's only one Cyrille Regis), John Richards, Graham Rix, Bobby Robson, David Sadler, Alan Smith, Ray Wilson, Sir Walter Winterbottom and Ray Wood. In addition, John Roberts made numerous useful suggestions – if you hurry to your local bookstore, you can still lay your hands on his book on the Busby Babes, *The Team That Wouldn't Die*. No better value for money can be found, providing you've already bought this book. Thanks too to Billy Watson and James Forbes for their support. Thanks too to my agent Tanja Howarth, who is great at putting the frighteners on and making offers people can't refuse. Keep on fighting.

All the Internet users out there should point their browsers in the direction of the greatest footballing site known to man, at *www.matchdayusa.com*, you know it makes sense – thanks to David and Richard at *Matchday* for their help and employment. Additional information has come from the publications listed in the bibliography, so my thanks and admiration go out to those authors.

Putting this together has been an especially fraught project, and without the help of a number of people, I would never have finished it. So you can blame them. Ian Preece has, as usual, been an editor *par excellence*, and a good friend in difficult times. My thanks to him, Angela, Thurston and Edie. Pete Nicholls has displayed his customary talent for drinking and talking at the same time, for which I am truly grateful. And Hackenbush sends greetings to Bryan.

Without Camille's encouragement, suggestions, arguments and early morning alarm calls, you'd have been lucky to get this before the next World Cup. Her critical appreciation and general interest in photography were equally vital. As was her ability to make me think. *Grazie mille*, Camille.

Most of all, thanks to Mom and Dad, for all the usual reasons and several thousand new ones.

To Mom and Dad

Nothing is more important than
friends you can believe in

Thank you
David

Introduction

'Only seconds to go here at Wembley Stadium, England lead West Germany 3–2. The hosts have one hand on the World Cup but the Germans come forward again. Beautiful interception by Moore. He looks up; he can see his captain making a run into the opposition half. Excellent through ball from Moore, slices the German defence in half. England's skipper has the ball deep in the opponent's half, there are some people on the pitch. He lashes the ball from fully 35 yards past the German keeper to give him his fourth of the game, what an incredible performance! England are the World Champions! And how fitting that this inspirational captain should lead his exhausted men up those famous 39 steps and take the golden trophy from Her Majesty the Queen.'

Of course, I was that goalscoring genius in a dream that persisted for about a decade. As I got older, Debbie Harry replaced the Queen, and she gave me the key to her hotel room rather than the World Cup, and that became a lot more exciting than football, but you get the picture. You probably have a similar memory; it's the enduring dream of kids all over England. Playing for your country at Wembley, and winning the World Cup for good measure.

Despite the combined efforts of Admiral, Umbro and the Football Association to undermine it with frequent changes and irritating amendments, are there any more powerful sporting images than that of the pristine England football shirt, any more potent symbols of achievement than wearing the three lions? They've been worn by the heroes of our national game, from Matthews to Moore, Bloomer to Shilton, Edwards to Shearer. The shirt has graced the stadia of the world, as England spread word of the game to the four corners of the globe and were repaid for this kindness by being overtaken by countries who quickly learned to play it better.

The history of the England team has spanned a period of massive change – in the game itself, in its organization and in the attitudes of the society that has shaped it. When the first ball was kicked against Scotland in 1872, it was the era of the amateur, on and off the field. By the time David Batty's penalty was saved at France '98, we were in the age of the professional superstar, the highly paid mercenary who can hawk his talents around the world, a world away from the wage slaves of just forty years ago. Today's players travel in first-class luxury on chartered jets where their pre-war predecessors stood up in third-class railway compartments. From turning up to play on the day of the game, tournaments are now prefaced by month-long training camps. But one thing has remained consistent, no matter what the changing times: the pride with which so many wear an England shirt. Bobby Robson, later able to dispense caps as the national manager, sums up the emotion: 'When you're selected for England, it's the biggest personal achievement; you have to be proud of that. You're being told you are the best player in the country at that time. I know it's a matter of the coach's choice but I was thrilled, it was something I'd lived for, worked for, longed for; it was wonderful. I felt very proud about it.'

The early years of England's footballing history were marked, disfigured, by a sense of superiority wrapped up in stifling insularity. The rudimentary travelling arrangements of the pre-jet age made international competition difficult and our island position made us more isolated than other European countries. Even so, it showed a chronic lack of vision to refuse to take part in the first three World Cup tournaments of 1930, 1934 and 1938, following the withdrawal from FIFA in 1928 over payments to amateurs during the Olympic Games. In truth, the view of the Football Association was that England need not be troubled by such second-rate competition, that everyone accepted our standing as the world's premier football nation. As World Cup winner Ray Wilson points out: 'The attitude was we'd invite the winners over, give 'em a good hiding and send 'em back home. Seems to me that if you're the best, you should prove it by winning the thing over and again. It's in the record books that Uruguay and Italy won the World Cup, not that we might have been a better team.' That short-sightedness meant a generation of giants such as Tommy Lawton, Raich Carter, Eddie Hapgood, Stan Cullis and Joe Mercer never graced the World Cup finals, nor picked up the medals that could have been theirs. It might even have given England the chance to become the first nation to win three World Cups and take the Jules Rimet trophy outright.

Nowadays, that suspicion of foreign competition has disappeared. The World Cup and European Championships are at the heart of our national aspirations and our self-image. Successes such as those at Italia '90 or Euro '96 galvanize the entire nation, making icons of the figureheads, men like Gazza, Stuart Pearce, Alan Shearer or David Seaman. The game is now central to the nation's emotional health, a faintly ridiculous but nonetheless undeniable position. And the pressures that rest on the shoulders of David Beckham, Michael Owen and Sol Campbell are often intolerable. But there is no shortage of young footballers desperate to take a place in the England side. The rewards are considerable but so are the perils. Who'd have wanted to swap places with Chris Waddle in 1990, Gareth Southgate in 1996 or Paul Ince in 1998?

In the days of the early pioneers – long-forgotten names such as J.C. Clegg, A.K. Smith, Ottaway, Chenery and Morice, England's first forward line – internationals were played for prestige and as friendship games (if any match with Scotland could be termed that). Largely battling the home nations, Scotland provided the only test, Wales and Ireland representing minor challenges. Now, every match is ripe with significance and, as each coach is at pains to tell us, there are no easy games left, mainly because England don't play Lawrie McMenemy's team.

International football is a multimillion-pound operation that lives on bogus promotion and dubious hyperbole. As we end the millennium, the football is in danger of getting lost beneath the onslaught of Adidas, Coca-Cola, World Cup diaries, xenophobic press reporting, satellite TV and the bizarre changes wrought on the game from the parallel universe inhabited by the denizens of FIFA. The truth is, if you can strip all that away, you're left with what football is really about, the glory game. And for any English boy, that glory finds its greatest fulfilment in winning the right to wear the three lions on the shirt.

I

In the Beginning

Curiously, given England's historical position as the birthplace of Association Football, the international game was delivered to an expectant world by the Auld Enemy, in Glasgow, at the West of Scotland Cricket Ground, Partick, on 30 November 1872. At least England were involved in the inaugural game, making a trip north of the border in order to do useful missionary work, aiding the spread of the game in Scotland, where rugby held sway. International rugby had begun earlier the same year, and the Football Association thought it might give football an important boost to emulate that event, generating greater public interest and awareness in the game. Organizing an inaugural fixture from scratch and without any precedent proved difficult, not least financially. There was no professional football in England at the time, so by definition the entire side was composed of amateurs. There were no match fees to pay, but travelling expenses had to be found. An impecunious FA prevailed on the clubs to pay for their players, perhaps explaining why nine different clubs were represented, Oxford University the only side to provide more than one player to England. Given the later treatment of poorly paid professionals, it's revealing that these well-to-do amateurs were subsidized, illustrating the masters and serfs philosophy within the higher echelons of the footballing Establishment that prevailed for at least a century.

Anti-climactically, the match itself ended in a 0–0 draw, the respected journal *Bell's Life* reporting 'a splendid display of football in the really scientific sense of the word and a most determined effort on the part of the representatives of the two nationalities to overcome each other.' With the Scots so supposedly backward in their development of the game, it was a surprise to many observers that they held their own so comfortably against the far more experienced Englishmen. What's more astonishing is that there were no goals, with England playing a 1–1–8 formation, the Scots a 2–2–6 line-up. How did fourteen forwards fail to find one goal between them? Possibly it was because the game was seen as an opportunity for the upper crust to indulge in a little 'hacking'. Lord Kinnaird was rated the finest player of his day, though he was never rewarded with an England cap, but was typical of many footballers at the time, famed for his ruthlessness. Talking to the one-time president of the FA Sir Francis Marindin, Kinnaird's mother expressed the fear that her son Arthur would some day come home with a broken leg. 'Never mind,' Marindin consoled her, 'it will not be his own.' Despite that kind of violence, or perhaps because of it, the game was adjudged a rousing success, around 4000 attending. A rematch was offered in England for the following March at the Kennington Oval. This time, the FA asked their member clubs to submit names for inclusion in the side and seventy names were put forward. With the FA Cup the only senior club competition at the time – the Football League did not come into existence until 1888 – measuring the merits of individual clubs and players wasn't easy. To address this trials were held in order to find the best players to teach the Scots a lesson. Why they were so keen to prove their credentials is a mystery given that tickets were not made easily available to the public. Instead, you could only get them from the secretaries of the FA clubs, and only then at the extortionate price of a shilling (5p). Fortunately, while the toffs were being allowed in in their carriages, large numbers of the great unwashed were able to sneak in and see the game for free. There was more goalmouth activity this time around, as England won 4–2, the teams changing ends after each goal was scored.

Many thought that England would now begin to assert their quality in future matches, but that was to prove the height of early

English supremacy. They lost four and drew one of the next five games between the two as the match became an annual event, the venue alternating between countries. The story of those games was of an English side based solely on individualism being regularly undone by the Scots, whose side was largely drawn from just two or three clubs and so had excellent teamwork to sustain it. Typical of the shambles that was the England side in 1875, the team all wore different coloured shirts. Not only that, goalkeeper Carr arrived late, but the ten men managed to keep the game goalless for the few minutes until he arrived. A pity he did, because England conceded two goals and only got a draw. Maybe if he hadn't turned up, they might have won. Things got worse three years later when England were taken apart 7–2, a correspondent of *Bell's Life*, signing himself 'A Disgusted Englishman', complaining that 'they played very selfishly, each one appearing to play entirely for himself and not for the success of the side.' England must have learned from that, because the following year they fought back from 4–1 down to win 5–4, recording their first win in this fixture in six attempts.

It was the Scotland game that mattered, even though the Welsh had also formed a national side by now. The fixture nearly came to a halt following a dispute in 1880 over the laws of the game. N.L. Jackson, founder of the Corinthians and assistant secretary at the FA, wrote, 'The Scots having refused to acknowledge the off-side rule as recently passed by the Football Association, Arthur Kinnaird and I, who were in charge of the team, had instructions not to permit our players to go on the field unless the referee and our opponents agreed to adopt the new rule. After a heated discussion which lasted until long after the time appointed for the kick-off, the Scottish authorities finally did agree, but unfor-tunately the referee did not adhere by the rule when it came to the point, and so unpleasant was the match in consequence that it almost led to a rupture between the two associations.' A 5–4 Scottish win did little to improve the FA's humour, but, fortunately, the breach was healed and the Scots were free to maintain their early dominance. England were in some disarray by now, for though they were able to beat Ireland 13–0 in Belfast, they lost to

Wales for the first time in 1882 in Wrexham. The Welsh having shown these new footballing credentials, the Home International competition was set up in 1883–84. Inevitably, it reflected that the balance of power within these islands lay in Scotland, as they won four and shared two of the first seven Championships, England managing to share it twice and win it once. England's sole outright success came in 1888, when they simultaneously achieved their first ever win in Scotland, 5–0, the *Daily Mail* reporting that 'England were trained to their work as never a team sent out by the English association were before.' The beginning of this English renaissance can be traced to the 1885 fixture, for although England only managed a 1–1 draw, it heralded a brief interest in tactics. England lined up with a 2–3–5 formation, the famous WM system that was to persist for another seventy-five years, not just in England, but over much of the world.

Essentially, the formation employed two full-backs, left and right, whose role was almost entirely defensive, though they played more centrally than the full-backs we know today. Ahead of them were three half-backs strung across the field, midfielders as we would known them now. Typically, they were the fetchers and carriers of the side, helping out in defence when necessary – Herbert Chapman was eventually to employ the centre half-back as a purely destructive stopper – attempting to break down opposing moves by tackling and interception, then setting their own forwards in motion once they'd won the ball. There were five forwards, comprising two wingers, whose job was to get crosses in for the centre-forward, typically a tall, powerful figure, good in the air. Alongside him were two inside-forwards who tended to be more creative players, able to carve out chances and score too. When it was first unveiled, the critics savaged the system as being too negative and ignoring the first principle of football, the need to score goals. Nowadays, any coach advocating a 2–3–5 line-up would be incarcerated in the nearest asylum for being too reckless.

Linked with the sudden desire to think more deeply about the game was the spread of professionalism through the 1880s and the eventual introduction of the Football League Championship in

1888. This led to a general improvement of the standard of football played, even though those footballers were not professionals in the sense that we know them today. Initially, at least, the pros had two jobs, getting paid to play and perhaps being rewarded with better full-time jobs, fixed by the football club into the bargain. As time moved on, some players were able to make a good living from football alone – West Bromwich Albion's England winger Billy Bassett earned a massive £43 a week! For all that they were making comparatively good money, the pros were still second-class citizens, not allowed to eat with the amateurs, required to call them 'sir' and defer to them at all times. Ultimately, the professionals had the last laugh, as the amateurs were squeezed off the field and into boardrooms and the corridors of power, where they've proved to be infinitely more dangerous.

Leading on from the professionalism that swept the land, the FA were forced, very reluctantly, to increase the England match fee from ten shillings (50p) to £1. Whether it was mere coincidence, or a reflection that superior talents demand rewards and will only then give of their best, can never be proven, but the 1890s were England's most satisfactory decade thus far. Rarely now were players drawn from smaller clubs, with long-forgotten names like Wednesbury Strollers, Birmingham Excelsior, Remnants, Clapham Rovers, First Surrey Rifles, Lancing Old Boys and Darwen. Instead the mighty clubs of the Football League, teams like Preston, Aston Villa and Blackburn, began to make their presence felt, imbuing the side with the professional disciplines and a greater adherence to team play. So strong were England that in both 1891 and 1892 they were able to play Wales and Ireland on the same day with separate teams, winning all four fixtures by 4–1 and 6–1 respectively in 1891 and winning both 2–0 in 1892. In the later years of the decade, these were treated as trial games, with Wales facing an all-amateur side and Ireland an all-professional eleven. But Scotland were the test and between 1890 and 1899, England won six and drew two of the ten fixtures, a massive shift in the balance of power.

England were winning comfortably, but all in the garden was

not perfect. The FA were required to ban betting by players and player discipline was also problematic, with frequent sendings off. There were frequent crowd control problems too. In 1894 too many eager fans besieged Parkhead, crammed into the ground, and there were injuries as barricades collapsed and people were crushed. Two years later, there were similar problems when an estimated crowd of 60,000 caused some to spill on to the perimeter of the field. They then had things thrown at them by those in the stands who resented their advantageous position and they had to be herded back on to the terraces. In a chilling portent of events eighty and ninety years later, the authorities of the day proved that while the money was coming in, they weren't interested in learning any lessons. Tragically, the inevitable happened at Ibrox in 1902. The capacity of the ground was an incredible 80,000, but there were more than 100,000 in the stadium when the game began. Six minutes in, the new stand partially collapsed. It was a wooden structure, planks placed on steel uprights, but the swaying of the huge throng caused seven rows, each thirty yards wide, to cave in, dropping the poor unfortunates standing on the wood fully forty feet, then to have further bodies crash into them fractions of a second later as they too fell through the floor. Twenty-six people died, 587 were injured. With all the compassion that is legion in Establishment circles, the footballers of both sides were forced back on to the field just 18 minutes later, to prevent the crowd asking for their money back. Unsurprisingly, the game was a damp squib, ending 1–1 as the players dolefully went through the motions.

Looked upon as England's first true superstar, Steve Bloomer of Derby County was a supreme inside-forward who scored goals at an astonishing rate and who could create them too. He was a key figure in improving English results. Ivan Sharpe was a club colleague who went on to play for the British Olympic gold medal winning team at the 1912 Olympics, then became a respected journalist. Writing of Bloomer, he recalled that, 'He was called "Paleface" ... his build was slim yet, at inside-right, he was master of them all ... he had the golden gift of splitting a defence with one arrow-like, pin-pointed pass ... he could shoot with sudden touch . . . but our Stephen was a tyrant. He said what he thought, and if things were going wrong, his partner had no pleasant Saturday.' Setting himself the highest standards, Bloomer did not suffer fools gladly, and if he had done the donkey work to create a gilt-edged chance, he wasn't shy about pointing it out to the errant forward. Another of Bloomer's admirers was Sir Frederick Wall, who was the secretary of the FA from 1895 to 1934. Writing in 1935, he noted that 'Bloomer, of course, makes mistakes like everyone else, but he was the superior of everyone I ever saw as a scorer . . . some of the men chosen for England in these latter days have not his intense desire to win. Bloomer wanted the ball near goal and men like G.O. Smith and Goodall saw that he received it. Bloomer lived to shoot.' Collecting 28 goals in just 23 games, Bloomer was one of the central reasons why England came out of the doldrums and were able to enter the new century in good heart.

Obviously, England and Scotland continued to vie for the Home International Championship, and though England's results against the Scots were decidedly mixed, they often managed to get a share of the Championship as the Scots squandered points against Wales and Ireland, fixtures where they were far less fired up. Ireland managed to share the trophy with England and Scotland in 1902, then the Welsh took the title outright in 1907. This was a reflection of the improved organization in the two 'minnow' countries. It also illustrated that pitting themselves against the best quality opposition was the surest way to improving the quality of their own play – although occasionally they would still find themselves on the wrong end of a terrible beating, in general they were able to give Scotland and England a decent game, keep the score down to respectable levels and, from time to time, pinch a draw or even a victory. While this was good news for them, for England and for Scotland it made much worse reading. The obvious implication was that by simply playing against the same three opponents, year in, year out, they were atrophying. There was no new tactical stimulus, the strengths and weaknesses of each side were well known, and, ultimately, the sides were cancelling one another out in terribly predictable games. With professionals now making up almost the entire England team, it meant that their clubs could have call on them during the summer months as well as during the season. And if the clubs could use them, so could England, thereby making it possible for the FA to send an England party overseas to play international friendlies, giving our footballers valuable exposure to Continental methods.

Vienna was the site of England's first foray abroad, as the party embarked on a four-game tour. It was generally assumed that British football was the best in the world, but, nonetheless, it was intriguing to see how our players would fare on foreign shores. In June 1908, the world had little to teach. England opened by beating Austria 6–1, then beating them 11–1 two days later. Two days following that, in Budapest, Hungary were humbled 7–0, and on 13 June, the tour was wrapped up in Prague with a 4–0 win over Bohemia. Obviously, the opposition was nothing to write home about, but England, remember, weren't flying across Europe, going from one city to the next in an hour or two. They had to trek across the Continent by train, hardly ideal preparation for any match, so victory by such massive margins was a genuinely impressive achievement.

England's party had a number of top-class footballers in it. Amateur Vivian Woodward proved an admirable successor to Steve Bloomer and helped himself to six goals, but it was in the fullbacks that England had a pair of all-time greats, in West Brom's Jesse Pennington and Blackburn's Bob Crompton, who amassed an amazing 41 caps in his career at a time when England seldom played more than three games a year. Crompton retained the rightback berth from his debut in March 1902 through to England's last game before the Great War in April 1914, missing just four games in all that time. Sir Frederick Wall said of him: 'No matter how the ball reached him, he could take and spurn it away with either foot. He placed his returns and made every effort to keep the ball in play by imparting screw. His idea was to serve his forwards.' At a time when full-backs were simply expected to kick the ball forty yards upfield if it came anywhere near them, preferably with the opposing winger still attached to it, the progressive intentions of Crompton and Pennington were revolutionary, and many fine England performances were built on that bedrock.

The two returned to Europe the following summer when England played two internationals in Budapest within three days, winning 4–2 and 8–2, and then won 8–1 in Vienna the following day. These were displays of considerable athleticism and skill in the circumstances. Having put a toe in the Continental waters, the FA decided that the quality of opposition was so poor, it wasn't worth sending England out there again, and the next time we sent a team to Europe it was to fight in Ypres and on the Somme.

Yes the opposition was poor, but the FA showed typical short-sightedness and insularity in curtailing this experiment, and in not venturing into other countries to see what they had to offer. It wasn't as if we were dominating on the home front and had no need of any fresh ideas. Wales and Ireland had both become harder to beat and Scotland were regaining the upper hand. Following the 1–1 draw at Hampden in 1912, Bob Crompton was forced to admit that, 'The Scots are better grounded in theory, more intelligent, more skilful and have better use of the ball. If they were as fast as they were clever, England would stand little chance with them.' England managed to gain parity on the basis of hard work and greater physical presence, but as is increasingly the case today, skilful teams can always graft on a little muscle to their play. It is technical quality that is the hardest thing to find, and England lacked it. Surely, even in hammering European sides, they might have picked up one or two wrinkles on and off the field that could have been of benefit? But that wasn't the so superior English way. It was our game, we invented it, so we knew best.

Oddly, results suggested otherwise, but the football Establishment seemed loath to take the hint. Good players were still being produced, such as Sunderland's forward, Charles Buchan. If we could find men as good as him, could there be a problem? Buchan may have had the ability, but was he given the opportunity or the incentive to use it? Despite an excellent record in a tremendous Sunderland side that would only just miss the Double by

13

losing the Cup Final in the 1912–13 season, Buchan was given just one chance to stake his claim. Unsurprisingly, the game went past him without him really stamping his authority on it: 'It is the unaccustomed atmosphere that, I think, accounts for so many failures on a first appearance for England. The player is keyed up to such an extent that it is almost impossible for him to produce his normal game. That is why I consider that a youngster should be given more than one game before being discarded. If he is good enough for selection, he is good enough for a second chance.' All perfectly logical, but Buchan was denied that next game, dropped immediately in spite of scoring England's only goal, though admittedly changes were inevitable once England had lost 2–1 in Belfast, a catastrophic result, England's first ever defeat at the hands of Ireland. Buchan was naturally upset at the way the game turned out, and his reaction might just have swayed the selectors against him when picking the next team: 'When I got into the dressing room, despondent at the defeat, I sat next to George Elliott, the free-scoring Middlesbrough centre-forward. On the other side of him was one of the linesmen. He passed some remarks to Elliott about the right-wing – Mordue and myself – that I could not help overhearing and did not like. So, with the hot-headedness of youth, I told him what I thought about him. He turned out to be a member of the FA Selection Committee.'

Buchan was further marked down as a trouble-maker when he went to collect his expenses: 'When I was called in the room to be paid, the FA member in charge crossed out one of the items, the last on the list. It was for a cab from Sunderland station to my home, which I had included in advance. As I would not arrive in town until six o'clock on the Sunday morning, I thought I was entitled to the ride home. But the FA member said, "I can't allow this to pass. You must get home by tram. They run in Sunderland, I suppose?" "Yes," I replied, "but not on Sunday mornings." Before the First World War, the first Sunday tram in Sunderland started off at midday. Eventually he paid out with a very bad grace. I remember the bill, including the international fee, return travel from Sunderland and meals, amounted to £12 19s 10d (£12.99).

He handed me thirteen golden sovereigns and said, "Have you the two pence change?" '

Under that sort of management, it's little surprise that the Englishmen often seemed to lack the desire of some of their opponents. In a phrase that was to become appallingly familiar over the following five years, England's players were lions led by donkeys. Football was put away for the duration of the Great War, though, ironically, it made a brief appearance one Christmas Day, when men came out of the trenches and we played our first ever international against the Germans on neutral ground in no man's land, a fixture the FA hadn't managed to arrange in peacetime. The score is unrecorded, but the Germans probably won on penalties.

2

Perpetual Change

When the hideous waste that was the Great War – billed as 'the war to end all wars', it didn't – finally ground to a close, it took some time before international football could be resumed. Following the incredibly enlightened isolationist policy that led to the political and economic circumstances in which the Nazis could flourish, in 1919 the FA decreed that England would not play against the Central Powers – Germany, Austria and Hungary – nor against any other nation that dared to play them. As a result, England spent the next couple of years locked in battle with the other home countries. It wasn't the most successful policy, for England didn't get so much as a share of the Championship until 1926–27, not winning outright until 1929–30. Inevitably, the First World War meant the end of a number of careers – Crompton was the most obvious retirement from the scene, though his defensive partner Jesse Pennington carried on briefly, going on to play in what he considered the finest match he could remember, against Scotland in Sheffield in April 1920: 'It rained throughout the game, we could hardly keep our feet, especially in the first half when we faced the wind and rain. We had four goals put past us, but our forwards had got two for themselves. I felt sure at half-time we might still win and I told the team this. I have never seen such great football from two teams in such conditions. This was to be my very last international, but it left a lasting impression, not for that fact, but because of the craftsmanship of both sets of forwards.'

England won the game 5–4, some consolation for having been beaten 2–1 by Wales at Highbury. Charles Buchan scored England's goal in that game, his second international, and was then immediately dropped, just as had been the case after his debut in 1913.

Here was an obvious talent, but one of which the FA were wary. At a time when professionals should be seen and not heard, Buchan would commit that most heinous of crimes, having his own mind and speaking it. He was forced to play in an England trial game in 1921. Sitting in the hotel beforehand, he was approached by an FA official who told him, ' "You will have to get out of that chair, Buchan, when Mr Lewis [an FA committee man] arrives" ... I thought it disparaging to professional players as a whole and would have done anything rather than give up the seat.'

When Stan Cullis got into the England side in 1937, little had changed in the FA's attitude: 'We were told to get to the game the best way we could. In other words, it was left to you to decide how you would go to Wembley!'

After his mutiny, Buchan was surprisingly selected again, for the summer trip to Belgium in May 1921, scoring the first goal in a 2–0 win. Again, though, he courted controversy, duly noted by those in authority, who dropped him like a stone once more. This time, his supposed misdemeanour occurred on the field: 'I noticed the Belgian goalkeeper always took three or four strides with the ball before making a clearance. So I awaited my opportunity and, as he was about to kick clear, I put my foot in front of the ball. It rebounded quickly from the sole of my boot, flew hard up against the cross-bar and bounced clear. If the ball had gone into the net, I think there would have been a riot. From that moment, the crowd roared every time I got the ball. You see, you are not supposed to go anywhere near a Continental goalkeeper even if he had the ball in his possession.' England won convincingly enough, but the fact that the margin was down to just two goals should have been an early warning that these damned Continentals were getting better at the game. The hint was taken, to a degree, and the Belgians were invited to play at Highbury. Fifty years and four months after England had played their first international, foreign opposition was finally welcomed to our shores. It wasn't much of a welcome, England winning 6–1.

At least England persisted in playing overseas, visiting France and Sweden in the summer of 1923. Charles Buchan was in the party and, amazingly, was selected as captain for the first game, in Paris. He wrote in his autobiography, 'After half an hour's play, Hegan scored the first goal for England. As captain I was so delighted that I ran across and shook Hegan's hand. Though I never thought about it for the rest of the game, I got a severe reprimand from the FA member in charge of the team after it was over. It seemed that hand-shaking was one of those things that wasn't done ... I do not like to see the congratulations business carried to excess. As for kissing, which has been known, well, I think that's a disgusting show of emotion ... after the match, some of the professionals came to me and asked if they were to get their expenses and match fee that evening. They wanted to go out shopping and, of course, to see the sights of Paris. So I went to the member in charge and put the matter before him ... he refused point blank to pay until we got on the boat for home the next day. I tried to make him see what I thought was reason, but he said, "I am determined they shall go back with their money in their pockets." Though we pooled our resources, I fear that some of the players had a thin evening on the boulevards.'

England's new captain, who had again got on the scoresheet in a 4–1 win, was dropped from the two games in Sweden, where admittedly below strength sides won 4–2 and 3–1. Nor did Buchan get back into the side early in the new season when English football was shocked to the core when we only managed a 2–2 draw in Antwerp. Again, a weakened side had been selected, the Belgians taking full advantage and emphasizing how quickly European football was progressing.

The miscreant Buchan was recalled to the colours for the sixth and final time, to play in the first ever Wembley international, against the Scots in April 1924. The way in which he got the news was typical of the treatment he had received down the years: 'I was walking home from business when a friend stopped me in the

Receipt

JCT

2 x 0		£2.99 -20%	£0.00	£4.78
	Total			£4.78

Cash: £5.00
Cheque: £0.00
Card: £0.00
Voucher: £0.00
Credit Note: £0.00

Date: 08/03/2013 12:48:17

Till: TILL4
Operator: 14

Change: £0.22

VAT No. 633 7316 45

* 0 0 6 4 4 3 0 9 *

street. "Congratulations, Charlie," he said, "and may the ball run kindly for you." Very surprised, I asked him what it was all about. "Don't you know?" he asked. "You're England's centre-forward at Wembley, I've just heard it over the air." True enough, the first announcement had been made by radio. I boasted only a "cat's-whisker" set in those days and more often than not it failed to work ... In those days, professional players had the choice of a match fee or a gold medal. I chose the medal. I'm glad I did, for it was the last time I ever played for England.' Six games, four goals, never played in two successive matches. You'd be forgiven for thinking he played through a golden age of English football, but he did not. Buchan was victimized for not knowing his place and England suffered by his omission.

Throughout the 1920s England achieved very moderate success on the home front, while further afield the gap was narrowing in some quarters. Even so, there were still plenty of easy pickings to be had on the Continent, and the summer tour of 1927 proved that, when England trounced Belgium 9–1, Luxembourg 5–2 and France 6–0. Given that in the 1930 World Cup Belgium lost to the USA and Paraguay, the French were beaten by Argentina and Chile, and that even today Luxembourg are still hopeless, these were not results to leave English supporters flushed with pride.

Looking at England teams in that decade, there are few, if any names, which echo down the century until the arrival of Everton's Dixie Dean in 1927. Perhaps that should be no surprise. The 1914–18 war exacted a massive toll on the youth of the nation, decimating a whole generation of young men from whose ranks the players of the 1920s would have been drawn, leaving many dead or seriously wounded. For those lucky enough to survive the war unscathed, there had been little chance to improve their footballing skills. Football had all but closed down for the duration, there were no wartime leagues as there would be during the Second World War. There was almost no opportunity for promising players to play the game alongside their military duties, as so many did twenty-five years on. Those who had played pre-war were too old to make a real impact in the 1920s, so the new players who emerged were starting from scratch, with comparatively few experienced players from whom they might learn the game, which in turn led to a fairly poor standard of football in the domestic game for several years.

That made the arrival of Dixie Dean all the more thrilling. Like Bloomer before him, the advent of a natural goalscorer lifted England out of the doldrums, though even with his presence, they had a disastrous year in 1927–28, losing to all three home nations, including a crushing 5–1 defeat against the Scots, the 'Wembley Wizards' as history knows them. Great a player as Dean was – and 18 goals in 16 games is pretty useful – no forward can survive without service, and England regularly failed to provide it. It was as well that Dean could capitalize on half chances, or England's record through the period would have been even worse. According to Ivan Sharpe, 'Dean's heading was magnificent, his judgement of the ball's flight perfection; he could force, guide or glide it past the goalkeeper.' But he was the figurehead of a team that changed with bewildering regularity. In eleven post-war years, the England selectors tried 145 different players, so it was hardly surprising that the team played with no method or cohesion. The folly of that policy was finally brought home in Madrid on 15 May 1929, when Spain became the first foreign nation to beat England, 4–3.

Surprisingly, there was no great outrage at the result. It was blamed on the heat and on the weakened side England had taken on tour – only the full-backs, Cooper and Blenkinsop, had played in the 1–0 defeat at Hampden a month earlier; only Blenkinsop and outside-right Adock playing in the next game with Ireland five months on. It was a decision that reflected the supremacy of clubs who wanted their best players to rest and the arrogance of a sporting Establishment who saw foreign nations as pygmies, not worthy of our best players, the English cricket selectors sending a similar second-string side to the West Indies for an inaugural tour the following year, with equally poor results. The simple truth was that in 1929, Britain saw itself as the epicentre of the footballing world, superior in every respect. The only international fixture that grabbed the interest was the annual grudge game between

England and Scotland, which the British saw as a sort of informal World Championship decider. No other nations mattered because they were never considered to be equals.

At least that result woke a few people from their slumbers and greater consistency in selection and tactics were employed. In December 1931, that Spanish defeat was avenged with a 7–1 win at Highbury, following which the Spanish keeper, Zamora, rated as the best in the world, was in tears. So we could still beat the foreigners in friendlies, but by now we had already missed the boat where the most important games were concerned. Following a dispute over payments to amateurs in the 1928 Olympics, England had left FIFA, not for the first time. Antipathetic towards the governing body ever since its formation in 1904, they had initially withdrawn in 1920, simply to make the point that in the eyes of the FA, FIFA had no mandate to run the game. Point made, they joined again in 1924, even though the row over amateurism was already in the air. Eventually the amateurs in the FA committee rooms decided that paying chaps supposedly playing as amateurs wasn't good form, and took themselves out of FIFA again, thereby missing out on a trip to Uruguay, saving a considerable amount of money that would otherwise have had to be spent on travelling and accommodation for the players.

The truth is that the FA showed little or no interest in the competition. We were England, we were the best – despite the regular defeats in the Home Internationals – and the world had nothing to teach us. If foreign nations wanted to come to England to further their education, that was fine, but why did we need to enter a competition taking place thousands of miles away, just to confirm what everybody already knew? We were the masters. While this remained the guiding principle, in fairness, the FA had become a little less parochial and had even begun to play against the Central Powers again, in the summer of 1930. The most famous members of England's party were keeper Harry Hibbs, who amassed an impressive twenty-five caps over the decade, and inside-forward David Jack, a veteran of the 1923 'White Horse' Cup Final and the first player to be transferred for a five-figure sum when he moved from Bolton to Arsenal for £10,890 in 1928, though one young man who was to have a great England future passed up the chance of visiting Europe. Eddie Hapgood 'was invited to tour Austria and Germany with the FA party in 1930 ... but turned it down when Mrs Hapgood told me our first-born was on the way.' Hapgood missed a tough tour, the Germans holding England to a 3–3 draw before we drew 0–0 in Vienna against an extremely strong Austrian outfit who had improved immeasurably from the side that England were so used to crushing before the war.

Greater examinations lay ahead. It was Austria who gave England their sternest test on home soil in December 1932 when the 'wunderteam' arrived to play at Stamford Bridge. It was still an England side waiting to find the players of true greatness who would transform fortunes during the rest of the 1930s, but on home soil, against Continental outfits, they remained indomitable opposition. The Austrians showed enviable technique and employed a high-quality passing game that far outstripped anything England could offer, but the home side drew on pride and determination to counter the threat. The game ended in a 4–3 victory for England, no mean achievement against a team widely rated as the best mainland Europe had to offer.

As encouraging was the fact that new players of genuine quality were coming through, even if the selectors were slow to notice them, as they had been with Buchan. Arsenal's great goalscorer Cliff Bastin forced his way into the team in November 1931 after a string of excellent performances. As he said himself, 'Modesty apart, there can't be much surprise in your selection when the national press has been prophesying it at you for the past seven days ... it is seldom, if ever, from the Football Association that a player receives the news he has been picked for an international. The first communication he gets from them is the itinerary, which arrives a day or two after the team has been announced ... unfortunately for me, the English selectors of those days were not particularly intelligent in their methods. With them, the emphasis always seemed to be laid on the individual performance of a player, rather than on how he fitted in with the team as a whole. It was a queer and unsatisfactory system.' Though England beat Wales 3–1, Bastin had a difficult game on the left, being paired with E.W. Hine of Leicester, who played in an advanced position very close to his winger, where at club level Bastin thrived in his partnership with the great Alex James, who played much deeper, thus creating space for both men.

Obviously Bastin was a quality player, so he dropped out of the side for eighteen months. But someone of his ability could not be ignored for ever, not even by England's selectors. Stan Cullis, later an England colleague, said Bastin was 'an ideal winger who could adapt himself to any style of play. Bastin was clever, with superb ball control and the ability to position himself in the right place. He could cross a ball as perfectly as Matthews or Finney and he could shoot with both feet as well as most centre-forwards.'

Along with Arsenal colleague Eddie Hapgood, Bastin was selected for the summer tour of 1933, taking in Italy and Switzerland. By now he had established a reputation that stretched way beyond north London, as a focal point of the all-conquering Arsenal side constructed by the legendary Herbert Chapman – Chapman actually travelled with the England party in an unofficial capacity and helped the side tactically during the trip, working on the use of the defensive, destructive centre-half, which had proven so successful at Highbury. Bastin was apparently the star of the show and, 'I was idolised right from the very moment I stepped off the train in Rome ... the Italians seemed to be under the impression I was going to play their international team on my own!' Bastin did not disappoint the crowd, scoring England's goal in a 1–1 draw against the side which would carry off the World Cup a year later in the same stadium. The game was not without its mishaps for England, for as Bastin recalled, 'At half-time, there was momentary panic in the England camp when Herbert Chapman could not recover the key to the dressing room, which he had so carefully locked up.' As the game progressed, the Italians warmed more and more to Bastin's play and the game was 'made memorable by the spectators' constant cry of "Basta Bastin! Basta

Bastin!" which, not being so rude as it sounds, means "Enough of Bastin!" '

Although England were travelling abroad more often, it was still tremendously exciting for the players to visit these new countries. After all, in the 1930s and 1940s, no ordinary working-class Englishman would ever get to see the eternal city – unless, as in the case of Bob Paisley a decade later, it was as part of the liberating force during the war, and not even Rome is worth the risk of getting killed for. The England squad made the most of their opportunity, and as Bastin wrote, 'We saw the mighty St Peter's, with its wonderful sculptures by Michelangelo, its magnificent chapel by Benvenuto Cellini; the Roman Forum . . . the Colosseum . . . the ruins of Pompeii and the Capitol Hill where the geese once shrieked to the city that the Gauls would soon be at its gates. But what left the greatest impression on my mind was the regimentation of the city. Everybody seemed to be in uniform: policemen, postmen, nuns, taxi-drivers, even the very street cleaners wore some distinctive attire. It was my first experience of the Fascist State.'

Our footballers were among the few who actually saw the impact of Fascism at first hand, and they were therefore among the least surprised when war finally proved inevitable. Bastin and company even had first-hand experience of Mussolini: 'We stayed in Rome for a few days after the game and had audiences with the Pope and Mussolini . . . Mussolini had evidently decided to keep us waiting. At last the bodyguards came into the room, and, eventually, the dictator himself entered, resplendent in morning dress. Never have I known such an astonishing personality. I have always considered Herbert Chapman to have been outstanding in this respect, but compared with Mussolini on this occasion he was an utter non-entity. Yet the man did nothing. Nothing whatsoever . . . it was an effect which I, for one, shall never forget.'

Disparate experiences such as this not only broadened the mind, they sharpened the footballing skills, and now England had a team that could compete in the highest company, making it even more disappointing that the FA again refused to make any concessions towards FIFA, and missed out on the 1934 World Cup. Instead, they embarked on a brief, disappointing European tour, losing 2–1 to both Hungary and Czechoslovakia, Bastin complaining that, 'There were too many players slow in recovery included in our team; men who would just stand still after they had been beaten in a tackle.' On returning home, some of that dead wood was cut from the team. Nevertheless, in his role as travel correspondent, Bastin enjoyed the trip, particularly Budapest: 'The city was alive. Everybody seemed to be happy, and at night time the Hungarians lived their bright, gay life in the wayside cafés ... it was a baking hot day when we met the dashing Hungarians. They proved themselves one of the finest sides I have ever played against.' In contrast, in Prague, 'The people were unfriendly and sullen and I missed the spontaneous good-fellowship which the Hungarians had displayed.'

England already had some stalwarts of the 1930s in place, men like Arsenal's defensive hard-man Wilf Copping, whose two-footed tackling would have made Tommy Smith blanch, and the silver-haired Raich Carter, an inside-forward of extravagant quality, a ball player with a wide repertoire of passing skills allied to which was his priceless ability to put the ball in the back of the net. Arsenal's supremacy was underlined by the introduction of right-back George Male and typically rumbustious centre-forward Ted Drake, best remembered for scoring all seven goals in Arsenal's win over Aston Villa in 1935. Also waiting in the wings was a young man by the name of Stanley Matthews, who made his debut against the Welsh in Cardiff in September 1934. He was notified of his selection by FA letter: 'Dear Matthews, you have been selected ...' How fortunate that diplomats of that quality were in charge of negotiations with the Germans throughout the 1930s, otherwise who knows what terrible things might have happened?

Despite scoring on his debut in a 4–0 win, usually the kiss of death, Matthews retained his place for the visit of the World Champions, Italy, to Highbury. The game deteriorated into one of the most brutal seen in this country. Cliff Bastin laid the blame for that squarely at the door of the Italians and their leaders: 'The

Italian team at that time was one of the finest in the world. They had won the World Cup earlier in the year and I knew that they would give us a very hard game. More was the pity, then, that Mussolini had offered them such terrific incentives [said to be £50 each] if they beat us that their play deteriorated in their over-eagerness to a patchwork series of clever moves and questionable tactics ... they were remarkably fit and tough and when I came into a tackle with one of them, it felt as if I had come up against a brick wall.'

Part of the problem can be ascribed to a difference in emphasis, however, for while the Englishmen complained about Italian cyn-icism, Hapgood found nothing wrong in 'Wilf Copping's famous double-footed tackle [which] was causing them furiously to think.' In Italy, such tackles were outlawed, so their attitude to Copping was one of horror. Even so, that did not excuse the calculated violence used by some of the visitors, notably on Eddie Hapgood: '[the ball] went high over me, and, as I doubled back to collar it, the right-half, without making any effort whatsoever to get the ball, jumped up in front of me and carefully smacked his elbow into my face ... they were kicking everything in sight ... it's a bit hard to play like a gentleman when somebody closely resembling an enthusiastic member of the Mafia is wiping his studs down your legs.' Hapgood was off the field for treatment for fifteen minutes (no substitutes in those days) but England clung on for a hard won 3–2 victory.

Eddie Hapgood was an emblem of the inter-war England team, much as Bob Crompton had been before 1914. A full-back and an excellent leader, he had the admiration of all his colleagues, Cliff Bastin writing that, 'Eddie had football developed into a meticu-lously exact science. His method of tackling was all his own. Never would you see him rush at an opponent hoping blindly for the best. If he did decide that a tackle was necessary, he would wait carefully until exactly the right moment and then ... presto: the ball was at his foot.' Stan Cullis backed that statement, adding, 'Every step he took had a purpose and every move carried the stamp of class ... I do not think I ever saw him completely mastered

26

by a winger.' Hapgood was fiercely proud of his place in the England side and was acutely aware of the rewards it brought: 'We were well rewarded for selection in the national side. Fee was £8 per man, while we were also allowed to keep our kit ... England shirts (with the badge taken off) are pretty good for cricket [and] you always had the option of a gold medal (value £8.8s).'

Scotland still provided a cornerstone of the fixture list, but the foreign challenge was now ever more important, and it was results against the foreign powers that were of the greatest interest. The summer visit to Austria and Belgium in 1936 was an especially taxing one, not made easier when the gullible English party fell for a con trick played by Austria's wily coach Hugo Meisl. Hapgood wrote, 'The morning of the match, [Meisl] called at our hotel and offered to show us the sights of Vienna. We jumped at the chance and set off on what became the longest tour I have ever made of any city – on foot. We walked for miles and I was beginning to bend at the knees when he said he must show us the birthplace of Johann Strauss. It was only round the corner said the wily Hugo. But that corner stretched another two miles.' Completely shattered, it was no surprise that England lost 2–1, going on to lose 3–2 in Brussels three days later. But it was typical of the shambolic organization that still dogged the national side. The great foreign nations like Austria and Italy had coaches who dealt with selection, tactics, teamwork, accommodation and so on. England seemed to lurch around the world like a bunch of package holidaymakers, with no one individual in charge of team affairs. The captain was required to give the team talk and Stan Cullis, later a successful manager himself, explained one such meeting: 'There was no team manager in those pre-war days, so the captain had to try to sort out the tactics. Stan Matthews would never offer suggestions, just sit there very quietly. I remember Raich once saying before a game, "Please talk to Stan, he never gives me the ball back!" and I said to him, "Never mind, just give it to him, and get into the penalty area."' Forgivable perhaps where a genius like Matthews was concerned, but far too simplistic for the increasingly complex world of international competition. Arsenal's Tom Whittaker often took

27

the role as trainer, but he was in no way comparable to Italy's Vittorio Pozzo, often regarded as the father of the modern game, a coach who recognized the value of tactical planning, of preparing to counter the opposition's strengths and of introducing new ideas to confound them on the field of play. International football was already a competitive business, and with Mussolini breathing down your neck, the incentive to mould a winning team was a powerful one. Pozzo was equal to the task, plotting games with the concentration of a chess grand master.

In contrast, because there was no tactical supremo, the England side remained wedded to the 2–3–5 format with seemingly little thought going into any possible alternatives. Our style of play was set in stone while the rest of the world was beginning to be more imaginative and experimental. Before the war, this was not so crucial – foreign sides had yet to come to any concrete conclusions, while England were carried along by a crop of excellent footballers who emerged together. The legacy of this smug insularity would not be fully revealed until our World Cup misadventures in the 1950s, but the seeds were sown in the pre-war years.

Scandinavia provided further problems in the summer of 1937. England thumped Norway and Sweden 6–0 and 4–0 respectively, then were set to wind things up in Helsinki, travelling by boat from Sweden. As Hapgood recalled, 'Our ship was held up for twelve hours on the treacherous rock-strewn waters of the Finland Archipelago. One scrape on the rocks and there wouldn't have been any more football for us.' Charles Buchan, by then a respected journalist, wrote, 'They were 24 hours late. They ran into fog during the Baltic crossing by boat and had an adventurous journey. I shall never forget reading the late L.V. Manning's story with headline streamers: £100,000 WORTH OF ENGLAND PLAYERS LOST AT SEA.' England took their irritation out on the Finns, winning 8–0. Having had such an easy run, the following summer the FA set England a far stiffer task with a tour of Germany, Switzerland and France, little more than a year before the start of the Second World War and amid the appeasement policy.

How sad that the game in Berlin is perhaps the most famous of

England's pre-war internationals, and mostly for the wrong reasons. Prior to the game, there was little inkling of what was to come as Matthews and his colleagues took in the city: 'What a trip that was! It took two days in the train to cross Europe, and once we entered Germany every other field seemed to contain an aerodrome ... we arrived in Berlin two days before the game and I went on a sightseeing tour with Bert Sproston. We did all the usual things and we were having a cup of tea in a café when suddenly everyone rushed to the exit. Women waved handkerchiefs and men stood stock still in the open doorway. Bert and I pushed our way through the crowd and on to the pavement to see what was happening. A column of SS motor cycle outriders appeared, followed by a couple of large black motor cars. It was Hitler. And wherever we went after that people wanted to tell us about him ... the people we met were absolutely mesmerised.'

The players were then given a tour of the infamous Olympic Stadium, site of Hitler's odious showpiece games of 1936. Matthews wrote, 'The shock came when we were shown to our dressing room. It was right at the top of a huge stand. We had to climb 200 steps to get there and it seemed to take for ever. We went up and down those steps six times that afternoon and believe me climbing steps can be hard work when the muscles are tired and cramp is setting in after playing on that lush turf.' Obviously the Germans were leaving nothing to chance in attempting to sap the energy and spirit of the Englishmen, but their efforts backfired amid controversy. Matthews recalled, 'The FA had decided that we should give the Nazi Fascist salute during the German national anthem. We were appalled ... I've never known such an atmosphere in an England dressing room ... the official view was that an international incident was to be avoided at all costs ... we were virtually under orders.' Matthews was appalled, but Bastin took a more phlegmatic view: 'Personally, I did not feel very strongly about the incident ... we gave our own salute immediately afterwards and it seemed to me that this palliated any indignity there might have been in stretching out our right arms in the Nazi fashion. If we had been requested to give the Nazi sign alone, then

I would have been angry. Certainly the German crowd appreciated our action. They cheered us to the echo.' In order to appease the angry Englishmen, the FA secretary Stanley Rous told the side, 'Win today, there'll be a case of cutlery for you.' That was the first time the FA had ever promised a bonus! It proved unnecessary, as the players were already indignant at their treatment and were determined to put on a good performance. Matthews recalled, 'The stadium was a mass of blazing red swastikas, thousands upon thousands of them – and the roar which greeted the German team was earsplitting . . . just behind our goal, in the middle of masses and masses of swastikas, two Union Jacks unfurled and a voice piped, "Let 'em have it, England!" What a moment!' In an incredibly tense atmosphere, England gave one of their finest displays, winning 6–3 to deny once again the spurious Nazi claims of racial supremacy, scoring a powerful political as well as sporting victory. And all this despite, as Bastin recorded, '. . . the odd garb of the referee. He wore leggings and a cloth cap. Neither of these facts upset us.' The ruthless focus of the professional athlete.

On the heels of the emotional turmoil of the Berlin game, it was hard for the side to regroup for a game against the Swiss in the altogether more congenial atmosphere of Zurich. Before the game, Stan Cullis remembered 'one of the FA party telling the lads in the dressing room before the match that, if they scored six goals, the crowd would still expect them to go for more.' That never became a problem, because England lost 2–1, in a game which Cliff Bastin 'would like to forget . . . a boys' match was played just before our own. This churned up the turf considerably. It is a villainous habit, this playing of "curtain-raisers" before a big game . . . it was quite the "dirtiest" game I have ever been unfortunate enough to play in.'

England got back on an even keel with a 4–2 win in France, but they were still attacked by the accompanying journalists for the defeat in Switzerland, causing Bastin to reflect, 'I have found that when England lose abroad, they are damned categorically; when they win, it is taken for granted.' *Plus ça change*.

The issue which the press should have concerned themselves

with was far more stark. As England were leaving Paris, the rest of the footballing world was converging on the city to participate in the third World Cup tournament, an event which England again treated with contempt. This crass stupidity had gone on for far too long, and it was surely time that it was addressed. But no, the FA, secure with their blinkered xenophobia, refused to countenance the idea that they might, just possibly, be wrong. Instead, we continued to busy ourselves with the Home Internationals, a series in which England had not distinguished themselves in recent years. Since the end of the war, Scotland had held the Indian sign over England, winning 11 and drawing 3 of 19 games, and England had not won in Scotland since 1927. England went into the 1939 game fresh from a 7–0 win over Ireland in Manchester, where Matthews had excelled himself. According to Stan Cullis, 'That day Stan ran Willie Cook, the fine Everton full-back, almost literally into the ground as he provided the passes which made all seven goals . . . I usually knew which way Matthews intended to go – but it made no difference. His reflexes were so quick that he always reached any given point before the unfortunate defender. He was an individualist who achieved his greatest triumphs without the help of any of his colleagues.'

Now going on to Hampden, Matthews had the privilege of trying to supply centre-forward Tommy Lawton, whom Cullis rated extremely highly: 'All in all, I think Lawton was a better player than either Dean or di Stefano . . . a wonderful sense of timing, which is born in a player, and an ability to keep his eye on the ball for every second of its flight helped to give Lawton his mastery.' Sure enough, it was Lawton who got the winner, though for him, the game was as memorable for his first exposure to the Hampden roar: 'It was fantastic . . . the noise echoes back and eddies around the great bowl to smash into your eardrums. It was hard to think.'

To say the Englishmen were thrilled with their 2–1 win would be an understatement, as Joe Mercer explained: 'We played under the shadow of these Scots. Frankly we were fed to the teeth with it . . . England players generally never feel the same way about these matches as the Scots do. With them it's inbred, part of the national character ... it's bound up with history ... but this 1939 match was the one exception. This time, as I say, we'd had enough of it. We wanted to beat them at least as much as they wanted to whack us. And we did. After that, it was a great night I seem to remember.'

Playing conditions at Hampden had been so bad, the England side had to change shirts at half-time and so broke the Scottish hoodoo while clad in borrowed, unnumbered Queen's Park shirts. So pleased were they to win, they'd have played as 'skins' if necessary, Charles Buchan recording, 'Never shall I forget watching Eddie Hapgood bursting with enthusiasm at the success of his team. He jumped up and down with arms outstretched like a Maori doing a war-dance. He said afterwards, "I've played all these years and this is the win I've longed for. I could have jumped over the moon in delight."'

Europe was on the brink of war, so it was surprising to see that England set off on tour as usual in 1939, still more amazing to find that they went to Italy. There, they were besieged in their Milan hotel by admirers in scenes more reminiscent of Beatlemania. Hearing the crowds below his room, Eddie Hapgood said to room-mate George Male, ' "I'll give them something to Viva about." With which classic remark, I threw open the window, stepped out on to the balcony and gave the crowd a quick flip of my arm, the nearest I could get to a Fascist salute. In a moment I wished that I had stayed inside. The roar almost knocked me back into the room and was redoubled as I vanished.' If you think of the uproar that now surrounds equally ill thought out stunts such as Paul Gascoigne's impromptu flute solo in front of the Celtic supporters while he was with Rangers, it's instructive to recall that footballers have always done daft things, like the rest of us. The players of the past weren't angels. They just used to get away with it.

With the match in Milan turning into another political event, neither side wanted to give anything away. England forged a 2–1 lead for themselves, until Italy scored an equalizer when the ball was punched into the net. Unfortunate, but in the circumstances, maybe a draw wasn't a bad result. England were then beaten in

Yugoslavia, but regained their pride with a 2–0 victory in Bucharest, in an ill-tempered encounter. Stan Cullis recalled, 'They kicked us from pillar to post . . . once, Vic Woodley and I were kicked into the back of the net . . . if you misbehaved in those days, it could finish your career. One of the Romanians took the sole off Joe Mercer's boot, and I saw Joe threatening him, so I had to tell him, "If you do anything, I'll send you off, never mind the referee. We're going to finish with eleven men and win." He refused to leave the field and with his toes hanging out, Joe kept going until Tom Whittaker, the trainer, could patch up the damage with a roll of sticking plaster . . . In addition to his tremendous ability, the bow-legged Joe possessed the heart of a lion. Together these two qualities combined to make him just about the most effective left-half-back I ever saw.'

Years of football stretched ahead of the nucleus of the England side. Frank Swift, tall, commanding, an FA Cup and League Championship winner with Manchester City, looked ready to fill England's goal for years, pulling off the one-handed saves that were a speciality, Tom Finney recalling, 'He had hands like buckets.' Stan Cullis, a dominant, no-nonsense centre-half; Joe Mercer, adapting the wing-half position to his own vision of the game, playing with flair and originality, always looking to create openings, but always ready to help out defensively. And the towering Tommy Lawton, as good an 'old-fashioned' centre-forward as England ever possessed, certainly the finest header of a ball that ever pulled on the white shirt. Dixie Dean's successor at Everton, Lawton took on that mantle with barely a second thought, showing a similarly phlegmatic attitude in England colours. And then there was Stanley Matthews, the genius on the right, leaving full-backs for dead and placing the ball so expertly on Lawton's forehead. But at a time when England were becoming a force on the world scene, that game in Romania was the end of international football for seven long years. It just shows what a bad loser Hitler was . . .

3

Summer of Discontent

For years, the Football Association had been an inward-looking organization, ignoring the rapid globalization of the sport and even snobbishly snubbing the first three World Cups. What use had England for the outside world? But then, on the 3rd September 1939, Herr Hitler made Neville Chamberlain the offer of a fixture he couldn't refuse, and the entire country suddenly found itself embroiled in another kind of world championship.

Inevitably, the war years brought an end to 'official' international football; not even the FA were sufficiently out of touch to invite the Italians over to Wembley. Even so, the coalition government of the time soon recognized the important effect sport could have on morale on the home front, and encouraged the footballing authorities to maintain some level of competition. Leagues continued in localized form, a wartime FA Cup competition was played and special games between the armed forces were also instigated. But to maintain a real focus, internationals were vital. The home countries, united against Fascism in Europe, continued to take to the football field and kick lumps out of one another. Proper caps were not awarded, because the sides were necessarily makeshift, with players unavailable because of military postings, but that scarcely mattered, for there was plenty of talent around. Joe Mercer, who lost so much of his career to the war years, wrote that, 'In these matches, everybody fancied himself a bit, everybody wanted the ball.' Played in the spirit that entertainment was paramount, the rules were so relaxed that Stan Mortensen, later to get 25 caps for England, actually played as a substitute for Wales against England at Wembley in 1943, after the Welsh lost Ivor Powell to a fractured collar-bone.

But, nevertheless, the games were fiercely contested, notably between England and Scotland, where crowds of up to 105,000 took brief refuge from the war. Matches were used to raise funds for the war effort, though even in their staging, the hardships of the time were apparent. In one 'Aid to Russia' game at Wembley in 1942, the Scots were so short of clothing coupons, they couldn't get new jerseys and had to use those worn by Tommy Walker over his career. (Fortunately, the Hearts inside-forward had played for Scotland on 20 occasions before the war, so there were enough shirts to go round.) Happily, the Englishmen weren't forced to take refuge in Fatty Foulke's cast offs, though his one England shirt would probably have clad the whole side.

With the war in its final days, games with foreign opposition became possible once more, and were an important signal that a return to normality was imminent. Many of England's finest lost swathes of their playing days to the war. Tom Finney did not make his Football League debut until the end of hostilities. But his genius surfaced at Preston, and he was able to make an international debut during wartime. He recalls, 'I was abroad from December 1942 to 1946 in the Army, mainly in Egypt. I was flown back from Italy to play against Switzerland in 1945. They were a neutral country, so you couldn't turn up in military uniform, we had to go in suits, so I had to fly back to Croydon Airport. I'd flown back in uniform, so Stanley Rous, the FA secretary, took me down to Moss Bros and got me a suit. I couldn't have got one on my own! Then I was allowed to fly out to Switzerland.'

For all that these international friendlies performed important war work, players and spectators alike longed for a return to the real thing, the sign that the horrors were behind them. That moment came on 28 September 1946, when an English side lined up for the first time in 2684 days, in Belfast. It was a massively changed side, only Tommy Lawton playing in the two internationals that bookended the war, though Raich Carter had also had pre-war experience. Even so, as Finney points out, it was scarcely a side of footballing virgins: 'We had some top-class players: Wilf Mannion, Billy Wright, Neil Franklin, Frank Swift, Laurie Scott. Most of us had played a few wartime internationals. It soon falls into place when you're playing with such good players: I always believe that the higher you go, if you've got the ability, then the better you'll play, because they understand what's to be done. It possibly helped that we were all in the same boat, and it was just so good to get back to normal sport again after so long. I'd only been out of the forces five weeks, demobbed early because I was in the building trade. So I was working as a plumber, and trained on Tuesdays and Thursdays at Preston.'

The FA had not used the seven-year hiatus to improve their communication skills, though. Finney 'was told I'd been picked by the local press, and then I got a letter from the FA – but the journalists were usually the first to know! The game in Belfast was on the Saturday, so I reported on Wednesday, we travelled across on Thursday, did a bit of training Friday, played Saturday. Then we went on to Dublin and played Eire on the Monday.' Such preparation looks incredibly skimpy today, but the results didn't suffer. England's first peacetime international ended in a 7–2 win, a Mannion hat-trick crowning the game. Such was the interest in the game, thousands of spectators spilled on to the pitch in a scene reminiscent of the 'White Horse' Cup Final of 1923. Two days later, Finney scored the only goal in Dublin to stony silence following a poor England display.

The national side played their first home game on 19 October at Maine Road, against Wales. Even in this post-war world, Finney remembers, 'The idea was to let the public see the national side. That was enjoyable and a good idea, to save people the expense of travelling down to London all the time. The very big games, like Scotland, were always at Wembley, but against Wales or Northern Ireland we played at the big grounds, like Maine Road, Hillsborough, Villa Park.' It remains a moot point, especially amid the controversy over Wembley's redevelopment, as to whether

36

England, and the fans, are best served by playing all their games in London. In the days of rationing and economic privation, it was imperative that the team went to the people. It did them little harm, Huddersfield's Leeds Road hosting an 8–2 victory over the Dutch in November, Lawton blasting in four.

The global conflict also pushed the FA into taking a wider view of the world. Overseas tours took on greater significance, often acting as a thank you to our allies and an olive branch to former enemies. The first jaunt came in the summer of 1947, to Switzerland, where England's first post-war defeat was inflicted, then on to Lisbon, where Billy Wright felt as though he were 'stepping into a baker's oven ... my clothes were as close to me as if I had fallen into a river'. The unaccustomed heat did not prevent an astonishing game. Already, in just a handful of internationals, a supposedly fierce rivalry had come into being between two of the greatest footballers England has ever produced. Tom Finney and Stanley Matthews were candidates for the number seven shirt, the outside-right berth. Matthews had wrested the shirt back from the younger man, but events in Lisbon offered a solution. According to Finney, 'I'd never played outside-left in my life but Bobby Langton got injured so I had to move there in Portugal. Walter Winterbottom, the manager, just called me over and said, "We've a bit of a problem, will you play outside-left?" I'd have played anywhere to play for my country. That was my introduction to that position and it started all the Finney-Matthews controversy, about whether we could both play in the same team. I suppose we gave the perfect answer because we won 10–0, and we both scored and played reasonably well. There was never any bother about it between me and Stan, it was just paper talk. We were good friends, travelled a lot together, often roomed together, and it was great to play in the same team.'

What a luxury to have both men in the same team, like pairing Best and Cruyff or Zidane and Ronaldo. Billy Wright was a committed fan and noted, 'Matthews tried to mesmerize the opposition. He got the ball between both feet, he had wonderful balance, and that's how he caught them off balance; they didn't know which way he would go. No player in the world could catch Stanley once he went a yard away from you. But Tom would do it every match. There were times when Stanley got kicked out of a game.' Nat Lofthouse, who arrived on the scene a little later, adds, 'Matthews could cross the ball so accurately he'd put the lace away so it wouldn't hurt you when you headed it ... but Tom Finney made more goals for me than any other player. He was the guy I always wanted to play with for England.'

Ironically, although England now had its first full-time coach, in the shape of Walter Winterbottom, a former Manchester United centre-half, it was not left to him to resolve the Finney-Matthews conundrum, hence the confusion. Selection of the England team was still in the hands of the International Committee, of which Winterbottom was just another member. The manager wasn't thrilled with this interference: 'The selection committee saw an England cap as a reward for loyal service and for players playing well. There was no attempt to build a team.' Finney adds, 'We'd play in November, then not again until May and the team, which might have done reasonably well, would have four or five changes. That made it obvious Walter wasn't in charge of selection. There was no continuity, no consistency, the way the Hungarians or some of the other Continentals had.'

Certain positions in the side were set in stone. Who could replace Finney, Matthews, Wright or Franklin? These players, along with others such as Mannion, Mortensen, Swift, Lawton, Scott and Hardwick, formed the core of the team in the immediate post-war years. Blackpool's Stan Mortensen, the hat-trick hero in the 'Matthews Cup Final' of 1953, was a prolific forward, who managed 23 goals in 25 England games. Although he lacked speed, he developed an impressive change of pace that often fooled defenders, added to which were ball skills comparable with Raich Carter, who he replaced in the national side. As the fifth member of England's most fearsome forward line, Wilf Mannion did not suffer by comparison with his colleagues either. Less of a goalscorer than Mortensen, he still managed 13 in his 26 games. But it was as a creator, by forensic passing or skillful dribbling, that Mannion really excelled. Playing the deepest of the forward line, Mannion was the link man between the half-backs and the forwards, his ability to spot a telling pass ahead of anyone else his greatest asset. And if the forwards were irresistible, then the full-back pairing of Laurie Scott of Arsenal and George Hardwick of Middlesbrough was immovable. Billy Wright described them as 'a classy pairing, not hard tacklers. George was a very good skipper, he was not a demonstrative skipper. I learned a lot from George.'

Domestically they were a powerful unit, but already England was waking up to the fact that the real challenges lay abroad. The first great test was waiting in Turin in May 1948 where the national side were to play one of our wartime enemies for the first time. Italy, twice World Champions, winners in 1934 and 1938, were *the* world power. Not only that, their players were on a bonus of £100 each to win, while the Englishmen got £20, win, lose or draw, though at least they were gifted a small sack of rice by the Italians, a useful gesture at a time of rationing.

To actually get abroad in the late 1940s was a thrill in itself – although many players such as Tom Finney had been posted over-seas in the forces, peacetime travel was an altogether more pleas-urable experience. He recalls: 'We travelled first class by plane, usually third class on the train, and, coming back from a game, there were many times I had to stand all the way to Preston! But the plane usually just had the England party on it, players, officials and journalists, sixty or seventy people, so that was exciting just after the war. We didn't see a lot of the places we went, normally our "free time" was spent at the English Embassy, and the tours were pretty concentrated, with probably three games in ten days.'

According to Walter Winterbottom, 'We arrived in Italy untested against the really strong nations of European football since the war, after a period when they had been playing remarkable football, and it was called the "Match of the Century!" We saw a film of them at a newsreel cinema before the game, and they were an extraordinary side, coached by Vittorio Pozzo. They asked the President how they thought the game would go and he said, "Being very modest, we expect to win 4–0," the score we thrashed them by! But we were fortunate. We had a Spanish referee I was amazed at; I thought they contrived two goals before we scored that were narrowly onside but were given offside. Then we broke away and Mortensen just ran through from a pass by Billy Wright and scored from a very narrow angle. A few moments later, Mortensen centred and Lawton cracked it in from the edge of the box. Then we played so well after that.'

Finney believes, 'The team that went to Turin and beat Italy, the World Cup holders, 4–0, were a really great side, best I ever played in. It was certainly one of the most exciting games I played in, our best victory, because we weren't given a cat in hell's chance of winning! First half, we were under tremendous pressure, big Frank Swift kept us in the game and then we scored against the run of play and came off at half-time winning 2–0. Had I been Italian, I'd have been very disappointed to come off losing after playing so well. In those days Continental sides seemed to fold if you got in the lead and in the second half we ran out comfortable winners.' The value of football on the international stage was brought home to Winterbottom when he was told by 'our ambassador that it was the best thing that could ever have happened, it would do our trade the world of good!'

Perhaps such realizations helped the FA shed their introspection. They announced that it was England's intention to qualify for the 1950 World Cup, to be held in Brazil, perhaps the single most important step forward made this century, the signal that the home of football recognized its invention was now the global game. In the light of that wonderful victory in Turin, a trouncing of the current holders, the home audience anticipated a triumphal sweep towards the World Cup. But that ignored the fact that Italy had recently suffered their equivalent of the Munich disaster, losing four internationals when Turin were involved in a plane crash. Equally, well though England performed, Finney for one was not blind to the implications of playing foreign sides: 'It was entirely new, they played the game a little bit differently than we did, we played as 2–3–5, but there were different systems abroad, with deep-lying forwards, which they had in Switzerland and so on.

Very interesting.' Writing in *Football Is My Passport*, Billy Wright stated, 'Walter Winterbottom, in my view, is one of the greatest men in world soccer when it comes to sizing up the teams that England has to play against.' But having had little playing exposure to the international game, England were no longer in the vanguard of tactical advancement despite the fact that, as Finney points out, 'Walter was a good coach, very well respected in Europe.' That said, Winterbottom was a victim of the dietary habits of the day, Wright noting that on one occasion, 'He personally went into the kitchens of one foreign hotel at which we were staying to show the chef just how English footballers liked their bacon and eggs.'

Most telling of all was the fact that that England side reached a peak in Turin. Only four of the players who beat Italy took part in the opening World Cup fixture two years later. The war years took their toll on a side in transition. Many who had played a little football before the war were getting too old. Those now young enough to play had little experience of the international game and so were sometimes exposed at the top level. Many of England's players were learning on the job, where players in countries such as Brazil or even Switzerland, less disrupted by the war, had more games behind them. England did have some good, even some wonderful, footballers, but as a unit, they were not head and shoulders above the rest of the world, as some claimed. Even England's selectors began to accept that changes were necessary and a little forward planning wouldn't go amiss with the World Cup looming, the games due to take place in strength-sapping conditions.

Tommy Lawton, though still a very fine player, was starting to show signs of age, and a new centre-forward was required to lead England's line. Among others, Jackie Milburn was given the chance to stake a claim, making his debut in Belfast in October 1948. The hero of Tyneside recalled that in the dressing room prior to the game, all his colleagues had given messages of encouragement, except for Stanley Matthews, the man he most wanted to hear from. Once the national anthem had been played however, 'Stan came waddling across and said, "The first time you see me heading down the wing, get away to the far post and just stop on the edge of the six-yard box. When I centre the ball, most of the time I put a lot of top on the ball to make it hang and fool the keeper, so that'll give you time to close in." I did exactly as he said ... this ball was hanging, literally hanging ... it came to me and – whey – the wife could have scored!' England recorded an emphatic 6–2 win, in what was Billy Wright's first game as England captain. Typical of the manner in which players were treated, Wright did not find out about his elevation through official channels. Returning home from the September international in Denmark Wright was 'carrying my gear, plus a huge ham which I had brought back from Copenhagen. I boarded the bus at the station to be greeted with the finest piece of soccer news ever given to me.' The clippie on the bus offered her congratulations and, when Wright looked bemused, she showed him the stop press column of the local *Express & Star*, which told him he was England's new skipper. Doubtless that's exactly the same way Alan Shearer found out.

Milburn had been a success on his debut, and it looked as though Wor Jackie could be the answer for England as he crashed in six goals in his first five games as England's number nine. But he suffered from injuries and found himself displaced from the side. Surprisingly, it mattered little to him: 'I won 13 caps, but I lost 20 or more through injury. Been selected and couldn't play. But it didn't mean nothing. It's lovely to have your first cap, but ... there didn't seem to be any atmosphere somehow. I remember playing me first game at Wembley against Scotland and when I walked out on to the pitch it was like a morgue.' Milburn was in a minority in his disinterest with England – it probably didn't help that he was soon shunted out on to the right wing – but his comparison between the passion generated at St James' Park and that at Wembley was an interesting one. Certainly playing England games around the country appealed to many of the players but Walter Winterbottom was adamant that 'that was something we had to change. We had to have a home stadium where we could be used to playing.'

England suffered their first defeat on home soil by overseas opposition at Goodison Park in September 1949 when the Republic of Ireland won 2–0, but otherwise, preparation for 1950 went well enough, though the lack of exposure to foreign opposition should have been a cause for concern. Italy were among the few visitors and though they were beaten 2–0, that owed as much to a brilliant goalkeeping performance from Bert Williams, described by Stan Cullis as the 'finest I have ever seen from any goalkeeper in the world', and a flukish goal from Billy Wright as it did to any English dominance. But at least qualification for the World Cup was never in any doubt. FIFA were remarkably obliging, given that it had been the FA who had snubbed them in the 1930s. Not only did they approve England's application for membership – as well as those of the other home nations – but they made the Home International Championship the qualification group. Even then they weren't finished, allowing the top two nations to go through, all but guaranteeing that England would reach Brazil. Sensibly the FA did not copy the ludicrous decision of their Scottish counterparts, who decreed they'd only go to the World Cup if they won the series. When the two sides met at Hampden Park, both had successfully despatched Wales and Northern Ireland. They were safe in the top two positions, so England had already qualified. The Scots had to avoid defeat to clinch a share of the Championship and a lucrative trip. They failed to do so, a Roy Bentley goal separating the sides in April 1950. So the UK sent just one representative, though Billy Wright suggested, 'It would have been for the good of British football if both England and Scotland could have gone to South America as partners.'

It might have been a psychological blow not to travel in hope with the Scots, but England were dealt a far more serious blow within a week of the Scotland fixture. English clubs still held their players on contracts that were little more than legalized slavery. Clubs could retain a player's registration, making it impossible to move to any club within FIFA's umbrella. The maximum wage meant that no player was ever going to get rich either. All was weighted towards the clubs, as Tom Finney recalls; 'I had an offer to go to Italy in 1952 but it never got off the ground because the club just said they wouldn't consider it, and they held my registration. They said, "You'll play for Preston or you'll play for nobody!" Players had no say. Once you were signed to a club, it ran for the rest of your career. It was a twelve-month contract, but they had the option to keep you, there was no freedom of contract. It was that that led to the George Eastham situation when he went to court and put a stop to it.' If a player wanted to make anything out of the game, he had to look abroad, and beyond the FIFA nations. In April 1950, a clutch of British players, including Neil Franklin of Stoke City, decided that their futures lay in Colombia (Franklin signed for Santa Fe for far better money than he'd ever make in the Potteries), effectively barring themselves from international football. Colombia were not members of FIFA, enabling their clubs to register the likes of Franklin and Manchester United's Charlie Mitten without having pay a transfer fee. With Franklin now playing in a non-FIFA nation, he was no longer eligible for international duty. For the individual, it was wholly understandable, but for England, it was a disaster. Tom Finney is adamant that 'Franklin was the best centre-half I ever played with. It was a body blow, gave the selectors a real problem in replacing him. And not just that year, but for several to come, and that was why Billy Wright eventually had to slot in there about four years later.'

Franklin was a thoroughly accomplished defender, an intelligent reader of the game, powerful in the air, comfortable on the ground, as befitted a former inside-forward. His decision to go to Colombia was ultimately disastrous for him. Returning to England later that year when he and his wife failed to settle, he was handed a six-month suspension and a spiteful transfer from Stoke, his move to Hull illustrating that the top clubs had been told not to touch him. Shattered by the reaction of the powers that be, at twenty-eight his career at the top was finished.

The devastation that Franklin's absence wrought was quickly in evidence on a brief tour of Portugal and Belgium in mid-May. Having beaten Portugal 10–0 just three years earlier, England were now reduced to scrambling through 5–3, courtesy of four goals from Tom Finney, including a couple of penalties. In Belgium they won 4–1, but by popular consent were lucky not to have conceded more. Billy Wright for one was unsure about the value of this trek into Europe, saying, 'It would have been better to have played the games earlier in the season and then allowed the "Rio Men" to have a rest before flying to South America.' England's right-back, Alf Ramsey, had different thoughts, however. Reflecting on those games, he wrote later, 'On many occasions it "clicked" so well that I thought with plenty of match practice it could be developed into a really first-rate combination.' As so often, Ramsey's thinking was ahead of its time. The England squad disbanded for four weeks, prior to getting together again for four days before flying out to Brazil. When they did finally regroup, Winterbottom had to arrange a practice game against an amateur side because 'all the clubs insisted their players had a month's rest. We couldn't use a proper ground either, because the pitches were being relaid or reseeded! And the players wouldn't take hard training at that stage of the year, they were programmed by their clubs to think they were tired. Those were the obstacles we were up against.'

After such skimpy preparation, the party flew out on 19 June. They flew to Rio via Paris, Lisbon, Dakar and Recife, a thirty-one-hour jaunt. They arrived on the 21st, jetlagged and exhausted and with their opening fixture just four days away. Tom Finney recalls, 'It was a big ambition to take part in the World Cup, something entirely new for us, and for it to be held in South America just made it more exciting. Nobody knew much about it, it wasn't like now, when everybody takes part, it was our first time. We were rated pretty highly, but all we knew about South American sides was what we'd read in magazines. It was a real eye-opener to go across to Brazil. It was laughable, really, before the World Cup, it took two days to travel there and we arrived a few days before we played our first game! Now they'd be there a fortnight to acclimatize. We found it very hard to play in temperatures of 90 degrees having come from a mild English summer, among mad keen supporters, a completely different environment to what we were used to. The altitude was a problem and we even had oxygen masks at half-time, which was completely foreign to us! Arsenal and Southampton had gone out there since the war on club tours and came back with reports on how skilful, fit and strong these players were, but we didn't know much more than that. We saw the opening game with Brazil and saw incredible skills, I was in awe of what we'd seen. It gave us an indication of just how good they were, when prior to that the general feeling had been that Europe reigned supreme, and that England would do really well in 1950.'

The change in environment was a significant one in those far off days before people, particularly professional footballers, treated jetting off across the world as an everyday occurrence. Winterbottom noticed that 'some players were discontent. It's miserable when you find that they're worried about the atmosphere they'll be playing in, scared to death of the supporters when, if you'd been there before, you'd have realized the crowds were simply enjoying themselves.' Some players took to their new surroundings immediately, Billy Wright saying, 'Brazil has a gaiety and charm about it which even on films doesn't hit you as powerfully as a visit.' But others were less sanguine, Matthews noting, 'Most of the players were eating bananas because the food didn't suit us.' Most players went down with 'Rio stomach' at some stage, just one of the many drawbacks in their hotel. Arsenal had staged a club tour to Brazil just after the war and had suggested the hotel they used would be ideal for the England party. But the demands of a close season tour and a World Cup are somewhat different and a hotel right on the Copacabana was hardly conducive to rest and relaxation prior to games. Players naturally wanted to use the beach but were forbidden since medical advice said the sun would cause lethargy. The hotel was packed with ordinary tourists, it was noisy, the food utterly different to anything they'd experienced. Again, arrogant English insularity had put the national team at a disadvantage. Stupidity didn't help much either, Winterbottom recalling another disaster: 'We asked to have special lightweight boots made for training and when they arrived, they were like heavy gardening boots, made from a sort of Wellington material!' Winterbottom almost lost inside-forward Stan Mortensen too. Taking a stroll, he managed to fall down a hole left by local municipal workers who had uprooted a tree but forgot to fill in the gap.

Footballers the world over are pretty similar, they just want to get on and play. So it was with some relief that on 25 June 1950, England played its first ever World Cup game, against Chile in Rio. England fielded a useful side, minus Matthews, who had arrived a little later in Brazil. Having been out of the side since April 1948, age catching up with him according to the selectors, Matthews had been a late choice for the squad and had already been sent out on a flag-waving trip with an FA party to Canada. He was thus required to make his own way to Brazil, his late arrival considered unimportant given that he was no longer a first choice in the side. Tom Finney continued at outside-right, with Jimmy Mullen playing wide on the left.

An introduction to the tournament via the weakest South American side was ideal preparation, and though England laboured, they registered a 2–0 win without ever being fluent. Tom Finney felt, 'After we won that game, we felt we had a great chance. We hadn't played that well, but we won easily enough and were in the competition. We had the USA to come at lower altitude, so we were pretty confident.' That was the sentiment of the entire footballing community. Even the Brazilians were anticipating a showdown with England and nobody paid the slightest heed to the USA. A ragbag of migrants from all over the world – captain Eddie McIllvenny, a Scot who had played for Wrexham early in his career. Though they had played well in losing 3–1 to Spain, surely they couldn't trouble England?

An unchanged side was named in spite of Matthews' availability, suggesting that England were not complacent, a sentiment Tom Finney echoes: 'We didn't take it easy, it was just one of those games where you can't score, a freak result, in the sense that we could have played them another ten times and won every one. Possibly with 2–3–5 our forwards weren't as clinical as we needed to be, because in England there were always chances coming along.

You got far fewer in internationals. We did the same against Spain, though Jackie Milburn had a goal ruled out for offside, even thought he shot past their full-back standing on the line! But it was a catastrophe. We were a laughing stock, the press were very critical, you just couldn't take it in that you'd lost to the USA, you just wanted to get home and forget all about it. But I'm still asked to explain it nearly fifty years later!'

As happens so often in the FA Cup, the more fancied side were brought down to earth by awkward conditions acting as a leveller between the teams, the Belo Horizonte ground hardly measuring up to the Maracanã. Equally, the American side was far more capable than many have suggested, certainly their best team until the 1994 series. Finney is right in calling the game a freak, but, equally, he was realistic enough to see it as a symptom of English decline: 'The whole tournament brought us down to earth and made us realize we had to think a bit more about this game, that other sides had studied it and were more advanced than we were, not just in the systems but in individual play, because there were some outstanding technical players. We had a lot to learn. Nowhere near the thought went into defending in this country as went into attacking. We stood still while others progressed, we kept thinking we were the best but we weren't. It still happens, especially in the press. In Euro '96 we were unlucky to go out on penalties, but over the whole tournament we weren't the best side, we were very fortunate against Spain, for instance. Obviously you ride your luck, but to the press, all that matters is the result, and that stops you learning.'

Even then, it took another three years before many would accept that England's standing in world football was perilously low. As it was, the World Cup wasn't yet over, even after the American defeat. A win over Spain would mean a play-off and possible qualification. Changes were made, Matthews, Baily, Milburn and Eckersley replacing Mullen, Mannion, Bentley and Aston. But morale had been shattered in Belo Horizonte and it was beyond Winterbottom and Wright to turn things around. Once Milburn had that goal disallowed in the 14th minute, it seemed the writing was on the wall and the players could do little but accept their fate. Billy Wright later argued that 'the English team that sunny June afternoon played some of the finest football I have seen from our National team ... the Spaniards for all their pushing, shoving and shirt-pulling, seemed to have little answer to our constructive football', but that seemed to be putting more than a little spin on events. Certainly England could have won, but once again, they didn't.

The country that had given the world its game was now a second-class citizen. Perhaps that wasn't surprising given the way the country treated its top players. Looking back on the series, double international Willie Watson – it was he who helped Trevor Bailey save a famous Test match at Lord's in 1953, thereby setting up an Ashes win – was less than elated at his treatment: 'We had training sessions in London and I asked permission to bring my wife down for the last weekend so that we could be together before I left. The FA agreed to this; and I remember putting in an expenses sheet covering a shilling booking charge on the first journey to London, and the excess fare for first class over third class, which we were allowed for the second journey. I travelled first class because the train was full and I didn't think it was right that I should all the way from Yorkshire to London prior to a most important training session. On my return from Rio, I received a cheque for £60 from the FA, being my fee for the trip – I didn't play in any of the three matches – and included in this letter was a note saying that I had overcharged sixteen shillings and threepence on expenses.' If you treated your greatest assets with less care than the Coal Board lavished on its pit ponies, it was hardly surprising if results weren't all you desired. It would be years before that lesson was learned.

4

It's the End of the World as We Know It

England's return from Brazil was a mercifully quiet one. Stepping off the plane, Billy Wright met a sole reporter, told him that he and the players were 'disappointed and looking forward to a jolly good rest' and that was the end of the inquest. Imagine how they'd be treated now – if the coach escaped jail, he'd be doing well. But that was a symptom of the times. For all that the English public were shocked by the American defeat – early reports of the 0–1 scoreline suggested that it had been a misprint and that England had won 10–1 – it was a nine-day wonder. After the initial stinging press critiques that castigated our forwards for their profligate finishing, interest in the whole tournament died down. With England out of the competition within three days of the USA débâcle, the defeat was swept under the carpet, as our sporting attention refocused on the Test series with the West Indies, where Ramadhin and Valentine were dismantling the English batting with ease. That was a real crisis, losing to the West Indies at home. With that as cover, the English footballers were able to slip back into the country almost unnoticed and allow their cricketing counterparts to feel the full fury of the press. The key difference in those days before satellite television was that a defeat at home, in front of your own supporters, stung far more than any in some far off country in a game which nobody saw. Out of sight, out of mind was the attitude, allowing people to dismiss the World Cup as a pretty inconsequential tournament. England had expected to see the Jules

Rimet trophy returned home, but since Wright didn't have it in his hand luggage, press and public alike effected a lofty disdain for the whole circus. Nobody had ever beaten us in England, so that proved we were the masters. Didn't it?

More intelligent observers realized that wasn't the case. Tom Finney accepted England were gradually slipping down the pecking order, while former international Stan Cullis later wrote, 'there was no doubt that we were a very weak footballing nation'. The real debate was over what needed to be done. On the one hand, Cullis and his Wolves side favoured a direct style of play, aimed at feeding the strikers as quickly as possible. Others, such as Walter Winterbottom himself, favoured a more studied passing game, arguing that tactics needed to be fluid and that possession was all in the new world of football.

Domestically the WM formation was still the staple. Some sides played a more sophisticated brand of it – the 'push and run' that won Spurs the League in 1950 –51 or Busby's Manchester United for example – but most sides were workmanlike. English football was extremely exciting, but technically very limited, certainly in comparison with the football played in Brazil. But that was how the crowds wanted it. Winterbottom ruefully recalls one international at Highbury just after the war when England had unveiled a passing game. 'Mannion was scything the ball around, we played wonderfully well. And I got a sheaf of letters from Arsenal supporters complaining that it wasn't exciting enough, that they didn't want this namby-pamby passing, they wanted the ball in the box.' The surreal thought of Arsenal supporters asking for excitement aside, that was the prevailing mood. Football was all about thrills and spills, games ending 5–4 or 4–3. As a modern-day spectator, it's easy to sympathize with that viewpoint at times, but it was never a philosophy that could carry England through against high-class foreign opposition. Winterbottom tried to alter that mindset, but as Finney shrewdly points out, 'I think we changed things a bit after 1950, but other countries improved as well. We beat Portugal 10–0 in 1947, then the next time we played in 1950, it was 5–3 and the games got closer and closer as teams thought about it a bit more. In Europe, they brought in coaching for teams and individuals a lot sooner than we did and paid more attention to it, particularly in places like Italy. It's only now with the Italians at clubs like Chelsea that we're having fitness coaches and dieticians and that type of thing, which they were doing right after the war.' Many English players still lived on the artery clogging fried breakfast, a packet of fags a day and a couple of pints at night.

The 1950–51 season was a mixed bag. The selectors continued to look desperately for a new Neil Franklin, the pack of forwards were constantly shuffled, but results were stubbornly unimpressive. Northern Ireland and Wales were beaten 4–1 and 4–2 respectively, but the Scots won 3–2 at Wembley. Even more worrying was a fixture at Highbury where England were again fortunate to hold on to their unbeaten home record against foreign opposition. Two early Nat Lofthouse goals had established supremacy, but the Yugoslavs fought back to secure a 2–2 draw. Lofthouse then missed the next four England games, highlighting the bizarre selection policies that ruined English chances. Yet when pride was restored in defeating a weak Argentina 2–1 at Wembley and Portugal 5–2 at Goodison Park, the wounds of the previous summer were forgotten. Against Argentina, though, England had looked at sea against a defence that simply funnelled back, conceding space all over the field except in and around the penalty area, where there were always spare men to pick up the English forwards. It was a tactic with which we were wholly unfamiliar and one which baffled the crowd.

The Portuguese game in May was most notable for the elevation of Alf Ramsey to the England captaincy. It was suggested that Billy Wright was missing solely because Wolves were going on tour and the club had insisted on having his services, but the truth was Wright had been dropped, as he admitted later: 'My football deteriorated about two months after the commencement of the 1950–51 season . . . frankly, I began to hate going on to the football field . . . The selectors dropped me. They were entitled to do so, and had in fact been most patient with me.'

People would now look at Wright's slump and ascribe it to the pressures of leadership and the arduous task of captaining England through an unhappy World Cup campaign. In 1951, the response to a player feeling jaded was that he should buck his ideas up and pull himself together. Critics called for Wright's head throughout the season and once they had it, were quick to write his professional obituary, pointing out that few England captains had ever recaptured that honour once lost. But that was ignoring the facts. Like anyone else, Wright was entitled to lose form at some stage of his career, he was only human. More than that, he was clearly the best man to captain his country. Wright was a student of the art, was a good motivator, sensible tactician when required, and a man who could lead by example. Typical of his style, he laid down three guidelines covering things he would not do: 'Shout or bully a player on the field; demonstrate by waving my arms in the air; assume the role of football foreman.' Wright was unassuming but commanded the respect of the side. Going to South Africa on that club tour and 'freed from the strain of competitive football, I slowly but surely began to regain all the confidence which had been lacking in my play . . . at the risk of being labelled swollen-headed I must say now that I knew I'd win back my place as right-half and Captain of England.' The job was returned to him for the first game of the new season when England met France at Highbury. 'I confess I nearly cried with joy and felt just as elated as I did on the first occasion England honoured me.'

But England's troubles were deeper rooted than their skipper's year-long malaise. Though the return of a revitalized Wright was like discovering a great new talent, the team were still unconvincing. The French held England 2–2, Wales and Northern Ireland offered greater resistance than usual and then they entertained a strong Austrian eleven at Wembley in November 1951, a game in which inside-forward Ivor Broadis made his debut: 'I was a bit fortunate to get my first game. I wasn't picked originally, but Stan Mortensen got injured on the Saturday. I played for Manchester City, but I lived in Carlisle, and we weren't on the phone. A local policeman had to come up on the Sunday to tell me I'd been picked and to go and join the squad the following day.'

As Argentina had exhibited new tactics six months earlier – the funnel defence which England immediately copied – so did Austria. Theirs were based around Ernst Ockwirk, 'Ockwirk the Clockwork'. Nominally the centre-half, he played just behind the attack and was what we'd now term the playmaker. To add to that, he packed a fierce shot. Recognizing the dangers Austria posed, Winterbottom got permission to bring the England party together for training a week before the game at Maine Road. Viewing Ockwirk as the threat, Winterbottom decided that it would make sense to nullify him by using an inside-forward who could not only create, but who could also tackle. In the training session, he asked Wright to take up that position, as he recalled: 'With the aid of some Manchester City players, and our own reserves, we worked on the principle that the side facing us was Austria, and Ray Barlow, West Bromwich Albion's lofty half-back, was asked to fill the "Ockwirk role". My job in this practice match was to try and snuff out Barlow, i.e., Ockwirk, from the inside-left position. They tell me I did quite a good job.' The tactic wasn't put into operation, a spate of injuries on the Saturday before the game meant Wright had to revert to his normal half-back position. Even so, the very idea created an unholy row, with the Wolves chairman contacting Winterbottom to express his disapproval at Wright being played out of position. He felt that if Wright played well in this new role, it might cause trouble when he returned to Molineux. Given that Wright was just about the last person to cause such a fuss, the accusation is ridiculous, but symptomatic of the blinkered thinking that blighted the English game.

When the game did take place, Austria showed themselves to be an inventive, accomplished unit, but were foxed by England's strategy of falling back into blanket defence. Nonetheless, it was the Austrians who took the lead just after half-time, one they held for twenty minutes. England then regained the initiative and Eddie Baily won a penalty. With England's unbeaten home record hanging in the balance, it fell to Alf Ramsey to square the game: 'As I walked towards the penalty spot I felt like a man going to the gallows ... my heart was beating madly, and as I bent down to place the ball on the spot the goal seemed to have shrunk to about half its normal size ... my legs felt like rubber, and just before my right foot made contact I noticed Zeman move slightly to his right. At once, like a boxer going in for the "kill", I side-footed the ball to the other side of the goal ... I was the happiest man in the world as the crowd roared. Then I had a sudden reaction and began wondering what would have happened if I had missed that all-important penalty-kick!' Ramsey was the star turn, for a few minutes later, he placed a free-kick in the path of Nat Lofthouse and England were ahead. That free-kick had been rehearsed time and again during the Maine Road session, perfectly illustrating the value of forward planning and sufficient preparation time, a lesson that went unheeded for many years. Austria snatched a late equalizer, but such were the reduced expectations prior to the game, simply avoiding defeat and retaining the prized home record was enough for most.

Ironically, England were about to enjoy something of a renaissance. Scotland were defeated 2–1 at Hampden Park prior to a tough-looking summer programme, taking in Italy, Austria and Switzerland. Most of the seasoned pros such as Wright, Finney, Ramsey, Lofthouse and Jimmy Dickinson were on board, but some newer names made the jaunt too. Ivor Broadis felt, 'It was an adventure to go abroad then. It was interesting to play in weather that you never played in over here, for instance, seeing different crowds, having new food.' Another newcomer was Ronnie Allen, who seemed amazed by the whole experience: 'Lying in bed it seemed amazing to me how we could leave London on Friday morning and now here I was in bed in Italy – and it was still only Friday. Also I was feeling very satisfied with the delightful meal which was served on our arrival at the hotel. Perhaps it was because of the ravioli, which I had sampled for the first time.' This may well be the first sighting of an English footballer eating pasta.

The Italian game was to be played in Florence. Italy had had a poor World Cup in 1950 too, and were as keen to rehabilitate their flagging reputation as England were. England got off to a bright start, Broadis getting his first goal for his country: 'I scored against

Italy very early on. It's like pulling on the England jersey for the first time, something you just don't forget, I was walking on air, and then I didn't play in the next two games!' Italy came back to get a draw, but it offered a satisfactory start to the trip. Alf Ramsey was disappointed at the performance of the Italians, writing that it was 'the most unpleasant international match in which I had ever taken part ... surely the time has come for these fellows, so charming off the field, to be told not to leave their good manners and sportsmanship in the dressing room when they trot on to the pitch ... do these sound like harsh words to be used by an England player? They're intended to be, for, like my colleagues, I do not stoop to dirty tricks or foul play.' Whatever the case on the field, the Italians certainly were charming off it, as Ronnie Allen recalled: 'As the players were leaving the pitch [at half-time] for the dressing rooms a small plane dived down over the stadium and dropped tiny parachutes each bearing a gift for the players and reserves. Thus I watched the second half with a dozen or more wristwatches in my lap, presents from the Italians and dropped out of the blue.' Sadly the fans did not behave so well towards their guests, Lofthouse narrowly missing a serious injury when a bottle was hurled at him.

Moving on from Italy, the Austrians looked set to offer a sterner test. On the evidence of the Wembley international, Austria were a real force in European football, if lacking a little of the penetration needed to back up their neat approach play. The game proved to be a tactical triumph for Winterbottom, who had his England side retreat deep into defence early on, inviting Austria to punch themselves out. At half-time, the score was 2–2, but as the second half wore on it became clear that the Austrians were tiring and becoming frustrated at their inability to turn possession into chances. They lost shape and discipline and committed too many men forward. Gil Merrick collected a cross, saw Finney unmarked and hurled the ball to him in the centre-circle. Finney immediately fed Lofthouse, who ran the 45 yards to immortality as the 'Lion of Vienna'. As Lofthouse struck the shot that won the game, the Austrian goalkeeper Musil came out to clatter him and, according to Wright, put him 'to sleep just as surely as if Rocky Marciano had clipped him on the chin'.

Tom Finney felt that wonder goal was just reward for a great player: 'Nat was outstanding; a wonderful goalscoring record. To average pretty much a goal a game is a fantastic achievement at that level. And there was a lot of competition, very good players like Jackie Milburn, Len Shackleton, Ronnie Allen, who barely got any caps. You get that in football, phases where there are a bunch of good players in similar positions coming along together.' An interested spectator was Ivor Broadis, omitted after his goal in Florence. His analysis of the sides is interesting: 'That Austrian team had some great players in it. They were more skilful with the ball than us – my theory is that we play through the winter, you get a bit of rain that softens the pitch, sometimes you get mud, and the mud helps kill the ball, so if you're going to trap it, mud helps deaden it. The Europeans tend to play on firmer pitches and it needed a bit more skill to do the things that we did in the mud, and I feel that's a great advantage to them. When I played at Newcastle, the pitch was sacred ground, we couldn't go on the bloody thing. On a wet day, we'd be running up and down the stands, the groundsman was Sandy Mutch, an old player, and we'd call down to ask him if we could have a game and he'd shake his fist at us! That was training – like playing snooker without a cue!'

The win in Austria was significant for morale beyond the football team, though as Wright recorded: 'Vienna was split into three zones and we had to play in the Russian zone. They were reputed to be number one in Europe, but they didn't count on the magnificent support we had from the British Tommys that day ... Nat cracked in a beautiful goal to make it 3–2 and everything was let loose. The referee blew his whistle for time, the British Tommys came running on to the pitch, grabbed hold of us, lifted us on to their shoulders and carried us off ... after the match they took us up to a wonderful restaurant right up in the hills, right in the Vienna woods, and we had a wonderful banquet.'

The Swiss were comfortably brushed aside in Zurich to complete a highly successful tour, but Broadis' observations are shrewd.

The following season the England side was not given the luxury of an extended build-up to internationals, except the customary week before the Scotland game, and that situation arose only because that game was played on a Saturday. The opportunity to build a cohesive side was lost in a season in which only four games were played, three against the home nations; competitive, but hardly instructive fixtures. Broadis again points out the absurdity of the selection system: 'You could be in or out at the whim of a director of a football club who happened to be on the FA selection committee. The strangest thing for me was I'd played against Austria in the November, played against Scotland at the end of the season, went on tour, came back and never played again until the Scotland game at the end of the next season. Then I went on tour again and exactly the same thing happened the next season: I didn't play until the next Scotland game! That was par for the course in those days, because half a dozen people were picking the side! It was ridiculous – and I might be maligning them, but there must have been a tendency to push their own players ahead of those from other clubs. Here in Cumbria, they've a sport called hound trailing, they put a drag of a scent down and let the hounds off. They'd say about some of the hounds that they could only run with the sun on their back, and I think the selectors must have thought the same about me because I only got picked in the summer!'

Broadis' return was timely, allowing him to score both England goals in a drawn match. It could have been better yet: 'I had a header cleared off the line as well. I had Nat and Tom on either side of me and if you couldn't play with Finney, you couldn't play; much the same with Nat. Finney was the best I ever played with, obviously, he didn't have a real weakness. You get one player thrown up every decade or so, and he was the one from that era. Along with Matthews, but they were completely different players, both exceptional, but Stan was that bit older.'

At least the FA made a stab at preparing for the 1954 World Cup, organizing a summer tour of South America followed by a game in New York. Over three and a half weeks, England also visited Argentina, Chile and Uruguay. Finney puts the player's viewpoint: 'It was only really on the summer tours that we got together. We had a pretty gruelling tour in 1953. It was hard, but to play these teams stood us in good stead, to see what they were doing.' Broadis agrees, though it was 'a mixed trip to South America, absolutely exhausting! They play the year round now and the wear and tear must be terrible, trying to keep them fit for such prolonged spells and to peak at the right time and for sustained periods must be extremely difficult. Apart from that trip to South America, which was a long one, we didn't play much in the summer, we generally had the best part of two months off. We watched an FA XI play Buenos Aires on the Wednesday and Walter left out most of the first-choice players because we had the full game coming on the Sunday. That was the first time I'd seen a deep-lying centre-forward. We were sitting round the touchline and he was deep with two inside men playing forward of him and he was picking up everything, destroying us in the first half – we didn't get that until Don Revie did it at Manchester City. It was a complete surprise to find a different system to play against and for our defenders, the centre-half had nobody to mark, or he was trying to mark two, and we lost 3–1.

'On the Sunday we played the full side and Arthur Ellis was the referee. On the way to the ground it started to rain, sheeting down. The ground had been bone hard – by the time we were ready and on the pitch, there were pools of standing water everywhere, and it was still coming down. We had our kick-in, the Argentines never appeared, and by the time they came on, we were liked drowned rats. Before long it was like a lake. Somebody clattered me after 15 minutes or so, so I clattered him back, and their players swarmed around me. Even now if I meet Nat, he always tells me that I ran out of the way, that I was on the outside looking in on this great mêlée! About five minutes after that, Arthur called the game off because the conditions were just impossible.'

Having performed so poorly in 1950, the English team were desperately keen to make a good impression in South America, and a 2–1 win in Santiago was an important result in difficult circumstances. Early on, a fierce Lofthouse shot hit a Chilean flush in the face. He collapsed and several of his team-mates attacked Lofthouse. The English reserves rescued him as the crowd showered them with oranges. After the game, England had a week off before playing in Montevideo. Several, including Alf Ramsey, put the time to good use by contracting dysentery. Again, in Uruguay the naïve Englishmen had another lesson in the cynicism of South American football of the time. Ivor Broadis recalls, 'It was all very pleasant before the game; they gave us all a pennant, with a smile and a handshake, and then spent the next 90 minutes kicking lumps out of you! Finney came in for terrible treatment.' England played well and were not in any way embarrassed by the World Cup holders who resorted to shirt pulling and vicious tackling that, according to the press, even had their own fans booing them. They got the result they wanted, though, seeing England off 2–1.

The tour ended in New York with the first meeting with the USA since the disaster in Belo Horizonte. The flight there was eventful: according to Broadis, as the team 'landed in Trinidad on the way it was on Coronation morning, the Union Jacks were out, so that made you feel good about representing England. We went to play the USA in the Yankee Stadium with the baseball diamond actually on the pitch!' For Tom Finney, one of four survivors from that infamous first game, 'It was nice to go there and win 6–3 to get some revenge! They were just making up the numbers then, the side was full of all nationalities, people who'd emigrated, so it was good to put one over on them.' Again, England had improved as a unit over the course of almost a month together, making it obvious to all but the most blinkered observer that preparation was crucial. Sadly the most blinkered observers happened to be running the FA.

Moving into World Cup season, one old campaigner worked his way back into the team when Tom Finney suffered injury. Following the magic of the Matthews Cup Final, Stanley returned to the England side for the first time since April 1951, again confounding those who had written him off as too old for inter-national recognition, in time to take on the Rest of Europe.

England's unbeaten record – the defeat against Ireland in 1949 was not considered to have been inflicted by truly foreign opposition – was placed under its severest stress yet, an Alf Ramsey penalty in the dying seconds grabbing a 4–4 draw. As Finney said, 'The unbeaten mantle was something you had to carry and it was a burden. Towards the end of that run, that was uppermost in your mind.' England didn't have to shoulder that burden much longer. In November 1953, the Hungarian national side paid a visit to Wembley. Just as he had been before the Austrian game a year earlier, Winterbottom was nervous about the quality of the opposition: 'Billy Wright and I met Harry Johnston, our centre-half, before the game and told him we had a problem with Hidegkuti. It was customary for the centre-half to follow the centre-forward, but Hidegkuti was playing a different game: I'd seen him lying deep against Sweden, I knew what he would do. So Harry asked me what the Swedes had done, and they'd just left him free and picked him up when he came through. Harry said he'd like to do that, to stay home rather than be pulled all over the field. And Hidegkuti wasn't the main destroyer at all, Bozsik was much more influential. But we were so old-fashioned in this country. In England, number five marked number nine. So if you put your left-back in the number nine shirt, your centre-half would have to play outside-right! That kind of rigid thinking had no place in the modern game.'

Certainly the Hungarians weren't bound by convention and had played all across Europe with a grace, fluidity and power that was awesome. Nor were they frightened to try new ideas, as Tom Finney points out: 'The Hungary game was a great awakening, it showed us things we'd never thought about, players coming out 20 minutes before a game with a ball each, passing it around, doing tricks.' Stanley Matthews said, 'Hungary had eleven great players and I don't know who could have beaten them at that time,' and it's hard to argue with that. For all that, the isolated English viewpoint going into the game was that Hungary were a good team, but that England would overcome them.

That required some reassessment when Nandor Hidegkuti put

them ahead with a fierce drive after 45 seconds. England pulled level, but by half-time the Hungarians had stamped their absolute mastery on the game and led 4–1. They had utterly dismantled the home side, even humiliating the national skipper with an astounding third goal, as Billy Wright was big enough to admit: 'The goal scored by Puskas will forever remain with me because the Hungarian captain beat me with a wonderful piece of footwork before crashing the ball fiercely past Merrick. It happened like this: I went into a tackle, firm and quickly, my eyes fixed on the ball at Puskas' feet. Ninety-nine times out of a hundred that ball would have been mine, but then I don't often meet a Puskas. Just as my boot was about to reach the ball he pulled it back with his left foot, I found myself in contact with nothing, and in one glorious movement Puskas completed a delightful piece of artistry by scoring a goal even I, the man he had so cleverly beaten, felt like applauding.' The image of that piece of trickery was seared on the national footballing psyche via newsreel footage and, more than anything, came to symbolize England's decline. England rallied a little in the second half as the Hungarians eased up, but the 6–3 scoreline is still one that's guaranteed to make players of a certain age wince.

The truth is it was an awakening that should have happened years earlier. England had hung on to the unbeaten home record with tenacity, but that clouded everything. The game had moved on, and friendly internationals were no longer the central plank of international football. Winning the World Cup was now the real issue, but few in England had woken up to the fact. All the while England remained unbeaten at home, it offered a comforting façade that all was well. But it was far from that. The 1950 World Cup should have brought that home to everyone, but because it happened thousands of miles away, we could comfortably ignore it. The Hungarians did English football the biggest favour it ever received by proving that the likes of Winterbottom were right. English football was not good enough, was Luddite in attitude and was falling further and further behind. Radical rethinking was required, and that would take years rather than the months that were left before the World Cup.

There were three games left to repair shattered confidence. In April, the traditional Scotland game took place at Hampden, a game that most of the players enjoyed above all others. Ivor Broadis, back in the team for the first time since the previous June, remembers, 'They were always keenly fought, it was war! I played two games at Hampden and the press up there destroyed the England team in the week before. None of us could play! In 1954, we went to stay at Troon and on the Friday we trained at Ayr's ground. We'd done the hard work in the week, so Friday was a more relaxing day, a few laps, few sprints, a bit of humour. I remember the Swedes had just started wearing their shorts a bit shorter, where we still had the long shorts and the high stockings. When we went out training, we were talking about it, so I rolled the sides of my shorts up and stuck my arse out, just clowning around. At breakfast the Saturday morning, Hugh Taylor in the *Daily Record* ran through the England team individually. He got to me and he said, "I saw him training yesterday and I've never seen anyone who looked less like an athlete!" We won 4–2 and I buttonholed him afterwards and asked him whether Willie Redpath, their left-half who marked me, agreed with his opinion!'

Two further games were lined up before flying out to Switzerland for the finals. The first game was in Belgrade, where England were beaten 1–0 by Yugoslavia, a result which caused plenty of excitement among the natives. According to Wright: 'Thousands of jubilant Yugoslavs lit newspapers and held them aloft like torches in triumph, before they joined up into a procession and marched back into Belgrade. I heard someone suggest there was grave danger of the stadium being set alight by fans in their ecstasy.'

Seven days later, following an opportunity to train as a squad, England were in Budapest to meet Hungary again. The match caused great local interest and Wright noted that 'Many [of the crowd] it was reported at the time had paid as much as £10 for a black-market ticket.' Tom Finney says, 'It was a shock to the system when Hungary beat us at Wembley, but it was an even bigger shock when we went out there and lost 7–1 in Budapest! It was a much changed side, and to my mind, nowhere near as strong as the side that lost 6–3, which I felt was a decent team. What exposed us was the deep-lying centre-forward. Nobody picked Hidegkuti up. He was what you'd call the playmaker now, he was directing operations, and that caused havoc. It was a lesson to watch them, as I had done at Wembley, just an education in the game. It was something entirely different and I still believe they were the best national side we ever played against. They were so good because they'd been together for years, they were majors in the Army, so they were together there, and they played as a team in the Olympics; they knew each other's game. But it made people think there was something sadly wrong with our game and that we needed to think a bit harder.'

Billy Wright also asked, 'What did we learn from this visit to Budapest? Firstly, it has impressed upon me that no International team can hope to go and play against the Hungarians as a "scratch" side. In Hungary they put the success of their National team at such a priority level they practise together, and have practice games against others with such regularity they have built up an understanding you cannot expect us to develop by an occasional kick-about.'

Ruminating on the difference between the two teams, Syd Owen, who replaced Johnston at centre-half, said, 'We couldn't get near them. They were like men from outer space.' For England to lose 7–1 on the brink of the World Cup was a disaster, Broadis adding, 'They were an incredible side, you couldn't see anyone stopping them winning the World Cup. It was very interesting in that World Cup, their preparation in Switzerland. They'd play school teams, win 28–0, clock up record numbers of goals. Whether it was a confidence measure or not, I don't know, but it was a very different thing to how we prepared.'

England prepared by having virtually a month between that game and the first World Cup group match against Belgium. When they took to the field against Belgium it was with an eleven that had never played together. It was Ivor Broadis' first experience of playing alongside Stanley Matthews: 'He was different to Finney. Inside to Finney, there was an amount of inter-passing that went on. With Stan, you gave him the ball to feet, he did his own thing, and you got into position for the end of it! But you had to enjoy playing with either of them. The better the player you play with, the easier the game is. The harder games were in the League, where you'd make three or four runs and get the ball once, where with Finney you got it nearly every time.'

Broadis benefited by scoring two goals, as England moved into a commanding 3–1 advantage with sixteen minutes to go. Belgium hit back, aided by the fact that centre-half Owen was carrying an injury. They squared the game with two goals in three minutes and took it into extra-time. Both sides scored again, but a 4–4 draw was very dispiriting. If ever an emphatic victory were needed it had been here, to dispel memories of Budapest. Instead, England were still in disarray. And they'd lost Owen. As Finney remembers, 'Billy Wright moved to centre-half. He was an outstanding foot-baller. After Neil Franklin went, they tried so many players there that didn't fit the bill, so they had to use Billy, and he just slotted in without any trouble.' England did seem more secure after these changes had been made and were able to weather the loss of Matthews and Lofthouse prior to the game with Switzerland, eventually cruising to a 2–0 win with goals from the Wolves pairing of Wilshaw and Mullen. England now topped their group and faced Uruguay, the holders, in the quarter-finals. Having played well in Montevideo the summer before, there was some cause for optimism, Finney pointing out, 'We approached it with con-fidence. I felt we played extremely well, had a couple of defensive mistakes which we shouldn't have made, and certainly shouldn't have lost 4–2. We were every bit as good on the day.' But English morale really had been shattered by the Hungarians, as Broadis agrees: 'If you look at that tournament, we went out to Uruguay and we could have got a result that day, we played well enough, certainly. It was something similar to Hoddle's experience in 1998 – the team was good enough to go further than we did. The coach can't come on the field, once you're on the pitch you have to sort it out yourself and I think one or two of our players were playing a bit below the standard that got them into the England team in the first place. I might have been one of them! It was a pity, but at that level, you can't afford to make mistakes because you're invariably punished, which is what happened to us.' Most accounts suggest that goalkeeper Gil Merrick in particular had a poor game – Brian Glanville described him as 'feeble', arguing that he should have saved at least two and probably three of the goals. But while England weren't defensively watertight, that ignores the quality of the Uruguayan side. They were the holders and played with the pride and determination that that position demands. They also had a host of good players. Skilful inside-forward Schiaffino was one of the players of the tournament, they had two fast, strong wingers in Abbadie and Borges, another clever inside-forward in Ambrois, muscular defenders in Santamaría and Martínez, an inspirational captain in Varela – who had lifted the Jules Rimet trophy four years before – and a resolute goalkeeper in Maspoli. They also had the incentive of becoming the first side to win the World Cup three times and so capture the trophy outright. They had beaten Scotland 7–0 in the group phase and would go on to take Hungary to extra-time in the semi-final before succumbing 4–2, so they could clearly play a bit.

And Uruguay were not averse to bending the rules. Wilshaw missed an easy chance thanks to what Glanville called 'a sly shove'. Had that gone in, England would have gone 2–1 up and the course of the game might have changed. As it was they went in at half-time trailing by that score when Varela scored from the edge of the box just before the break. Almost immediately after the restart, it was 3–1, Varela drop-kicking a free-kick rugby-style into the path of Schiaffino, who scored. Finney pulled a goal back after 67 minutes, but when Matthews hit the post, that was the signal for England's challenge to peter out. Ten minutes after Finney's goal, Uruguay's two-goal advantage was restored by Ambrois. To push them so close reflected no little credit on the English team, but their brittle self-confidence, so massively undermined by the twin Hungarian humiliations, meant they found it hard to recover from set-backs.

Put simply, England weren't as bad as some suggested, but they weren't a top-class international outfit either. But most damning of all was the comment that came from the England captain, Billy Wright: 'We hadn't really learned much since 1950. We were still playing as individuals rather than as a unit, because our domestic game was used to chances being created by individuals rather than by collective play.' To fail to learn anything in four years is a shocking indictment of a game that was smug, insular and thoroughly out of touch. The challenge over the next four years was to redress that balance and re-establish England as a power. Ironically, it was a Scot who would do more than most to help.

5

The Real World

English football was clearly in crisis. Certainly its achievements did not match up to its self-image; in fairness a problem not restricted to football alone, but one that has now dogged the nation for fifty years or more. But just as the Conservative Party is dead on its feet because of a refusal to accept the existence of the outside world, so English football continued to be stifled by its insularity. In spite of the harsh lessons of two World Cups, the governing bodies still refused to see the value of European competition. Not only was the England side subservient to the clubs, when the clubs had the chance to dip a toe in European waters, they were denied the chance. Chelsea, Champions in 1954–55, were ordered not to enter the inaugural European Cup competition and did as they were told. Thankfully, a few clubs had rather more guts and saw the benefits of playing sides from the Continent. As Tom Finney points out: 'It certainly helped that we started to look outside England, when teams like West Bromwich Albion and Wolves started to play foreign opposition. You've got to measure yourself against these people, to find out how good you are. If you're isolated in your own country, you don't progress. Manchester United went into Europe, against the League's wishes, but that was a very forward-thinking move by Matt Busby.'

The Busby Babes and their sorties into Europe were to have a fundamental impact on the make-up of the domestic game, just as massive talents such as Roger Byrne, Tommy Taylor, Duncan

Edwards and Bobby Charlton came to full footballing maturity in the cauldron of the European Cup. Had it not been for Busby's ambition and the breadth of his vision, English football could well have stayed trapped in its own time warp for a further decade. On a personal level, Busby must, at times, have reflected that it would have been better if he'd never heard of the European Cup, but for the good of the English game, the decision to take part was a seminal one.

England came back from Switzerland with a major rebuilding job on their hands. One early change was to replace Gil Merrick with Ray Wood of Manchester United: 'I was originally picked to go to the World Cup in 1954 but hurt my wrist and missed it. I made my debut in Belfast, and seven of us got our first cap then. Roger Byrne and Bill Foulkes from United played, so that was helpful, and Ray Barlow, Don Revie, Johnny Haynes all played. I'd played at Under-23 level and for the Football League three times, and played for England B against Scotland, so I had been in amongst the players. I had to play for United on the Saturday before the game and we had to phone the FA at 11 o'clock on the Saturday night to check who'd been picked to play and to report whether we were fit or not. So I was in a public call box in Manchester on the Saturday night trying to find out if I'd been picked for England! I found Walter was a smashing bloke. He'd played a bit, but he gave you a lot of theory; he knew what he was talking about. But we were never together very long – to play on Wednesday you'd report on Monday, and for the game in Belfast we spent the best part of a day travelling. The difference between then and now is people knew what they had to do in the positions they played, because most teams played the same WM formation. The inside-forwards would alternate – if one was up the other was back – the wingers stayed wide and didn't come chasing back, the wing-halves were always supporting the inside-forwards, so it was just a matter of doing the job you did normally. It's harder to do that now because there are so many different formations.'

Even for the hardened professional, the opportunity to play with the legends of the game is enticing, as Wood recalls: 'It was wonderful to play with Billy Wright and Stan Matthews; you think about these things but don't imagine it's going to happen to you. Northern Ireland had a decent team too: Danny Blanchflower, his brother Jackie, Jimmy McIlroy, that rogue Peter McParland! We won 2–0, but the reports were that the only two who had a good game were Billy Wright and myself! Of course, you don't see the game the same way as the supporters or the press, so you often wonder if they've been at the same game! England had a lot of good players at that time. Ray Barlow was a great player, and he only got that one game – it was Bill Foulkes' only international – so for players that good just to get the one game shows how strong we were.

'After that match we played Wales. It was great to play at Wembley. Everybody has their way of going abut things. I was very quiet, trying to concentrate, so I didn't wave to the crowd or look for anybody in the stand, because once you've lost your concentration, you're going downhill. We'd made a lot of changes and that didn't help, but I think after the World Cup they were trying out new players to give them experience, because we didn't play as many international matches as they do now. But it was hard to think you'd had a reasonable game and then find yourself left out of the next one just to give someone else a chance.'

England had a good pool of talent and the strength was exemplified by a convincing 3–1 win over the World Champions, West Germany, at Wembley in December, though Wood missed out: 'They left me out and brought Bert Williams back because they didn't think I was experienced enough, and we murdered them. Len Shackleton had a great day; he was brilliant, too clever for everybody.' Billy Wright was upset at the grudging praise for this achievement and wrote, 'Some folk claimed it was in reality a "hollow victory" over a German reserve team, conclusions which again caused me to ask myself the question, "Just what does an England team have to do to win a little praise?" Yes, I'm still awaiting a fair answer to that one!'

England did play well, but that victory then gave the selectors the chance to illustrate precisely what was wrong with their mentality too. The English goals had been scored by Roy Bentley, Ronnie Allen and Len Shackleton. None were in the team for the next game and Allen and Shackleton never pulled on an England shirt again. In fairness, it wasn't all bad, for in that next England international, at home to Scotland, Duncan Edwards made his debut at the age of 18 years and 183 days. Edwards was already such an accomplished all-round footballer, many wondered why it had taken him so long to get a cap. Tom Finney remembers that 'Duncan was exceptional, a bit like Michael Owen in the 1998 World Cup in the way he just came straight in and was an international player right away.' Billy Wright's contemporary assessment of him was that, 'Here is a youth who has everything necessary to put himself among the great players of our time . . . a footballer of the Elizabethan mould . . . first and foremost Duncan Edwards is a thinker . . . he is light on his feet; recovers quicker than most defenders; wisely believes there is no such thing as a defender but that every man on the field is a footballer who should be able to attack and defend.'

Edwards started what looked set to be a glittering career by helping England to a 7–2 win, but England were clearly in transition, as an ill-fated summer tour in 1955 made clear, with defeats in France and Portugal sandwiching a draw in Spain. The defeat in Portugal was hugely symbolic, indicating just how rapidly some European nations had improved while England had failed to achieve similar growth. Having won in Lisbon by 10–0 in 1947, eight years later an admittedly weakened England side were defeated 3–1, a pretty rapid shift in comparative fortunes. In fairness to the English hierarchy, it is always easier to gain rapid improvement from a low starting point. Simply by embracing modern tactical philosophies, particularly the introduction of defensive disciplines, a poor side with little attacking flair can, at the very least, make itself difficult to beat, a phenomenon still being shown today by the nations of the Middle and Far East, for example. But this improvement made it all the more important that England should work harder to stay a step ahead of the game. England needed to embrace all that was new at the 1954 World Cup – Hungarian teamwork, West German efficiency and national planning, the sweeper system – but failed to do so. Reactionary clubs continued to play the WM formation and were happy to stay in a rut.

The fact that England were struggling so badly did little to advance the cause for abolition of the maximum wage. As the figurehead of the nation's game, the national squad's failings gave critics the perfect opportunity to claim the players were getting too much. Ivor Broadis, by now out of the England reckoning, thinks, 'It was more of a normal job then, there weren't the rewards. You got £2 for a win, £1 for a draw in the League, and you worked to get that. Now there's so much money before you've kicked a ball, it's very difficult to come to terms with it. We knew we were being exploited – you'd get 64,000 crowds for big games; where did the money go? Good luck to them today, but it changes the way people view the game.'

On the other hand, Billy Wright balked at the thought of getting big money to captain his country: 'To receive £100 for playing ninety minutes' football sounds crazy to me. I do not know of one England player who would put financial reward before the honour of playing for his country ... once a footballer begins to think perpetually in terms of cash, instead of soccer, the time has come for him to hang up his boots.' From Ray Wood's recollection, Wright's assessment of the players' pride was correct: 'Some players now get more in a week than I made in twenty years! Somebody else was getting their hands on the money when we played! We got fifty quid for playing for England, less tax. I played in the first ever Under-23s for England and that was £15 and a tie, but playing for the Football League was better because you got £20 in your hand! So we weren't playing for the money, it was for the honour, and if you were injured, you still made sure you turned up to play if you could.' Tom Finney confirms that, adding, 'Nobody was concerned with money, it was never mentioned, never thought about. You got £20, then it went to £30 then up to £50, but there were no bonuses or anything like that. And often we'd play

Continental teams on good bonuses to beat us. But I don't think it entered our minds to question it.' At a time when the average working wage was around £10 or £12, the footballer's maximum wage of £20 was quite reasonable in comparison, though of course they were in a precarious career. At a time when full employment meant that ordinary workers could at least rely on having a job for life, a footballer was finished in his mid-thirties with no obvious career move open to him unless he was able to stay in the game in some capacity.

Things changed a little later as the maximum wage was abolished, Blackburn winger Bryan Douglas, Stanley Matthews' eventual successor in the England side, admitting, 'We had no idea what we should be asking for, there were no agents to guide you then. So we used England games to get together and find out how much the different clubs were paying!' Most spectators would give their right arm to play for England – though some ineffective players who've worn the shirt appear to have given their right leg – and would do so for no reward. They've a right to expect the players to give everything, and perhaps if there were no match fee, it would dispel the ludicrous terrace rumblings that the players only play for England for the money. However, England players are the élite few, the cream of the country's talent. If you're among the best in your trade, be you a footballer, lawyer, designer, accountant or whatever, you would expect to get the top rate for the job. The argument that players shouldn't be well paid is a spurious one and an insult. Had our top players been better paid after the war, at a time when many of their foreign counterparts were receiving excellent wages and healthy bonuses, perhaps England's results would have been better. Which is what everyone wants, isn't it?

Money or no money, England gradually came out of the doldrums. There was a brief flirtation with the 'Revie Plan', essentially a variation on the theme of the deep-lying forward built around Manchester City's Don Revie, but it was never as successful in international football as domestically, simply because foreign sides knew how to cope and refused to concede space by following him deeper and deeper. Through 1955–56, there were good wins over

Spain, and even Brazil were comfortably beaten at Wembley, 4–2, Tommy Taylor helping himself to two goals and confirming that he was the obvious successor to Nat Lofthouse. Equally important was the emergence of Fulham's Johnny Haynes, a tremendously gifted footballer, but one often dogged, unfairly perhaps, by controversy.

To many, Haynes was a footballing equivalent of Geoffrey Boycott, utterly self-absorbed and set apart from his team-mates. Billy Wright, though, would have none of that: 'Johnny is a credit to football and to himself. As to those stories we've read at some time or another that Johnny doesn't fit in with the England players, it is all moonshine and must never be taken at all seriously ... a great footballer who sets himself a tremendously high standard.' Maurice Norman, more an Under-23 player than senior squad member through the late 1950s, remembers that, 'Many of the moves revolved around Johnny Haynes; he was a good distributor of the ball.' Haynes quickly became the playmaker, and looking at the party that travelled on the 1956 summer tour, England suddenly had the nucleus of a good side coming together. In addition to Haynes, there was Duncan Edwards, Roger Byrne, Tommy Taylor, Ronnie Clayton, alongside stalwarts such as Wright and Finney.

The goalkeeping position was up for grabs, or so it seemed, with Ray Wood coming back into the picture: 'That summer we should have played Russia but the game was cancelled and we played Finland instead. We went to Sweden, Finland and Germany and I played in Helsinki. We got a nice smart blazer, £2 a day spending money, it was great! Two years later, the taxman sent a request for his cut of the spending money – I'd had £28 for fourteen days and he took a bloody slice out of that! We had good hotels, good coaches to take us to and from training and games. I could have had a few more caps, such as when we were out in Germany and Reg Matthews got injured but carried on anyway – and he'd done the same a couple of weeks earlier against Brazil at Wembley! So I could have had five caps instead of three, but it was great to get the three. I got one or two injuries at the wrong time, but there were lots of good keepers about – Merrick, Williams,

Ditchburn, Baynham, Hopkinson, Matthews, there was no shortage of choice. And with the committee picking the team, they probably didn't want too many players from one side in the England team and United were pretty well represented. There was no consistency – in the three games I played, there were 26 different players!'

After the confidence booster against Brazil, a good tour was imperative to set England up for World Cup qualification in their group with Denmark and the Republic of Ireland. There was a solid 0–0 draw in Sweden, then Finland, a team of similar quality to Denmark, were hammered 5–1, a promising portent. Finally, England travelled to West Germany for a hugely symbolic game, as Ray Wood recalls: 'It was the first time England had gone to West Germany since the war. We were taken through the Brandenburg Gate and into East Berlin by the Lancashire Regiment, who were stationed there. They gave us a tour. Stalin Alley was just a showpiece front, one main street and behind it was just rubble!'

The game went well, a 3–1 win on the World Champions' home turf, Duncan Edwards scoring his first England goal following a powerful run and shot – quintessential Edwards. Ray Wood is effusive about his team-mate: 'Duncan was a huge lad for his age, he was a man when he was a boy. He'd frighten the life out of some players, because he'd go in hard if he had to, but he had a lot of skill. He could play centre-forward, wing-half, centre-half, wherever you wanted him to play; had a fierce shot. It's such a pity that Munich happened because nobody saw the best of Duncan, nor that United team. You never knew what they could have done. They were all full of confidence; big teams aren't afraid of games, they just go out and play.'

As the tour had illustrated, suddenly England had a team again. There's no doubt that the English clubs were beginning to become more open-minded about the Continental influence and that Winterbottom's coaching and general approach were starting to bear fruit. Not for the last time though, it was the Manchester United influence that was pre-eminent, both in terms of personnel and

75

style. As Spurs had done in the early 1950s with push and run and as Liverpool were to do in the 1970s and 1980s with pass and move, so the late 1950s saw Manchester United transform the face of English football. After Wolves had had success with the long ball game, United took the decade by the scruff of the neck with their grace and power, passing the ball, prizing possession, valuing intelligence. Edwards epitomized the two ends of the game, as Bobby Charlton recalls: 'Duncan was head and shoulders above everybody else ... he had a passion, he loved the game, had the ability to play sixty-, seventy-, eighty-yard pinpoint passes. It's a shame there are no great TV pictures of him because he's without a doubt the greatest all-round player I've ever seen.' Wolves boss Stan Cullis, whose side were displaced at the top by United, was quick to concede that 'Edwards "read" a game – a precious asset – as well as any player whom I recall.' It was an accolade that could be applied to most of the United side who were now set to start their apprenticeship in the European Cup. Unquestionably the experience they gained from the opening of the 1956–57 campaign through to the snows of Munich saw them mature rapidly, as it should. After all, even a player as experienced as Billy Wright was moved to remark that, 'Looking back over my career I'd go so far as to say that I probably learned more as a young player through playing abroad than I ever did through playing top-class soccer at home!'

Following a disappointing draw in Belfast, England went on a triumphal march through the 1956–57 season, beating Wales, Yugoslavia, Denmark, Scotland, the Republic of Ireland, Denmark again, and ending with a draw in Dublin to seal qualification for the following year's World Cup in Sweden. The senior internationals were then given the summer off, in the hope they'd come back fresher for the rest. Sensibly, the FA had arranged for an Under-23 tour into Eastern Europe, so that the young guns could stake a claim for a place in the side. One member of the squad was Tottenham's Maurice Norman. He was keenly aware of the honour in representing his country: 'I come from a very simple and humble background, born in a cottage in Mulbarton with a population of

470 then, near Norwich. When I joined Spurs at 21 (I was sold because Norwich needed new floodlights) I'd never even been to London! For the tour all members of the squad received the FA booklet with general notes and information, were advised on what clothes to wear and given a limited amount of foreign currency. We got travelling expenses to London and an allowance of £2 per day while abroad. Players got a match fee of £30, reserves got £20. We weren't allowed to talk to the press, comment on TV, nor write about or criticize colleagues, opposition or referees in any way! England played a man-to-man marking style, where Spurs incorporated a slow build-up with one-touch passing and fast wingers cutting inside. It was quite a difference and hard for all the players to adapt to that from their club styles. The first time I flew was on that tour. Once the plane was above the clouds I found it a magical experience. Travelling abroad was wonderful, filling your mind with so many unique and invaluable situations. You play against foreign sides in some amazing stadia, in temperatures vastly different to our own.

'To go behind the "Iron Curtain" was enlightening. Bulgaria was such a poor country, poverty stricken. Sofia was drab, dull, depressing, the hotel was poor, their first class more like our third class. On one occasion we asked for boiled eggs but when they arrived they were raw, they'd just been dipped in cold water! For me it was an abrupt awakening to the misery endured by many people, the realization of how fortunate we were in England. We travelled through to Romania by sleeper train and it was a much more pleasant place, happier atmosphere. They were still poor, and their way out was to achieve "greatness", so sport was very import-ant to them. We went to see *Carmen* at the Opera House and watched the European Gymnastic Championships. Duncan Edwards was on the trip and he dominated the game in Bratislava, scored twice from about thirty yards! I made good friends on that trip and remember it with pride – I still have some cut glass from Bratislava to this day.'

With the exception of a defeat at home to Northern Ireland – who had perhaps their finest ever side at the time, a team that was to do well in Sweden – England swaggered through the start of the 1957–58 season, hammering Wales and then France 4–0. New players were gradually being introduced, such as Bryan Douglas: 'It was unexpected. I took over from the great Stanley Matthews. Mind, he was in his late 40s at the time! I didn't know, you didn't get a letter until after it had been announced on the news. I went in to training one morning and Bill Eckersley congratulated me and I asked him, "What about?" It had been on the news that morning. My first game was against Wales, to be played on a Saturday. I travelled down with Ronnie Clayton by train from Blackburn on the Monday; we trained in London for a couple of days then we were allowed home on the Wednesday! We had to reassemble in Porthcawl, and I went down there on the Thursday by car with the great Tom Finney, which itself was a terrific thrill – only a couple of years earlier I'd been watching him from the terraces. Tom was playing centre-forward for Preston at the time, but with England he was on the left wing.' Another newcomer, this time in the French game, was West Brom's Bobby Robson, who scored twice on his debut. When the French were so easily brushed aside – a team that would go on to finish third in Sweden – it looked as though England were going to the World Cup with genuine expectations rather than false hopes.

Those expectations died in Munich in February 1958 when Manchester United were decimated by that tragic air crash. Even at this distance it seems crass to talk about sporting disasters alongside such overwhelming personal tragedies, but as Walter Winterbottom says, 'Munich took away the spine of the team.' It's impossible to overestimate the effect Munich had on English football. For the players, it was hardest of all, as Maurice Norman says: 'I lost several good friends, as we all did. It meant the England team travelled in two planes for some time after that.' Three established internationals perished: Tommy Taylor had notched twelve goals in his last eight internationals; Roger Byrne might well have replaced Billy Wright as England captain. And Duncan Edwards ... there were no limits to what Duncan Edwards might have achieved. Bobby Charlton reckons that 'he was on the thresh-

78

old of probably the greatest career of any England international'. Reflecting on the loss, Bryan Douglas recalls that, 'I had three or four games with the United boys who perished. Tommy Taylor was my room-mate in France a couple of months before the crash, when we had a great result. I couldn't take it in when I heard that they'd died. Duncan was a great guy. His potential was never really realized, but he was a bit like Owen is now, the big star. He was a big guy, a mountain, a leader. I often wonder if we hadn't lost him, would Bobby Moore have got so many caps? Bobby was a wonderful player, but Duncan would have made him wait.' At a stroke, England's chances in Sweden were halved, for hard though players like Derek Kevan and Bert Slater tried, they were thrown in at the deep end and didn't have time to settle before the World Cup was upon them.

And for those replacements, it was a difficult emotional experience. Jim Langley replaced Byrne and was happy to admit, 'If Roger Byrne hadn't gone west in the Munich disaster I wouldn't have been capped in the first place, but Don Howe and I got drafted into a largely experimental side at Hampden and we got a dream start, tonking the Scots 4–0. It was the usual paper thing. On the Friday evening before I shouldn't have been picked according to people like Bernard Joy. On the Monday afterwards I was a hero! Walter Winterbottom picked an unchanged team in the next international against Portugal at Wembley and luckily good old Bobby Charlton saved my blushes in that one. His two goals ensured that we gained a 2–1 win after I had missed a penalty ... my favourite trick was always to feint to shoot inside the left-hand post with my left foot and then place it in the right-hand corner. It only partially worked this time. The keeper moved the wrong way OK but the ball smashed against the right-hand post.'

With the World Cup fast approaching, the England electors needed to take every chance to find new players. Thus far, Maurice Norman had a clutch of Under-23 caps, and recalls, 'In the back of your mind, you always think an Under-23 cap is a stepping stone. I played in a game for an Under-23 Past & Present XI against the England World Cup XI at Stamford Bridge in May, and the headlines were NORMAN & CLOUGH LEAVE NO DOUBT. Then I was in the squad that went on a Continental tour to Yugoslavia and the USSR prior to the 1958 World Cup.' Bobby Charlton had arrived on the scene to carry the torch for Manchester United and scored three goals in his first two games, both played in Britain. Inevitably, for Charlton the test would come when England needed to fly abroad. As Maurice Norman remembers, with savage irony, 'We flew out to Belgrade and this was Bobby Charlton's first flight since Munich, and we were playing on the ground where United had had their last match before the crash. At Zurich, we were held up for three hours by engine trouble and were transferred to another plane. Bobby was reasonably calm, but very quiet.'

Yugoslavia had also qualified for the World Cup and this was the first step of a two–leg tour that would end in the USSR, who shared England's first-round group in Sweden. It was an interesting trip, according to Norman: 'Before we flew out, the Russian ambassador met us at a reception in London and told us, "You are the best ambassadors. The result of the match is not important. The main thing is to improve the relationship between the two countries." Walter Winterbottom told him, "The result does matter. We want to win as a successful preliminary to the World Cup in which we meet you in the first round." On arrival in Belgrade, four hours late, we were told, "Be careful what you say and do," and there were police and soldiers all over the streets.'

England gave one of their most disappointing performances since the war. Norman watched from the sidelines: 'It was a sticky, humid afternoon, the pitch was bumpy, but as Walter Winterbottom simply said, "We were outclassed." We weren't considered quick enough in thought, anticipation or positioning. We'd been valued at a total of £500,000 on the transfer market, so we were very disillusioned, unhappy, shattered. The selectors were upset too, because they intended to keep an unchanged team for the last game before the World Cup. They'd actually given the reserves like myself some time off to go shopping, but because of the result, that was cancelled and we all had extra training. It was a bad result, but the Yugoslavs were a good team, rugged, geared to play for 180 minutes, flat out. One of their players, Crinkovic, at 14 had been fighting with partisans in the forests!' Jim Langley shares the assessment, telling *The Footballer* magazine: 'I seemed to spend half my time trying to mark two or three of them, as our tactics collapsed. I never played for England again but I swear I wasn't helped by some of the lads getting sloshed after the match, failing to pay a taxi out there and trying to charge the fee to my account . . . it all started as a bit of a joke but rebounded on me and the top brass were not amused. I could always call Bobby Charlton as a witness. At the time of the incident he was strumming his balalaika on the hotel balcony and I was trying to croon in Italian!'

It was a blessed relief to get out of Yugoslavia after such a hiding, though Moscow hardly seemed to offer much respite. But as Maurice Norman points out, 'They were very hospitable and the programme was crowded with receptions and the like. We visited the Kremlin, Red Square, Lenin's tomb in the morning, then had a training session in the afternoon, then on to see *Prince Igor* at the Bolshoi in the evening. We had to go around in pairs, followed everywhere by the "secret service". People clamoured for anything from us: shoes, clothes, money, razor blades! Walter had a row over the training ground we were allocated. He wanted to train at the 50,000-capacity Red Star Stadium instead of the Youth Stadium, a bumpy meadowland, where the pitch consisted of clover inter-spersed with tufts of grass six inches high. In the evening, it was pitch dark as floodlights weren't available, the only illumination came from a street light 200 yards away. Haynes fell heavily on the dewy rough pitch, so we did a few simple running exercises instead of ball work. Finney, who was 36 then, trained alone on a track because he was worried the treacherous pitch might cause a muscle injury. Tiredness, unaccustomed foods, and a sudden drop in temperature was taking a toll: Billy Wright and Bert Slater went down with stomach trouble, so I thought I'd get a chance, but they were eventually fit!' Tom Finney, a veteran international by now, was still excited by the opportunity of seeing the world. 'It was interesting to go there because very few Europeans had at that time. We saw a bit of the country, they made a thing of showing us round the universities they'd built, and it was a big propaganda thing for them, because they wanted us to think everything they did was the best in the world.'

The game in Moscow was the final friendly before the real business began. Bryan Douglas remembers, 'You'd get an inkling of what the team would be by the way the practice games were arranged, and Brian Clough played at centre-forward. Like always, Brian had an opinion and I think he upset a few people, but he was left out of the game in Moscow and [West Brom's] Derek Kevan played instead. There were rumours he'd had words with Winterbottom, and when the final squad for Sweden was selected, Brian wasn't in it.' Norman bears that out, though he adds that the switch in personnel might well have been a simple tactical adjustment: 'Derek Kevan was subdued because of heavy criticism for his performance against Portugal, but he was smiling again when Walter announced the team and said our tactics had changed. Every forward had been turned into a potential goalscorer. Haynes had to modify his deep-lying game to support this new policy. Walter had one or two secret plans up his sleeve, one of which was to encourage Kevan to develop his simple but effective strategy of bursting through the middle. When the game was played, the pitch was well below international standards, both penalty areas were waterlogged, though we were pleased the ground was softer and it was cooler. The Lenin Stadium was a fantastic place, held 100,000 people, and the palace had swimming pools, a cycle track, basketball and tennis courts. England were unlucky, their equalizer looked like hand ball, but Derek Kevan had scored and at least we came home in good spirits.'

This goal marked a turnaround in Kevan's fortunes. Like most forwards, he suffered in comparison with the prolific Tommy Taylor and initially suffered by being asked to fit into a system that had been designed with Taylor's gifts in mind. Where Taylor had represented a change in tack away from the typical English centre-forward, Kevan, nicknamed 'The Tank', had more traditional virtues; he was a strong, bustling forward who used his physique to good effect. With the shift in tactics that Maurice Norman has already noted, Kevan felt more comfortable with his role and registered two of the four goals England managed in Sweden.

Following the lengthy and traumatic domestic season, the merits of this brief tour were widely debated. As Maurice Norman says, 'There was a feeling in some soccer circles that tours out of season were a waste. The theory was that players needed the summer off for relaxation and renewal ready for the domestic season, instead of touring the Continent or even further afield wearing themselves out, so that when the new season opens they're stale or tired. At this point England still had to go to Sweden, tired or not.' Bryan Douglas suffered the effects of nine months of hard work: 'That year Blackburn got to the semis in the Cup and we'd got promotion, so we'd had a particularly hard season. This is often a problem for England with the World Cup, because it's always played in the summer when some nations are fresh and we're just at the end of a long season. I was a bit jaded, physically and mentally tired, and I think that applied to most of the players. After the tour, we only came home for a week before we reassembled and went out to Sweden, so it was pretty exhausting. The aircraft weren't like they are today and especially the ones behind the Iron Curtain. The cold war was at its height then and you had to be a bit on your guard, it was always in the back of your mind that you were in Communist territory. So it was mentally tiring too.'

With that exhaustion allied to the debilitating psychological effects of the Munich disaster, England were always fighting an uphill struggle. But at least the preparation was the best yet for a World Cup series. According to Norman, 'We met in Roehampton at the end of May for training at the Bank of England Sports Ground. Tom Finney got injured, which was a worry. Walter had a gift for organization, a quiet intellectual man, great thinker, always planning for the future, insisted on planning things in depth. He was quite relaxed; if anything, he was too nice, sometimes we could have been pushed harder. There was no great need to be a disciplinarian then because players seemed to toe the line. During his time, practices were changing dramatically, but he was still frustrated by the club before country situation. We were away about a week and then flew out to Gothenburg on 5 June and played the USSR three days later. In Gothenburg, the hotel was almost millionaire class. The facilities were good, and we were so near the Arctic Circle that we had the phenomena of the "midnight sun", so there were twenty-two hours of daylight in midsummer. The press surrounded us, but as friends – there didn't seem to be any hounding as there appears to be today. They were part of the set-up and travelled from place to place.'

In a telling example of the way the press has changed over forty years, Douglas recalls, 'Just before the World Cup, the lads found out Billy was going out with Joy Beverley from the Beverley Sisters, and we kept it quiet. But the story broke during the tournament and he had to deal with the press over that. He was a wonderful guy, great captain. He wasn't one of these players who shouts all the time, he'd give encouragement, gently put you right.' Wright got little bother from the press, despite having a relationship that was the 1950s equivalent of David Beckham and Posh Spice.

The England side that opened its campaign against the USSR in Gothenburg was certainly pretty useful, containing the likes of Finney, Haynes, Robson, Douglas, Wright, Kevan and Howe. How much more could it have achieved with the dynamism of Edwards, the goalscoring instincts of Taylor, the authority of Byrne. England even chose not to use the brilliant Bobby Charlton, Tom Finney reasoning that, 'I think they felt he was still suffering after Munich.' Having played the USSR in Moscow three weeks earlier, England knew what to expect, but found themselves two down just before the hour. Derek Kevan gave renewed hope with a flicked header after 66 minutes, but with time running out, England looked out of it. With five minutes to go, they were awarded a penalty and Tom Finney was given responsibility: 'I was 36 in 1958, I'd had a good run in the England side, so I knew it would be my last World Cup. To face Lev Yashin was a bit of pressure because he was known for studying how players took penalties. It was a great relief to see it hit the back of the net. That was virtually the last thing I did in Sweden, after that I was out with an injured knee for the rest of the tournament.' England also had a Bobby Robson goal disallowed for a supposed infringement on Yashin: 'The ball was played into Yashin and he and Derek Kevan went for it, there was a half clearance that came to me and I put the ball in. The referee, Zsolt, was a Hungarian and that was at the time when they were being suppressed, threatened by the Russians, so there was controversy about his appointment. Whether that had anything to do with him disallowing a perfectly good goal, I don't know!'

Maurice Norman again watched from the sidelines and felt 'the atmosphere was much the same as any international away from home, very little hype', Bryan Douglas adding, 'We played in Gothenburg, in a new stadium and the crowds weren't bad, but the level of interest wasn't anything like it's become. And people didn't travel like they do now. The crowds at all the games were mainly just the Swedes. People didn't follow their team abroad. There was a bit of TV from Sweden, but nothing like as much coverage, nor as sophisticated as it is today.' Maurice Norman concedes, 'The team didn't really play to their ability. The first game promised a lot, we fought back and could easily have won. But in truth, we were behind the Continentals, their style of play was different. We were more physical, they were developing a slower, stylish game with room for individual flair. And foreign referees had a different concept of taking notice (or not) of shirt pulling, tripping, bodychecking and all those other little obstructional devices.' Bryan Douglas is more direct: 'The Russians were pulling the shirt off Finney's back all the way through.'

Brazil, another team yet to win the Jules Rimet trophy, were next on the agenda. Norman admits the tactics were unadventurous: 'We planned to keep it tight at the back and come away with at least a point, and then look to beat Austria. But however good they were, you had to treat them as just another team, not to be in awe of them, which isn't easy when faced with Didi, Santos and the like.' Bobby Robson was again in the forward line and confesses to one great regret: 'Pelé didn't play in that game, which I was very sorry about because it would have been nice to be able to say that I'd played in the same game as him! But he didn't come through until later in the tournament. We drew 0–0 against Vavá, Zagallo, all those guys; so they could play, it was a great experience and I found it a very difficult game. I think of all the games I ever played, that was the hardest I ever had, didn't touch the ball too many times because they kept it so well. It's a pity there wasn't so much TV exposure then because it wasn't until the 1970 side that the Brazilians got portrayed around the world, but that team in 1958 was a very, very good side. Even then, we could have had a penalty when Derek Kevan was brought down in the box, so we did OK.' Walter Winterbottom goes further, pointing out that, 'Brazil were just kicking the ball out of play to waste time, happy to get a draw,' though having already demolished Austria 3–0, it would have been absurd if Brazil had risked defeat with the tricky USSR fixture to come.

Victory for England over Austria would have seen them through to the next phase, and with Austria not having managed a goal in their two games it didn't seem too taxing a proposition. But, as Tom Finney says, the whole tournament seemed jinxed: 'Things did run against us in 1958 – there was the Munich disaster, I got injured, we had goals disallowed, and Austria, who hadn't scored in three games, suddenly scored two brilliant goals from long range against us. We just felt we were unfortunate because we did very well against Brazil to draw 0–0 – the only team to stop them scoring – and played well in other games, but you go through spells when everything goes wrong and all you can do is keep going.' Ultimately, England were happy to get a 2–2 draw, twice coming from behind through Haynes and Kevan, though Bobby Robson had another seemingly legitimate goal chalked off.

With Brazil beating the USSR, it meant England had to meet the Soviets for the third time in a month to decide who would advance to the last eight. Changes were made, Bryan Douglas conceding, 'I was tiring and I missed the play-off game and Peter Brabrook came in. He hit the post and he played particularly well and even had a goal disallowed.' Peter Broadbent replaced Bobby Robson. As a student of the game, Robson admits, 'We didn't create the chances to win it, it was a close game and we lost 1–0, not much in it.'

So that was another World Cup gone by, though at least this

time there were signs that England had begun to learn how to play international football. Along with others in the squad such as Eddie Hopkinson, Peter Sillett, Bobby Smith and Bobby Charlton, Maurice Norman didn't get a kick: 'I was Billy Wright's understudy and learned a lot by just being in the company of older more experienced players such as Billy and Finney. It helped me mature and get a new outlook on the senior game, becoming aware of the need to study opponents and their tactics. It's always difficult to be an understudy. The need to keep yourself ready in mind and body, at the peak, just in case, is never easy. Naturally it always comes as a let down when you're not needed. It was disappointing not to play, almost heartbreaking having to sit on the line or in the stand when you just want to be out there. I don't think it changed my game because I didn't play, but being around the squad was a positive experience. Touring means leaving behind the family and being single-minded, dedicated and disciplined. But you see different countries, different cultures, new foods, landscapes, scenery, how the rest of the world lives. It changes your outlook, affects your life and how you interact with people.'

Such open-mindedness was encouraging, as was the impact of Winterbottom on the likes of Howe and Robson: 'Walter urged Don and me to go to Lilleshall to take up coaching under his guidance.' Tom Finney adds, 'Bobby and Don were always deep thinkers about the game. If you've any idea, you learn from the best, and at the World Cup they studied what was happening in the games; like the rest of us they wanted to become better players.' Given the contribution those two have subsequently made to English football, it's obvious the Swedish adventure was not all in vain. The team returned, escaping fierce criticism, simply because the spectre of Munich and football's most frustrating question, 'what if?' hung over the entire campaign. Next time, after three World Cup failures, there could be no excuses.

6

....

Chasing Rainbows

Ever since World War Two, international football has run on a four-year cycle. In more recent times, European nations have had that augmented – some might say disrupted – by the burgeoning importance of the European Championships. But it is still the World Cup that dominates the thoughts of international managers. The long haul to Chile in 1962 began with the customary round of Home Internationals plus a game against the USSR at Wembley, where revenge was gained with a thumping 5–0 win that came four months too late, further evidence that England genuinely were disadvantaged by playing at the end of a long and extremely gruelling season. Too little notice is still taken of that, but at least we play more internationals now. In 1958–59 England managed the grand total of four, including three Home Internationals, prior to the summer glut. What sort of preparation is that for learning from, then taking on and beating the world? None, according to Bobby Robson: 'I played five years for England when I was pretty much a regular and I reached the magnificent total of 20 caps! Now a regular for that length of time would get 60 caps. It was hard to keep the level of intensity, because between World Cups you'd have two years where you'd play just the Home Internationals and then the odd friendly, because there were no European Championships then.'

Because of the World Cup cycle, it was time for some England players to say their farewells. Nat Lofthouse played his final game against Wales at Villa Park in November, a month after Tom Finney had bowed out against the USSR. Finney accepts, 'It was on the cards that I'd be replaced by Alan A'Court or Bobby Charlton or someone. They didn't give me any indication that the Russia game was my last, but they were starting to look ahead to the next World Cup; you just expected it. It was a shame to have to finish, but my whole England career was a great experience. It's the pinnacle, it must be if you've any ambition at all.'

Another great managed to soldier on right through the 1958–59 season. England skipper Billy Wright boosted his tally of caps to 105, his one hundredth coming in a 1–0 win over Scotland at Wembley. The move to centre-half had undeniably lengthened his England career, but given that he was 34 when the side returned from Sweden, the case for continuing to select him was a little shaky. Maurice Norman believes, 'Billy was a great player, no question about it. He was only 5ft 8in but could jump amazingly. But without any disrespect, I feel he won his last few caps because the selectors wanted him to reach 100 caps, and that he should have stepped down earlier. When Billy hung up his boots, I hoped my chance had come, that seemed the general opinion. But suddenly I was forgotten and Brian Labone, Trevor Smith, Joe Shaw and Peter Swan all got their chances. Between 1958 and 1962, I was an understudy on at least 14 occasions! That was the period of Spurs' greatest success, the Double year and so on, so it was disappointing not to play for England and I felt the chance getting further away.' Naturally Norman had a vested interest in seeing Wright removed, but his observation is logical, and exposes the lack of forward planning at the heart of our football, the greatest casualty being Walter Winterbottom, whose reputation suffered for reasons beyond his control.

Billy Wright's swansong came in the summer of 1959 when, following a 2–2 draw with the Italians at Wembley, England embarked on another South American tour. One notable absentee was Bryan Douglas: 'I got injured in 1958, had a cartilage operation, which was a four- or five-month job then. I was advised to rest the summer of 1959 and missed a South American tour, because they didn't know it was a cartilage problem then, they just thought it was wear and tear and needed resting. But the first game of the next season, my knee went again, but they still didn't operate. I rested it and played after three weeks, and it went again. Eventually I went to London to see a specialist, the guy that did Denis Compton's knee. In those days it was a revolutionary technique to do an X-ray that gave you a blow-up of the knee, and they found the cartilage problem. When I got back we were short of an inside-forward because Roy Vernon had gone to Everton, and I took over at inside-left. After that I didn't get back in until the summer of 1960, but I still played outside-right for England!'

Douglas' knee was a pretty decent judge of when to miss a tour, because it was an unmitigated disaster, with three successive defeats in Brazil (2–0), Peru (4–1) and Mexico (2–1). The only bright spot came in Los Angeles when the USA were thrashed 8–1, Bobby Charlton claiming three while goal poacher supreme Jimmy Greaves, in his third international, couldn't get any. But that was a hollow victory and by the time the new season rolled around, drastic surgery was clearly required. Billy Wright announced his retirement and, along with Greaves, other promising youngsters such as Brian Clough and Burnley winger John Connelly were drafted in. But it wasn't easy for Winterbottom to make these changes: 'The selection committee could always overrule me. We'd tried to put a young side together; playing Wales in 1959 we had the youngest forward line ever fielded – Connelly, Greaves, Clough, Charlton, Holliday – and they played well and we drew 1–1. We had the same team against Sweden at Wembley and I tried to tell the committee to be prepared for a poorer performance because these were young lads getting experience. We lost 3–2 and the next time there were five changes!'

One beneficiary of that bizarre policy was Scottish-based Joe Baker, who came in for Clough, whose case wasn't aided by the fact that he played for unfashionable Middlesbrough in Division Two: 'I was amazed to get picked by the committee, because I didn't think they'd have heard of me! Funnily enough, I'd already played for Scottish schoolboys against England, so I thought everybody thought I was Scottish. But before 1967, at senior level you had to play for the country where you were born, so I wasn't eligible to play for Scotland. Nowadays you can qualify for half a dozen countries depending on your family, which is terrible, it should be your birthplace or the nationality of your parents.'

Baker's first game was against Northern Ireland, a triumphant debut: 'I got a goal at Wembley, I'd only turned 19, but I'd got a couple of years' experience in the top division in Scotland. I was up for the game but it was all very strange, the environment. I'd never seen the England players before because there wasn't much TV then, so it was very difficult to adjust. But when somebody can play football, it takes you ten minutes to get used to the other guys, and it's easy to play with good players. The big problem was they could never understand my accent – but they took to me well. When I first got to the hotel, they didn't know me from Adam, I was just sat in the corner and they all passed me by. When I got my first cap I was playing in Scotland for Hibernian, and so nobody knew me in England, the public were saying, "Who is this guy?" It was the first time it had been done. There was plenty of banter back at the grounds in Scotland after that. And to play against them at Hampden in my second game was a strange thing, calling for the ball from our team in a Scottish accent! It was one of those times when you couldn't win! It was a great honour to get an England cap because there were some tremendous players around; we weren't short of footballers. The side had Haynes, Greaves and Charlton in it, and they'd be great players in any era. It's hard to compare then and now because of all the facilities, better equipment, the lighter ball, but if the likes of Bobby Charlton had those advantages, he'd still be the best.'

While Baker was going through his version of culture shock, so was a young left-back, making his debut against the Scots, Ray Wilson: 'From Huddersfield to Hampden for my debut! But that was no problem because if you're going to survive at that level you've got to be able to cope and I always looked forward to those places. I think I had my best games in places like Brazil, with 100,000 people there, and generally away from home. That's important for internationals because there's a massive difference between playing First Division soccer and moving up a level. It really isn't a matter of how you can play because you wouldn't get in the team if you hadn't got ability, it's purely and simply a matter of have you got the bottle to play at the top? It's the same in most sports, when it comes to the big championships there are some players who can win the Open or Wimbledon four or five times, and others who you might think are better players who can't seem to win the big events. That has to be purely and simply in your mind, nothing else. When I first got in as a kid at Huddersfield, I'd look at the players a bit older than me and think, "I'm as good as and a fair bit better than them," and I had that attitude throughout my career. I didn't see anything that frightened me.' Alf Ramsey was later to prove beyond doubt that the mental toughness of a footballer was every bit as important as his ability on the ball. Wilson was rock solid, never upset by the conditions or the opposition. But how do you spot those characters? As Wilson points out, 'It was a big problem having the selection committee pick the team. You had people who wouldn't know a ball from a tomato picking the side. They chose players they'd seen having a good day. So sides changed rapidly. There were a few who got some caps – Wright, Finney, Haynes – but the rest of the side got picked on how they were doing at the time, which is a bit silly. It has to be better to get a squad together, and then you do get to know the players. That came in a bit later, where Alf identified the players he wanted and picked them for the squad, whether they were having a good time for their club or not. I remember Len Shackleton had a great game against West Germany in 1954 after they'd won the World Cup, and he said afterwards, "I bet only five or six of us play next time," and that was so. There was no squad. To survive at that level, how you perform for your club doesn't come into it. When I eventually left Huddersfield, I had 30 caps and six First Division games, because Huddersfield wouldn't give me a transfer! My first four years with England, I was in the Second Division – when I first got in in 1960, very few people knew me.'

In the summer of 1960, England set out on another tour. Joe

Baker was still in the set-up, having scored again in a 3–3 draw with Yugoslavia at Wembley: 'We went on tour to Spain and Hungary, and, again, as a youngster it was hard to slot in, and the results weren't good because Walter was rebuilding again, and the team was just bits and pieces, really. We had good players, but as a unit we hadn't really got it together. The press hammered us after those games. It is a problem in England, because if you get the wrong side of the press, they're the worst in the world.'

Losing 3–0 in Madrid and 2–0 in Budapest, things were at a very low ebb for the England team, but those who chose to criticize were ignoring the fact that a nucleus of good, still fairly inexperienced footballers was coming together – Wilson, Armfield, Baker, Charlton, Greaves were all in the team. Inevitably, young players do not have the consistency that their older counterparts can achieve, but how better to get experience than by playing in the world's greatest stadia? Of the players who played on that trip, five were still in the squad six summers later, when it really mattered. That said, as far as results were concerned, England were in disarray. Since the World Cup, they'd played 16 games, lost 6 and won just 4, those coming against the USSR, the USA, Scotland and Northern Ireland, not an impressive bag. Taken in isolation, the 1959–60 season looked worse yet – played 7, won 1 (Northern Ireland), lost 3. Those statistics make the events of the following season even more astounding. Suddenly Greaves and Bobby Charlton in particular came alive in front of goal. Northern Ireland were beaten 5–2 in Belfast, Luxembourg 9–0 away, Spain 4–2, Wales 5–1 and, most incredible yet, Scotland 9–3, then Mexico 8–0, all at Wembley. The side got a decent draw in Lisbon, won 3–2 in Rome before finally ending the run with a 3–1 defeat in Vienna. Nine games, won 7, lost 1, 45 goals for, 14 against. The value of keeping faith with youngsters was beginning to bear fruit and England had found a nice blend of youth and experience in the shape of Bobby Robson, Johnny Haynes and Bryan Douglas.

And that Scottish result! Bobby Robson recalls, 'The Scottish match was always a big occasion – I got the first goal, so that was a special match. Those games were extremely competitive, keen rivalry, very hostile at Hampden especially; no prisoners taken!' Bryan Douglas adds, 'Before that, we always used to hear about the "wee blue devils", but after that game we never heard much about them again! They blamed the keeper; I believe he emigrated. An amazing game, every time we touched the ball, it went in the net.' With 13 goals in the eight games he played (he missed the Mexico game) Jimmy Greaves had made himself England's greatest menace. Bryan Douglas reckons, 'He was just a natural, so cool in and around the box. He wasn't a workhorse, but if you're putting the ball in the net as regular as he did, what did it matter? People talk about Owen and Fowler now – Fowler's very like Jimmy – but Jimmy was the best I've seen at putting the ball in the net, no doubt about that. He was very unassuming, modest, a funny guy, but on the field, when the ball was in the penalty area, look out, Jimmy was about!'

One England regular who had to look on the carnage from beyond was Ray Wilson: 'I went out to Spain, played in front of 100,000, then Hungary, who were a massive side in 1960. It was a pretty awesome tour. On that tour, I went down in training with a knee injury, got through the tour, but when I got back to Huddersfield I went to see a specialist. He said there was nothing wrong. But our first game was at Sheffield United and it went right away, cartilage problem, so I was out of the England side and they started to put a good run together. Then Michael McNeil, who replaced me, got injured, so I was back in at the start of 1961– 62. I was delighted to get back in the side for the last qualifier for 1962, against Portugal, because obviously I wanted to go to the World Cup. They were a good side, with Ron Flowers, Peter Swan and Jimmy Armfield at the back. Perhaps they peaked too early, when they beat Scotland 9–3, but they'd just started playing this 4–2–4 system and that was bemusing sides. By the time we got to Chile, people had cottoned on. Then Bobby Robson got injured as well, which was how Bobby Moore got in, and that was him in for ever! Robson was a massive influence at that time, because the 4–2–4 revolved around him and Haynes; they were running the show.'

Haynes, in particular, was the fulcrum of England's play; everything was channelled through him, allowing him to use his impressive array of passes to maximum effect. Robson was an equally astute reader of the game, if not as eloquent a user of the ball as Haynes. The two complemented each other well, both highly creative footballers, thoroughly adept at feeding the disparate requirements of forwards as distinct as Greaves, Charlton and Smith.

Again, qualification for the World Cup was a straightforward affair. Luxembourg were twice beaten comfortably, England avoided defeat in Portugal, who were then beaten 2–0 at Wembley. But Wilson's point that England had passed a peak was valid. Luxembourg put up sterner opposition in the return and restricted their defeat to 4–1, Wales and Northern Ireland got draws and the Scots won 2–0 at Hampden to get a measure of revenge for the previous year's débâcle. Austria and Switzerland were both well beaten at Wembley, 3–1 each time, but the fluidity of the previous year had largely gone. The central figures hoping to put England back on the rails were Walter Winterbottom and skipper Johnny Haynes. Perhaps neither was quite the right personality at the right time. Of the manager, Wilson says, 'Walter was the old regime. He knew the game, but to run a side at that level, I think you need to have been an international.' Maurice Norman is a little less critical, pointing out the difficulties he operated under: 'Walter was a good manager and had he had responsibility for selection, etc, I think things could have been better. He understood the theory, practice and politics of football, defended his players, cared about them, was intensely loyal, though he seemed to take notice of the press, so that if any member of the selection committee backed somebody who was getting good write-ups, Walter could be swayed into going along with that view and not standing up for players he preferred. He allowed too many to come and go without a real chance to show what they could do.'

There were still fewer questions about Haynes' ability as a footballer, but the first £100 a week player, following the abolition of the maximum wage, continued to be beset by questions as to his temperament and his suitability as a leader. Ray Wilson says, 'I can understand some people describing Johnny as selfish, but in many respects you have to be to reach the level that he did. He was a massive player. Probably, if he'd been at his peak in Alf's time, Alf would have controlled that. A lot of people thought he was running the show, and he may have been, but that might not have been a bad idea, some liaison between him and Walter was fine. I'm not being critical, because he was a great player and a good skipper, but possibly he had too much influence. John had a short fuse, but if he'd been Alf's captain rather than Walter's, it might have worked a lot better.' Maurice Norman agrees that, 'Johnny was a little absorbed in his own game, but he loved the game fervently, gave his all and always wanted the ball. He did find it hard to put up with the mistakes of others, because he set such high standards. He was always working, passing the ball with relentless precision; he specialized in the long, accurate ball through the middle.' The final view is that of Bryan Douglas: 'Johnny was a different captain to Billy Wright. I thought he was a great guy, great player, but he was aggressive. Not as a player, not as a tackler, but with his own players. If you weren't doing your job, he'd let you know about it. I didn't mind that; though some of the players may have done. But I found him an excellent captain, and he led by example. He did want the ball all the time, but there's nothing wrong with that, it's the guys that hide that I'm against. John was a terrific passer with both feet. He didn't beat people, but he could find the open spaces and he could distribute the ball left, right and centre. He didn't suffer fools and he was a bit aggressive with his tongue, but I didn't mind, I just admired his ability; I was always happy to play with John.'

And if England were to do well in 1962, they certainly needed the likes of Haynes at his very best. England still had to set the World Cup alight – first-round casualties in 1950 and 1958, beaten quarter-finalists in 1954; hardly the record of a proud footballing nation, still less one that had given the game to the world. Playing in South America was never going to suit European sides, but England could call on arguably the strongest squad they'd yet taken to a finals series. Goalkeepers Ron Springett and Alan Hodgkinson looked reliable, leaving Gordon Banks as the stay-at-home reserve; the full-backs included Armfield, Wilson and Howe; centre-backs Swan, Norman and Flowers were all resolute defenders. In midfield, there was a glut of talent – Haynes, Robson, George Eastham, Stan Anderson and a young man yet to play for his country, Bobby Moore. And how much more talent did you need up front than Greaves, Charlton, Douglas, Gerry Hitchens, Connelly, Roger Hunt and Alan Peacock? To take the crown from Brazil in their own part of the world was a stiff assignment, but the squad approached it with some justifiable confidence. And, again, preparation had moved on in the four years since Sweden, as Maurice Norman could testify: 'I was picked in the squad again, though this time as understudy to Peter Swan! The set-up hadn't changed much, just a turnover of individuals. Walter was as earnest and emphatic as usual. No problems over money, though there were discussions between players about club and personal contracts. I was still on £20 per week at Spurs. For the World Cup in Chile, the match fee had risen to £60. It was said that had we won the competition, we'd have received a "very substantial sum", probably around £1000 each.

'The build-up was more professional, the World Cup was viewed far more seriously, and it was the first one where TV was really used. We copied many countries by going to a camp away from the outside world and the media. Before we left, Harold Shepherdson packed over two thousand pills to combat stomach disorders; we took boiled sweets, 8 lbs of tea, sauces, all sorts of things. Walter said, "If the team does well in Peru, it will remain the same for the first match against Hungary in Chile." Walter had been out to watch Austria play Bulgaria and announced the team and again, I was understudy to Peter Swan. Later that day, I went to the Hospital for Tropical Diseases at St Pancras with Jimmy Greaves and Bobby Moore to get yellow fever jabs. On returning to Roehampton to prepare for the flight to Lima, I found the squad was to fly in two planes, the first team in one, the reserves in another. I was on the first team plane because Peter Swan had tonsillitis, a temperature of 102, but was still travelling. The flight to Peru was a long one, we touched down in several countries, had thirty minutes in Lisbon to stretch our legs and walk off the meal we had on the journey (smoked salmon, caviar and crab washed down with champagne cocktails, not really to my taste). Back on the plane, the night was short as we were near the equator; Dakar was hot even in the middle of the night. We had some sleep as we crossed the ocean, which took four and a half hours. We had breakfast – scrambled egg – then touched down in Buenos Aires. The last leg was two and a half hours, we had to pass over the Andes, and arrived in Lima Airport in time for more breakfast! The atmosphere is very different to a club tour, the team were established internationals, and you knew if you were picked, you only had your place for that game. I was very aware of that! When we arrived, we had a telegram from Prince Philip: "With best of luck to the England team." '

Tales of altitude training, heat acclimatization and the like are staples of today's footballspeak. Ray Wilson's not so sure about it all: 'We played Peru on the way out and we were there about a week before the first game, but the business of acclimatization seemed a lot of codswallop to me; it never seemed a problem. I think if nobody had brought it up, people wouldn't worry about it.' For other members of the side, such as Maurice Norman, the visit to Lima would be one never to be forgotten, allowing him to pick up his first cap after four years in and around the England squad: 'For me it was now or never on that trip. I was playing well, had just played in a Cup-winning side that got to the semis of the European Cup. There'd been a definite rise in my confidence following the European games, but also getting married to Jacqueline in March 1961 made a big difference. We married on Monday – my day off – I trained the next day, played Chelsea on the Saturday and had a great match, heading the winner which clinched the Championship. That marked a change in my fortunes and I owe a lot to her and her family as well as my own for allowing me to be so single-minded in pursuit of my football. I didn't know if I would be playing until we had trained in Lima the day before the game. So that meant Bobby Moore and I got our first caps. I received telegrams from Tottenham's directors, Bill Nicholson, some press-men, friends, relations. Bill said, "At last, you have waited long enough," which was good of him, as I knew it would make life even more difficult for him, as we already had eight players on international duty.

'It was the culmination of all I'd striven for. It was here at last and it was a continual revelation for me to think I was a footballer, doing the one and only thing that came naturally to me and the only thing I really wanted to do. Being able to see the world, famous places, famous people, the good and the bad, the best hotels, playing in great stadia and getting paid for it; it was a dream come true, the dream I'd had all my life. I felt all my patience, determination and discipline had been worth it. There is nothing better than playing for your country. The 50,000-seater stadium had been the site of savage bullfights the previous Sunday and only a wire fence separated us from some tempestuous fans. The Peruvian players earned about £60 a month and were mostly taxi drivers!

'We won 4–0, our first win in South America since 1953, and it was nice revenge for the five survivors of the team who lost 4–1 there in 1959. Jimmy Greaves scored three in 14 minutes in a half-empty stadium. We wore a new all-red strip and we meant to win. There were deafening firecrackers to greet the Peruvians but we were on top throughout; they were fast but with little forward movement. Even I went up into our forward line and created a chance for Gerry Hitchens, which was kicked off the line. I was used to Blanchflower and Mackay at Spurs, but having Bobby Moore and Ron Flowers instead didn't pose any problems; you must adapt quickly.'

The win in Peru boosted English confidence, but their hopes were dealt a nasty blow a couple of days later when Bobby Robson got injured: 'Nineteen sixty-two was a great disappointment for me because I was in the team when we set out, and Walter took young Bobby Moore, who was 21 then, as cover. We played in a friendly in Peru and won 4–0; I didn't play and Walter gave Bobby a run out, to save me for the World Cup. We had a practice game and I fractured my ankle, got a crack in it, which was a three-week job, and Bobby Moore played instead of me. And that was Bobby in for ever, 108 caps! We played Brazil in a knockout game and I was fit for that, but not match fit, so Bobby stayed in. I was despondent about that, so upset, because I felt I'd been playing so well.'

Having endured the mammoth journey to Peru, the trip on to Chile was no picnic either, another 2000-mile jaunt. Bryan Douglas remembers, 'Lima was as far as the 707 aircraft took us, and from Lima we went by prop to Chile and it took us hours. We arrived in Santiago and then had another horrendous coach journey on to Rancagua, and then eventually up to the hills. By then we were just thinking, "Where the hell are we going?"' Ray Wilson points out how antiquated the tournament was then: 'It's staggering how things have moved on. When we were in Chile, we stayed in a village up in the mountains! Our group was Hungary, Argentina, us and Bulgaria, so that was three of the top eight in the world at the time, and I don't think the gates were any more than 8 or 9000. It was like playing in a village, a little stand on one side and a hut on the other, and that was it! We travelled in by coach and train from the mountains. It wasn't until later on when we got to Santiago that things were more normal, but can you imagine a World Cup like that today?! I hope I'm not being unkind, but I can't imagine a country like Chile getting the World Cup now.'

Keeping players happy during a World Cup is a crucial part of the manager's job, often one that will cause him greater difficulty than his selection and tactical approach. Each player is an individual and while some will enjoy the training camp set-up, others will find it suffocating or dull. Maurice Norman and Ray Wilson had differing views, Norman's first: 'The party moved to a training camp at the American Braden Copper Company Camp in Coya, which some players weren't happy with. Personally, I felt it was ideal, a perfect setting for training, perched high up among the snow-capped mountains of the Andes. It was an oasis, covered with tall cacti and cut off from the world, a paradise. We lived in three adjoining miners' houses, two to a bedroom. On one side of the camp was a hydroelectric plant, on the other a South American cowboy, sitting sleepily on his horse wearing a broad-brimmed hat and a poncho. We had a specialist cook brought in, we ate mainly roast beef, chicken and rice. George Robledo, the Chilean who had played with Newcastle in the 1950s, was helping to iron out wrinkles in the team whilst in Chile. He said we had the best camp and the best climatic conditions – high up in the mountains, not too hot, with plenty of rain. But the problem came in the evenings for some. There were no TVs, pubs, cinemas, although there was a nine-hole golf course, swimming pool and beautiful gardens. We were met by the local band, who played "God Save The Queen", very out of time!'

Ray Wilson was a little less impressed by the facilities on offer: 'I'll never forget when we got on the train to go into the mountains and it was the train they used to go out to the old copper mines. Every time we turned a corner, George Eastham sat back saying, "Bloody hell, not another!" We thought we'd never get there, it was in the wilderness, the foothills of the Andes! Thinking back, I never thought about people like George or Roger [Hunt], who went all that way and never got a kick, and I feel somewhat ashamed about that, that I didn't realize how the people on the edges of the team felt; "Am I playing?", not being able to sleep the night before it got picked. I never even thought it was going to happen to me, which really does sound awful! But to go there and not play in 1962 must have been terrible because the place was awful, there was nothing to do. The highlight was to go to the cinema at night to watch a French film with Spanish subtitles! So if you were just training and not looking forward to playing it must have been terrible. And there was nothing financial about it. If you were a reserve – there were only two reserves – you got £30, but if you didn't play, you got nothing! The only financial thing they got was £2 a day expenses.'

As Bryan Douglas points out, 'We played in a little village, dust streets, our training place was up in the mountains, in the Andes. We were based by an American copper mine. Five miles away from the village they had their complex, up in the hills. We were expecting Wyatt Earp to go past! The only way out was a little diesel train that used to carry the workers up to the mine. It took about twenty minutes on that to Rancagua. Apart from coming down to play and train, we were just stuck up in this mountain, by this little shanty village. There was a British lady, who was a cook, who looked after the team; we weren't in a hotel or anything. There was a bowling alley there and that was about it, it was really boring, to be honest.'

The World Cup was now ready to begin in earnest, and England had as good a chance of doing as well as they'd ever had. As Norman notes, 'Walter was said to be pleased with the defence after Peru, and said in the press that if I did what I did for Spurs, I was in for the World Cup. Then Peter fell ill again and was hospitalized. There were some facilities at the camp, but we didn't have a doctor with the team.' Essentially, that meant that the side who had played in Peru was now the first choice and, following such an emphatic victory in Lima, confidence was high.

The opener was against the Hungarians, long England's *bête noire*, having won the previous three fixtures, rattling in fifteen goals in the process. Nobody in the party was going to underestimate the East Europeans, even though their greatest days were now behind them and the giants of 1953 long gone. England's strength was clearly in the front line, with footballers of the quality of Greaves, Bobby Charlton, Gerry Hitchens – a brave, free-scoring centre-forward good enough to be earning his handsome living with Inter Milan, a radical change from his early working career as a miner in Shropshire – and Bryan Douglas. Behind them, Johnny Haynes was required to make the bullets, augmented by the young Bobby Moore. That was initially England's problem. Moore was not yet the great figure he became, though Norman points out, 'At the beginning, he was underestimated, he had strong positional sense and was dependable and determined, with youth on his side. He read the game well and as he developed he became calmer and showed many good skills, especially in distribution.' But the loss of Bobby Robson was a serious blow. He and Haynes worked superbly together and were the fulcrum of the team and the Moore–Haynes tandem was less effective.

The first game was played in Rancagua. Bryan Douglas recalls, 'Accrington Stanley went out of the League playing in front of bigger crowds than we got for those games!' Maurice Norman remembers that 'the ground held 25,000 but the crowd was about 7000, as the ordinary people couldn't afford tickets. The Hungarians played well, displayed superior tactics and ball skills. The ground was slippery, which caused mistakes. For me, it was probably an even more intense game than the 1961 Cup Final, when Spurs won the Double, because a defeat would mean we had virtually no chance of progressing, as Argentina had already beaten Bulgaria in their first game.'

Ray Wilson felt England were unlucky to lose the game 2–1, but it was telling that England's only goal came from a Ron Flowers penalty. Though Hungary were the better side, it was an unfortunate mistake that cost the game when, in the pouring rain, Flowers slipped and allowed Florian Albert through. It was a disappointing opening to the campaign, without doubt, but England recognized they could improve and that they had certainly not been annihilated. And it was as well that they weren't given time to dwell on the defeat, the crucial match with Argentina coming just two days later. It was a game that England had to win, but the selectors weren't pushed into panic changes, the only difference being the replacement of Hitchens with Alan Peacock of Middlesbrough, a tall man whose strength in the air would be exploited to the full both by England's wingers and by the overlapping full-backs, Wilson and Armfield. Argentina had begun to perfect the cynical savagery that was to dog their football throughout the decade and managed to put two of the Bulgarians out of the tournament, so England knew a physical game was in store. But the likes of Wilson, Norman and Flowers were hardly shrinking violets, and they could put themselves about as well as the next man. Maurice Norman felt the Argentines would be a real threat: 'They were probably the biggest side I ever faced, all above 6 feet, with very fiery temperaments. We arrived only 40 minutes before kick-off because of a delay in travelling to Rancagua. We'd been allocated a one-track railway train, but due to a motionless goods train, we were delayed! It was hot, humid, the hottest day since we'd arrived. We played firm and strong, much the better team, so we got back into the World Cup.' Ray Wilson admits to some trepidation before the match: 'The game was crucial and that was against another favourite, Argentina, because they were virtually at home. The one thing in our favour was the game did draw a crowd, about 10,000 people! And the Chileans made it feel like we were at home because they were massive rivals, they absolutely hated the Argentineans. We played them off the park.'

This was, indeed, one of England's best World Cup performances to that point. They took charge of the game from the outset, with Flowers scoring after 17 minutes, his second successive spot-kick. Bobby Charlton, playing wide on the left, scored with a trademark shot from distance just before the break and Greaves secured things just after the hour with a typical piece of poaching in the six yard box. Argentina got a late consolation, but England had won with ease and underlined their credentials as genuine challengers.

By the time England were set to play their final group game, against Bulgaria, they knew exactly what they had to do. Hungary had thrashed the Bulgarians 6–1, then simply shut out Argentina in a 0–0 draw. England could not top the group, but avoiding defeat would see them qualify at the expense of Argentina. For Ray Wilson, it was a nerve-racking experience: 'The worst for us was the last game because we had to avoid defeat, and at that time I can honestly say players weren't equipped to play for draws, it wasn't in our culture. Nobody had really played seriously in Europe except Manchester United. At Everton, a few years later on, we'd go away into Germany or Spain, or wherever, and play like we did at Goodison and get arseholed every time, come back 2 or 3 down and then have to pull it back. So the idea of keeping it tight away from home hadn't come in. Bulgaria were the bottom team and weren't a very good side. I don't know whether Walter or Johnny Haynes decided it, but we decided a 0–0 would see us through. I remember Bobby Charlton shouting, "What the hell's going on, get the bloody ball up here!" If we'd gone at them like we had in the first two, we'd probably have made it much more simple for ourselves, but that was a frightening game, one of the worst I've played in. Because they didn't want to come over halfway either, we were in our half, they were in theirs, and it was like playing tennis. I can't remember anyone having a shot and it must have been the most boring game of all time!'

As Glenn Hoddle can now testify, getting the right place in your qualification group is absolutely essential. Because of the poor start against Hungary, England were condemned to face the World Cup holders, Brazil, in the quarter-final. Had England managed to top the group, they'd have been able to stay in Rancagua and play against a strong, but not unbeatable Czechoslovakian side. England could take a little comfort from the fact that Pelé was injured and would be missing from the Brazilian line-up, but that was about as good as it got against a team that still contained Didi, Vavá, Amarildo, Zagallo and Garrincha, of whom Jimmy Armfield says, 'He seemed to have a limp, slightly hunched, but was very quick over five yards, like Matthews in that respect. Once he went, that was it!' England also had to trek across country, not a great distance, but an awkward trip nonetheless, but at least one which gave them a chance to see something of the country. Ray Wilson recalls, 'You did get extremes of poverty and wealth, very little in the middle. Certainly in the village we stayed, they were lovely folk, but I couldn't describe them as anything other than peasants.' Maurice Norman was equally struck by the economic conditions in Chile: 'It was hot and dusty, the majority lived in poverty, their houses huts and shacks, yet the landowners lived in the lap of luxury. The Brazil game was at Viña del Mar, on the coast, with swank hotels, top restaurants, casinos, nightclubs, dance halls and swimming pools. The people were friendly but deep in poverty, the vast majority lived in tiny houses, huts or holes in the walls, these poor native people in their shanty towns, hovels where people spent a lifetime in terrible conditions. Then a few yards down the road, the rich were living in luxury. It had a profound effect on me.'

It's surprisingly rare for England's footballers to be so touched by any nation, simply because they don't often get to see it. As Ray Wilson points out, 'People say to me, "You must have been everywhere, Ray," and I say, "I have, but I've been nowhere!" You get on a plane, go to the hotel, train. You might get the odd bus trip round the city, because you're there to play, but you can't go walking round for two or three hours, so you're pretty restricted. On tour, or in a competition like the World Cup, the thing you have to beat is boredom. You're relatively fit, so you're not training much, so there's nothing to do; it's a matter of killing time. You can't go night-clubbing – not then, anyway, we couldn't afford it! I don't know how much that's changed, there's always been the odd player who liked a drink more than anybody else, but most were pretty level headed; they were decent drinkers but they did it at the right time. That's the important thing with most things in life. Good pros have to mix socially and have to work hard, and I did that. I certainly wouldn't dream of going out two or three nights before a game, but after the game, especially if we'd had a good result or if we knew full well that we'd got that night free, I'd stay out with anybody, I'd probably still be sat in the nightclub when the sweeper-upper came round! I can't deny we used to enjoy ourselves, that's for sure. We probably were closer to the press than they are today. They'd stay in the same hotels, travel with us, but I can't remember a problem, I can't remember anyone going out the night before the game. As long as you did things at the right time, you didn't have any trouble.'

Bryan Douglas sympathizes with Wilson's view, and adds, 'I do feel sorry for some of the present day players and the treatment they get from the press; but they are film stars now, they're high profile and that's not going to change. When we went abroad, we had to do everything together. We all had to go to the British Embassy, our hosts would arrange some sightseeing tour if there was time, or we'd be taken to a show. On the day of the match, there'd be a reception after the game and you'd be left to your own devices then to have a drink, but it was often with the press – they were our hosts sometimes! So that never got in the papers!'

The quarter-finals of the World Cup was a rarefied atmosphere for England, only the second time they'd got that far in four attempts. There were suggestions that Bobby Robson might return for the game, but though he was now over his injury he certainly wasn't match fit, and England could not take a risk with him in such a big game. So the same basic ten players took to the field again, with the injured Peacock replaced by Hitchens, the rotation between those two players being the only changes England had made in the four games.

Prior to the game, Maurice Norman remembers, 'the stadium was covered in sea mist from the Pacific. Walter told the press, "We know this is our Final, we are full of fight, we know this is our greatest game. No more funny business, there must be complete preparation and absolute execution. I want to emphasize we are not suffering in any way from fatigue." In fact, we were suffering, tired at the end of a long season, battered and bruised from the other matches. Our confidence was reasonably high, we thought we had a chance. We wanted to keep it tight against great players like Didi, Vavá, Garrincha, Amarildo. The ball was lighter and the ground hard, they were specialists in bending it round the wall in free-kicks. The Santos brothers, though in their mid-30s, were as fine as pair of full-backs as I ever saw. The star was the bow-legged Manoel Garrincha, the "Little Bird", who scored after half an hour.'

Ray Wilson remembers that goal vividly: 'I was man-marking Garrincha and they took a corner – Zagallo took it from the left – I was on the line and Garrincha ran right along the back, into the six yard box, nobody marking him at all, and he headed it in. And we had a long discussion about it afterwards, and I said it had to be changed. What's the point having a defender on the line and the guy he's supposed to be marking left free? We had Hitchens and Bobby stood on the halfway line not picking anybody up. Now they'd be back doing some defending.'

England hit back within 7 minutes, Hitchens pouncing on a rebound, and at the break there was cause for some quiet optimism. Bryan Douglas remembers that, 'We were doing quite well. I had a bit of joy against Djalma Santos, Bobby Charlton was having a good time on the other wing and it was 1–1. Garrincha had scored for them, he was a bit like Matthews, helluva player, but at half-time we felt confident. But they got a free-kick and it hit Ron Springett in the chest and ballooned up and Vavá got to the rebound and scored. Then Garrincha hit one from thirty yards and it flew in. Ron was good keeper when they came at him in the penalty area, but from distance he had a bit of difficulty, I think.'

By the hour mark Brazil were 3–1 up and out of reach. Maurice Norman recalls that it was 'a very different atmosphere, 18,000 people, they had strong support in red and blue uniforms, they kept up an incessant beat with single drums, steel bands, whose instruments included frying pans, biscuit tins and coffee drums. The game was held up when a dog came on the pitch, until it was finally coaxed off by Greavesie. I remember vividly Garrincha beating Ray Wilson on halfway, then coming at the penalty area like lightning. My heart was in my mouth as I went to tackle him, but I beat him, though he was a wonderful player. But we lost and were out. No excuses, we were very dejected, we really felt we had the chances to win. We all know how great Brazilians are, but it's not until you see their skill for yourself that you see how unbelievable they are. They were supposed to be playing 4–2–4, but they often had seven in defence when needed and the same in attack when they could, they were so fluid.'

As Maurice Norman says, 'We didn't get a warm reception at home – the World Cup is supposed to be a sporting occasion, but with so much at stake in politics and prestige, the sport can be forgotten.' Again, England were found wanting technically and tactically, and as the public became more interested in this exotic World Cup idea, so they were losing patience at failure after failure. Wasn't it time we won it, especially if we were going to host the damned thing in 1966? Walter Winterbottom could take some comfort in the realization that slowly but surely the gap was closing. But he would not be around to gather that particular harvest. On England's return, it was announced that Winterbottom would be stepping down from the post as England manager after seventeen years in the job. English football, as ever, was looking for a quick fix, a saviour. And lo, the golden child came to lead England to the New Jerusalem, and he didst come from ... Dagenham.

7

A World to Win

It was apparent that England's approach to international football needed fresh impetus. Winterbottom had done a solid job, introducing new ideas, better organization on and off the field and a greater appreciation of the strengths of foreign opposition. But simply by virtue of the fact that he'd been in the job seventeen years, it meant that he was accepted as part of the furniture. There was only so far he could push for change before he came up against the FA's constant and immovable objection: 'But, Walter, you've been doing it like that for years, so why change?' That knee-jerk reaction to new ideas had held England back for too long and things were now getting very serious. In 1960, England were awarded the honour of hosting the 1966 World Cup. After four post-war attempts to win it, the public were thirsty for, if not ultimate victory, then at least a side that might challenge and acquit itself well. And, as ever, when the public begins to turn, the Establishment begins to fear for its own safety and reacts.

Walter Winterbottom's decision to step down from his post as England manager had been an open secret for some time, but had he not gone voluntarily it's likely the FA would have pushed him. Seventeen years in one job is a very long tenure and the time was right for change. That's not necessarily a reflection on Winterbottom's ability to do the job, merely an acceptance that however open-minded a coach might be, there are certain basic principles to which they will adhere. After such a prolonged period of time, a new man with new ideas will offer a breath of fresh air.

For Winterbottom too, it was time for a change. It was apparent that down the years, he had become increasingly frustrated with the job of running the England team. The regular battles with the selection committee offered one problem, but it was not the only one. He had little time to work with the side except on summer tours, when a number of players he wanted to use were made unavailable by clubs who wanted their stars to rest. Whenever Winterbottom introduced any tactical innovation, there was inevitably an outcry from the clubs back home who felt this would cause unrest among players who were being asked to play in different ways for club and country. However committed, for anyone, there comes a point when banging your head against a brick wall becomes too much.

Once it became obvious that Winterbottom would be leaving the England job, it seemed likely that he would take over the vacant position as secretary of the Football Association, a job which Winterbottom particularly coveted. The position became open when Sir Stanley Rous took over as president of FIFA, and Winterbottom looked the ideal candidate to overhaul the outdated structure and principles that held sway at Lancaster Gate. A good administrator too, here was a football man with a massive store of knowledge on international football. Who better than Winterbottom to take on the mantle? And because Winterbottom was the ideal choice, the man who could bring English football into the twentieth century, he didn't get the job. The reactionary hierarchy outvoted Winterbottom, installing Denis Follows instead, a hard-working, conscientious administrator, but an Establishment man. When he left the job a decade and more later, one tribute to him from the Minister of Sport, Denis Howell, read, 'Denis is much more of an amateur soccer man than a professional ... University sport is still his great joy.' And that was a recommendation for running the English branch of the world game?

So Winterbottom was out. But who would replace him? There were candidates like Burnley's Jimmy Adamson, who had been Winterbottom's assistant in Chile. Adamson had been named Footballer of the Year in 1962 and he was an intelligent, thoughtful player. He had captained Burnley to the Championship in 1960, in much the same way that Danny Blanchflower had led Tottenham to the Double the year after, then led them to the runners-up slot in both League and Cup in 1962. Clearly an impressive footballing intellect, Adamson was just 33, still playing, had no managerial experience as such and no international caps. It was surprisingly forward-looking of the FA to approach him for an interview, but Burnley weren't keen to release him and Adamson didn't want to force the issue.

Bill Nicholson, who had assisted Winterbottom in 1958, might have been another choice, but such was the success he was enjoying with Spurs, at home and abroad, it would have been impossible to shift him from White Hart Lane. Denis Wilshaw, who had played in the 1954 World Cup, was also under consideration, but again he was a reluctant nominee. With the obvious personal and professional attacks that would attend failure in 1966 at the forefront of everyone's minds, not for the last time, the England manager's job was seen as a poisoned chalice.

Winterbottom held the fort through three games, including England's debut in the European Nations Cup (guess what? we hadn't entered the inaugural event), then played as a straight two-legged knockout competition. England were pitched against France, who hadn't even qualified for Chile. The first leg was at home, a game Maurice Norman has particular cause to remember: 'I played against France at Hillsborough and was dropped afterwards. I wasn't surprised because I was booed whenever I touched the ball because the Sheffield fans wanted Swan or Shaw in the team. I felt very dejected and my form at Spurs suffered too.' A radically reshaped England, with four changes in attack and midfield, managed an unimpressive 1–1 draw – Flowers scored his third penalty in five games – in a match that saw Jimmy Armfield replace the injured Johnny Haynes as captain. Maurice Norman saw Armfield as 'a quiet, deep thinker, good captain. An attacking full-back who'd go into the front line if circumstances warranted it. Not a talker, but a tactician, like Danny Blanchflower. He had tremendous confidence in himself, cool and calm, with a firmness that meant he always had complete control of the team. He could be blunt and never used more words than necessary but you weren't left in any doubt as to what he wanted and what he thought of the team's performances.' Winterbottom took the side through easy wins over Northern Ireland and Wales before bowing out.

Finally, the Football Association had settled on his successor, Alf Ramsey, who'd had a distinguished playing career with Spurs and England and who, as manager of Ipswich, had steered the backwater club from the depths of the Third Division South to the League Championship within seven years. Few in the game doubted he was a master tactician, but the fact that he was at best third choice hardly inspired confidence. Paradoxically, the very difficulties the FA faced meant that Ramsey's hand was strengthened when it came to negotiating terms and conditions. He insisted he would not take charge full-time until May 1963 so that he could properly discharge his obligations to Ipswich, a meticulous and thoughtful move typical of the man. More important still, Ramsey was able to ensure that he would have sole charge of all team matters, including absolute control over team selection. In its way, perhaps this was the single most important step forward in English inter-national football. Fair enough, it meant if we had a lousy manager, we'd get a lousy team, but at least the players knew who they were performing for, a consistent selection policy was possible (if not always delivered) and an élite group playing to a preordained method could be worked with. As Walter Winterbottom says, 'In 1982, for instance, Italy had eleven players from Juventus; they built solidarity out of a club. You can't do that in England. Even before the Continentals came into the game, our league was servicing the five home nations. What Alf did was to get unity by consistent selection, something I could never do.' He also chose to raise expectations ahead of the World Cup in a manner not universally popular with his players. According to Ray Wilson: 'If I've got anything agin Alf, it was sitting in the house watching him on TV saying, "We shall win the World Cup." I thought, "Shit! What do you want to say that for?" '

Ramsey certainly approached the job with an open mind. Only three of what were to be his core players – Bobby Charlton, Bobby Moore and Jimmy Greaves – took the field in the European Nations return leg with France, where England were soundly beaten 5–2. On the way off, Ramsey asked Armfield, 'Do we always defend like that?' The captain got the inference: 'We weren't going to defend like that again.' Ramsey immediately drafted Gordon Banks into the side, and he became a fixture under Ramsey until the car crash that cost him an eye. The improvement was soon apparent, for though England lost 2–1 to Scotland, defensively they looked more solid.

That was obvious in a 1–1 draw with Brazil at Wembley, when Ray Wilson was restored to the team: 'I'd been injured and was probably lucky to miss the games I did because they were poor results, though if they'd gone well, I might never have got back in. Alf didn't like my attitude, thought I was arrogant, a big mouth. I was fiercely competitive, that's for sure, and he admitted later he'd made a bad judgement before he really knew me. My first game with him was against Brazil on the Wednesday, but I had to play for Huddersfield on the Monday. I got there for training on Tuesday. He came over to meet me and asked me how I wanted to play. I said I liked to use the ball, but he was just letting me in. When I'd finished, he said, "You'll bloody play how I want you to play!" '

Maurice Norman had been recalled by Ramsey and noticed an immediate difference in the ethos: 'Alf demanded more *for* the team in every way but also expected more *from* it. He did not put *anything* before the players. This made you want to give more, try harder. He made you feel good about yourself, your game; he inspired you to give more. I felt I could have run through a brick wall for him. He wanted an international team to be like a club side – similar outlook, spirit and understanding between players. Many found him cold and aloof, but I always got on well with him. He was always fair, never slated you in team talks, but took you aside and discussed your mistakes privately. He was a perfectionist, believed that to develop the team's understanding you needed frequent meetings, discussing all aspects of the game, opposition. He had endless practice matches to try new ideas; every match was a new challenge, a battle of wits, speed and skill. He used to say, "No team can improve by gaining easy victories over poor sides." However good the opposition, he would never let us believe we couldn't win; no time for inferiority complexes.'

Ramsey's first real exposure to the job came with the summer tour of 1963, which went into Eastern Europe and then on to Switzerland. Culturally, Norman noted, 'There'd been a slight improvement behind the Iron Curtain since 1958 – not much, though we weren't followed around so much until we went to East Germany. There were a lot of propaganda speeches during this trip, which was often the case in Iron Curtain countries, and we were kept away from the ordinary people. Politics was a very touchy subject, you had to be very careful. It was an experience to visit the Berlin Wall and realize all the misery it was causing; it made me think a lot about the differences between East and West!' For all the political dimension, Wilson points out, 'With Walter, we always had to go to the Embassy. We had nothing in common with the people there, they didn't know who we were, why we were there, but we had to go and talk to them. Alf put a stop to that. He'd go with officials or Harold Shepherdson.'

Freed from some of the more onerous touring tasks, England got down to playing some bright football against relatively moderate opposition. The arrival of a new manager seemed to concentrate a few minds and with everyone playing for their places, England achieved some good results. Czechoslovakia, World Cup Finalists a year earlier, though now in transition, were beaten 4–2, then East Germany overcome 2–1 in Leipzig. The tour was then crowned with an 8–1 win in Basle, Bobby Charlton getting three. Bryan Douglas also scored, yet as he remembers, 'When Ramsey came on the scene that was pretty much the finish of me. He wasn't too familiar with the international game but he did his homework and eventually it paid dividends. But when he came in, he had to sort things out. He decided he didn't want wingers and that put paid to me. I got three goals in three games for him and then he dropped me. I was still an inside-forward at Blackburn, but a winger for England, and Ramsey continually told me off for not staying on the wing. If I wasn't getting the ball, I'd come inside to get it and I suppose I was spoiling the shape of the team as he saw it. But I had a few games with him and I knew my days were numbered. When I got home from that tour, I told my wife, "That's it, I think." And it was.' Douglas was replaced with Southampton's Terry Paine, who was probably stronger in the tackle, an early indication of the multi-purpose footballer that Ramsey prized, though Paine himself was to fall by the wayside as wingers were phased out, and the yet more adaptable Alan Ball came into his own, the first of the wide midfielders, as opposed to an out-and-out winger.

Although Alf had wrested control of selection, he still found himself beset by the conflicting demands of the Football League, and he rarely came out on top. In the 1963–64 season England again played just four games until the summer. The only Continental opposition came in the form of an FA centenary celebration game against the Rest of the World, which England won 2–1, against a side bristling with talent but totally lacking in cohesion, causing Maurice Norman to remark, 'We played extremely well and showed our skill and superior tactics.' These matches were scarcely the sort of test England required if they were going to make the kind of progress necessary to fulfil Ramsey's prophecy of ultimate success in 1966. At least he could look forward to a busy month through May and into June when England would cram in seven games, three against top-class South American outfits and also a stop off in New York.

Having introduced Banks and Hunt to the nucleus, he now had to replace Jimmy Armfield, who dropped out of the reckoning with a serious injury that was to cost him the England captaincy and a place in Ramsey's first eleven. As an adventurous, elegant, full-back, Armfield gave Ramsey the extra attacking option he required, adding to that a quiet authority that kept the team in order. Had Ramsey not been able to find such a capable replace-ment for Armfield, he would surely have returned for the World

Cup, perhaps even as captain, though Moore's later assurance would have made that unlikely. As it was, in George Cohen, Ramsey found a new right-back who matched his needs perfectly. He made his debut in a game with Uruguay at Wembley: 'They were very defensive, so it helped me feel my way into the side; steady game, nothing heroic. But I'd been around a while by then, I'd played my first senior game for Fulham at 16, and became a regular at 17, had played a Cup semi-final against Manchester United in 1958 after Munich, and played in front of two massive crowds. So I had a fair bit of experience already and reputations didn't bother me. I was a pretty confident youngster, a bit of a big head, no doubt! And I'd already played with very good players like Johnny Haynes, Bobby Robson, Roy Bentley, so the big names with England were no different.' With such confidence, Cohen was an ideal Ramsey man, his self-belief never preventing him from following Ramsey's instructions to the letter, allied to which was his ability to play a dual purpose role: 'My main asset was I could sprint, so I loved getting into the attack and then getting back into defence.'

On the other flank, Ray Wilson was not dissimilar, though an even better player, as good as any left-back in the world. While many were resolutely talking down English chances for 1966, hindsight makes it clear that we were suddenly producing a clutch of genuine world-class footballers. In addition to Wilson, we had Banks, Moore, Bobby Charlton and Greaves, an impressive spine around which to build. So events prior to England's departure for Portugal to start the summer tour could have been quite catastrophic.

Ray Wilson recalls, 'Before the tour, we met up in dribs and drabs. Bobby Charlton knew somebody who was opening a club and asked if we wanted to go. So him, me, Bobby Moore, George Eastham, Gordon Banks, Johnny Byrne and Jimmy Greaves all went. We got back a bit late and we found our passports on our beds, so we knew Alf knew we'd been gone. I suppose we should have asked him, but it was all pretty innocent, nobody got legless; we weren't that late. But Alf never said a word 'til we were in

Portugal, then he gave us some real stick! He had a meeting, then at the end said, "There are seven players who would like to have a word with me." So we went to see him and he said that if he'd had enough players available, we wouldn't have come, so we were put down pretty firmly! Then we won well, more easily than the 4–3 score, and Johnny got three, Bobby Charlton the other, so maybe we should have asked him if we could always prepare like that. He'd have liked that!'

Though Ramsey was a disciplinarian, he was also deeply pragmatic. Had he sent them home, he'd have created a press incident, which he was always keen to avoid. The seven could have become martyrs, forcing him to either eat humble pie, so weakening his position, or freeze them out for good. And what manager would imagine he could win the World Cup without Moore, Charlton, Banks, Wilson and Greaves? Had the players been fringe members of the squad, perhaps Ramsey would have acted on these threats. As it was, he was stymied by the wholesale nature of the mutiny. In retrospect, the seven did their manager a favour, as George Cohen explains: 'Alf's word was law, because of the famous passport incident. So the word was out that if you messed around, you were out. I respond to discipline, so the regimentation didn't worry me, and if you can't behave when you're with the England team, you shouldn't be there. We had a good crop of players at that time, as we'd always had, but it needed a figure like Ramsey to take on the FA, introduce the proper disciplines and establish England at the top. There'd have been no dentist's chair under Alf! Young people are always going to look for some fun, whatever they class fun as. But when you were with Alf, you were expected to behave like adults. His attitude was absolutely right, the idea that surely he wasn't asking too much. And that kind of discipline is needed. You all have to toe the line because otherwise it has a bad effect – if there are guys doing the right thing and they see other players getting away with murder . . . It's bad for the reputation of the side and the country. Equally, if you had that discipline, Alf knew you would get injured but get up and carry on, that if you were knackered, you'd keep running.'

ABOVE An early England line-up from 1895. Steve Bloomer is seated first from the left *(Hulton Getty)*

BELOW Dixie Dean attacks Spain's Ricardo Zamora, Highbury 1931 *(Hulton Getty)*

THIS PAGE

ABOVE The Blackpool connection:
Stanley Matthews and Stan Mortensen,
October 1953 *(Hulton Getty)*

RIGHT The Preston plumber, Tom
Finney, February 1947 *(Hulton Getty)*

FACING PAGE

TOP Captain Eddie Hapgood shares
a joke with the Duke of Kent. Willie
Hall (far right) is amused; Stan Cullis
(next to him) isn't. Highbury,
November 1938 *(Hulton Getty)*

LEFT The party that visited Italy
and Switzerland in 1948. Left to right:
Frank Swift, John Aston, Alf Ramsey,
John Howe, Billy Wright, Neil Franklin,
Bill Nicholson, Henry Cockburn, Tom
Finney, Tommy Lawton, Wilf Mannion,
Bob Langton, Stan Mortensen, Stan
Pearson, Stanley Matthews, Laurie
Scott *(Hulton Getty)*

ABOVE England's greatest performance? Tom Finney makes it 4–0 against Italy in Turin, May 1948 *(Hulton Getty)*

BELOW Nat Lofthouse ponders the value of a shoulder charge, England v Rest of the World, October 1955 *(Hulton Getty)*

Billy Wright captures Tiddles the Cat, training session, Brighton, November 1949 *(Hulton Getty)*

Training prior to the November 1957 fixture against France, which saw Bobby Robson's international debut and Duncan Edwards' final cap, three months before the Munich disaster *(Hulton Getty)*

Trainer Harold Shepherd-son dispenses advice to Jimmy Greaves, Bobby Charlton and Johnny Haynes, April 1961 *(Hulton Getty)*

Walter Winterbottom reminds Brian Clough that he's the manager, training session prior to England v Sweden, 1959 *(Hulton Getty)*

Happy families: Jack and Bobby Charlton, April 1965 *(Hulton Getty)*

Ray Wilson, supported by George Cohen, keeps Uruguay at bay, May 1964 *(Hulton Getty)*

ABOVE
World Champions.
Back row: trainer
Harold Shepherdson,
George Cohen, Martin
Peters, Gordon Banks,
Alan Ball, Bobby Moore,
Nobby Stiles. Front row:
Bobby Charlton, Roger
Hunt, Geoff Hurst, Ray
Wilson, Jack Charlton
(Hulton Getty)

LEFT
Geoff Hurst leaps
as England overcome
Argentina in the '66
quarter-final *(Hulton
Getty)*

Maurice Norman follows Cohen's line: 'I suppose players were different. There was less freedom to go around alone, we went everywhere as a group, supervised most of the time. Players were settled in their habits, earned good money for the time, but nothing to compare with today. And in a lot of the countries we visited, the political situation was dodgy, so we kept quiet. The press were different, mostly looking on the bright side, dealing with tactics and games, not off-the-pitch behaviour or personalities. Alf wouldn't have stood for bad behaviour. Anything unprofessional could lead to you being sent home and probably never selected again. Football itself has changed, there's so much more money, players and their expectations have changed, and winning at all costs is the attitude very often. It sometimes seems that pulling an England shirt on meant more to players in my day, and there is so much more in the lives of current-day footballers.'

The differing reactions to touring within the squad illustrated the way in which English society was changing. For Liverpool's Peter Thompson, 'It was strange. I was from a council estate and suddenly I'm flying first class across the world and staying in the Waldorf Astoria!' George Cohen was a little more phlegmatic: 'I'd had some experience of going abroad – my first club trip was to Italy in 1958 when we went by train, and we had a fascinating tour of the Tuscany valley, went to Venice, but those club trips were a lot more relaxed than England tours. To go to South America and America was still unusual in 1964. I didn't go overboard about New York, I found it a bit threatening. We were there ten days; there were some nice restaurants, and we found one called Mama Leone's that sold jellied eels, which I'm very partial to! It was a fascinating place, but I'd hate to live there!' Maurice Norman feels that, 'We were going along nicely that season, and seemed to be on top of the world. We flew out to the USA and played them in New York and won 10–0, so confidence was sky high. We had nearly two weeks in New York, it was tiring but inspiring and enjoyable because going abroad was still far from the norm then. We saw some of New York. I didn't like it a lot, there seemed so little air, light and sunshine, it was claustrophobic, probably because of the narrow streets and the skyscrapers. I remember us training then going to the hotel to watch multi-channel TV, which was a novelty to us then.'

The basis of the tour was not the trip to America, however, but a tournament in Brazil, the Little World Cup, featuring England, Brazil, Argentina and Portugal. The scheduling left a great deal to be desired, indicating just how little attention was paid to anything other than events on the field. George Cohen explains that, 'We had a long flight to Brazil and then played within thirty-six hours. And it exhausted me, after 25 minutes I couldn't raise my legs. We actually outplayed them for quite a while and then suddenly in the second half the whole team just died. I was particularly poorly, and the doctor said it was down to the flight, the hours in a plane at 60,000 feet followed by a hard game so soon afterwards. I couldn't play again on that tour. I was just ill, had to have a walk around the town with Dr Bass, took me up Sugar Loaf Mountain to have something to eat and drink, and I just couldn't play again on that trip.'

If you're going to play against a Pelé-inspired Brazil in the Maracanã, you need to be at a peak of fitness. England weren't and Brazil exploited that, even before the game kicked off. Wilson recalls, 'We were sat in the dressing room for two hours before they arrived at the ground, so we started playing about four in the morning our time! We did well for an hour and then collapsed.' Norman continues, 'Football was almost like a religion and their supporters were fanatical, using fireworks to create atmosphere. They had a six-foot-deep concrete moat around the pitch, which they flooded if there was any trouble. Our best game was against Brazil, it was only in the last 20 minutes that the damage was done. There's little more I can add about Pelé, but as we were running out of steam, he seemed to take over! We'd contained them well enough then all hell let loose. I'd never seen skill like it, it was genius, he had all the tricks in the book. He didn't need to play the full 90 minutes at full pace, he waited his moment, struck, and you couldn't answer him!' Brazil thumped England 5–1.

Although the football was going a little sour, there was still plenty to interest men newly exposed to South America. George Cohen says, 'It was a fascinating tour if you were interested in politics, because that country was very near to Communism at that time. The police were Fascists, the way they treated people was brutal; it was appalling. I'd seen deprivation at home during the war and just afterwards, but when you saw the way they lived in Brazil, you realized we'd been well off! We'd had ration books, all they could do was scavenge around rubbish dumps for food. It's a beautiful country, and we went to São Paulo, which is a remarkable mix of extreme wealth and abject poverty. We went up to see this wonderful statue of Christ, but I remember thinking about how much it must have cost and how that money could have been spent on the people. And then we saw these incredible precious stones being cut, some unbelievable wealth there.'

Maurice Norman adds, 'One of my most lasting memories is of the statue of Christ on the Mount as we flew in. The mountain and the statue dominate the skyline – apparently at least thirty people a year jump to their deaths from this mountain top. The sky was always cloudless, it was burning hot, the sea was blue, the waves gigantic . . . the huge Sugar Loaf Mountain. We'd look out of the window on to the Copacabana and see hundreds of youngsters kicking a ball around. From dawn until dusk it went on, they spent all their time learning anything and everything about football. We had a kick about with some of the lads and they beat us, showing fantastic skills.' Peter Thompson was able to spend some time on the beach and remembers those youngsters: 'We were lying there and these Brazilian kids played with little rag balls, doing all these incredible tricks, and they came over to us and asked us to do them, great players like Bobby Charlton, but there was no way we were going to be embarrassed!'

After a five-day break, a little pride was regained in São Paulo with a 1–1 draw against Portugal, before England completed their labours against Argentina. Ray Wilson sees that game as a vital part of the learning curve towards 1966: 'We lost 1–0. Rattin refereed it, it was incredible. They were very physical, very nasty, but we learned something from that. A couple of years later, Alf said they were animals, but that was a little unkind to animals. They were gangsters. Rattin was awesome, a big man, always around the referee, sticking his nose in everything; it was painful. Which was a shame, because they were a good side. I thought they'd be a problem if we met them in '66. But by then we'd got into the habit of playing Alf's way. In '64 we kept pushing and that suited them – we had 80 per cent of the ball and they won 1–0. In '66, we didn't do that, we played their way, keeping the ball. It must have been an awful game to watch.'

It's important to note that while critical lessons were drawn from failure, the great success of the tour was soon to fall out of Ramsey's first eleven. Peter Thompson 'was thrilled to get picked and I got off to a fabulous start. In Portugal and then in South America, I had a fabulous run. The competition was probably the best four teams in the world and they picked a team out of the four at the end and I was in it. They started calling me the white Pelé! When I got back home, Shanks called me in after four terrible games and said, "The white Pelé? More like the white Nelly!"' Thompson was to be a casualty of the transition to the famous wingless wonders, suffering, as Bryan Douglas had done, from his lack of defensive qualities.

The Little World Cup seemed to indicate that England were still out of their depth as an international force, but like pretty well every press proclamation about the fortunes of the national team, that was way too extreme. They had been victims of a ludicrous schedule and weather they weren't fully acclimatized to. Against Brazil, they had held their own until fatigue destroyed them. These were not issues that would trouble them in 1966. The potential for trouble came from two sources. The genius of Pelé – and what could anyone do about that, other than hope to beat him with close marking? – and the rugged organization and technical ability of Argentina. Each of these would suffer the same kind of climatic and cultural difficulties that beset England in Brazil, so taken in that light, the situation was less desperate than it was painted. Crucially, Argentina had also provided Ramsey with a blueprint for success. Although he had introduced a greater degree of organization than previously, his philosophy with England had still been an aggressive one, looking to score plenty of goals. Results had generally been good, and if your team scores four, eight, even ten goals in a game, it's hard to criticize. Yet although England were generally winning, analysis of the goals against column suggested frailties that could be exploited. Allowing the likes of Northern Ireland and Portugal to grab three goals had to be cause for concern. Once England came up against a ruthless unit like Argentina, whose first rule of philosophy was 'if they don't score we don't lose', they were asking for trouble. Ramsey accepted England had to adopt similar principles.

It was a slow process, but one which gradually unfolded over the 1964–65 season. England tended to play two wingers, but Bobby Charlton was not always one of them, a good move according to George Cohen: 'I first came up against Bobby Charlton in a Cup semi-final in 1958, just after Munich, and I thought he was some mature player even then. Bob used to get chewed off by the crowd at Wembley when he was on the wing, but moving him into the middle, like George Best, gave him greater freedom. He had that great acceleration, beautiful balance that gives the great players half a chance at goal when there isn't one.'

Moving Charlton had further implications for the shape of the team, though these were only to become apparent later. Ramsey's first preoccupation was to get the defence working as a unit. It took time, with results through 1964–65 generally uninspiring. Following a 4–3 win in Belfast, after which Ramsey tore into the side for their indiscipline, England were lucky to get a 2–2 draw against Belgium at Wembley, Peter Thompson pointing out, 'They murdered us. I never got a bloody kick!' A draw in Amsterdam did little to improve perceptions of the side, but in fairness to Ramsey he was struggling with injuries. Bobby Moore missed a couple of games and Ray Wilson was out for much of that season. By the time he returned against Scotland in April 1965, things had changed dramatically: 'I got an horrendous injury in '64 and got to the stage where I thought I wouldn't play again. I tore the muscles in my groin off the bone. They didn't X-ray it, just gave me rest. But it was getting worse, so I finally had some X-rays and they found the bone was calcifying inside the muscle. That put me out till spring '65 and when I got back, the back four was sorted out – Banks, Cohen, me, Moore, Jack Charlton and Nobby sitting in front. Me and big Jack were mouthy players and it's very important that people talk. We never used to break, we tried to keep the back four solid, we never tackled until they got round the penalty area and the other lads put them under pressure, so they couldn't squeeze a ball through. If one of us had tackled on the halfway line and missed, it's mayhem. Someone has to come across, that leaves a space, it's like dominoes going down.'

Jack Charlton came in partly because Maurice Norman 'was moved to full-back at Spurs. You never give up trying, especially with the World Cup in England on the horizon. I lost a stone to give me more speed and all went well. Then Spurs played a friendly against a Hungarian XI and I broke my leg. Alf told me later I'd have been in the twenty-two, so who knows what might have happened? It took me three years before I was fit enough to lead a normal life; I had to have rebreaks and bone grafting.'

It was the elevation of Stiles to the national colours that was both most interesting and most revealing. As Cohen notes, 'We could see what the shape was as it started to come together with Jack and Nobby coming in. Jack had something that Alf felt he needed – he was terrific in the air, a single-minded so and so, bit contrary at times – and he gave us security, until he came up against Torres of Portugal. We could see the little pieces being bolted together and the only uncertainty was who would supply the crosses and how, so we could see where we were going, but we weren't there yet. I don't believe he finally came to his conclusions until the tour in '66, when he settled on his nucleus of about fifteen players and his tactics. It's not recognized that Nobby was a very good distributor of the ball, but he fed Bobby Charlton time and again. Bobby could see Nobby go into a tackle, was confident he'd come out with the ball, move into space and Nobby would find him. That was a very good partnership.' It also made it all the more important that Charlton moved away from the wing and into a more central role. So seven slots were now filled, and surely Jimmy Greaves would make it eight. The improvement was almost immediately apparent. After getting a 2–2 draw with Scotland, England's next ten games through to the next meeting with the old enemy saw them concede just seven goals, three of them coming amid an aberration against Austria.

By May 1965, things were starting to get serious as the countdown to the World Cup began in earnest. The very fact that England managed to fit in ten games in twelve months made it clear that Ramsey was getting his way, and grabbing the necessary preparation time. A summer tour saw the defence bedding down nicely, with a 1–1 draw in Belgrade, then a 1–0 win in Nuremberg, with the first real use of the 4–3–3 system, and a 2–1 win in Sweden. It was quickly apparent that the back four and Stiles were going to form as tight a barrier as any in the world. But in sacrificing one midfielder to an almost entirely destructive role, it meant that creatively England were a little short. Now the task was to adjust the balance.

Importantly, the team were starting to realize they could compete with the best. According to George Cohen: 'Alf was terribly confident, he knew the type of player and the type of characters he needed, and he knew he could get them. He made us incredibly hard to beat and if you're not losing games and not conceding goals that gives you the confidence to go on and win them. Towards the end of '65 the defence had taken shape, the squad was settled, you knew damn well that he knew what he was doing. He didn't overburden you with detail or facts and figures; if he said something to you, you knew it was pertinent. His attitude was, "I've picked you because of the way you play for your club, just do that and any other little things I ask, and we'll get on fine!" '

A 3–2 home defeat against Austria in October 1965 gave critics plenty of ammunition, but perhaps it didn't do any harm, damping down any rising expectations. The key game in England's preparation came in Madrid in December 1965. England again played what has been called 4–3–3, though it would be better termed

4–1–3–2, Stiles as an advance sweeper, Bobby Charlton with a comparatively free role in midfield, Alan Ball and George Eastham providing the industry and a degree of width, and just two forwards, in this case the tireless Roger Hunt and Joe Baker. Baker had returned from the wilderness with a goal in the previous game against Northern Ireland, in the absence of Jimmy Greaves who was suffering from hepatitis. 'I dropped out of the team through circumstances, really, when I went out to Italy. It wasn't until I came back and went to Arsenal, in the spotlight, that I got back into the reckoning. I came back in 1962 and started popping in some goals and then Alf Ramsey took notice of me.' Baker scored early on and felt comfortable in the new style: 'People make a fuss about tactics and formations. The first time we played 4–3–3 was in Madrid, but there was no special training for it. Your own intelligence as an international means you should know what to do. If the manager says we're playing 4–3–3, the players know what they're supposed to do, you don't need lectures. Alf just put a side together, said, "You're left-back, you're left midfield, you're right midfield," and we just got on with it. So you've got your back four with two centre-halves, they know that if one goes forward, the other stays behind, you should be mentally attuned to do that, it's not difficult.'

That 2–0 win in Madrid (Hunt scored the second) was a seminal moment. Ray Wilson remembers that, 'We toyed with them. It was purely and simply the system, their defence didn't know who to mark, there were no wingers, they got caught ball watching and we murdered them. I'd have fancied us against anybody away from home; we were best equipped to play away.' Wilson's assessment was underlined by a 1–1 draw with Poland at Goodison in January, when a similar line-up struggled against a tight defence, though conditions scarcely helped. Joe Baker reckons the match 'should never have been played; it was a mudheap, a quagmire, a terrible game. Nobody played that night, you couldn't kick the ball ten yards. But I don't know what happened after that, I just disappeared out of the picture. That's what I didn't like about Ramsey, that he didn't explain things man to man. If he'd said, "Look, Joe, I've decided on the system I'm playing and I think Roger and Jimmy play it best, I'm the one who gets the stick if it fails, so I'm sorry I can't have you," I could accept that, but not to get a call or a letter was awful. Like all managers he had his favourites, and my face didn't fit. Maybe he didn't like my accent! But I couldn't relate to him. I call a spade a spade, but he wouldn't talk back to you after a game, to tell you what you'd done. He wouldn't say, "Right, you were crap," he'd just quietly drop you out of it without telling you what you'd done. When he selected the twenty-seven, I never got a phone call, a letter or anything to say why I wasn't considered, and I thought that was wrong. I got a few goals for him then just disappeared off the scene.'

Peter Thompson has a similar story from that period: 'I had two really poor games and where Shankly would have a go at you, Alf just came over, touched my knee and said, "Very disappointed," and walked off. I was nearly crying. His big criticism was I didn't look up, which was fair, but I couldn't change my style. Tactically, I was hopeless. At Liverpool, we'd come in for a team meeting, Shanks would say, "Right, boys, these are the tactics. Tommo, you can go because you never bloody listen anyway," and I could leave. Alf wasn't like that.'

Though Thompson remained in the squads, Baker was not picked again and, by the time of England's next friendly against West Germany at Wembley a month later, he'd been replaced by Geoff Hurst. As Baker says, 'I don't think Geoff was a great centre-forward, by no means was he a great footballer – if you use the word "great" properly, about Pelé or Eusebio. Geoff was a big powerful guy, up the middle, lots of hustle and bustle, and he did it very well. And he slotted nicely into the way the team played, next to Roger Hunt. I always played alongside guys like Geoff for my clubs, people like Frank Wignall or Geoff Strong – they'd win the ball in the air, I'd make runs off them. You form partnerships, but it doesn't take long. Intelligent players read what the other guy is doing and play according to that. Where Alf was right was to avoid having too many individuals in the side, because you're playing a dangerous game there. He had the blend – Nobby to win and then give it to somebody like Bobby Charlton that could play, the same with Jack and Bobby Moore.'

Hurst entered the side with some trepidation: 'I arrived as a nervous 24-year-old. Alf was very formal, thanked you for coming. He had an extremely strong character, which is probably the essential element when you have the press and 50 million people telling you who to pick. It's very easy to get sidetracked, but he didn't. Alf's only priority was his players; we were aware of it and responded. As a newcomer, I was more concerned about my own performances; I was happy just to be in the reckoning. I didn't expect to be picked ahead of Jimmy or Roger, I wasn't really thinking about winning the World Cup, more just getting in the team. It wasn't hard to settle in, we had good characters who wouldn't go under. He picked players who weren't the best, necessarily, but ones who could work in a team and who were the right sort of characters.' Nor was Ramsey averse to a little mischief at the other side's expense. Thinking back to the fluidity of the Hungarians of the early 1950s and the confusion they wrought, he played Stiles with a number nine on his back against West Germany, though Nobby played his traditional harrying game. The irony was, he got the only goal of the match and the game was written up as though he was England's new attacking weapon!

The side overcame Scotland 4–3 at Hampden, then Yugoslavia 2–0 at Wembley. They then took a break through much of May prior to settling down to the proper preparations at Lilleshall. It was not the easiest of regimes, Ray Wilson suggesting it 'was like doing National Service again. It was gruelling but it was worth it. We were in the middle of nowhere, we had to get on with each other and the team bonded together. We got incredibly fit and saw the benefit when things went ever so well on the tour. But it was so boring, 27 virile young men cooped up together where the high spot was playing tennis! Success does bring you together, but when I meet the guys now, there is a special feeling between us, that you went through something together, like being in a war!'

George Cohen agrees, saying, 'Lilleshall only needed a moat! It was a long way from the nearest pub, so nobody bothered – Jack might have! We knew why we were there, it was a momentous thing, we knew that and everybody reacted correctly. I'd been badly injured at Fulham towards the end of the season, severed my knee to the bursa, and that interrupted my momentum and I didn't have a great World Cup because of that, so I had to train hard under Les Cocker and Harold Shepherdson; they worked me like mad after training. Alf wouldn't allow the press access to us, except on certain days that he specified. He wouldn't tolerate them interrupting our preparations. He helped them where he could but once he'd given interviews or the players had done the same, he just wanted them to go away so we could get on with the job. I think the press found it hard to understand him, and he was certainly different to Walter, who had always been very open with them. But Alf didn't feel any obligation towards them, only to the team and to the preparation. Things are different now, and it would be difficult to run things in quite the same way because the teams are tied to sponsors and they have contractual demands. But the idea is to win football games, and I don't think players should be so easily available, nor should they be giving opinions on who should or shouldn't be in the side, because it undermines the dressing room.'

The month at Lilleshall was extremely intense, but then on the eve of England's best ever chance to win the World Cup, it should have been. The players Ramsey had assembled understood the task in hand, as Hurst explains: 'It was difficult under Alf's strict discipline, but I'd just got in the squad, it was lovely to be there, you're on the verge of the World Cup, only a centre-forward for two years after Ron Greenwood converted me from wing-half, it was an adventure. If we'd been there six months, that would have been fine. It's not a hardship because you're at home, privileged to play for England, and because we had the right characters. We didn't have people who would have been disruptive, or detrimental to the squad as a whole; the wrong people were weeded out. No moaning, no bitching about the length of time, we were a professional unit, accepted everything. The discipline was there, without him having to be a disciplinarian, another great knack.'

To increase Ramsey's choice and as back-up in the event of injury, there were twenty-seven players summoned to Lilleshall, so the axe hovered above a number of fringe candidates. Among others, it fell on Peter Thompson: 'My biggest disappointment was not getting in the twenty-two for the World Cup, because he picked three wingers in preference to me. Then the very next squad afterwards, I was back in. As part of the twenty-seven, we were all getting free suits, free this, free that, the cars were full. The day he named the team, a firm had come with these white macs, we all tried them on. Then Alf pulled the six of us over, Bobby Tambling was nearly crying. I was very disappointed. Alf said, "I'm so sorry, I had to make a decision, I feel the twenty-two I have picked will win the World Cup. Any questions?" So Johnny Byrne from West Ham said, "Can we keep our white macs, Alf?"!'

The omission of Thompson, even though there were three other 'wingers' in the party, made it clear that Ramsey was interested solely in people on whom he could rely 100 per cent. Thompson was as gifted an individualist as anyone in the country, but by his own admission, there were days when the magic just didn't work. On those occasions, he was no more than a passenger. Ramsey had no time for luxury players, only eleven players who would do exactly as he asked time and time again. If you look at the wingers he did choose – Callaghan, Paine and Connelly – only Connelly was a traditional winger, the other two were able to fill in as midfielders. Ramsey had not entirely dispensed with wing play, particularly since he felt that in the group games, England's opponents would employ blanket defences which might require width to open them up. But it was apparent that, especially in the light of the success in Madrid, they held only a peripheral interest for him. With the timely arrival of Peters and Ball, England had a new way forward that did not hinge on the traditional virtues of pace and trickery on the flanks.

Following Lilleshall, there was a brief tour of Scandinavia and Poland, embracing four games in ten days, the kind of punishing schedule England would face in the tournament proper. Finland, Denmark and Norway were comprehensively beaten, but it was the game in Poland that was critical. Everyone anticipated that England's first-choice side would play, so there was consternation when Martin Peters was selected, underlining the message that Ramsey would not have much use for wingers when the going got tough. (The side that played Poland was the team that eventually won the World Cup, with Hurst replacing Greaves.) England won 1–0. Ray Wilson recalls, 'We were so comfortable, we looked a really good side. That was the first time I thought to myself that we really had a chance.'

It wasn't an opinion shared beyond the England camp. In the build-up to the tournament, England were rated as little more than outsiders by the pundits, Jimmy Hill going so far as to say that, 'It's not Alf Ramsey's fault, nobody could win the World Cup with these players.' England were routinely quoted as 10–1 shots, out-rageous odds for a home nation widely acknowledged to have three of the world's greatest footballers – Bobby Charlton, Banks and Moore – in their team. Returning home from the tour, Ramsey gave the squad a couple of days off to return to their families, a decision he later counted among the most critical of his reign. The England party reconvened on Friday 8 July, prior to their opening fixture against Uruguay on the Monday, the game that would start the eighth World Cup.

In the years since then, we've come to expect that the first game will be a damp quib. Each team has to carry the burden of expectation, not only of their own nation, but of the world which, after four years of waiting, is desperate to see a festival of football. Admittedly the build-up to the 1966 tournament was nothing like that which we see today, but it was the first World Cup of the serious television age, with the games screened live all over the world. That meant the opening match was under greater scrutiny than ever before, with an inevitable increase in tension. The teams had to endure a lengthy wait in the stadium as the opening ceremony was played out for the cameras, before the Queen officially declared the start of the tournament. All these peripheral events were very much part of setting the scene, but they were irritations the players could have well done without. Uruguay were under pressure, but for England's eleven, the atmosphere just got more unbearable with every passing minute. George Cohen recalls, 'We'd been preparing for the World Cup for months, we'd been looking towards it for years, then the day comes and all you want to do is get on the field and start playing. All the ceremony that goes with it is unavoidable, and of course it's a great thing to be playing before the Queen, but you really are just desperate to get stuck in!'

There was little to enthral the watching millions, nor convince the home nation that England would be contenders as they struggled to a goalless draw in the opening fixture with Uruguay, an early collision between supporter expectations and footballing realism. As Ray Wilson says, 'If a team puts eleven men behind the ball, it's not hard to get a o–o if that's all you want. Our supporters didn't understand that, they didn't want tactics, they wanted action. But football wasn't like that any more.' George Cohen expands on the theme: 'It didn't upset us because they only wanted a draw – for great chunks of the game Gordon was the only guy in our half. We knew we wouldn't concede because Ray and myself covered: we were quick, Jack was always there and Bobby would move ahead or behind him according to the situation. We didn't have a flat back four, which is a load of rubbish! Anybody who gets caught flat deserves to lose. We got a lot of stick, but we knew we'd done all the work and that it was one of those days when it wouldn't go in. The important thing is not to lose that first game, and we hadn't.'

The Mexicans also managed to frustrate England for long periods of the second game, but a typical Bobby Charlton screamer from outside the box finally broke the tension and carried the side to an important win. The French were then defeated 2–0 in another stuttering England display, two goals from Roger Hunt ensuring that the home team topped the group, and giving him three of England's four goals, a pretty good return from the man many wanted to see dropped. In spite of Hunt's personal success, the game was not without an unfortunate legacy, as George Cohen explains: 'Simon got the ball and tried to sell a dummy and Nobby was late, just went straight through him. Didn't look nice, but it wasn't malicious in intent, just clumsy. The FA tried to get Alf to drop Nobby, and Alf refused. The story goes that he said if they required him to leave Nobby out, he'd resign. Nobby was made a scapegoat, there were far worse tackles in that tournament, such as the systematic ill treatment of Pelé, and plenty of diabolical tackles from Argentina.'

Ray Wilson adds, 'Nobby was always going to be in the side. But there was never a more unlikely looking international. What kids today must think when they see a picture of him, I don't know! He looks like Woody Allen.' On the face of it, even more serious than the mysterious affair of Stiles was the injury to Jimmy Greaves. He sustained a nasty gash to the leg and it was immediately apparent that England would be without one of their true world-class players for the tough-looking quarter-final with Argentina three days later. It had long been assumed that if England were going to win the trophy, it would be Greaves who would provide the goals. In spite of a sluggish start to the tournament – perhaps a result of the lingering effects of his bout of hepatitis – he was still regarded as *the* threat. To lose him just as the competition was reaching this stage seemed a calamity. But, as Geoff Hurst points out, 'Sometimes an injury can be a blessing in disguise. We saw it in 1986 when Robson was injured and Wilkins sent off and the balance was suddenly better because of enforced changes, and maybe that was the same in '66 when Jimmy got injured.'

Hurst, of course, was the beneficiary of Greaves' ill fortune, but it's not impossible that Ramsey was already toying with making that switch, and that the enforced change suited him. As Ray Wilson points out, 'Bringing Geoff in gave us an option: we could give sharing balls into the box instead of always trying to pick a way through. Away, most games were played in our half and it was easy for Jimmy and Roger because they were nippy. At Wembley it didn't work, so Geoff gave us something else.' George Cohen adds that 'using conventional wingers didn't seem to work with Alf, though Alan Ball played in a wide position when we went 4–4–2 when Jimmy got injured, so we could use Geoff and Roger to their best.' This was a significant change because England had used one winger in each of the three group games without conspicuous success. Now, with a midfield three of Charlton, Peters and Ball in advance of Stiles, suddenly England were fluid, adaptable, rugged and creative. Mind, Argentina were pretty useful as well.

It is possible to make a case that Argentina were as strong as any country contesting the 1966 Championship and, had they been the hosts, it would have been extremely difficult to stop them. Even so, as Geoff Hurst suggests, home advantage is a double-edged sword: 'It does help, but I think it's unfair to say we wouldn't have won it away from home. For about four or five years we were the best team in the world, we could compete with anybody, anywhere, as we showed in 1970 against Brazil in their own back yard. But there is huge pressure at home – England are always expected to well, no matter what. And people did come to play very negatively because you're seen as the big threat. Argentina were like that, very tough, they played in a physically aggressive manner, certainly against us. They were an outstanding team, and if I were to criticize them it was because they tried to kick us out of the game rather than play us out of it. Had they played their football, they might have got a better result.' Ray Wilson agrees with that summary, adding, 'They seemed to get more satisfaction out of niggling. If they'd set their stall out to play, they could have been a massive side.'

The game is infamous for the sending off of their captain, Rattín. As he had in the Little World Cup, Rattín felt it was the captain's role to harry the referee at every turn, acting as an intermediary between the official and his team. In fairness to him, that was an accepted part of the game in Argentina and his actions were nothing out of the ordinary, all part of the dramatic spectacle. But, as George Cohen says, to European eyes, his behaviour was extraordinary: 'Rattín wanted to run the competition, harassed the referee on everything, and he wasn't having it; it got quite painful in the end. He was an outstanding player, so if anyone had to go, I'm glad it was him! Technically they were brilliant, but they deteriorated into a mob if things didn't go right. There were some bloody late tackles going on, there was the pat on the shoulder that turns out to be a wrench of the ear, or pulling the short hairs on your neck. Spitting in your face wasn't nice, running back and having someone rake your Achilles tendon ... It was very unpleasant.'

In spite of being reduced to ten men, Argentina found it relatively easy to hold out – a feat that still surprises many. Yet if you limit your horizons to not conceding, even with just ten men, it's not impossible by any means. Eventually, though, it was the new system that prevailed. With thirteen minutes to go, Martin Peters, now making a midfield berth his own, floated in a beautifully weighted cross that was begging to be headed in. Hurst obliged, ghosting in between two defenders to put England into the semi-final. The game over, the traditional swapping of shirts began, George Cohen happy enough to take part. 'As far as I was concerned, once it's over that's it, but by the time I had it over my neck, the guy could see Alf coming and he was pulling at it! Alf had arrived and said, "You're not changing shirts with these people." By that time the sleeve was three feet long! Alf knew what had been going on, he recognized the nastiness that wasn't obvious to the ordinary spectator who followed the ball. He was incensed and then he gave the famous quote about Argentina as "animals".'

While the controversy raged around that remark, the England camp quietly went about its business of preparing for a semi-final with Eusebio's Portugal, against whom they already had a very good record. Few backed England but to George Cohen, 'If you look game on game, we were coming to a peak. And look at the record, we'd never been beaten by West Germany, almost always did well against Portugal, so we were becoming more confident.' Ray Wilson concedes that 'Portugal had a wonderful side, played great football. They had a go, so it was like playing away from home. After Argentina, we started to believe, we'd got to the stage where we hadn't let anybody down – that's your big worry at home. And the crowds started to get behind us, which was encouraging because there was always an anti-north influence at Wembley, so if there were a lot of northern lads in the side and we weren't doing well, the crowd would get on to them. We didn't want to go to Goodison for the semi. Wembley suited us, we were so fit and the Wembley occasion is very draining because of the atmosphere and because the pitch is so spongy.' With Portugal committed to attack, England were almost the away side, a situation which fitted their style to perfection. Although Portugal had players of the highest quality, notably the towering Torres and the mighty Eusebio, England always felt they could win. Eusebio was obviously the danger man, so Nobby Stiles, the villain of the piece a week earlier, was detailed to man-mark him. By the end of the game he was the hero of the hour, as George Cohen accepts: 'Nobby had his best game for England, he did a terrific job on Eusebio, he got so fed up he went out on the wing! He was six inches taller, four yards faster, but Nobby shunted him, shadowed him, shielded, pushed him into dead ends, did one helluva job. But when he had the ball, he used to find his mate Bobby Charlton. Bobby was always looking for when Nobby had the ball and as soon as he had it, Bobby was in space to receive it. Big Jack says that there wouldn't be a Bobby Charlton without Nobby. I don't know that's strictly true but I'm not going to argue with big Jack!'

If Stiles had a wonderful game, so too did his Manchester United team-mate. Bobby Charlton gave a display of almost perpetual motion, shuttling from one penalty area to the other, making tackles, carving out openings and scoring two cracking goals. Although England finally conceded a goal, a penalty after Jack Charlton had been forced to handle the ball, they stood firm for the last few minutes and were into their first ever World Cup Final, where they would meet West Germany.

In the four days leading up to the game, debate raged around Jimmy Greaves. Would he be brought back into the team? In many ways, simply asking the question showed a marked lack of understanding. Greaves was a goalscoring genius, no question. But he simply did not suit the team as it was structured, certainly not at Wembley. England had only begun to play once the midfield balance was altered to accommodate a changed forward line. With Hurst and Hunt covering acres of ground, their movement not only offered umpteen options for the midfielders, but created the space for Bobby Charlton to burst through from deep. Greaves was simply not that kind of player. However high the stakes, it was simply inconceivable that Ramsey would recall him. Even so, Geoff Hurst is realistic enough to admit, 'That was a major decision, with no substitutes, to keep me, with just 5 or 6 caps. It was very brave. I don't recall being under pressure from Jimmy, because I was just happy to be there. Jimmy was the outstanding goalscorer of his, or perhaps any other, generation, and it was unthinkable that if you picked a team to win the World Cup, Jimmy wouldn't be in it, but circumstances changed over that week or so. The reasoning was good, but what would have happened to Alf had we lost 3–0 and Roger or myself missed a couple of sitters each?! So for the Final, nothing changed. The outstanding memory, or non-memory for me, a crazy thing, is I can't actually recall Alf telling me I was playing. I know Martin was told at the cinema and I'm sure Alf told everyone privately and asked them to keep it quiet. Then that night in our room Martin and I were talking and blurted out we'd both been picked.'

England had essentially perfected the system they were to use, but as George Cohen explains, the West Germans made adjustments: 'They made a fundamental mistake, as their manager, Helmut Schoen, admitted, using Beckenbauer to follow Bobby Charlton. We did the same! They cancelled each other out, but their sacrifice was greater: he was their major playmaker, he was a great attacking threat, he worked well with Uwe Seeler, they combined superbly and they lost all that on the day and didn't have anyone else as creative. Though Bobby had a quiet game for us, we still had Alan and Martin in the middle to create things, where they didn't. They were a very good side, though we'd always had good results against them. We kept our shape well as a defence against them, we held our width and depth, so that if, say, Emmerich came up against me and then ran inside, I'd follow him for a few yards and then pass him on to Jack or Bobby and get back into position, so I didn't leave a whacking great piece of real estate behind me on our right.

'Alf just filled in a few little details, but I knew Held was a sprinter who you could run into blind avenues, that Emmerich had a great shot but no speed, so you react accordingly. I knew Ray Wilson's game, we knew that one of us could be last man, so we'd keep an eye on one another, so that if Ray stepped up, I'd be alert to the fact that I had to stay last man. Jack's contribution was terrific too, covered the ground so well, very fit, but he gave us so much confidence because nobody, except perhaps Torres of Portugal, could match him in the air. For a full-back, he was reassuring because he was a no-nonsense player. If the ball needed the boot, it got it, if he could make a pass, he made it, but he never tried to do things he couldn't. Then once you brought the team out from the back, Bobby Moore would take charge, very calm and collected, it was a very well thought-out side. If you look at those players who won the Final, I don't know who else Alf could have chosen to have done a better job. We were well regimented, we knew what we had to do, but we were flexible too, able to cope with the unexpected things that were thrown at us. We did well because we functioned as a team, and ⁺ᴸ ᴜd disguise the quality of the individuals a little bit, but if we hadn't had Bobby, who could be explosive, or Ballie to run them ragged – and on the day nobody was better than Alan, he had an outstanding game – we couldn't have created goals. Roger Hunt would never have been off my team sheet, he was one of the leading scorers in Europe with Liverpool and he and Geoff worked like clockwork. And if it looks too bloody easy, you're labelled as mechanical! But if it looks easy, it seems to me that you're doing something right!'

There is no better documented game in English footballing history than the 1966 World Cup Final. The West Germans took the lead early on following an error from Ray Wilson ('I was livid, but all you can do is carry on playing and not do anything else daft'), but a smartly taken free-kick by Bobby Moore soon found Geoff Hurst drifting in across the box and the scores were level. As the game progressed into the second half, England became increasingly dominant and finally got their reward when Martin Peters was quickest to react to a looping deflection and fired them ahead with 12 minutes left. Inevitably the West Germans then threw everything at England, but didn't look like beating Banks. In the final minute, they won a free-kick on the edge of the box. According to Ray Wilson, 'The referee was naïve to give it against big Jack. Then when it came in there were ricochets and it all went in slow motion. I went for the ball but Seeler stepped across me so I had to stop and go again. I stuck my leg out but it ballooned over it and in. We'd overrun them, battered them for the last half-hour and should have won it. That was devastating, much worse than the first goal. For the whistle to go immediately, you had to fancy them, you always feel that.'

Geoff Hurst concurs with that view: 'You have to think the side that sneaks the late goal becomes favourites. But because of the characters, we shrugged it off, got on with it. Alf came on, said, "We've won the World Cup once, go and do it again." He'd done his job by picking the right players, didn't have to say anything else.'

The rest, as they say, is history; the images still vivid. Alan Ball hurtling down the right like a man possessed to screw the ball back into Hurst's path, the shot thundering against the bar, Roger Hunt claiming the goal, a moment of suspense, then pandemonium when the goal was given. Moore collecting the ball, splitting the defence, Hurst outpacing Overath and cracking a shot into the roof of the net, Moore wiping his hands before collecting the trophy, Stiles dancing his jig, Bobby Charlton in tears. These are some of the most famous pictures of the century. What was it like to be in the middle? Ray Wilson remembers, 'My first reaction was, "I'm bloody glad this is all over!" because it had been stressful mentally as well as being physically tiring. I thought we had a chance after the tour before the tournament. I could feel that we were coming to terms with it, we were blending, we had a side. I was delighted to win it, but I can't say I was overjoyed. I'm certainly glad we didn't lose the Final, but at that time, at least in getting there, I felt we'd achieved something.

'We weren't riotous in the dressing room, it was a sense of relief, I think. I think the actual finish to the game overpowered how you could feel. If it had been a mundane game and you'd sneaked through, perhaps if they hadn't got the equalizer in the 90 minutes, we'd have been more riotous. In many respects it was a dour game as a spectacle. If it had finished at 90 minutes, it hadn't had much sparkle. In fact we should have finished them off in the second half, we were much fitter, we missed two or three good chances, but the last-minute equalizer – was it a foul? Did the third goal go in? – then Geoff's goal with the last kick, it suddenly went from a pretty ordinary game to the most exciting World Cup Final of all time! When I think back, if they hadn't equalized, it wouldn't be Sir Geoffrey! Kenneth Wolstenholme goes to sixty dinners a week off his "they think it's all over", so it's amazing how life can change!'

For George Cohen, the emotions were similar: 'I just felt really tired. Fulham had just gone through another crisis in the League, I'd spent ten days in hospital with a knee injury at the end of the season. I was so tired, I didn't put up much of a resistance when Nobby knocked me over and gave me a kiss – it was right in front of the Royal Box, it must have looked terrible! The feeling was, really, "Thank God, it's over, we've done it." The feeling was far better a couple of days later when I'd had a rest, got over the occasion and realized the enormity of what we'd done. It is the greatest thing that's happened to English football, and it did change our lives. It's hard for me to understand what people are thinking when they say, "There's George Cohen, he was in the World Cup Final," but I still get that all these years later.'

Ray Wilson is phlegmatic about the acclaim he still receives: 'You have to be realistic about it. The area where I live, it's out of the way and I don't get bothered by people. If I do, it's in places where it's pretty sensible, you can answer the questions easily enough. I just take on board that I was part and parcel of the most important time in English football history, and you've got to be reasonable with people when they ask questions, you can't just brush them off. If you've achieved that, you've got to accept the things that go with it and I don't have a problem with that at all. I might do if I were the likes of Bobby getting it day after day, but fortunately I don't!'

Being an England player during those turbulent times was not a universally happy experience, however, as Joe Baker explains: 'I don't think playing for England did me any good; I'd have been better off playing for Scotland, because I am Scottish, really. I was only six weeks in England! So I burned the bridges, really. The first night I went down to play for England, I read a guy called Desmond Hackett writing in one of the papers, saying, "Why get a Scot to play for England when we've got all these great centre-forwards?" So that was a nice welcome! Then I came back up to Hibs and started getting stick because I'd played for England! I think if I'd been able to play for Scotland, I'd have played for years with Denis Law, which would have been ideal for me. I finished up staying in Scotland when I finished playing and I think had I been a Scottish international rather than an English one, it would have helped me to stay in the game.'

One final observation on the World Cup of 1966 must revolve around money, as it is now seemingly the only currency in football. As Ray Wilson says, 'In them days you had no money to throw about. We got £2 a day expenses. Some of the lads went through the thirty days at Lilleshall without getting any money. If you didn't play in the World Cup, you didn't get any money. We got a £22,000 bonus for winning it so we decided to split it equally between the twenty-two.' Joe Baker agrees that, 'Money has changed things. I don't begrudge players the money – I went to Italy, after all – but I don't think they always play for the jersey any more, a lot have an eye on the endorsements, the bonuses.'

And, finally, there is the matter of George Cohen's World Cup medal. When he chose to sell it in 1998, some commentators decided that it showed a lack of pride in his achievements and in his country; pretty rich assessments from some of the same writers who do so much to ruin the nation's reputation with the hyperbolic xenophobia that taints so much international football reporting here. But Cohen is big enough to look after himself: 'I don't owe anybody an explanation. I looked at my pension and felt it needed a boost. But, equally, I have two sons who I love dearly and who are equal in my life, and there is no way you can cut a medal in half; I cannot give it to one of them. We talked about it and the one boy said, "Anthony should have it"; the other said, "Andrew should have it"! So I felt it was practical to put its value into my pension, then after that its value would be theirs. I'm not a rich man, nor am I a poor man, but I am a practical man, and this seemed the best solution all round, and we can all benefit. Kevin Keegan rang me while he was in France for the World Cup and said that Fulham would be delighted to have it and asked if we could come to some arrangement, and ultimately I decided it should go the club. Kevin was very good about it, it's always available to me for charities or if the family want to see it, but it's always available for people to see, where if it had gone a collector, it would be in a vault somewhere.'

The practicalities of inheritance aside, should Michael Owen win a World Cup medal some time in his career, it's hard to imagine him having to sell it to top up his pension. Which is as it should be, isn't it? Maybe some of today's footballers aren't so overpaid, after all. Or at least, not if they achieve the ultimate.

8

....

Kind of Blue

After the Lord Mayor's show comes the bloke with the bucket. What do you do after you've won the World Cup? For many, life after that would be an anticlimax, but such were the characters that Ramsey had assembled, there were no thoughts of resting on their laurels. Instead, Ray Wilson's view is typical: 'Having won it, I was disappointed I wasn't Alan Ball's age. I'd have liked it to happen earlier, to give me that reputation – that gives you a tremendous edge before a game's even started. I was 32 then and it spurred me on in many respects, I wanted more of that.'

In typical Ramsey fashion, the manager stayed loyal to the World Cup-winning team for the first three internationals after the Final, his first change being made when Jimmy Greaves finally returned for Roger Hunt in the 1967 game with Scotland at Wembley. As England struggled with injuries during the game – Jack Charlton and Ray Wilson were virtual passengers for most of it – the Scots gained sweet revenge for the year of misery they'd been forced to endure after England became the World Champions, by winning 3–2 at Wembley, in the first England game since Ramsey had become Sir Alfred.

Not only did Ramsey keep faith with many of the individuals, he kept faith with the system that had served him so well in 1966. Though Nobby Stiles faded out of the picture, he was replaced by Alan Mullery of Spurs, an equally adept anchor man, but a more creative force and someone always likely to pop up with a crucial goal. Elsewhere there were few changes in personnel and it wasn't until the 1967–68 season, as preparations were getting underway for the European Championships, that new faces began to be drafted in. One of the first newcomers was Manchester United's David Sadler who, along with Everton's Brian Labone, was competing for Jack Charlton's shirt.

Sadler's first game was a 2–0 win against Northern Ireland at Wembley, where he partnered the inevitable Bobby Moore at the heart of the defence: 'He was an amazing man. The thing about Bobby was that obviously he was a very good player in the normal First Division games, but that's all he was; he wasn't clearly head and shoulders above everybody else. But when he put on the England shirt, he was a giant, he was one of those people that as the stage gets bigger, they get bigger. For England he was quite phenomenal.

'It was interesting to be around Sir Alf. I knew a bit about him, I'd been to a few training sessions. He was very placid, not very demonstrative at all; all he asked you to do was perform as you did for your club. He didn't ask you to do anything you weren't already doing, and I think that was the secret of his success with England. But the atmosphere has to be a little different. Being successful on a day-to-day basis at your club is a great thing, you're with your friends, there's a bond there, and to play at Old Trafford in front of those huge crowds was a marvellous thrill. To play for England is a slightly different thing and, certainly to start with, it's a more personal situation, you want to do well for yourself as much as for the team, because you're not as integrated into the side and you don't know that you'll get more opportunities.'

Ramsey was frustrated by the recurring demands of League football over this two-year period. In deference to them having allowed him additional internationals and unprecedented access to his players in the run-up to the 1966 finals, there was no full tour in the summer of 1967, meaning there'd been just six games in that year. The following season, there were just four matches prior to the two-legged qualifier for the European Nations Cup with Spain. While it's easy to criticize Ramsey for failing to experiment with new players and ideas, it's only fair to ask just exactly when could he have done it? And England were carrying the added burden of World Cup holders, meaning every other team in the world was especially keen to beat them, so the manager had a special responsibility to protect his side's reputation. Even so, by the time England took on Spain at Wembley in April 1968, it was a very familiar-looking side, Mike Summerbee replacing the injured Hurst, Mullery established as the new improved Stiles, and Cyril Knowles taking the place of George Cohen.

Cohen took the end of his career in his stride: 'My England career was very important to me. I played for a smallish club – Fulham were never going to reach the great heights, we weren't going to win the League or the Cup. In a way, it would have been a mundane career without the excitement of playing for England, and it would have upset me not to achieve that. When I finished playing for England, Alf said if I ever fancied going to a training session to do so. He made me welcome at any functions I attended with the team. I met him in a private capacity afterwards, and I liked the man even more. He was a very correct person, I liked the way he handled himself, always as a gentleman. There would have been no nonsense like the Hoddle diary with Alf. I can't remember him criticizing players in public, he wouldn't be dealing with faith healers and saying they could make a difference to the result! I don't think you could imagine Greavesie or big Jack taking all that seriously!'

England laboured through that game against the Spaniards, winning thanks to Bobby Charlton's goal, and giving themselves a slim advantage to take to Madrid. The game brought back memories of the early stages of 1966 when England struggled to defeat a packed defence. So many of England's poorer displays were reserved for Wembley and they remained an infinitely better side away from home. But the fact that the home fans saw the worst side of England led to them being labelled dour and unadventurous. There was a degree of truth in that, but like so many generalizations, it was far too simplistic, as Ray Wilson points out: 'We weren't just a defensive side in the 1960s, we played some good football and got plenty of goals at a time when the game was more defensive than ever before, because sides were picking the bat up off Italy.'

English superiority away from Wembley was underlined by another excellent performance in Madrid, when Spain were defeated 2–1, with Peters and Norman Hunter getting the goals. That put them through to the semi-final stage, which was to be held in Italy a month later. In preparation, there was a friendly with Sweden at Wembley, a satisfying 3–1 win, and then there was a trip to Hanover to play West Germany, Colin Bell getting an early taste of international football, after a typical apprenticeship: 'Alf included you in the squad for a couple of years before you got the chance to really establish yourself in the team.' The game showed just how commercialism was starting to make its presence felt in the game. Though the maximum wage was now long gone and, by normal standards, top footballers were getting well paid, they were still a long way from the millionaire status many now enjoy. So if a boot company decided to throw a few quid at the England side, they were only too accommodating. As a result, in Hanover, many of the side sported brand new Adidas boots and came off the field with feet covered in blisters. Needless to say, Sir Alf was not amused, especially as England suffered their first ever defeat at the hands of West Germany, losing by a single goal, hardly an auspicious omen on the verge of the Nations Cup semi-finals. Nor was it comforting to hear Ramsey change his traditional policy of asking a player to do exactly what he did for his club. Peter Thompson was the victim: 'I wasn't that comfortable with him, he wanted me to play more for the team, not as an individual, which was my game. We were playing in Germany and he said, "Play the same way as you do for Liverpool, but don't hold the ball." That was my game! Saying that was like tying my legs together. I had a shocker. After then I was never confident of getting in.'

This made it clear that Ramsey knew that he would have to adapt the 1966 style in order to win again in 1970. Over a four-year period, any tactics can be worked out and countered. Ramsey wanted to use the width of the field once more, and was keen to employ Thompson's trickery, but, as ever, he wanted to graft the work ethic on to the player. When Thompson proved incapable of changing his style, Ramsey put greater store in the use of overlapping full-backs, with good results in Europe, though they were to fare less successfully in the heat of Mexico.

The European Nations Cup had never really excited a great deal of interest in England, not surprising given our normal attitude to all things European. But as World Champions, it took on a new dimension, particularly as the finals were to be held away from Wembley. However comprehensively England had won the 1966 Final, there were still those whispers of doubt, suggestions that Wembley and the home crowd had played as big a part in the eventual triumph as the footballers themselves. As Ray Wilson says, 'It would have been lovely to have won the European Championships as well, it would have been proof of how good we were.'

Oddly, though, England's personnel, and even their tactical shape, were in a state of some flux when the tournament actually rolled around. There had been a run of injuries and loss of form, while other players such as Cohen, Wilson and Jack Charlton seemed to be at the end of their England careers. The side that took the field against Yugoslavia in Florence for the semi-final lacked the beautiful balance of '66. The back four was solid but the midfield lacked the verve and inspiration of before. Though Ball and Peters were still there, and though Mullery was perhaps an improvement on Stiles, the fourth member of the quartet was Norman Hunter. Hunter was a better player than many gave him credit for, and wasn't simply the assassin of 'bite yer legs' folklore, but as a creative player, he was not in the Bobby Charlton mould. Charlton himself had been moved into a striking role, just behind Roger Hunt, while Geoff Hurst was rested. In a physically brutal game, the Yugoslavs gave as good as they got, perhaps better, though it was an England player, Alan Mullery, who was sent off. England were now having to compete in an increasingly physical world game, though in fielding the likes of Stiles, Hunter, Mullery and Jack Charlton, it was a climate Ramsey had done much to foster.

Ray Wilson remembers, 'They were an inferior side, just sat back; we were never out of their area. We should have won comfortably, but they hit us on the break.' It was a rare Bobby Moore error that allowed Yugoslavia to score, and that was the end of England's challenge. Once again, they had been utterly frustrated by a side who had played a packed defence. England's quality in an open game was illustrated in the third place game against the USSR, a 2–0 win hardly flattering a side that 'paralysed the Russians, because they came to play football' according to Wilson. But the world community knew that if you gave England space, they would use it. So they concentrated on denying it. Picking the way through locked and bolted defences would be the major challenge of the rest of Ramsey's reign.

One attempt to address that issue came in the selection of Francis Lee, a typically self-confident character so admired by Ramsey: 'He just gave me a free role, go where you want, support Geoff, carry on as normal, which was a good start. I went out and enjoyed it, it was my life's ambition to play for my country, so why not enjoy it? In fact, Joe Mercer used to ask me if I could arrange to play as well for Manchester City as I did for England!'

As one England career began, so another came to a close. Ray Wilson had played his final England game in the Nations Cup tie with the USSR: 'I got injured at the start of the '68–69 season, my right knee collapsed, I was 34 and I was realistic enough to know I was finished at that level. I'd had a life and a job that I couldn't wait to get out of bed to do. I'd been pretty fortunate to be around with a good side at the right time, 63 caps, and I knew that what had been on offer to me, I'd achieved. I knew that I was going to be going backwards from then on, and I wasn't looking forward to that, so I wasn't too unhappy about finishing. Very quickly after I'd finished, I'd forgotten about it, I'm pleased to say I don't look back and say, "Oh, I'm better than this lot playing now." I go to reunions, which is what you do at my age, and some of them think they can still play now!' In the long-term, England were fortunate to find an excellent replacement for Wilson in Terry Cooper, who played the overlapping full-back role to perfection.

Initially, however, it was just another destabilizing factor as the team started to prepare to defend its World crown in Mexico.

There's no question that the face of football changed radically throughout the 1960s. The success of the England team in 1966 had had an impact, notably in the sudden disappearance of wingers from our domestic game, a move not to the taste of many. But there were other, cultural changes. The abolition of the maximum wage had improved player lifestyles and footballers were now fêted as pop stars. The most obvious manifestation of that trend was Northern Ireland's George Best, but England had its own versions. Chelsea, because of its proximity to the King's Road and 'swinging London', was the show business club and players such as Alan Hudson and, particularly, Peter Osgood were always in the limelight. Osgood had been in the forty named for the 1966 World Cup, and though it's unlikely he would have made the twenty-seven, let alone the twenty-two, it was good for him to know Ramsey was watching him at such a young age. A broken leg had put his career back, but by the 1968–69 season he was recapturing his very best form. As with so many before him, he had to wait in the wings before Ramsey gave him his chance: 'It was frustrating in the late 1960s, to be honest, I was just missing the squad, then when I got in the squad, I was just missing out on the team. But I accepted that I was just a member of the squad, because I respected all the players around me. I was a big fish at Chelsea, I suppose, and in the papers a lot, but you'd look around and see players with World Cup medals and you'd realize you had to excel to replace them. All I ever wanted to be was one of the lads, and when I went into the England camp, they accepted me straight away.'

The 1968–69 season provided a pretty mixed bag with draws home and away against Romania, a home draw with Bulgaria and a 5–0 thrashing of France. That French game and then subsequent success in the Home Internationals suggested that Ramsey had found a new team, building on the strengths of the still young core of 1966 and refreshing it with new, and in some cases greater talents. As Francis Lee says, 'During that period, Alf was lucky because he could put five or six names down straight away, people like Ball, Hurst, Peters, Banks, Moore, Bobby Charlton were all fairly young in 1966 and were improving going into Mexico.'

To that nucleus you could add the likes of Lee himself, Cooper, Mullery and Bell. The season's real test would come in the summer, however, when England flew out to South America and internationals in Mexico, Uruguay and Brazil. Obviously the football was important, but it was as much a fact-finding mission as anything else. The facts they found were not terribly reassuring. In spite of orders to conserve energy as much as possible, the players suffered very badly through both heat and altitude, and by the end of the tour Bobby Moore was on the point of collapse. The conditions made it very apparent that England would have to look again at their pattern of play. The tremendous industry that characterized the victorious side of 1966 was just not repeatable in Mexico. Retaining possession would be more important than it ever had been, so Ramsey wanted to ensure he used players who were utterly reliable and would make as few errors as possible, further fuelling the burgeoning flair versus commitment argument. There was no question that Ramsey was open to players of individual quality if they could be harnessed to the side – how many players better than Bobby Charlton has England ever produced? – but teamwork was his central credo. And that teamwork would be vital for any European outfit in such tortuous conditions.

A Mexican XI was thrashed 4–0 in the opening fixture, then England played out a grim goalless draw against the full national side in Mexico City. With substitutions now entering into the game, they would be critical in the heat, and this provided Ramsey with a particularly taxing problem. Always a believer in a fairly rigid tactical structure, the fact that he could now tinker with it mid-game was a temptation he was not entirely happy with, particularly as it meant the opposition could also suddenly change their shape without warning and without Ramsey being able to adequately brief his players. His first dabble in this new idea came against the Mexican XI when he asked Peters and Ball to run themselves into the ground in the first half, and would then replace them with fresh legs for the second half. Injuries to Jack Charlton and Bob McNab in the second half did little for that plan and subsequently he reverted to a more cautious use of his options.

Having played Mexico, the next game was in Montevideo. Lee recalls, 'We had an horrendous trip out to Uruguay, via Peru. We were travelling 24 hours, got there in the middle of the night, up for training at ten, played the following day and won, and it was the worst preparation for any game I ever had!' Goals from Lee and Hurst meant a satisfactory 2–1 win had been achieved, an excellent morale booster before going on to the real meat of the tour – a game at the Maracanã. Brazil had had their problems in 1966 when Pelé had been kicked out of the competition and an ageing unit had been unable to withstand the battering of stronger, fitter sides. This time around, they were constructing a side of breathtaking talent, and were clear favourites to win the World Cup and claim the Jules Rimet trophy as theirs by right for a third victory.

Entertaining the current champions, and keen to get a psychological edge on them, Brazil weren't above a little gamesmanship either. According to Francis Lee: 'We were in the tunnel ready to go out and Alf asked, "Where are Brazil?" They replied, "You have started too early, go back in the dressing room, we start in half an hour." Alf said, "If that team is not in the corridor shortly, we are going home." Five minutes later they shuffled into the tunnel!' England controlled the early exchanges with some ease and were ahead until late in the game thanks to a Colin Bell goal. But Ramsey's usually sure tactical touch deserted him and, failing to make substitutions, he saw his team visibly tire and concede two late goals – this brought home to him that, in South America at least, football was a thirteen-man game, though a year later he would come to rue learning that lesson. For all the disappointment in the Maracanã, England had gleaned valuable intelligence from this trip, some of a purely tactical nature, but much, much more on general health and fitness that would inform the nature of their preparation in 1970.

One thing the tour had made clear was the advisability of finding younger legs better able to withstand the climate. So even a Third

Division player, Rodney Marsh, was included in the preliminary forty: 'I'd got 44 goals for QPR and Alf looked on me as, "OK, a flair player, but if he can score goals, I might change him into a Geoff Hurst type!"'

With youth in mind, players like Jeff Astle, Emlyn Hughes and Peter Osgood were drafted into the side. Following stuttering performances home and away against the Dutch and at home to Portugal, Osgood received the call in February 1970 for a game in Belgium: 'I got a call on the Sunday from Dave Sexton to go to Hendon Hall. I was a bit fed up of it, so I said, "I'm not going to carry the bags again." But Alf had told him that if I went, I'd play, so I went, played and we won 3–1. Half an hour before the game, Moor said to Alf, "OK if we have a drink now?" and this bottle of brandy came out! So this fantastic captain had a good swig and I thought, "If it's good enough for God, it's good enough for me!" Afterwards, they were great. Alf came up to me and said, "Well done, welcome to our team, go and have a good drink." So we went out to this club and the atmosphere was a bit funny in there. After half an hour, Bobby Moore went up to the bar and dropped his trousers. He'd realized it was a gay club! Playing for England was everything. When I got in the squad, they were World Champions, so how many people can say they've played with them? It was unbelievable to be in the dressing room with Charlton, Hurst, Peters, Moore, Banks, all legends.'

The League season had been organized to finish earlier than usual to give England extra time to jet out to South America and complete their preparations in good time. Before then, there was one important task to be fulfilled – recording the team's single. As Osgood says, 'It's no good just working hard and training hard, you need to have a bit of fun as well to get the team spirit going and doing something like "Back Home" was funny. I don't think we'd profess to be singers or anything but we had a laugh and got on *Top of the Pops* and all that; it was great fun.'

The party of twenty-seven flew out at the beginning of May, a full month before the first game. As David Sadler says, 'It was typical of Ramsey, he'd been very meticulous with his preparation, certainly for those days. We went out very early to acclimatize and that was very necessary.' Peter Osgood remembers that 'when we got to Mexico, we couldn't train at first because of the altitude, so we had a mini-Olympics. Colin Bell – Nijinksy – won everything, he was so fit. Then, suddenly, you're through it, you're OK.'

The conditions were so difficult that even the super fit Bell found it 'very difficult to breathe, probably took us nearly a fort-night before we could start to think about training because it was so hard to breathe. In Colombia it was amazing, you ran 10 yards and you'd stop and put your hands on your knees. You couldn't play a one-two, it was like having asthma.' Part of the accli-matization plan was to spend time at different altitudes, so that by the time they opened their campaign against Romania, they would be coming closer to sea level.

They started at 7349 feet in Mexico City, but found themselves staying in a hotel with the Mexican squad, much to Ramsey's annoyance. This drove him to further introspection and the England camp started to adopt a siege mentality. Matters weren't helped on the opening training day as Peter Thompson remembers: 'We were Champions and we were in our first training session. There was lots of interest, so Alf gave the press an hour to take photos, ask questions, whatever. Alf stopped it, we started a training run and as we ran, the press followed us and as we turned round, we just ran into them. It went on and on and Alf lost his temper, so they took photos and you had "wild man Ramsey" stories.' To that were added other PR disasters, such as the insistence on bringing in an English-made bus to ferry the players around, and a refusal to eat local food, the crowning stupidity coming in a decision to fly in fresh fruit to Mexico! Francis Lee remembers that 'one of the papers said, "If you're thinking of throwing tomatoes at the English team, always wash them first!"'

England were to fly out to Colombia for their first warm-up game, then on to Ecuador. When the side reached Bogotá, they went to their hotel, the Tequendama. Killing time in the hotel foyer, Peter Thompson says, 'We all went in a jewellers, laughing and joking, looking at earrings at £10,000, and me, Moore and

Charlton were last in there. I went to get some mail from reception, twenty yards away, and by the time I got back this woman rushed out screaming that somebody had stolen a bracelet. Within five minutes there were police, cameras, press, it was just a set-up.'

A similar incident had happened with the Brazilian side a year earlier, so England were prepared for the possibilities. Ramsey appeared to have smoothed out the problems and the team simply got back to the football. There were comfortable wins from each fixture, 4–0 in Colombia and 2–0 in Ecuador, and encouraging signs that the team had modified its style to take on board the forensic passing game that was so necessary. The squad flew back to Mexico from Ecuador, having a brief stopover in Bogotá. David Sadler remembers, 'We arrived in Colombia and were there for several hours. We went to watch a film, I think it was *Grand Prix*, while we were waiting to catch a connecting flight. We came out and Bobby was missing and the ruckus had started. We had to get the plane without him so we were very concerned for him and about what would happen to the team, because we were only a week or so away from the start of the competition.'

Peter Osgood best sums up everyone's attitude to the affair: 'The Bogotá thing was unreal. Mooro would never do anything wrong; he was an absolute gentleman, it was a privilege to be his friend. It was an obvious set-up. But it was lucky it was him and not Bobby Charlton, because Charlton would have come back like Yul Brynner by the time he'd got out of it; he was a worrier. But Mooro took it in his stride. It's odd, you look back and wonder if it happened. If it had been anybody else, we'd have been up in arms, but because it was Bobby, he was so cool, so relaxed, it didn't seem so serious.' Moore was placed under house arrest, and his room-mate, Peter Thompson, was left to field his phone calls, including one from Sean Connery, who thought that Thompson was the England captain's butler.

Moore had to retrace his movements for a reconstruction of the alleged theft, but two days later was given a conditional release. By now, the England squad were already in Mexico, so Moore had to make his way to the training camp in Guadalajara. The whole fiasco was not allowed to interrupt preparations, for as Geoff Hurst says: 'Alf had picked professionals who would get on with the job. In Bogotá, Bobby managed it incredibly well, from being under house arrest, then coming into a World Cup and, against Brazil, giving the best performance I'd ever seen from a central defender. He could raise his game to another level, had a magnificent tussle against an amazing forward line.'

There was no suggestion that England summon a replacement for Moore, but there was one late addition, as Roy McFarland explains: 'Before Mexico there was talk of Jack Charlton, Brian Labone, David Sadler; and I was the understudy to them. I was on standby. We went on an Under-23 tour, with Ron Suart in charge and Les Cocker as coach, and we had a very good tour in Belgium, Holland and Portugal. We were away a week or so, while the team had gone off to South America. We had to be prepared to go out if necessary. Peter Shilton was on standby too. We got back to London, Peter and I got the train back and we were both shattered. We'd had a long season, had the tour, and both felt we had nothing else to give. As I got back to my digs in Derby, a newsflash came on that Peter had been called up to fly out to Mexico. An hour earlier, we'd been saying we almost felt that we didn't want to be called up we were so tired, though as soon as I heard it, I thought, "Christ, I wish that was me!"' By the time Shilton arrived, a lot of hard work had already been done. But there was time for relaxation too, essential under the conditions. Ramsey gave his squad one night off, imposing a curfew, which was broken. The following morning he called the players together to tell them: 'You all let me down. It doesn't matter how famous you are, next time I'll just give you your ticket home. Thank you for joining us, and you can go.'

But as Peter Osgood points out, that was very much a mild, one-off event: 'Players knew where they stood with Alf. If he'd been in charge in France in 1998, Teddy Sheringham would have been kicked out, gone. Gascoigne wouldn't have got a look in. Alf didn't mind you having a beer at the right time, and he made sure we knew when that was. We had three weeks out there working to start with, no drinking, just the odd day off to play golf, when we all stayed together. We weighed in every day, took our tablets, ate and drank together; we knew we had a job to do. Let's be fair, I liked a drink as much as anybody, and there were people like Mooro and Ballie around, but we stuck to the task and left the celebrating or commiserating until later.'

David Sadler agrees with that level of discipline: 'When you're given the opportunity to be at the peak, it seems to me that you would be foolish to do anything that would jeopardize that. It's hard enough to get in the squad, then in the team and then stay there without courting trouble. I'm sure the press has changed from my time in the limelight, then they were our friends and were only really interested in the football; they weren't looking for reasons to knock people. Having said that, players shouldn't give them the opportunity, they know the rules, they know what will happen. You do have to make sacrifices, make concessions, but it's worth it to play for your country, what can be better than that? And certainly the rewards now are colossal.'

Before the tournament proper began, Ramsey had one unpleasant task to discharge; the dropping of six players from the twenty-eight. He sacrificed both the wide players, Ralph Coates and Peter Thompson, young forward Brian Kidd, defender Bob McNab, Peter Shilton whose late journey had been in vain and David Sadler. These were tough footballing decisions, honestly made. Sadly, the announcement was bungled. Because of the time differences, Ramsey informed the press early so they could meet the deadlines back in England. The pressmen in Mexico were told to keep the information to themselves and did so, but their editors back home were less scrupulous. According to Thompson, 'Local reporters went to people's houses, looking for quotes. They wanted the wives to say, "Alf Ramsey's a bastard," or whatever. David Sadler's wife phoned him from England to tell him he was out; my wife told me! That was so disappointing to find out that way. There was a terrible atmosphere, David got hold of Alf in the corridor and said Alf should have told him and Alf's head dropped, he was embarrassed and then he called us together and apologized.

Alf asked the six to stay on but only me and David did.'

David Sadler was realistic about his fate: 'When I was picked in the twenty-eight, it was really as cover for Brian Labone and big Jack. I was in there because I was a bit younger, both of them had turned 30 and Alf wasn't sure how they'd react to the heat and the altitude. So when we set off, I knew where I was in the pecking order. But once you get under way, you always hope you'll be chosen. I acclimatized quickly, coped well with the altitude. Training was good, I played in one of the games on tour, so you start to build your hopes up. The decision had to come and when it did, to be left out was very disappointing, but that's the way of the game. Alf then invited us to stay on with the team if we wanted to, and Peter Thompson and I stayed and were very much part of the set-up, though obviously we weren't going to play. I just took the view it was a great opportunity to stay with the team and also to see a World Cup at first hand.' Despite the upset, according to Osgood, the spirit remained good in the camp throughout the punishing schedule: 'I roomed with Hurst and Astle and Astle is a funny, funny man. He had this record, "Spirit In The Sky" [ironically the record that 'Back Home' ousted from the top of the charts], and he kept playing it and playing it, and in the end me and Hursty had to break it. But Astle was very funny, the squad was good, our preparation was spot on.'

Osgood had every reason to feel good, because he was in the form of his life: 'We'd had a B side v the A side game and we'd won 3–1. I got two past Gordon, I was nutmegging Nobby Stiles. I came on as a sub against Romania and it went well, I was flying. Mooro came up to me and said, "Alf's told me you'll start against Brazil." We had the team talk and Alf said it would be the side that finished against Romania, but then he started going on about Franny Lee, who I'd replaced. So Bobby pulled him up, said, "Hang on, Alf, you said Ossie was playing." Alf just said, "Sorry, Peter," and I wasn't even on the bench. It broke my heart, it really hurt, and I went out that night and got pissed and missed training the next day. I just thought it wasn't on, it wasn't the way to treat somebody.'

In that Romanian game, England had eased through with the only goal, scored by Geoff Hurst, a result that set them up for qualification and also prepared them for the encounter with Brazil, who had been awesome in their first-game demolition of the Czechs. As expected, Ramsey reverted to the tried and tested for this psychologically important game, Brazil's fans trying to tip the scales. Lee remembers: 'The night before we played Brazil was a disgrace. There were thousands in the streets, jumping on car wrecks, hitting them with sticks. You could not sleep at all.'

It became a World Cup classic – Banks' save from Pelé, Moore's brilliance in defence, the flair and drive of the Brazilians, Jairzinho's lashing drive into the net. England lost by a single goal, but could easily have won. Lee had a good header well saved and missed another excellent chance; Ball struck the crossbar; Astle shot narrowly wide from the edge of the box; whereas Brazil had few clear cut chances, despite looking more assured in open play. In a game where sheer genius was on show wherever you cared to look, this was a game that belonged to Bobby Moore, a man who just a few days earlier had been under house arrest. If any coach wants to conduct a master-class in every one of the defensive arts, he has only to show his pupils film of Bobby Moore on that June day in Guadalajara. Defending as art form.

Although disappointed to lose the game, England had made it abundantly clear that they were serious about defending their title and that they had the quality to do so. As Geoff Hurst says, 'It was possibly a better squad than 1966, extra flair, with Francis Lee and Alan Mullery in their respective roles. We'd broken the back by winning it, which is important, you then always believe you can do it again.' Francis Lee adds that Brazil, the champions elect in many people's eyes, 'did not want to play us again'. The greatest worry for England was the climate. However well they prepare, northern European athletes can never feel at home after just a month in a country like Mexico, for as Lee points out, 'It was so hot a guy like me could lose 7 or 8 lbs in a game and it takes a lot, about a week, to really get over that. It was so demanding to play up front with just two of us that Alf had to rotate the forwards.'

Accordingly, Osgood had been the sub for Lee against Romania; Astle had done the same against Brazil. With qualification all but sealed, more changes were made against the Czechs. Astle and Clarke started the game, Osgood replacing Astle later on.

Astle and Clarke looked a good pairing. Astle was exceptionally strong in the air – he'd learned his trade from the great Tommy Lawton – and had a powerful shot in both feet, as he proved when getting the winner for West Brom in the 1968 FA Cup Final from outside the box. Clarke, in contrast, was a predator, very much in the Greaves mould. Nicknamed 'Sniffer' because he was always sniffing around for half-chances in and around the six-yard box, he was incredibly adept at picking up the pieces, thriving on knock-downs from a target man, or pouncing on loose balls and deflections. It was his penalty that won the game against Czechoslovakia. With England needing only to avoid defeat to go through and the Czechs already demoralized and disinterested following defeats against Brazil and Romania, a dour, dismal match ensued, in which the controversial penalty decision – the handball that conceded the penalty looked to be accidental – offered the only real hint of colour.

Second place in the group meant a demanding quarter-final with West Germany. With their new goalscoring sensation Gerd Müller – a man as lazy and as deadly as Jimmy Greaves – the West Germans had looked good in the group phase, but there was no reason to imagine England couldn't overcome them in Leon. Confidence was inevitably dented in the couple of days before the game when Gordon Banks fell ill under suspicious circumstances with stomach trouble. As Osgood points out, 'We all ate and drank exactly the same things, so to this day I'm convinced somebody in the hotel got at Gordon Banks to make him ill.' In the run-up to the game, Ramsey was desperate to ensure Banks would play and even put him through a farcical fitness test where the ability to stand up straight was virtually the only criterion. Banks was initially named in the side, but during the team meeting before the game, he succumbed to illness again and Peter Bonetti stepped into the breach.

Despite these disruptions, England started well, though it was clear that the Germans were the better suited to the conditions, passing the ball crisply while England ran and ran. That running saw England to a two-goal lead after 50 minutes of play and an apparently serene passage to the semi-finals and a showdown with a none too impressive Italian team.

It was as well they had that cushion, for as Peter Thompson points out, the team were tiring: 'I was in the stand and at half-time I was soaked to the skin. I went down at half-time and they were totally exhausted. Another five minutes and they'd have been asleep.' On the hour, West Germany had to gamble and made a substitution, to Thompson's distress: 'Criticism only comes from results. They brought on Grabowski and I'd been compared with him. England were so tired because of the heat, he tore us to shreds, so they all said I should have been in! Nobody said that in 1966 when we won it! But to ask the full-backs to do two jobs, to defend and to keep joining in the attack, was too much; it was too hot. By the time Grabowski got on, Terry Cooper could hardly walk. I'd have fancied playing against him then.' Exploiting the space left by the flagging Cooper, on 68 minutes Beckenbauer drove out to England's left and pushed a cross shot past Bonetti.

Beckenbauer, who had been attending to Bobby Charlton once more, had had to leave him to his own devices and revert to a more attacking role in the attempt to get his side back in the game. Rather than leaving Charlton on to exploit this freedom, as Beck-enbauer's shot went in Ramsey pulled Charlton off and sent on Colin Bell: 'I came on to fill Bob's spot. The temperature and the climate take a lot out of you. The theme was just fresh legs.' Within a minute Bell had created a chance for Hurst and had a good shot saved, so close were England to re-establishing a two-goal cushion.

England continued to hold their own until, with 10 minutes to go, Peters came off for Hunter, a sensible move to stiffen the midfield, it seemed. Almost immediately, Schnellinger's centre looked to have eluded its target, but Uwe Seeler arched away, stretched his neck and managed to head the ball goalwards, with no real intent. The ball looped over Bonetti and nestled in the corner of the net. As Francis Lee says, 'If I'd been Seeler, I'd have bought a lottery ticket after the game.' Bell agrees, adding, 'You can't say anything except it was just meant to be. Seeler's goal was a fluke. That changed the whole game, got them on a roll, got them motoring.' As four years before, England had won the game once. But could they win it again? They could not. After 109 minutes a Grabowski cross was headed across the face of goal by Loehr and there was Gerd Müller to slam the ball past Bonetti. Game over.

The inquest is still going on. Were the substitutions the root of England's demise? Francis Lee doesn't think so: 'The effect of the substitutions has been overdone. Colin came on and played well, we needed fresh legs and at that heat and altitude you needed to use the subs.' Peter Osgood adds, 'Bobby had lost 10 lbs against Brazil and Bobby was the jewel. After the quarter-final, the semis were three days later, so Alf tried to nurse him. And you couldn't ask for a better player to come on than Colin. It's just the other side of the Greavesie decision from '66: one worked, one didn't.' Was Peter Bonetti to blame? Perhaps Banks might have done better, but then Banks was the best by a long way, a goalkeeping deity. As mere mortals go, Bonetti did his best and was not helped by the lack of preparation, concentration time that was denied him by Ramsey's vacillating. Peter Osgood is particularly sorry for his Chelsea colleague: 'Peter Bonetti was a great goalkeeper, the best pro I ever worked with, trained right, ate right, never went out. It just annoys me that he had twenty years at Chelsea when he was second in the world to Banksie and he's remembered for one game.'

In the dressing room, there were no recriminations. Francis Lee remembers, 'We were knackered, devastated by the result. When you've blown it in a competition like that, there's no point having rows about it. It's the pinnacle and if you haven't done it, you don't need anybody to tell you've dropped it.' Geoff Hurst was similarly disconsolate: 'For all the world it looked like we'd get back to play Brazil in the Final – I think we'd have beaten Italy in the semi-final, it was only the fatigue from the game against us that let them beat the West Germans. The West German game was probably the most disappointing day of my life, a hard game, difficult conditions, the altitude, heat, feeling dizzy during the match and then having won it, to have the game effectively over but to lose, was devastating. I just wanted to get away, just leave it. I had a seven- or eight-hour car journey, we all went off in our own directions because once it's over, it's over, there's nothing left to do, and I went to Acapulco, drove with Brian Glanville, just to get away.'

Patriotism aside, it may have been good for the wider game that England did not make the Final, for they would have given Brazil a harder game, certainly a cagier game, and football would have been denied what was a dazzling Final. Not exactly a sentiment you'd have wanted to air with any of the England players, but perhaps a fair one. In spite of the disappointment, England came home from Mexico with their reputation at worst intact and probably enhanced. There was no reason to imagine that with the next four-year cycle entirely based in Europe, England weren't on the brink of another glorious chapter in their history. Oh dear.

9

Please Don't Let Me Be Misunderstood

When England returned home from Mexico, it was to a climate of disappointment – little wonder when the West German defeat had, according to popular mythology, helped lead to the election of Ted Heath. For the public at large, it was difficult to know how to feel about the England side and their performances in Mexico. On the one hand, they hadn't inspired too much excitement, especially in the professional but lacklustre victories over Romania and Czechoslovakia. Set against the genius of Brazil (not exactly a fair comparison, it's true) and the neat passing moves of West Germany, England looked little more than a functional unit. Paradoxically, though, they had played particularly well in the games against those two sides and had been unfortunate to lose, so there was still something in Ramsey's method. The difficulty came because it was very hard to feel any warmth towards the England boss and particularly towards his style of play. England were rarely as negative as they were painted, but nor did they thrill the crowds time and again.

If a team can excite its followers, can seduce them with tremendous football, they will forgive the occasional lapse. But if that side's only appeal lies in its relentless ability to grind out result after result after result, where's the residual satisfaction when they falter? If you live only for pragmatism, if you don't allow a dream to flourish, what's the point in failure? If you give the world some footballing romance, some hope, then even in failure you've achieved something worthwhile – the Scott Fitzgerald school of tactics. Look at more recent examples. Keegan's Newcastle existed to entertain as much as anything else. So when they fell short of the title, the fans were forgiving because they'd had a hell of a ride on the way. But under George Graham, Arsenal existed only to win trophies and, bung controversy aside, when the trophies dried up, it was time for Stroller to walk away. In 1970, Alf Ramsey was beset by that same problem.

There were further issues to be addressed. The Charlton brothers were finished as internationals, Stiles dropped out of the squad, and though they still had plenty left in them, the likes of Moore, Hurst, Banks, Lee and Mullery were all getting towards the latter stages of their England careers. Who could tell how long they could be prolonged, or how much more susceptible to injury the players might become as the general wear and tear of professional football took its toll? Some of the potential replacements were good players, but not *as* good. Martin Chivers, for example, was good in the air and a useful leader of the line, but he lacked Hurst's all-round vision, deftness of touch and eye for goal. Allan Clarke was an excellent goal poacher, but lacked Francis Lee's ability to link the play between midfield and attack. He didn't have Lee's mobility around the field, but instead was more like Jimmy Greaves, in that he tended to stay upfield waiting for the ball to come to him. Lee would go and get it, thereby creating spaces for the likes of Ball and Peters to burst through from deep. And if Paul Madeley was a classy, accomplished defender with Leeds United, adaptable enough to play in literally every position for Don Revie's team, that very versatility was problematic, preventing him from truly establishing himself in a particular role. Ramsey used him in defence and midfield, a mix and match process alien to him in the past, and one which did Madeley little good either.

Other players who had come into the squad did not fit Ramsey's identikit of an international, for whatever reason, be it ability or character. Osgood was one such: 'I did well in Mexico and then never got picked again until 1973. I thought the world of Alf but the one thing I hold against him was he wouldn't pick flair players –

Marsh, Hudson, Bowles and the rest. I thought we should have been given a chance, but he had his way of playing. To be fair to Alf, Revie came in and picked a party of eighty-one and I wasn't even in that! If they don't like you, what can you do? If Lawrie McMenemy had been manager, I'd have got 60 caps.'

Missing training in Mexico, however understandable a reaction, was surely something that rankled with Ramsey. It's the only logical explanation for Osgood's regular omission at a time when England was crying out for a player of his talent and vision in front of goal. That mistrust of the 'character', of footballers who sprang from the rock'n'roll generation, led Ramsey to reject a number of players who could have offered England something. In fairness, it's far too simplistic to say that had he picked Osgood, Bowles, Hudson and Worthington, all England's difficulties would have been solved. As Geoff Hurst says, 'The flair players in the 1970s didn't compare with the likes of Bobby Charlton and Bobby Moore. There's talent and there's genius!' And some, such as Bowles, were undeniably unreliable and, as Roy McFarland points out, 'Alf looked at players like Hudson and Marsh and felt he couldn't hang his hat on them, couldn't rely on them to play well every time. There is a step up from club football and his assessment of who could bridge the gap wasn't far wrong.' Nevertheless, there was a marked lack of imagination in some selections.

The emergence of McFarland was one early ray of light following Mexico. An accomplished centre-half, commanding in the air and with excellent distribution, he was thrilled to get in the England side in a Nations Cup group game against Malta in February 1971 – only England's second international after Mexico: 'Playing for your country becomes the ultimate ambition, but at the time you start your career, it's the last thing on your mind. Targets come one by one – you want to get in the club team, then you want to stay in it, then you start to learn what's required and, if it goes well, you look at playing at a higher level. It's like every job, it's an apprenticeship to start with, and once you've passed the early tests, then you start to look ahead. I'd been at Tranmere as a pro for twelve months and Brian Clough came to sign me. In his talk to persuade me to sign for Derby, he said, "In twelve months, you'll be playing for England." That was the first time I'd ever thought about it; what was he talking about? He was a month out! It took me thirteen months to get in the Under–23s. The best thing about that was the players were in the same boat, it's not the full monty, but it's nice to be with players of your own age, because in the full squad you're surrounded by senior pros who've done everything and it can be intimidating. That helped me relax into the set-up, to play with Royle, Shilton, Hughes and to forge relationships with players as early as that and then go on into the big squad with them meant you felt comfortable.'

His assessment of the junior teams is backed up by John Richards, now chief executive at Wolves: 'The Under–23s were useful, it got you used to fitting in with different players, some of whom progressed with you into the full side, and it wasn't such a culture shock. We went on a tour of Eastern Europe in 1972, which was great experience, because we had a lot of very good players in there – Shilton, Keegan, Channon, MacDonald – and the tour was a good way of meeting everyone. And visiting those places at that time, you were very restricted in what you could do, so it turned you in on yourselves and you had to make your own entertainment, pull together and get to know each other. And that was all a good learning experience, a good introduction to the importance of team spirit.'

Travelling with England was another part of the wider England experience. According to Roy McFarland: 'Travelling with England is a stark difference from going abroad in the summer with your wife or girlfriend! Everything is done for you, you have the best flights and hotels, you don't have to show your passport, at airports you are treated well, you get pampered, you become spoilt. It's lovely! That's the first thing that hits you. You think, "I must be a bit special, a bit important," and it gives the feeling of being wanted and that's a good feeling to have. You're expected to keep your discipline but you are made to feel different. Even so, you don't get the same feeling with England as with your club, you can't get together a couple of days later and discuss the game, which is a shame. But the spirit was good. Alf was thorough, he loved his players and we returned that. We knew his attitude, how meticulous he was, how he'd get you prepared. In training he'd pull a player to one side while you were getting ready to do some stretching exercises and make a quiet suggestion, things to make you think rather than direct criticisms, always something helpful. I found the same with Cloughie, though others didn't, some found him dogmatic and a bit frightening.'

It's a regular complaint from footballers that spectators aren't always aware of the quality or value of certain players, that they don't see the overall picture clearly enough. So it's nice to know that even internationals can be taken aback by the talents of their team-mates, as Roy McFarland recounts: 'On my debut against Malta, Joe Cini got away from me late on, got in a good header and Banksie made a terrific save, which was an eye-opener. What a goalkeeper: hadn't had a thing to do for 80 minutes then makes a brilliant stop. He was special. My first game was alongside Norman Hunter. I count myself fortunate that in that party there were five players who had won the World Cup and had distinguished themselves in Mexico. It was easy for me as a youngster to fit into that side, then soon after that I was playing with Bobby Moore and I felt our relationship at the back was strong and solid. Maybe Alf did hold on to one or two of them too long, but they were top international players. People ask who was the best player I've played with and as much as Bobby had class and great quality, much of what I learned about the game came from Dave Mackay, who was a great example. I idolized him, I lived with him for a couple of years in Derby, travelled with him, ate with him, learned a lot from him about what was required to be a footballer. Then to come into the England team and play with Bobby was a finishing school. At Derby I played on the right because Mackay was left-footed, as I was. For England, Bobby played on the left, though he was right-footed. It never caused a problem, we were never caught out; he was such a talented player.'

England were gifted a particularly easy qualifying group for the Nations Cup, pitted against Malta, Greece and Switzerland, hardly giants of European football. There was a little disquiet that the established names continued to crop up on the team sheets against the Greeks and Maltese, in particular. If ever there was an opportunity to experiment, surely that was it, though as Mick Channon points out, 'People talk about friendlies and games against small nations, but there was no such thing for England, everybody wanted to beat us. Alf was a very proud man, he loved winning and he did it with class, with dignity. Alf didn't swear much, but when he did it was an aggressive adjective to say we'd stuff 'em!' But couldn't Marsh or Hudson have got a game at that stage, to see if they had anything to offer?

Instead of experimenting with attacking players, Ramsey's attempts to look at fresh faces only extended as far as the likes of Tommy Smith and Larry Lloyd, again both very good players, but England's problems lay not in destruction, but in creation. Yet there were always reasons for Ramsey's caution, as Roy McFarland explains: 'Alf liked the tried and tested. He tried new players and if they fitted in, if their standards were good, they stayed. If not, he moved them out. There was always a rotation, but the solidness of the squad was strong. It was evolution, not revolution, and that's how he got loyalty from us. Alf was warm, quite funny, the frostiness with the press wasn't there with players. He would never say anything uncomplimentary about his players.'

The squad was fiercely loyal to their manager and whatever problems might beset them, England could never be criticized for a lack of effort. Once a player had proved to Ramsey's satisfaction that he could be trusted with the England shirt, he took some shifting. According to McFarland: 'I was a regular, barring injury, missing the odd game in the Home Internationals, because that was the time Alf could rotate and give a few other players a game against whoever we played in the midweek. But he always had his strongest side out against Scotland. He always wanted to win that, as much as they did, he had that lovely passion which rubbed off on us.' A later recruit, Mick Channon, reinforces that view: 'The Home Internationals were like another league at the end of the season. I think it was good for English football to have three meaningful games at the end of the season, where the manager could have a look at a few players in matches that have an edge, more than playing a friendly in Turkey. But the best team always played against the Jocks because he fucking hated them! Not nasty, but just because he wanted to match the passion the Scots had. He instilled that in me and, even now, if we beat Scotland, there's nobody happier than Mick Channon!'

With three straight wins – two against Greece, one against Malta – England entered the 1971–72 season with one foot already in the knockout stage of the Nations Cup. A 3–2 win in Basle cemented qualification, though a 1–1 draw with the Swiss at Wembley took some of the gloss off the achievement, and a 2–0 win in Greece did little to pacify the doubters. The time for experimentation had passed and England didn't look much closer to finding a reinvigorated team. And they certainly needed one, for the quarter-final draw had pitted them against the West Germans in a two-legged tie. The folly of Ramsey's selectorial intransigence became apparent, for in England's most critical games for two years, he was forced to consider Rodney Marsh, who he had been studiously ignoring over the previous two years. Marsh had come on as sub against Switzerland in November 1971 and would again be on the bench for this quarter-final: 'He didn't like my attitude to football. I played off the cuff, always did. If you've got a player like that, you either discard him or build a team round him, because you can't harness a player like that to a system. He was very dogmatic, the team was 4–4–2, the forwards had a specific job and shouldn't deviate from that. He tried to change at the end, to bring in more flair, but I think he'd gone past his sell-by date, the world had caught up and it was all a bit late. But you can't second guess managers. His philosophy was 4–4–2 with a certain type of player. People suggested me, Ossie, Hudson or whoever should have got a longer run. But then it wouldn't have been Alf's team. If you wanted us to play, you'd have had to have a different manager.'

Ramsey was also hurt by the late withdrawal of Roy McFarland through injury, unbalancing the central defence, since Hunter and Moore never looked comfortable together. Injury problems were becoming an increasing theme for Ramsey, and as Allan Clarke points out in *Bremner!*, 'I never knew this at the time, but Don Revie probably stopped me from winning more than 19 caps for England. He used to phone the England manager and say, "I'm sorry, Alf, the boy's had a knock so I'm not sending him."' Revie was probably not the only culprit.

The game against West Germany at Wembley Stadium had enormous repercussions. As Colin Bell says, 'They murdered us. They couldn't do a thing wrong; they were all buzzing. There was nothing you could do about them. They were just a crack side at their peak.' Geoff Hurst agrees, adding, 'Netzer was superb, Müller was an outstanding forward, Beckenbauer was fully matured, they were a great, great side.' What was most disturbing from an English point of view was not that the West Germans had simply played better on the day. They had given England an education in the modern game, much as Ramsey's side had given them a lesson six years earlier. The West Germans had their trademark efficiency and organization down pat, but more than that they played with style, with purpose and with panache. Rarely has Wembley been graced by a better individual performance than that given by Günter Netzer, who was just astounding, giving a display so good that Zidane would be proud to claim it as his own. He ran the entire game from the centre of midfield, never wasted a pass, always picked out the right target, orchestrated total West German domination. When you then remember that the Germans also had the likes of Beckenbauer, Uli Hoeness and Gerd Müller to capitalize on Netzer's work, it's apparent that England weren't beaten by mugs. But nor could anyone deny that the Germans were on a completely different plane. Not since 1953 had England been so systematically undressed by a visiting nation. And though the Hungarians had administered an incredible shock when they won 6–3 to destroy England's unbeaten home record, the West Germany's 3–1 win had a similar impact. In 1953, at least there had been some sense that England weren't the great power after the catastrophic 1950 World Cup. But when the West Germans destroyed them in 1972, this was just six years after we had been crowned World Champions, only two years after we had given a good account of ourselves in Mexico and had been, by popular consent, the second best team in the competition. To have fallen so far, so fast, was a bitter pill to swallow and difficult to comprehend. England remained wedded to the 4–4–2 system that served them well from 1965 to 1970, but the system was beginning to creak. Much of it was based upon traditional English verities of hard work and a never-say-die attitude, qualities that could carry a side so far but no further. Against more technically gifted sides, England needed more than that in order to prevail.

There were two prime reasons for English decline. Firstly, Ramsey's system had changed little down the years, so opponents were able to copy and counter it. England were now too predictable, too obvious in their approach. They lacked the flair, the spontaneity that unlocked defences at international level. The national team was staid, outmoded. Even so, the system might have managed better results had we not lost a clutch of great players all at once. The 4–4–2 formation was workmanlike, but while Bobby Charlton was at the centre of it, England had a genius who could suddenly change the course of a game with one visionary pass, or one thrilling burst of pace followed by a ferocious shot. There was no Bobby Charlton any longer. Nor was there any sign of a new Geoff Hurst, described by Jimmy Armfield as, 'The finest all-round centre-forward we ever had.' Perhaps Ramsey could have made better use of players such as Osgood and Marsh, but they were never going to be Ramsey type players. Sir Alf had his own style, his own beliefs and his own principles, honed over thirty years in the game. He wasn't going to change them overnight. So for them to continue to succeed, he needed to find players with both the skill and the character of Bobby Charlton. And they come along very rarely. In their absence, Ramsey needed to go back to first principles, see what talent was available to him and formulate a game plan accordingly. But in dismissing the likes of Marsh, he imposed heavy restrictions on himself, almost left himself straitjacketed into the 4–4–2 of old. And that was simply too obvious now.

Did England have the talent available to make the necessary

changes? It's a moot point. There's a powerful argument that says truly great players define the shape of the team around them, that they force managers to employ them to their best advantage. Ramsey himself had done that with Bobby Charlton. Helmut Schoen did the same with Franz Beckenbauer. In giving him a role as sweeper, Schoen allowed him to play with the game in front of him, thereby allowing him to maximize the value of his terrific reading of the game. Beckenbauer saw matches unfold and, by using his brilliant tactical brain, could then dictate their course, offensively and defensively. And, just as England had in 1966, so West Germany had a batch of world-class performers come to maturity at the same time in 1972 – goalkeeper Sepp Maier, Günter Netzer in midfield, razor-sharp Gerd Müller in attack, all of whom owed much to Beckenbauer's running of the game.

For the Dutch, it was Johan Cruyff who dictated matters. Perhaps the greatest European footballer of all time – George Best might put up a pretty persuasive counter-argument – Cruyff has always been an individual who wanted to be in the thick of everything. Given that Holland had no footballing reputation of any kind, the sudden arrival of Ajax on the European scene in the early 1970s was startling. The most exciting aspect of their rise was the prominence of number fourteen, Cruyff. One minute he'd be waltzing past three defenders on the left wing, then he'd be making an interception at right-back, then he'd turn up at centre-forward to crack a shot past the keeper. Total football was already a part of the Dutch vocabulary, but to see Cruyff play it put flesh on the philosophy. And again, circumstances conspired to allow a generation of great talents to emerge together and put a revolutionary plan into action, each player seemingly comfortable in possession in every area of the pitch. Holland had Cruyff, the commanding, defensive elegance of Rudi Krol, the midfield vision of Johan Neeskens, the goalscoring flair of Johnny Rep, and a host of technically accomplished footballers who were not frightened of the ball, wherever and however they received it. Holland were the inheritors of the Hungarian mantle, not bound by shirt numbers or positions on the field, but a team of footballers who played the game. Certainly each knew he had to work within a team structure — if the nominal right-back went off into central midfield, a team-mate had to cover for him — but every individual was given the freedom to play as such. To use a cliché, the Dutch themselves rarely knew what they were going to do, so what chance did the opposition have? Great players, genuinely great players worthy of the term, render systems redundant.

If you don't have great players, can you devise revolutionary tactics? Probably not. Look at the success of Norway in recent years, or that of Watford in the 1980s and Wimbledon in the 1990s in our domestic League. None of those sides have great individuals, certainly not in comparison with the competition. So, instead, they have all chosen to play the percentages, reducing the chances of error at the back, pressurizing in numbers at the front. Hardly the game to please the purist, but modern, noisy and effective all the same. And that was what England and Ramsey were reduced to by 1972, simply because we lacked great footballers, and those we had who were potentially great were *personae non gratae* at the court of King Alf.

Just as the defeat in Mexico had rung down the curtain on Bobby Charlton's career when he was substituted, so it was against West Germany at Wembley for Geoff Hurst: 'I think all pros are the same, I didn't feel I'd been that bad and that I shouldn't have been substituted by Rodney Marsh; I didn't feel I was the worst of the six midfield and front players. The strange thing about my finish with England was he picked a couple of younger players for the second leg and it looked like I was finished, then a couple pulled out and I was called back in and it looked as though I'd play, which would have been my fiftieth cap, but then I got a back problem and was pulled out and never got picked again! I understand from the grapevine that he wanted to bring me back six or eight months later, I was playing pretty well, but I heard he felt that it wouldn't be good for me personally to play a few games and then have to be left out again. I don't remember getting told I was left out, I just didn't receive a selection letter for the next game. We'd wait for the letter to come and it didn't! We've seen over the years a lot of top players who've been left out without a word and have said it shouldn't finish like that, and I think one has to look at that comment. It was never a problem for me.' As Hurst departed, it was to be replaced by Rodney Marsh: 'We were getting paralysed and I came on in desperation with 15 minutes left. I did think I was in the team on sufferance. That night, 100,000 people in Wembley were calling for me and he had to put me on. I don't think he liked that much. But to get stuffed at Wembley was the turning of the tide.'

To all intents and purposes, the Nations Cup was over – to beat West Germany by two clear goals in Berlin looked an impossible dream, even to the greatest optimist. Many pundits wanted to see England at least go out in a blaze of glory, and Ramsey was exhorted to pick a young, adventurous side. Predictably, he didn't, though for good reasons, according to the returning Roy McFarland: 'In Berlin, there's no doubt we were physical. The stinging criticism had been felt: they were a good team, Netzer had been unbelievable, they were much better than us at Wembley. They kept possession, it was an onslaught in Berlin, we had to chase the ball, so we decided to be solid, and it was a game for experienced players. As a defender I look back on the 0–0 with some pride, even though we didn't play much football. But against a world-class eleven, we got some pride back.' To get a draw in West Germany wasn't a bad result, but it was not enough and England were dumped unceremoniously out of the tournament. For the first time, people were openly speculating about Ramsey's position, and even about England's ability to qualify for the World Cup in 1974. But that was just being alarmist, wasn't it? England not qualifying for the World Cup? Unthinkable . . .

Just as Hurst had gone, so too did Francis Lee, immediately opening up further vacancies. It's a moot point as to whether Moore should have gone too, because, as Peter Osgood suggests, 'Alf was too loyal to his players, he let them get old like Matt Busby did at Manchester United.' Colin Todd would surely have been a more than adequate replacement, but, of course, Moore was more than just another footballer. He represented everything that

Ramsey had achieved, was a monumental figurehead. For Ramsey to leave him out would not only need an irrefutable footballing argument. It would require the manager to make a hugely emotional decision, one he was not ready to make, for as Mick Channon says, 'Moore was very like Alf, did everything in a quiet way, he took Alf on to the pitch, if you like; very competitive, but never showed it.' In his darkest hours, Ramsey, like us all, needed a friendly face, an ally, someone he could rely on completely.

That was all the more apparent when he lost Gordon Banks to the car accident that took his eye. Ramsey was lucky to have two excellent young goalkeepers to fight over the position in Ray Clemence and the eventual winner, Peter Shilton. Inheriting Banks' jersey in such circumstances could have been embarrassing, but Roy McFarland rejects that: 'As far as Peter was concerned there was no awkwardness after Banks' injury. Shilts always felt he was the best. He trained that way – for all that's happened, good and bad, in Peter's life, he took his football very seriously. No matter what anybody else said, he thought he was the best. That's a big thing in football, that self-belief. When Ron Greenwood alternated him and Ray Clemence, I felt that was the wrong way to approach it, and Peter didn't like that.'

Shilton's utter and very obvious dedication to his football endeared him to Ramsey. Rodney Marsh's more cavalier style did little for him: 'There were plenty of games when we were doing well when he'd take me off. I never got to play the way I could. The closest was against Wales at Ninian Park, where I had an outstanding game, scored, did all the things I did at Manchester City, but afterwards Alf didn't even speak to me.' In mitigation, Francis Lee points out, 'Rodney was deaf in one ear, so maybe Alf was talking to the wrong side!' There was never any great warmth between Marsh and Ramsey, and the end for the mercurial Manchester City player came when England played Wales in a World Cup qualifier at Wembley: 'I made a sarcastic comment in a team talk to Alf. Before the game, he said to me, "You don't work hard enough. If you don't work harder tonight, I'll pull you off at half-time." I said,

"Christ, we only get a cup of tea and an orange at City." He looked at me and I think it went over his head. But I didn't play again!'

Other youngsters were coming through to challenge for the forward spots, players who fitted the Ramsey mould better than men like Marsh or Worthington. These included Kevin Keegan, and Mick Channon: 'When Alf was in charge, he used the Under–23s to have a look at you, then he'd move you up and leave you in the stands for a while. The hardest thing was getting in the fucking team in the first place! Once you got in, it was because he'd sussed you out, knew you were the right type of player, and then it was as hard to get out. Some thought that was a fault, but I don't think so; if he thought you were good enough, he'd persevere with you. Alf wasn't worried about your weaknesses, he wanted your strengths. If you have to coach the best players in the country, you've got a problem. He knew who he wanted for the job and people respected that – when he went round the old First Division, the buzz would go round the ground, "Alf's here today, I'll show him I can play!" OK, you need time for set pieces and general organization, but not coaching! If you have to coach 'em, they shouldn't be internationals.'

Another player who only got the most fleeting of opportunities was Wolves' John Richards: 'There were a lot of good players and England play very few games, so although you really need four or five games to settle, you're very aware you have to take the chance straight away, because there might not be another. If you came from a "smaller" club, you were generally a big fish in a small pool, so it was a big difference to get into the England squad and be right down the pecking order. It wasn't as difficult as you might suspect because Ramsey was very good at introducing newcomers – there were good lads in the squad, they tried to make it less daunting. I got my cap at Goodison against Northern Ireland, which was a bit of an oddity because it was their home game, but because of the troubles, they couldn't play in Belfast. I got called in late because of injury to Allan Clarke – I was in the main squad of twenty-two for the Home Internationals but for that first game Alf had only called in sixteen, with the rest of us to join up later.

So I went into the sixteen and straight into the team. It was fortunate because I'm from Warrington originally, so my family were all able to get to the game very easily and see me make my debut. It whizzed past, like a Cup Final. I remember feeling proud to get the shirt and then pleased to win. I was a bit disappointed in my performance, I was out on the left of Chivers and Channon, which wasn't my natural position, so I don't think I did myself justice. But it was a great occasion, even better because it was near home.'

Having been played out of position, it seems unfair that Richards never got another chance, particularly bearing in mind Colin Bell's comment, 'It took me a few games to understand international football, it was a game of patience, feeling each other out and having to hit them on the break.' Richards agrees with the wider view, strongly held in the midlands in particular, that 'It was a definite disadvantage not to play in the so-called strongholds of Liverpool or London and, to an extent, Leeds at that time. There wasn't such widespread media interest in football and the papers concentrated on those centres, and that did help those players get more prominence.'

The most pressing issue on England's agenda was qualification for the World Cup of 1974 – problematic given that the team was clearly in a state of transition with no obvious new sense of direction. England were in a three-team group along with Wales and Poland, superficially a reasonable draw, but one fraught with danger, especially since in such a small group there is little time to retrieve a bad result. The Welsh games were played first. England stuttered to a 1–0 win in Cardiff, then were fairly fortunate to escape with a 1–1 draw at Wembley. Such results brought further complaints that England were too negative, but Roy McFarland denies that: 'I never felt we were negative under Alf, because we had Peters and Ball in the middle. Alf said Martin was ten years ahead of his time, and people like Malcolm Allison ridiculed that, but Martin was an excellent player, creative, likely to score goals, doing some of the things David Platt did later. I think the problem was finding someone to score the goals. When you've had Hurst,

Hunt, Greaves and Lee, they take some replacing! He struggled to get the balance, maybe the likes of Keegan and Channon weren't quite ready, so it was a struggle for him.'

The opposite view is put forward by Peter Osgood: 'We couldn't beat teams at Wembley because they packed their defence and we hadn't got the flair to get round that. Alf wanted to play to a system and wouldn't trust anyone who wouldn't conform. He had players who had the potential to do a better job but he was afraid to use them.'

The crunch games for qualification were with Poland. England had a summer tour organized for 1973 which would take in Czechoslovakia, Poland (for the first leg of the qualifier), the USSR and then Italy. Roy McFarland points out the folly of that: 'You do need to get your schedule right. It didn't help going to Poland after a long hard season, because, make no mistake, the English season is exhausting. You do need your rest. May and June isn't a good time for us to play internationals.'

So it proved. There were none of the much-touted 'flair' players in the party and England continued to turn out frustrating performances where they controlled many of the games, but could not score the goals their superiority warranted. In Prague they managed a 1–1 draw, reasonable if uninspiring preparation for the Poland game. McFarland recalls, 'We were ready for them, Alf had picked out the good players. I felt they had pace up front, which could be dangerous at Wembley, but in Poland I thought they feared us. And to lose 2–0 was disappointing. I felt we were better than them but we didn't take our chances. The same happened at Wembley, but the real disappointment was in Katowice. I felt comfortable, didn't feel they could hurt us. Then when we went a goal down, we had to over commit, and they caught us with a sucker punch. Then the frustration came out with Alan; he got sent off because he genuinely felt we should have won.'

Part of the problem was the fact that Ramsey had chosen to field a more defensive line-up, omitting Mick Channon: 'My big disappointment was to miss the game in Poland, when he played Peter Storey instead, but he never left me out again. I played in all the others leading up to it and he left me out on the morning. He pulled me aside and said it was just a tactical switch to play another defender and not give anything away, no reflection on me. I remember hearing later he thought it was a mistake, but he never told me! Katowice was a horrible bowl of a stadium, a cold place. They had a good side, Domarski, Lato, Gadocha, a very hard team to play against.'

Defeat in Poland was a savage blow, though some might argue it was just reward for going into a game with such low ambitions. Poland were a very good side, but had England been more adventurous, then they might well have got a better result. Instead, having fallen behind, they lacked the invention to force their way back into the match. Afterwards, the camp was understandably downbeat. According to McFarland: 'There was nothing to do after the game, so we all went up to the room Bobby Moore and Alan Ball had, because it was the biggest. We all sat there with a couple of beers and Alf knocked on the door and said, "Do you mind if I come in?" He sat down and had a beer, and talked about the game. He said their first goal was his fault and we couldn't convince him otherwise, though it was nothing to do with him – Colin was out of position, Bobby and I hadn't organized quickly enough for a quickly taken free-kick. Then he got up, said, "Enjoy yourselves, lads," and went out. Moments like that are important to your education. I feel privileged to have been sitting in there with Moore, Peters, Bell, Ball, Shilton and Alf, and to just be talking about football, which is what we were there for.'

Following such a disappointment, the squad would happily have flown home, but there were obligations to discharge. In their way, these responsibilities helped lift the gloom. McFarland remembers, 'We had a long flight to Moscow, which wasn't great, but once we started training again the atmosphere lifted, Alf was very positive. It was a big help to me to be amongst the senior players. It was a bad defeat and it would have been easy to get depressed by it, but they'd seen it all before, they carried us along and lifted our spirits. Then we got a good result in Russia, winning 2–1. And it was an interesting trip in itself; we were going to look at Lenin's tomb in

Red Square, we went in St Basil's cathedral, so that was an education too. But Alf just wanted us to concentrate on the football. We were there to work. And that meant not much time off, which kept you out of mischief! When they go abroad now, the news reporters go out too. Situations are often set up and that's a sad reflection of the way newspapers want to interpret society.'

The tour finished in Turin, a 2–0 defeat, though the mood was improved by the creation of a little piece of history, Bobby Moore winning his 107th cap and going past Bobby Charlton's record, though it virtually signalled the end of his career, winning just one more cap against Italy in November 1973. Again, McFarland sees that game as part of his wider footballing education: 'That game gave me a real understanding of international football, and about what the Italians were like. They hit you on the break, everything was counter-attack, and that was new to me. It's a learning process at that level. They'd let you have the ball in areas of the field where they felt they didn't want it or that you couldn't do anything with it. Then when you got near their area, they'd make it very hard to squeeze through and they were exceptionally good at hitting you quickly on the break. I remember I made an interception in our half and there was an Italian two yards away, but he just turned his back and walked out to the touchline. It wasn't his job to win the ball, but to find space. So when they won it again, he came alive, looking for it.' That was a luxury which Ramsey denied his forwards, expecting them to track back, to chase defenders down, to hustle and bustle. But that was looking increasingly like yesterday's view of the game.

When England got back home, there were signs that Ramsey wanted to evolve a new style, based more upon the Continental, neat passing model. Tony Currie was introduced as an English version of Netzer, and the signs were good, initially at least. As a warm-up to the Poland return, Austria travelled to Wembley and were thumped for their troubles, England rattling in seven goals without reply. Had Ramsey found a solution to the goalscoring question just in time? That result offered some optimism, for England now knew exactly what they had to do to qualify – beat the Poles at Wembley in October. For the biggest game England had played since Mexico, the preparation was hardly idea. (Roy McFarland 'was playing at Old Trafford for Derby four days before the Poland game. It's not the way we should have prepared but that was how things were. Alf had talked about the need for time and preparation and people laughed at him, they thought it wasn't necessary. As much as we invented football, it's the rest of the world that does things that are more professional. The Germans and the Italians left clear weekends before big games, but it took us another fifteen or twenty years.' (The only argument against that comes from Mick Channon who thinks, 'People didn't seem to get injured then. I played for twenty-two years, 600 or 700 games. If I'd waited until I was properly fit, I'd have played 100; certainly wouldn't have played 46 for England. A niggle, dead leg, strain, didn't stop you playing football. The only thing that mattered was playing. We were fit – you want to be fit, you will be.')

Apparently, Ramsey's team talk at Wembley didn't vary much from the norm, as Channon recalls, 'The other side didn't matter; it was what we did. He'd say, "Number five, he's got a good left foot," and he might be talking about Beckenbauer or Cruyff! He didn't build them up, he made them look human. He believed we were the best.'

The 1–1 draw with Poland is another part of football folklore: Tomaszewski, the goalkeeper dismissed by Brian Clough as a clown, hurling himself all over his penalty area to pull off incredible saves; shots bouncing off the frame of the goal; Hunter's slip and Shilton diving over an innocuous shot; Clarke's penalty; Kevin Hector's last-minute miss. All vivid pictures in mind. The Polish goal seemed protected by some lucky charm or force field, and this more than twenty years BD (Before Drewery). Mick Channon is still exasperated by the very thought of the game: 'We were criticized for not being more patient. How can you be more patient? We had complete control of the game, constantly shooting in on their goal, what difference would it make? Just one of those days when it won't go in. If it had been any other game, if the result hadn't been so crucial, you'd have been happy with the performance!'

Roy McFarland felt the disappointment very keenly: 'I'll always reflect on qualification for 1974, and it came down to that game at Wembley. On the day we deserved to win, but the best team doesn't always win the match. It was just one of those fluke occasions. I've never been in a dressing room like it afterwards: players were crying, I may have been one of them, I can't remember. But I do remember how disappointed, how low I was, especially as 48 hours before, Cloughie had walked out on Derby! That was the worst week of my career. The one thing I wanted was to play in the World Cup finals; I was desperate to go to West Germany. I had a good chance early on – Peters took a quick free-kick, which was a West Ham standard. He put his hand on the ball and then, without looking, just flicked it over the wall. I ran clear. I was on a bit of an angle and thought, "Should I shoot or pull it back?" I pulled it back. I look back now and think "Should I have shot?" I still think about it, that game is so embedded in my mind. I saw it again not long ago and I kept thinking, "We've got to score here!" It is a very fine line and, generally, the ability gets through, but this time it didn't. We couldn't have played any better, all we could have done was finish better, been more clinical.

'Had we got through to the World Cup, with the squad we had, I think we'd have done well. We weren't a magnificent side, but we were a decent team, hard to break down. Poland ended up third and I think we were better, we'd have been close. Driving home that night was the most miserable night I've had in football. One header from Kevin Hector and it would all have been different – why'd the bastard hit the post!?'

England's failure to qualify was obviously a major blow to national sporting prestige, but for the players concerned it was a savage professional blow. Colin Bell gives a good summation of their feelings: 'I was probably in my prime for 1974. It had taken six or seven years to become an established England player and I felt I was just ready to go on the stage at the World Cup, to show what I was made of.'

Having fallen at the final fence, it was almost inevitable that Ramsey, the man who had won the World Cup just eight years before, would have to go. Bizarrely, the change didn't come at once. Instead he soldiered on through a couple more games – a 1–0 home defeat against Italy and a goalless draw in Lisbon, in which he unveiled a radically different side, only Channon and Peters surviving from the Polish draw and new faces like Stan Bowles, Colin Todd, Trevor Brooking, David Nish and Martin Dobson winning caps – and even named the party that would go on the 1974 summer tour. Then, in April 1974, the Football Association put on the collective black cap and pronounced sentence. Ramsey's ties with the England team were immediately and completely severed. Roy McFarland 'felt it was a mistake. Times were changing but with all his knowledge, he would still have succeeded.' George Cohen, who knew Ramsey's methods, his strengths and weaknesses as well as anyone, argues that, 'It was absurd to sack him, we lost all continuity. It would never have happened on the Continent.' And to simply dispense with his services did seem ludicrous. After eleven years in the job, Ramsey had a huge store of knowledge and information which could have been passed on to his successor – many felt that a younger man should have been given the coaching position with the national team with Ramsey acting as an advisor in the background. But as has so often been the case, the FA preferred a scorched-earth, Year Zero policy. Worked well, hasn't it?

....

10

Never the Same Way Once

Far be it for me to suggest that the Football Association couldn't run a raffle and that it didn't know what it was doing when it sacked Alf Ramsey, but think about this. There's little doubt that once the Poland game ended in a draw, Ramsey was finished. That was 17 October 1973. So the official decision and announcement wasn't made until May 1974, but Ramsey was dead in the water six months earlier, and everyone at the FA knew that. As Roy McFarland says, 'The FA said from day one that Brian [Clough] would never get the job. He was too outspoken, he'd have turned the place upside down, upset people, said things. That wasn't what they wanted. They didn't want a yes–man, exactly, because Alf was never that. But Alf was interested in his team and nothing else. So when we didn't qualify and Brian was out of work, maybe they did think, "Christ, we can't sack Alf, Cloughie will be up for the job and he's the last bloke we want." That possibly kept Alf in the job another few months.'

That's a pretty shrewd judgement. So the FA had six months to sit on their hands, waiting for Cloughie to get safely out of the way. You might have though that *the* organization in English football, knowing there was a vacancy coming up for the top job within that organization, might have had plans in hand about the succession. They might have taken informal soundings as to who might be interested in the job, for example, might even have made informal approaches to their target. But apparently not. Instead, the decision to sack Ramsey seemed to be thrust on them from on high and they began to thrash about in utter confusion, eventually choosing to appoint a caretaker manager to get the England team through the summer. Does all this sound strangely familiar? But we should not have been surprised. After all this is the organization of whom Ted Croker wrote, on taking over as secretary in 1973, 'I soon discovered that it was extremely difficult for the man in the street to discover how to buy a ticket for an England game. The FA telephone number was ex-directory.'

England had a hectic programme ahead of them, with the three Home Internationals and a home game with Argentina – the first since the infamous 'animals' encounter of 1966 – then a three-match tour of the Eastern bloc, taking in East Germany, Bulgaria and Yugoslavia, an itinerary that had been intended as a nice warm-up for the World Cup. Now they were meaningless friendlies that only served to emphasize English inadequacy and all that we were missing. Who cared what we did in East Germany or Yugoslavia? They were going to the finals, we weren't. The mood within the English game was resolutely suicidal – this was the first time we'd failed to qualify for the competition we used to think we were too good to enter. And not only had we failed, we'd bored people into the bargain. Our self-esteem was a notch below Kafka's, and it desperately needed improving.

As an interim measure, just to get the side through the summer – using the squad that Ramsey had already picked – the avuncular Joe Mercer was installed as caretaker manager. In fairness to the FA, they couldn't have found anyone better to hold the fort. Mercer was universally liked by press and public alike. At the end of his career in the game he no longer had any burning personal ambitions, so there was little pressure on him. Where Ramsey's tenure had ended with him carrying the weight of the world on his shoulders, Mercer had no such worries and communicated the same carefree attitude to his players. As Roy McFarland notes, 'Joe was the elder statesman. His team talks were simple: "I'm not telling you how to play. You wouldn't be here for England if you didn't know how to play. Go and enjoy yourselves, get on with it." Joe loved football and loved to see players playing the game. I think he thought he'd come in with a smile on his face, crack a few jokes, put a smile back on the team, lift the side after things had gone wrong. It worked well for the short time he was there.'

McFarland only experienced the Mercer touch for a couple of games, picking up a serious Achilles injury in the Home International with Northern Ireland, but Mick Channon was pretty much a regular: 'Joe was a lovely bloke, just came in to keep it together, ticking over. He put a few new faces in, made people smile a bit. He made it a bit more enjoyable than it had been for a while, because there was nothing riding on the games except getting back some pride and some fun.'

One of the most interesting aspects of Mercer's time at the helm was the personnel he used. Suddenly England teams were packed with the likes of Frank Worthington, Trevor Brooking and Stan Bowles, the flair players that everyone wanted. The perception was that this was Uncle Joe putting his stamp on the side, saying football should be fun; but this was Ramsey's squad. The selections emphasized just how radically Ramsey had been looking to change before his time ran out. Whether it was a genuine reassessment of his own priorities and the direction in which international football was going, or a simple stab at self-preservation by appeasing the press is a moot point. What it did reveal was that England lacked players of genuine world class. Ironically the footballers who came out of Mercer's stint with their reputations enhanced and international places more secure were the more industrious types, such as Kevin Keegan and Emlyn Hughes.

The Home International series was a mixed bag, the customary wins over Wales and Northern Ireland followed by a disappointing 2–0 defeat at Hampden, a cruel reminder that Scotland were on their way to the World Cup and England weren't. An entertaining 2–2 draw with Argentina – both their goals coming from a young Mario Kempes – improved the prevailing mood as well as diplomatic relations between the two countries, and then it was time to tour.

Eastern Europe would have been an ideal location to prepare

for the World Cup, three taxing games sharpening the side perfectly. But as the venue for a meaningless tour with little or nothing riding on the results, it left a lot to be desired. Disappointment at missing the World Cup mixed with exhaustion after a long hard season and an inevitable desire to let off steam. The average age of the England side had been considerably reduced, some of the 'playboy' footballers were included and many of the senior figures had gone. With Mercer not exactly the strictest disciplinarian either, there was always the potential for an off-the-field problem or two. When it came, it was in unexpected fashion. Having drawn 1–1 in Leipzig, then won by a single goal in Bulgaria, the party flew from Sofia to Belgrade to complete the tour. In the airport, Liverpool full-back Alec Lindsay climbed on the luggage conveyor and started to walk against the belt, as in a silent movie. A security guard came over, pulled off the belt and threw Lindsay against a wall. Kevin Keegan had been watching and found it hilarious until he too was grabbed by a guard. In his first autobiography, he wrote, 'As I struggled, in a state of shock, an armed guard appeared in front of me and joined the attack ... I could feel myself being dragged away, choking from the power of the guard's arms around my neck.' Keegan was taken into an office and by his own account, 'I was punched, clubbed and kicked, and when I thought he had stopped, he came across and repeated the treatment again.' Keegan was then faced with a list of charges – sexually assaulting an airhostess, assaulting a security guard, disturbing the peace and causing an obstruction. It transpired that the guards didn't realize Keegan was with the England party because they were dressed casually rather than in England suits or blazers. The team threatened to pull out of the game, but that would have jeopardized Keegan's safety further, so he was released on the understanding that the game went ahead.

Keegan insisted on playing and grabbed a late equalizer to give England a creditable 2–2 draw and bring down the curtain on Joe Mercer's reign. It had been fun while it lasted, but those final days showed how football, its image and its reporting were to change. Though no fault of his, the Keegan incident alerted the newspapers to the fact that an England might not just fill the sports pages, but the front pages too. Things would never be quite the same again.

During the summer of 1974, while the rest of the footballing world cast its eyes towards West Germany and the World Cup, the FA were hunting Ramsey's full-time successor. When the appointment was made, it shocked nobody. Working on the basis that the England manager had to be an Englishman – and that was so obvious in 1974 that the question never even arose – if you wanted someone with a proven track record, the choice was Brian Clough or Don Revie. And it was never going to be Brian Clough, because the FA, in their wisdom, felt he would tarnish their reputation. Something Revie would never do . . .

Revie's reputation as an astute technician had been made as a player in the 1950s, when Manchester City were successful with the Revie Plan. He played as a deep centre-forward, much the way the Hungarians operated in the mid-1950s and with similar results. Thereafter, Revie went into management and had taken Leeds United from the Second Division to a position where they were the most feared team in the country, not only because of their talent, but because of their uncompromising physicality and ruthless cynicism. Admittedly they had been shaking off that tag in the last couple of years of Revie's reign when they were able to play some quite sublime football, though, as Roy McFarland says, they could still 'hurt you both ways, physically and with their football. To be hurt physically and to get a point out of the game wasn't so bad, but to be hurt physically and mentally was hard. They were a tremendous team that never got the credit they deserved.' That's a fair point because the side that won the Championship in 1973–74 remains one of the very best to grace the English League. Yet for all their consistency, that League title was only the second they won under Revie in a period where they could and should have dominated as Liverpool were to do. For all his talent, Revie was a worrier, deeply insecure about himself and his team, and many said that financial motivation loomed much too large in his life. It was that which encouraged the cynicism, that unease and lack of self-belief which so often communicated itself to his players, causing them such anxiety that they regularly fell at the final hurdle, far too often for a team of their quality.

Revie was only too aware of his detractors, and had seen the way in which Ramsey had ultimately been destroyed by the press and by his refusal to assist the fourth estate. It was an example that only served to fuel his paranoia. Revie decided he should go out of his way to get the press on his side. He was open to them and, in time, even his judgement would be swayed by them. As Mick Channon says, 'When Don came in it was all change. You were very conscious of the media, of image; it was a different environment. Once Alf went, everybody got a run: we'll try anybody! Since Alf, they've never really put a settled team together. I honestly don't think Revie ever picked the team he wanted, it was what the press said ... it got to the stage when it was said you could soon buy England caps at Woolworths, they were being dished out too readily. He lost control.' Following the complaints over Ramsey's intransigence and his unwillingness to introduce fresh faces, Revie immediately set out to show that he would never be so blinkered. Before a game had been played, he called a get-together of the players he said he would be considering for England duty. It had been a matter of faith with Alf Ramsey that the England manager only ever had around thirty players that he could realistically choose from. Revie dismissed that from the outset. He called a meeting of eighty-one players – more than seven full club teams!

Roy McFarland was among that number, in spite of his Achilles injury: 'He liked get-togethers. The first one, the hotel was packed with footballers! We met in Manchester, but it wasn't a select group. You sat in the room and looked around wondering what was going on! It's all right to have a wide range to pick from, but do you need it? He could have halved that, and looked seriously at say thirty names that he'd whittle down to a final twenty-two for a big game or tournament. I suppose he gave all the players the feeling they could get a cap, and maybe one or two did who shouldn't have. You didn't feel special as an England player any longer, and that's an important consideration.'

Phil Neal made a similar point in his autobiography: 'Revie was a great believer that the squad should be one big happy family, and some couldn't cope with this. A number of them were very miffed when Don asked them to give a hand with the hoovering or bring in the coal.' Even so, McFarland still recognized many of Revie's better characteristics: 'after I'd done my Achilles, I was out for most of the '74–75 season, but Don kept in touch, told me that if I got fit, I'd be in his squad. That's exactly what happened, I had six games for Derby and was in the squad. It was a shame because Colin Todd was in the side a lot and we knew each other inside out; I think we would have done well together for England. But it probably took me three years after the injury to feel right and, by then, age starts to catch up. Don wanted me to play and talked about me being captain, which I would have loved, but it wasn't to be. Don was a very good communicator, talked to the players, discussed everything with them.'

One thing he discussed early on was money, to the annoyance of some players who felt he was turning an honour into a job. Revie's intention was clearly to offer further motivation, but some plainly felt the England cap was enough motivation of itself, the likes of Alan Ball and Martin Peters later complaining vociferously about Revie's apparent obsession with money. In 1974, he announced that the basic fee for playing for England would henceforth be £100, with a bonus of £200 for a win and £100 for a draw. A year later, in the midst of qualifying for the Nations Cup, the team was offered £5000 a man for winning the trophy.

The problem is, it doesn't matter how much money you offer, it's talent that wins cups, not greed. And, as Ramsey had found, the talent pool was not as deep as some imagined. Initially things went well: a useful Czech side was summarily dismissed at Wembley, 3–0; West Germany, World Champions, were embarrassed 2–0 in a friendly; then Cyprus hammered 5–0, Malcolm MacDonald helping himself to all five, equalling the individual record set by Steve Bloomer, G.O. Smith and Willie Hall and raising hopes that England had found another great goalscorer.

Sadly, against better quality opposition, Supermac was found wanting.

There were some imaginative team selections – the early introduction of Kevin Beattie and Gerry Francis for example – and the side played some positive, progressive football. When the 1974–75 season was closed with a magnificent 5–1 win over the Scots at Wembley, Gerry Francis looking every inch the midfield general England required, it put the seal on a very satisfactory first season for Revie, marred only by the failure to be a dismally defensive Portugal at Wembley in another qualifier.

But with seven points out of eight already in the bag, that didn't look like it would be critical. And then the wheels started to fall off. The first sign that things were going awry came when Revie dumped Alan Ball. Not only did he drop the England captain, he did so by letter, which he didn't even sign, Ball finding out from a journalist's phone call before the letter had even arrived. What a surprise when Ball, never the most placid character, reacted angrily all over the press – who could have expected that? So Revie's honeymoon was well and truly over. Ball had been sacrificed to make way for Gerry Francis, around whom Revie wanted to build his new team, and it was a particularly savage irony that after just eight games as captain, Francis started to accumulate the series of injuries that eventually ended his career, his final game coming at the end of the 1975–76 season.

Revie's original thinking was, in its way, understandable enough. Looking to the 1978 World Cup in Argentina, Revie had to be thinking about team building and about the players who could make an impact out there. At 33 Ball would, by then, have to be a borderline case, so Revie at least escaped the charge levelled at Ramsey of standing by the old guard for too long. But the decision as to when best to dispense with quality is a fine judgement, and Revie possibly erred on the other side of that line. Roy McFarland believes that much: 'He was criticized for getting rid of Alan, especially, a bit too early, but, like most managers, he wanted to stamp his authority on the job and get players they've introduced into the team. He was losing experience, and in the case of Ball and Peters [who never played for Revie], two world-class players. And Don had a bad run with injuries – myself, Colin Bell, Gerry Francis – and that did disrupt his plans. Losing Colin was a big blow because he was becoming a very, very good international. I'm not sure Don knew what his best side was, because of losing players through age or injury, being a bit unlucky, making a few wrong decisions. Maybe what was left wasn't quite of the highest international class; good enough to survive, but not good enough to make a real impression or win things at that level.'

McFarland is right to point to those injuries as hammer blows to Revie's hopes, though all three were available for the crucial return trip to Czechoslovakia. Mick Channon fired England into the lead and, for a time, they were in control. They then conceded a goal shortly before half-time and, as the Czechs began to dominate thereafter, England were on the rack. It was no surprise to see them concede a second goal, leaving England to struggle to qualify for the quarter-finals. To compound the misery, Colin Bell had played his last international, his career soon to be ended by injury. This was a terrible blow to Revie's plans, for Bell had long been a mainstay of the England midfield. Although never quite in the same class, Bell had been the closest England had come to replacing Bobby Charlton. Like Charlton, Bell was astonishingly fit and could cover the ground for 90 minutes without any problem, shuttling from box to box, linking defence and attack with deft passes. He made intelligent runs all over the field, was always available to a team-mate and regularly scored important goals. An archetypal Ramsey player in that he was both creative and a workhorse, Bell was still at his peak when the end came.

England went to Portugal knowing that they had to win to have any hope of denying the Czechs, but could manage no more than a 1–1 draw. Revie could point to the fact that the Czechs ultimately went on to win the competition and were far better quality opposition than the English media gave them credit for, but after the disasters of the tail end of the Ramsey reign, the public wanted results not reasons. Most telling was the inability to beat Portugal in either game. England could still not score goals against teams whose only ambition was not to concede. How much of that was Revie's fault? As manager, the final responsibility was always his, but how many alternatives did he have to a forward line including Keegan and Channon? His error came in his selection further back in the side, often packing the midfield with defensively minded footballers, betraying his siege mentality and his overpowering fear of defeat. With defenders all over the pitch, there was little room for creativity, few who could make the opportunities for the forwards.

Not only were tactics and selection sometimes suspect, so was the whole approach. The climate of fear was stifling. Roy McFarland remembers Revie was 'meticulous, but maybe too much so, because players weren't used to it. As a manager myself now, I'll put together a dossier on the teams we're playing. Don would have a dossier the same size on each individual player we were facing. And if you were up against two players, you'd get two dossiers. I won't say you had to read them, but they were there for you. I don't think the players took to it, they didn't like it, thought it was strange, even though he'd done it at Leeds for years. If you read them, you knew if the player was right footed, two footed, a good header, comfortable with the ball, couldn't pass, where you should press him to get the ball. But you could read them and think you were up against a great player. If one of the forwards was reading about a centre-half and saw "good in the air, will kick you, strong in the tackle, good distribution, a very strong all-round player", you'd put the dossier down and think, "Bloody hell, who am I playing against? This is the best player in the world!"' Mick Channon backs that assessment, saying, 'He went overboard with tactics. I don't think he needed to do that. Alf simply said, "This is what we're going to do, you take him," then we'd have a couple of free-kick routines and that would be the end of the story. Eventually, your mind would be full of too much, you could end up a nervous wreck ... players aren't really that intelligent, they don't need all that. They just want to play football.'

And it wasn't merely the tactics that caused unrest. Some players felt their general treatment while on England duty was faintly ridiculous. Mick Channon wasn't wildly impressed: 'He wanted the England team to be his boys, like at Leeds. But we were England. It was unfortunate he got it wrong. Once he fell out with someone, he couldn't forgive. Of course we used to sneak out. I used to rebel against being told what to do. You treat people like children and they'll behave like them.' Phil Neal reflected on Revie's attachment to parlour games such as bingo and carpet putting: 'I found it an amusing eccentricity the first time but after a while it began to get on my nerves. I felt we were being treated like children. Players always seemed to be finding excuses to cry off international duty. Some said it was because clubs wants to give Revie a taste of his own medicine. He'd never been slow to withdraw Leeds players from midweek games to ensure they were available for League games the following weekend. Now other managers who'd released their players in the past and suffered for their patriotism were delighted to turn the tables.'

As a Leeds player, someone like Trevor Cherry could better understand Revie's thinking, but he also concedes it was flawed where England were concerned: 'He'd have liked to run England on Leeds lines, but it had to be different, it didn't work out with England. There's a lot more politics involved, in the FA, with the press, the players aren't yours, you're just borrowing them, so he couldn't get the same feeling with England. He had problems adjusting to the way other players conducted themselves: he found the southern lads were from a different culture compared with the spirit he'd created at Leeds, and I don't think he came to terms with that. And the press never really gave him a fair crack of the whip, because Leeds were never very popular. We never really had a settled team for various reasons and that was probably the thing that cost us the most; too many changes.'

Revie's world had been turned upside down within twelve months, a fact underlined by England's visit to Hampden. The Scots were thirsting for revenge after the 5–1 pasting at Wembley and turned the tables to win 2–1. That England were on the skids was emphasized by Scotland's winner from Kenny Dalglish, a trundling shot that was virtually a back pass, which squirmed through Ray Clemence's hands, through his legs and just had enough strength to cross the line. Roy McFarland recalls, 'Ray was gutted when Dalglish put the ball through his legs. Good players do make mistakes. Bobby Moore lost the ball as last man in Poland in 1973 trying to dribble when he shouldn't and we went two down and that was the end of the game. But that's a great player. Ray was a top-class keeper. Shilts has always been criticized for not saving that shot against Poland at Wembley that went under him. We've all done it – that Dalglish goal, I dived in on Joe Jordan just inside our half when I shouldn't have. Alf taught me to stand up, not to sell myself. I dived in, didn't get the ball and that was the move that eventually ended up with Dalglish. So I should have done better. But that was symptomatic of Don's time, things just seemed to go against him. I don't think the team was right, and I don't think he ever resolved that.'

Revie did try to introduce fresh faces, including Trevor Cherry: 'I played in the Football League team in Scotland and I already knew Don from his Leeds days, and Les Cocker told me then he was going to have me in the big squad. It was everything to play for England, the only time in my life I couldn't sleep, and the only time I ever worried about getting injured, really.' Cherry made his debut in a 2–1 win in Wales and proved a hugely valuable addition to the squad for his versatility: 'I played in midfield first of all, but I was always more comfortable at the back, but even Ron Greenwood felt I could do a job there. Being adaptable can be a drawback, I felt I was best to the left of the centre-back, but I played in midfield and both full-back positions too.'

With an influx of new players such as Phil Thompson, Mick Mills, Ray Wilkins, Ray Kennedy, Phil Neal and Stuart Pearson, Revie did his best to refresh his flagging team. This was a marked difference from the way in which Ramsey had put his teams together. Ramsey decided on a way of playing and then picked footballers to service the plan. Jack Charlton and Roger Hunt were not necessarily the best, most gifted players in their particular positions, but the way in which they played dovetailed perfectly with Ramsey's system and the other players he selected. In contrast,

Revie seemed to have no specific plan. So meticulous in other areas, in selection he was strangely indecisive. Certainly he yielded to the obvious temptation of picking the 'best' players, seemingly without any thought as to whether they would gel as a unit, partly because of his desire to please the press and public by producing an attractive team. Revie, always such a sharp tactician at Leeds, now seemed to believe that the best players didn't require a system. That might have worked had these 'best' players been extravagantly gifted, but Revie had the misfortune to be labouring in a period when the cupboard was bare, and our best did not compare with the Dutch or the West Germans. Equally disruptive, he was often swayed by form. If a particular player was enjoying a hot streak at any given time, he might suddenly find himself with an England cap at the expense of a tried and trusted regular. With all due respect, should Colin Viljoen ever have played ahead of Mick Channon, for example? Revie had clearly never heard the phrase 'form is temporary, class is permanent'.

Yet at Leeds, that was a maxim to which he always adhered. He picked a side in August and those eleven were still taking to the field the following April, injuries permitting. And nobody dared injure a Leeds player for fear of Norman Hunter, Johnny Giles or Billy Bremner exacting their own special kind of retribution. Revie got the England job at the wrong time, just as he was changing the Leeds method from one of brutalization to one which played the beautiful game, like the Corleones moving out of the protection racket and back into the strictly legit olive oil business. Maybe this Damascus-like conversion indicated a wholesale change in his footballing philosophy, or at least a reversion to his earlier beliefs – after all, as a player he had instigated the very modern Revie Plan, based on the Hungarian deep-lying centre-forward. But at Leeds, Revie had the players to do the job, notably in the midfield masters Giles and Bremner, neither of whom was English. As Leeds went from success to success by playing bright, attractive football, maybe Revie saw that as the way forward, especially having seen Ramsey savaged for his supposed negativity. Perhaps he felt that, with all of England to choose from, he'd be a failure if he couldn't pick a winning side that played with style, in much the same way that Graham Taylor was to lose sight of the qualities that had made him successful at club level. If he did, it was a miscalculation, an idea rendered even more unworkable by the loss of some of his most cultured players – Bell, McFarland, Gerry Francis, Todd – through injury.

A trip to America to compete in a tournament to celebrate the American bicentenary – how obvious that there should be a football competition to celebrate an American anniversary – offered a degree of encouragement. The side played well in a narrow defeat against Brazil, then beat Italy 3–2 with goals from Phil Thompson and two from Mick Channon. Not only was it good to beat major opposition again, it was an excellent piece of psychological warfare because, typical of Revie's bad luck at this time, England had been drawn in a World Cup qualifying group that also included the Italians. And when did they ever fail to get to the finals? (Apart from 1958.) Also in the group were Finland, and England flew out to Helsinki and returned with a comprehensive 4–1 victory, allowing fans to enjoy the summer with a little more optimism than they might have imagined possible.

But it was to prove a false dawn, a case of England shining in fixtures which the opposition treated as little more than a training exercise, then getting unnecessarily excited by unrepresentative results. England started the 1976–77 season with some of the most dismal performances in their history. They drew with Ireland at Wembley, then struggled past Finland at Wembley 2–1 in a display that was so bad that Revie was forced to apologize to the crowd via the press. Hardly the best preparation for the key trip to Rome. By now Revie's own confidence was shattered. There were already rumblings emanating from the FA – notably the ever-genial Sir Harold Thompson – about Revie's future, the press were on his back and the key elements of his side were crumbling. And, like his predecessors, he was getting precious little help from the clubs. Revie believed he had thrashed out an agreement with Alan Hardaker, secretary of the Football League, on the postponement of matches prior to key international fixtures. He made a speech implying that was the case, forcing Hardaker into a corner. After the ritual denial, Hardaker had to agree to bring games forward to the Wednesday from the Saturday, a minor, if important victory. Later, he got the concession that he should have players for nine days before a midweek international providing he released them to play on the Saturday, again a very marginal compromise from the clubs.

What kind of team to take to Italy for a game England couldn't afford to lose? Trevor Cherry remembers it as a 'very poor side, really, it was very negative, there were too many of us who were defenders playing out of position, and we gave them the game. I think the boss just got his selection wrong for that game.' Roy McFarland disagrees to some extent: 'I wouldn't say we went to Italy looking for a draw, though the midfielders weren't our most creative. Keegan, Bowles and Channon were up front and they were shackled, they never got a kick, but if you're playing those three and Trevor Brooking in midfield, you're not that defensively minded. It's ultra critical to say we got no help from the forwards because you should give credit to the defenders, they played man to man with a sweeper. They kicked them, spat at them, pushed them, the referee was a bit lenient, they didn't get the protection. But the Italians knew their job and stuck to it.'

England were well beaten 2–0, leaving goalkeeper Ray Clemence to complain, 'It could have been a lot worse.' He was right – England were lucky to get nil. If that were not enough, England were then even more thoroughly humiliated at Wembley by a Dutch side that handed out a lesson every bit as comprehensive as those dished out by Hungary in 1953 and West Germany in 1972. Once again, world football had moved on to another plane without us noticing. A 2–0 defeat was scarcely an accurate reflection of the huge gulf that existed between the two teams. By now, the writing was on the wall for Revie. England were in chaos, they weren't going to make it to the Argentine finals without a miracle, and given that the Pope lives in Italy, that looked unlikely. Scotland came to Wembley at the end of the season and won 2–1. The Tartan Army then took the Wembley turf apart, wrecked the goalposts and left the citadel in ruins. How's that for a metaphor?

The England squad were relieved to be getting out of the country, on a fact-finding mission to South America that had originally been booked in the fond hope that it would be a useful exercise prior to returning the following year. It certainly was for Mick Channon who 'went to Manchester City after Peter Swales tapped me when I was playing for England in Brazil!' Surprisingly, as Trevor Cherry says, 'We had a very good tour and played particularly well against Brazil in their own back garden, drawing 0–0. In Argentina we drew 1–1, which was encouraging too, even though I got sent off. It couldn't have worked out better for me because I got exonerated and the lad who was sent off with me, Bertoni, got a six-match ban. It was just the politics over there that if a player from the home side went, one from the other team had to go as well! He'd whacked me in the mouth!'

The tour finished with a 0–0 draw against Uruguay, but, in truth, the results didn't matter much by then because only the most wide-eyed optimist could see England returning to the continent twelve months later. Mick Channon remembers, 'I thought something was going wrong with Don. He didn't turn up in Brazil until just before the game. That wasn't like him. He was supposed to have been watching Italy, I think.' In fact, though Revie had said he'd gone to watch England's opponents, he'd flown out to Dubai to discuss a deal to take over as manager of the United Arab Emirates. Knowing the axe was coming, Revie's pragmatism – some would see it as greed – got the better of him. Seizing an opportunity to stay in work and provide for his family, he accepted the UAE offer. Then, stupidly, he announced his decision to quit as England manager through the pages of the *Daily Mail*, a move guaranteed to turn an already miserable situation thoroughly poisonous. The rest of the press were livid that Revie hadn't chosen them for his exclusive and tore into him, calling him a traitor, a money-grabber and a cheat. The FA weren't overly keen on him either, immediately introducing a ten-year ban to prevent him working in English football, though this was later reversed in the courts following a restraint of trade case.

In the end, Revie was defeated because he didn't know what he wanted to do. Did he want to entertain? To please the press? To excite the fans? To make money? To win matches? In the end, in trying to do everything, he achieved nothing. As Roy McFarland says, 'It was sad the way Don left. His teams at Leeds were the hardest and best sides I ever played against – they were tough, strong, had ability. Had they had Peter Shilton in goal, they would have won everything. I liked Don as a man, I've got great respect for him, he gave me his time when I had a serious injury, he was very helpful. I'd have loved to have played for him, but never really got the chance because of injury.'

As Revie himself said later, if he'd stuck to his first principles, the principles that made Leeds United great, maybe he'd have had a chance. His team wouldn't have been pretty, but they'd have won more games, which was all that seemed to matter by 1977. How would he have done it? By creating 'a real bastard of a team.' Ah, the poetry of the beautiful game.

11

Am I Getting Through?

Having botched Alf Ramsey's sacking, at least the Football Association could justifiably argue that Revie's departure had taken them unawares – four months unawares to be exact, because they'd have sacked him in November once England had formally failed to qualify for Argentina '78. Lancaster Gate must have been haunted by a touch of déjà vu because, once again, when the vacancy needed filling, one Brian Clough was hovering in the background. Having rehabilitated his reputation after his forty-four days in the Elland Road wilderness by dragging Nottingham Forest to promotion in the 1976–77 season, Clough was the people's choice once more. And not only the people's choice. According to Trevor Cherry: 'I played under Brian, I thought he was a brilliant manager, he treated me very well, and he was the favourite to replace Don, but he was never going to get the job, to be honest. He'd have had to change the FA committee and turn the place upside down. No disrespect to Ron Greenwood, but Cloughie was the right man for the job.'

The FA went through the necessary charade of having Old Big Head in for an interview, but Cloughie could have turned the Thames into wine, walked on it, cured the lame (or at least Kevin Beattie), and then for an encore turned Wembley into a modern football stadium and he still wouldn't have been made England manager. Although the eventual appointee, Ron Greenwood, made a decent enough fist of the job, the International Committee should still be ashamed of their cowardly actions in denying Clough the chance to turn England into a world power again. He'd have made life bloody difficult for them, but so what? Their brief was to ensure England had the best opportunity to succeed in world football, not to give themselves a cushy life. Apparently nobody had pointed that out to them.

Ron Greenwood initially took the job in a caretaker role, simply to complete the now hopeless World Cup qualification series. The FA insisted that then, they would look again at the position. Just a smokescreen. After Revie's departure, the FA wanted a steady replacement, someone who would not embarrass them, whether he was the best candidate or not. And Clough would have embarrassed them, would have told the world that the committee men knew nothing about the game. He'd have reorganized the FA from top to bottom – and reorganization was long overdue – and had the hangers-on slung out. Ron Greenwood, on the other hand, would live and let live. Let him pick the team and let the committee get on with whatever they wanted to do. Which was fine by them.

In fairness, his managerial credentials weren't bad, even if his greatest successes were a long time past. He'd been a member of the West Ham academy, had overseen the development of a team that exploited the skills of Moore, Hurst, Peters and that had won the FA Cup in 1964 and the European Cup Winners' Cup a year later. Those were useful achievements, but on the other hand, shouldn't a side that boasted three World Cup winners have done rather more than that? West Ham had never realistically challenged for the Championship, so for all that Greenwood's sides could entertain, the question of their resolve was never satisfactorily answered. Did his sides always have a soft underbelly, or was it simply the purist style had no place in the modern world? His results at international level would help answer that conundrum.

With three matches at his disposal – a friendly against the Swiss then qualifiers in Luxembourg and at home to Italy, Greenwood decided he'd have little time to impose his own ideas on the side, but instead saw himself in the role of morale booster, much as Joe Mercer had been three years previously. Sensibly, rather than trying to bring a new side together, he chose to build around one club, the incredibly successful Liverpool. There were six Liverpool men in his first selection, plus Keegan, who had left Anfield that summer. That was an experiment that did not bear much fruit, a 0–0 draw with the Swiss hardly acting as the rousing start he'd sought. He kept faith with the policy in Luxembourg, though Keegan was missing, and England eked out a 2–0 win. Coming into the Italian game, popular support for Greenwood, which had never been that high, was ebbing away. Had England been humbled by the Italians, the clamour for Greenwood to be replaced might have been irresistible, even though he made a good impression on the players, as Trevor Cherry recounts: 'When Ron came on board, I thought that was me finished, that he wouldn't like my style, but we got on very well. He liked people to play good football but he knew you had to win the ball as well.'

The Liverpool experiment was shelved, though as the premier side in the country, they still provided three players plus Keegan. It was no surprise to see Trevor Brooking, an archetypal Greenwood player, drafted in to play alongside Ray Wilkins in central midfield. What was more intriguing was the introduction of two wingers, in Steve Coppell and Peter Barnes, to feed a target man, Bob Latchford. It would be wrong to suggest that Italy were playing flat out, for they knew that as long as they avoided a catastrophic defeat, England could not prevent them qualifying for the World Cup. But even so, England were fluid, attractive and impressive in carving out an emphatic 2–0 win. Ron Greenwood sealed his position as team manager and a few more optimistic souls were scenting a new dawn for English football after seven long years of failure.

That breath of fresh air continued through the rest of the season, when results were pretty decent – a narrow defeat in West Germany, a draw at home to Brazil, three straight wins in the Home Internationals, then a thumping 4–1 win over Hungary who were on their way to Argentina. With a settled side and some very talented youngsters like Peter Barnes, Steve Coppell, Viv Anderson, Laurie Cunningham and Glenn Hoddle either in the full side or starring at Under-21 level, the cynicism of the Revie years seemed a long time ago.

Friendlies are one thing, serious competition quite another. After nine months in the job, Greenwood had yet to be put under any pressure. That started with the 1978–79 season, when England were confronted with qualification for the European Championships again. Proof that luck plays a huge part in the game came with the draw. After Ramsey and Revie had been pitted against really top-class opposition, Greenwood found himself in a group with Bulgaria, Ireland, Denmark and Northern Ireland, useful teams, but all eminently beatable. In fact, the biggest alarm came in the opening fixture in Denmark. Despite Keegan giving England a two-goal cushion by the 23rd minute, the Danes were level before the break. England then extended their lead through Latchford and Phil Neal, before Denmark pulled a goal back and ensured a fraught final four minutes. Thereafter in qualification, England were very rarely in any danger, dropping only one point in eight games when they travelled to Dublin. There were some exceptional results and performances in there too, such as a 3–0 win in Bulgaria, a 5–1 victory in Belfast then a 4–0 home win over the same opposition. More importantly, England were playing with a degree of style, even swagger, that they had not managed since 1970. Greenwood had established a settled side built around a nucleus of Clemence, Neal, Mick Mills, Phil Thompson, Dave Watson, Wilkins, Keegan, Coppell, Latchford, Brooking and Barnes. These players offered a nice blend. At the back, there was a strong Liverpool element, Clemence, Neal and Thompson all well aware of one another's strengths and weaknesses, all vital cogs in the miserly Championship-winning side of 1978–79 that had conceded a mere 16 goals in 42 games. With both Mills and Watson offering plenty of experience to complement the utter reliability of the Liverpool men, defensively England weren't going to concede much. Greenwood certainly scored over Revie by employing width. Coppell was no pure winger, more a wide midfielder who was willing to tackle back, but even so, his great stamina allowed him to get forward and offer an additional attacking threat, while on the other flank, Peter Barnes was in the classical mould, only attacking thoughts in his mind. The left-sided pairing of Barnes and Mills was ideal, in that Mills did not commit himself forward, giving Barnes licence to attack, a freedom he exploited well early in his career, though the story of his England days was really one of potential unfulfilled. Wilkins and Brooking manned central midfield. Brooking struck up an excellent partnership with Kevin Keegan that verged on the telepathic at times and which was to harvest many goals over the years, Brooking either furnishing Keegan with a telling through ball to allow him to finish an intelligent run with a strike on goal, or breaking from deep to allow Keegan to repay the complement. Wilkins tended to lie deeper, though he was hardly the archetypal anchor man in the Ince or Batty sense. That was the benefit of having such a solid back line, for even if the midfielders did concede possession a little too easily at times, there was always Watson or Thompson ready to mop with with a no-nonsense tackle.

Greenwood saw the role of the midfielders as a largely offensive one, the wide players trying to supply Bob Latchford in the air, Brooking looking to play more sophisticated passes to Keegan. Keegan was by now the focus of the side, his time in West Germany with Hamburg SV acting as something of a finishing school for a player who'd already enjoyed a wonderful career at Anfield. Learning how to cope with Continental markers on a weekly basis, Keegan was a revelation when he came back to play for his country. Those eleven were effectively the first choice through 1978–79, but other individuals were offered the occasional taste of international duty.

While the football was going well, the international side was also undergoing one of its most significant cultural developments. Over the previous couple of seasons, some extremely talented black youngsters had been making their presence felt in the English First Division. It was only a matter of time before England had its first black international, and there was huge media interest in the issue. For some time it looked like the sublime Laurie Cunningham would be the first to claim a full cap, but because of Greenwood's attachment to Peter Barnes – people have been sectioned for lesser eccentricities than that; Barnes' promising beginning having quickly evaporated – Cunningham had to bide his time.

So it was Nottingham Forest's spindly right-back Viv Anderson who claimed the place in the record books when he was picked to play against Czechoslovakia at Wembley on 29 November 1978. Just as he was at the time, Anderson is keen to down play the wider significance of his selection, understandably so. After all, Anderson would prefer to be remembered for the quality of his football rather than as some kind of symbolic figure: 'I was pleased to be called up but I just focused on playing well. Ron Greenwood told me early on that I'd be playing, so I was really trying to concentrate on that. There was a lot of debate about it, I was getting telegrams from people like Elton John, from Laurie Cunningham's family, but I just wanted to think about the football, to do my best for me, my family and my friends, and the rest of it could go by the wayside, really. Of course it was a big thing, but I was so nervous about the football that I never really gave the race issue any thought. It was reassuring to have Peter Shilton and Tony Woodcock around the squad, it's easier to settle if you've got friends in there. Ron was a quiet man, told you what he wanted of you; a good tactician, showed you where you should be and where you shouldn't be. He knew his job, all the aspects of the game, a total football man, but you couldn't have had a greater contrast with Brian Clough, who was my manager at Forest! I remember going on the coach to Wembley: all the lads like Kevin Keegan, Bob Latchford, all having a little word with me, all trying to help settle the nerves, giving advice, it was a great help. But really, it was a relief to get on the pitch. It wasn't the best of days, frosty on one side and soft on the other, so I had to wear studs first half and rubbers in the second, so it was a strange game. But it went well, we won 1–0, I had a hand in the goal; I couldn't have asked for much more.'

Back in the late 1970s, there weren't that many top-class black players around and each had to deal with the inevitable publicity in his own fashion. West Bromwich Albion's Cyrille Regis – one of Albion's fabled 'Three Degrees', along with Cunningham and

Brendon Batson — was one of the most prominent, and he accepts, 'We were breaking new ground. Once you're in, you don't think about making a stand for blackness, you're thinking about playing at as high a level as you can for as long as you can, to stretch your talent as far as it can go. But there was another dimension to it, the press would pick up on it, young black boys would pick up on it, so you became very aware that you were breaking down barriers, but that wasn't the focus. I didn't go out saying I'm going to break down barriers for black people, but you have to accept that side of it. You do become a role model, you are an example, you do destroy myths, but that comes off the back of stretching your talent. It was difficult because there weren't too many black players around. Now, racist chants have virtually disappeared compared with the late '70s when you had 5000 or 6000 people shouting, "Nigger, nigger, lick my boots ... Pull that trigger, shoot that nigger," the monkey chants, the bananas. What you learn is to turn that negative into a positive. If they're going to give you stick, you go out there, score goals, show them how to play. And maybe that determination helps push you further. If the racial aspect had affected my wife, my parents, my kids, it would have been a different story. But it was always confined to the stadium, apart from the usual run of the mill racist things that happen to black people, period. But if the hooligans had targeted my family, it would have been different. As it was, I could handle it.' And let's face it, none of the cowards shouting from the stands would have gone within a mile of big Cyrille, a player with so powerful a physique he was compared to heavyweight champion Joe Frazier.

When Regis finally made his full England debut in 1982, on the eve of the game he received a bullet through the post. What the fuck is wrong with these people? The irony was that Regis had actually *chosen* to play for England: 'I got into the Albion team in October 1977 and had a fairly good year. I had dual nationality; I came from French Guyana, my father was from St Lucia and had a British passport, so I was eligible for France and England. St Etienne came in for me at the end of that season and offered about

£750,000, with the idea that if I did well for them, I'd play for France. In the end I decided to stay at West Brom and pretty quickly got picked in the England Under-21s. That was the French team of Platini, Tigana and Giresse, but I don't regret the decision. You make your choices at the time, and we had a very good team at Albion; I'd only been in the game a year, and I felt this was the place to stay. Within twelve months I was in the Under-21s with Laurie, Hoddle, Rix, Cowans, Robson and Statham; it was a good squad. We went to Denmark, Sweden and Bulgaria and we travelled with the full side and it was interesting to be around the likes of Keegan, McDermott and Brooking. But you had to wait your turn, very rarely would you get in after a year of playing well. The senior pros were in, Ron Greenwood was very loyal to them and it took a lot to shift them, because they were good players. The turnover's higher now, but it took me nearly five years of playing well in the top flight to get in.

'It's a cliché, but football is about opinions, and it was Ron Greenwood's that counted at the time. He had Keegan, Mariner, Woodcock and Francis; they were an experienced side and it wasn't easy to dislodge them. You are at a disadvantage at a club like Albion because you don't get the media coverage that you do in Manchester or London. But I enjoyed it here and I've no regrets that I didn't move.' There's a lot of truth in that, given that Bryan Robson, who had clearly been the best midfielder in the country for two years, didn't really establish himself in the England side until he went to Manchester United. Then, miraculously, overnight he became a regular. There were exceptions that proved the rule, of course, notably the inclusion of a Nottingham Forest contingent, though given that they were League Champions then double European Champions over a three-year period, it would have looked pretty odd had they not been represented.

Greenwood did have a settled side and was very loyal to his squad, in a way reminiscent of Ramsey. Despite one blip, when they lost 4–1 in Wales, England seemed to be building very nicely towards the European Championships, which, for the first time, would be held World Cup style, eight sides slugging it out in Italy.

England went to Barcelona and beat Spain 2–0, then outplayed Argentina, the World Cup holders, at Wembley, winning 3–1.

England were drawn in a group with hosts Italy, Belgium and Spain, a tough proposition, given that only the top team would progress, directly into the Final. Nevertheless, there was a groundswell of optimism as England tackled their first major tournament since Mexico in 1970. Yet even before they went, the perplexing machinations of the FA threw things into chaos once more. For reasons unfathomable, England had agreed to play in Australia at the end of May, playing in Sydney just twelve days before they were due to meet Belgium in Turin. Trevor Cherry 'captained the team – it was half the squad that was going on to the European Championships in Italy. That was a thank you from Ron, to let me captain the side, though it was Bobby Robson who actually took the side. Everything was first class – travel, hotels and all that – but the FA committee men don't skimp either! But touring with England is hotels, airports and training grounds and that's about it. It sounds daft, you travel the world but you don't see it! But you're not off on holiday or on a sightseeing trip, you're there to work.'

Flights to and from the other side of the world, even if most of those who made the journey were just back-up members of the squad, isn't the best preparation for a major tournament, and it again raised the question of just how professionally our game was being run. In footballing terms the Australian trip was totally worthless, offering up a meaningless 2–1 win and a bit of flag waving. Ludicrous.

On the home front, attention was quite rightly focused on the coming Championships. Belgium offered the first challenge. Their recent record had been as depressing as England's, but at least Belgium wasn't saddled with an inflated sense of its own importance, nor over-optimistic ambitions. England, on the other hand, were expected to win and win well. Before a pathetic crowd of just 7000, England took the lead just after the half-hour mark through Ray Wilkins, but Jan Ceulemans equalized within a matter of minutes. It then became obvious that of the 7000 fans, an unhealthy proportion were English thugs, who took out their disappointment on the locals, though how the morons managed to work out that Belgium had equalized is uncertain. They were quickly quietened by the local police, using copious amounts of tear gas, though the gas had to be turned off for several moments when the wind blew it on to the field and the players were left fighting for breath. Understandably, the game, which had never been a classic, petered out thereafter and ended 1–1. As Trevor Cherry says, 'When the hooligans cause trouble, it doesn't help. It doesn't change the way people treat the team, they realize it's nothing to do with us, or with football, really; they understand it's a wider social problem, but it is upsetting, no question about it.' Viv Anderson recalls that 'we got caught out by the trouble in the Belgium game, because it wasn't expected. The FA had to make a statement about it – I think it was Bert Millichip – but as a player, you're left to concentrate on the football.'

By the time England played again, Belgium had beaten Spain, who had managed a 0–0 draw with Italy in their opener. As a result, England needed to beat the hosts, who themselves were smarting from some pretty aggressive criticism after the Spanish game. England had much the better of the first half, but were unable to make their superiority tell and after the break Italy began to exert more pressure, finally breaking English resistance ten minutes from time with a Tardelli goal. Viv Anderson remembers 'losing to Italy 1–0 and being so disappointed, having played pretty well. But it meant I got in for the Spain game, so that was a thrill to play in such a major competition.' England's tournament was effectively over – perhaps poetic justice for giving Margaret Thatcher, the woman who wanted to destroy football with her mindless identity card scheme, an odious photo opportunity just before they left.

England made six changes for an unimportant fixture that had no real bearing on the group table, and won through 2–1, but, as Trevor Cherry says, 'The Championships were just a disappointment. We went out feeling we had a reasonable chance, but we didn't really perform. It was our first test for ten years and the lack of experience told, particularly in such a hotbed of football.

I was very disappointed not to play, but that's how it went.'

Cherry's point is a good one. Just as we have seen our clubs struggle to catch up with their European counterparts following the Heysel ban, England's ten-year absence from the very peak of international competition meant that we were inevitably going to struggle against the very best. The European Championships of 1980 had been an important stepping stone for what was still a relatively young squad. The level of expectation going into the tournament had been too high, but playing there meant that England would be far better equipped for the World Cup in Spain in 1982. Assuming they got there.

The qualification group wasn't one that should have held any fears for England, particularly as two sides went through. Hungary, Romania, Switzerland and Norway were all middle-ranking nations at the very best and none of them had made it through to the European Championships. Failing to get through that group would be a national disaster on a scale far exceeding the mishaps under Ramsey and Revie. The squad was also in good shape, with very few of the regular names dropping out of the reckoning. One that did was Trevor Cherry: 'Ron was a gentleman. When I was coming to a finish with England, I said to my wife, "Ron will ring this week because they announce the squad on Monday." Sunday night he rang to tell me I wasn't in it and we proceeded to talk about players for three-quarters of an hour. He treated me like a son.'

The self-imposed departure of Liverpool's Ray Kennedy was rather less amicable. He wrote in a Sunday newspaper: 'I feel more pride in the red jersey than in the white shirt of England ... I'm resigning here and now as Greenwood's bridesmaid. I refuse to be an England convenience again and I want that worry off my back ... I am sick and tired of the treatment I've received ... I never felt I was playing in a team for England. There was no unit and I was out on a limb. The set-up was not my scene. I found it hard to perform in the role I was given.' Having collected 17 caps, most as a sub, from 30 call-ups, Kennedy suffered the anguish of the peripheral squad man who was an automatic choice back at his club. It is a difficult adjustment to make, as Viv Anderson concedes: 'It was frustrating to be in and out of the side, but people forget what a smashing player Phil Neal was, and there was Mick Mills too. Everybody wants to play every game and you think you're the best player, so it was difficult not to get a run in the side. It's a matter of luck as well – some players come through when there's no competition, then other years there's three or four players after one place. That said, I haven't got a complaint or an ounce of bitterness about it in me, I'm more than delighted to have got 30 caps.'

To his credit, Greenwood was never afraid to draft in new talent. For the first qualifier, at home to Norway, he introduced Arsenal's Graham Rix: 'Liam Brady left Arsenal after 1980 and I suppose that put me more into the spotlight, though it was a blow to lose Liam; you couldn't replace someone like him. Don Howe was the coach at Arsenal and with England, and he knew me inside out, which works both ways. If I was playing well, he was there to put my name forward, but if I wasn't performing, he knew that as well, so there were pluses and minuses in that. I'd played a few Under-21s, but nothing can really get you prepared for playing for your country in a full international; it's a big step up. As well as that, it takes a while to get used to playing with new players; you're never sure who you'll be playing with, what their reactions are in certain situations, what they're thinking. Before that game, there'd been talk that I'd play, my mom and dad came down; it was a big, big night for me. And we won 4–0; I made the first goal, pulling the ball back for Terry McDermott to smack in. I was pleased with the way I started but I felt I had more to offer. People seemed generally happy with what I'd done, and thought it had been a good selection. Then we went out to Romania, we lost a big game 2–1 and a lot of people questioned me, questioned whether we should have had more experience! OK, we had a young midfield at that time, good legs, players who could keep going, like myself, Robbo, Ray Wilkins. We had a good mix, with Keegan, Brooking, Shilton, Thompson: it was a handy to have them around, because we were whippersnappers at that level. Ron Greenwood was a very easy going sort of bloke, nothing ruffled him. I think he relied a lot on Don Howe, who was the disciplinarian, wanted things done the right way. Ron was softly spoken, knew the game, had a good rapport with the players, let us get on with it to an extent. But I'd played Cup Finals for Arsenal, we played a lot in Europe, so the occasion didn't worry me. The hotels weren't great, there were no dirty tricks, but it was all very basic, but I was prepared for it. We just didn't play.'

Defeat in Bucharest gave some cause for concern, but it was hardly a fatal blow. More worrying than the result was the performance. Throughout the 1980–81 season, England continued to falter, beating the Swiss 2–1, then going six games without a win, including a 0–0 draw at home to Romania, then losing 2–1 in Switzerland to throw their group wide open. Not only did our footballers let us down in Basle, so too did our supposed supporters, causing mayhem on the terraces. As Graham Rix says, 'England have a small percentage of followers who behave like idiots, but unfortunately they're the ones you see and hear on TV. We all want to win, but we can't have win at all costs. If things don't go our way, we have to accept it, you can't just smash a bar up or start fighting. Although once you're on the pitch you just want to play, it is in the back of your mind, "I hope it doesn't kick off today." We all have responsibilities – players and fans – we're all representing our country, after all.'

The poor results were symptomatic of general confusion in the English camp. Having had success using two wingers, Greenwood had jettisoned Peter Barnes for many games and played a more defensive 4–4–2 line-up, expecting his wide midfielders to give more to the side defensively and not play as out and out wingers. Out on the left, Graham Rix 'had a run of games in the summer of 1981. We lost 1–0 to Brazil, played well, deserved a draw. Then we lost to Scotland 1–0, John Robertson got a penalty and I missed an absolute sitter with my head. Steve Coppell picked me out from the right and I tried to glance it in but headed it wide. Jimmy Hill said at the time, "You shouldn't be playing for England if you can't score from there." ' Which, presumably, is why Jimmy Hill never played for England. England were weakened by Keegan's absence for much of the season. And then there was the Glenn Hoddle question. Hoddle had been given his debut against Bulgaria in 1979, scoring a wonderful goal from the edge of the box. It was a trick he performed regularly for Tottenham where, alongside Ossie Ardiles, he ran the team. Most pundits felt that Hoddle should be allowed to do the same for England, but Greenwood never showed that kind of faith in him. Instead of being England's playmaker, Hoddle was expected to simply hold down a midfield berth, a role that never suited him. It was a situation reminiscent of the Ramsey–Marsh stand-off of a decade earlier. A player of that kind of flair and vision must, by definition, be inconsistent simply because he has the ambition and the audacity to try the extraordinary. If the radar is slightly off, it doesn't work. The manager has to bite the bullet and either construct a team around him or ignore him. There can be no satisfactory compromise. English history is one of compromise, then disenchantment, especially in the last thirty years. Rodney Marsh has spoken of Ramsey seeing him as someone who might be converted into a Hurstlike goalscorer, rather than a creator around whom the team could be built. Hoddle was often picked, seemingly on sufferance, then asked to play in an assortment of midfield roles, often out wide, but was rarely given the central playmaking role he coveted. And by playing Hoddle out of position, he was rarely able to produce the performances his talents warranted, causing him to lose faith in the England set-up, demotivating him, leaving him yet more ineffective when the call came again. In defence of England coaches, the team play so few fixtures that every result matters and to select an inconsistent performer is a big gamble. But it is only in giving these visionary players the security of a run in the side that their true talents can come out, as they learn the needs of their team-mates and they, in turn, come to appreciate the qualities the playmaker can bring to the side. Like so much in English life, the long-term good has often been sacrificed to short-term expediency and the headlines in the next day's press, a mistake that foreign opposition rarely seems to make. The history of other nations, on the other hand, is littered with success stories such as Platini, Beckenbauer, Zidane, Gerson, Neeskens, Socrates, et al. A moral there somewhere?

The defeat in Switzerland was part of a two-game tour at the end of the season, both of which were qualification games. As already noted, playing important games in the summer is fraught with danger for any of the home nations. Yet, as Viv Anderson points out, it does have advantages: 'At that stage we still played in the League on the Saturday and met up on Sunday for the Wednesday game, so the summer tours always gave you the chance of working together properly. After you'd been together for a fortnight, it was more like a club set-up, you could put the work in and then see it come to fruition in a game. In the season, that didn't always happen because there wasn't time. It's good to have two or three weeks clear that are just focused on winning a particular game or series of games.'

England were now given a week to prepare for the away game in Hungary, a game they had to win. Defeat would mean that they'd lost three straight away qualifiers, with just Norway left to visit. Against the Swiss, England had been unfortunate to fall behind, but conceding against the run of play sapped their self-belief and within a couple of minutes they were two down. In the midst of such a run of awful form, it's always difficult to see where the next positive result is coming from, but it simply had to come in Budapest. Greenwood made four changes, the most significant being to restore Brooking to the side after a lengthy absence – it was the first time the highly successful Keegan–Brooking partnership had operated in these qualifiers. They did not let their manager down, Brooking scoring twice and Keegan once in the 3–1 win in the Nep Stadium. The first goal seemed to confirm that England had turned a corner, a mishit shot from Brooking squirming its way into the net. The game was surprisingly open for such a key fixture and the Hungarians grabbed an equalizer on the stroke of half-time. England were able to regroup in the dressing room and came out in confident mood, Brooking restoring England's advantage with a thumping shot on the hour, Keegan ending Hungarian resistance with a penalty after 73 minutes. Evidence of how quickly fortunes can turn in football, England now knew their task – wins in Norway and at home to Hungary would qualify them for Spain.

Nevertheless, the squad faced some merciless criticism from the press, who were particularly concerned at the manner of England's recent performances. After the adventure of Greenwood's early days in the job, England were becoming increasingly defensive – prior to the Hungary game, they scored just one goal in five games, against generally moderate opposition. This was a throwback to the dourest Ramsey days, with the additional drawback that England weren't as defensively watertight. Whether Greenwood was the right choice as England manager, he was an eminently decent man with little taste for the vociferous attacks he was forced to weather. According to Phil Neal's autobiography, on the flight home from Budapest, 'Ron stunned each and every one of us by announcing he proposed to use his news conference to announce his resignation. There was a silence for a moment then loud protests. Ray Clemence was one of the first to chip in: "If you quit then we might as well throw our boots away." Ron looked genuinely puzzled by the depth of feeling ... it was unthinkable from our point of view that he should consider himself personally responsible for our failure ... it was touch and go for several minutes.' With England back in control of their own destiny, a sacrifice was no longer necessary, and Greenwood was eventually convinced that he should see the job through to the bitter end. Pick up the two wins, and nobody would even remember the turmoil England had been in. In a World Cup qualifying group, results are, ultimately, all that counts.

England flew out to Oslo for their first game of the 1981–82 season on 9 September, with a very different system to that they'd used the year before. They now played with three midfielders – Robson, McDermott and Hoddle – and three forwards – Keegan, Mariner and Francis, though Francis was pushed out on to the right wing. It was the more attacking line-up the press had craved, but in probably the wrong game. Hoddle was generally at his best as the advance man in a midfield four, with the security of ball winners behind him. In Norway, he was expected to play wide on the left, and was also required to get plenty of tackles in, which was never his game. Not only that, but the surface in Oslo was a disgrace, little better than a park pitch, hardly the ideal environment for him to display his full repertoire of passing skills. Really, the game in Oslo was one for experience and for grafters. That was just another of a series of catastrophic misjudgements made by Greenwood. After the Football League offered to cancel the First Division programme the Saturday before the game, he asked them to play on so that the players would get match practice. Brooking, Watson and Coppell all got injured.

But after 16 minutes in Oslo it didn't seem to matter as England took the lead with a Bryan Robson goal. Gradually, though, it became painfully obvious that the unbalanced midfield just could not operate together, their uncertainty spreading to the defence, where Russell Osman, so accomplished with Ipswich, was continuing his unhappy England career. He had no glaring technical deficiencies as such, but seemed to lack the innate self-confidence required to make the step up to international level, the stubbornness that allowed apparently less skilful players such as Jack Charlton to make the transition and carve out highly successful England careers. Norway's Albertsen was left unmarked to turn a cross past Clemence, then four minutes before the break, a terrible error by Terry McDermott pushed the ball into the path of Thoresen who had the easiest of tasks to put the ball past Clemence. Even Greenwood's substitutions were ill judged.

Replacing Hoddle with Barnes at least gave him a natural left-sided player, but instead of addressing the problem on the right, Francis was left to his own devices and, instead, Paul Mariner was replaced by Peter Withe. England huffed and puffed, but they could not blow the Norwegian house down. The game lost, the Norwegian commentator was left to run through a litany of English heroes and Maggie Thatcher, to inform them that 'Your boys took a hell of a beating.'

Since Greenwood had promised his players he'd see the job through, he withstood calls for his head and prepared for the final game with Hungary, though at the time it seemed like it would be a meaningless fixture, Hungary and Romania having surely booked their passage by then. But by the time that game rolled around on 18 November, the Swiss had beaten Romania, then held them to a draw in Bern. England needed just a draw to go to Spain. Greenwood made four changes, restoring Shilton for Clemence, Coppell and Brooking for Francis and Hoddle and bringing in Alvin Martin for the unfortunate Osman. The midfield was immediately more cohesive and once Mariner had given them the lead on 16 minutes, the game was over, against a Hungarian team that couldn't have cared less anyway. England were off to Spain, but it was scarcely a great national triumph to come through second in a very mediocre group. Still, after two humiliating failures in the recent past, the travelling meant nothing. The getting there was all important.

It was obvious though that England needed to find some new players who might give them a fighting chance on the world stage. With central defence a particular weakness, Greenwood was happy to find that Terry Butcher had better international credentials than Osman. He continued to experiment with Hoddle but could never find the right role for him, while Alan Devonshire disappointed. A first senior cap was also given to Cyrille Regis against Northern Ireland: 'To get that first cap was fantastic. To think that five or six years before I'd been on a building site, playing part-time in the Athenian League and then to have an England shirt on in front of 90,000 at Wembley, it's a great climb, a lot of self-satisfaction, lot of pride to reach those heights. I got 20 minutes, he just let me play. At that age and making your debut, you've got so much going on in your head that any instructions go in one ear and out the other. You just want to get on and play. I got a couple of half chances against Pat Jennings, but it wasn't to be. To get in the England set-up is a totally different thing, the football's different, the mentality's different. People say you need four or five games to get settled and you do. If you can get those games – get your toe in, get a bit of confidence – but you can't really do that in just one game. It's hard to tell how much is down to being in the right place, having a bit of luck at the right time. Some players are allowed that run even when their first few games are nothing special, but they gradually get to grips with it, and some go on to have good international careers – Chris Waddle had a slow start, I think. Staying in there is hard.

'The football is totally different to what we have day to day in the Premiership, you need to be more precise, keep the ball much better. You'll play one way for your club, then when you get to England, you'll be asked to do something else, you'll have to adapt to the style of international football and to the style of the team. Ronnie Allen was manager at Albion, he'd been an England player, and he realized that stamina was my problem – John Sillet used to call me a Rolls Royce with a Mini engine! I had power, pace, but not stamina. So at West Brom, I didn't have to defend, Ronnie didn't want me to come back past the halfway line and I got him 25 goals. But with England, I couldn't do that, so I had to change my approach, learn to pick my runs, pace myself, retain possession, otherwise I'd be running around all day!'

As ever, there was a late scramble to fill the last few places in the twenty-two. Graham Rix was one of those on the fringes: 'The 1981–82 season I had a lot of trouble with my Achilles and I was playing when I shouldn't have, really. I wasn't training, just going from game to game. I wasn't really fit, pulled out of a couple of squads, and it did reach the stage where I thought I was going to miss the World Cup. And while I was out, Alan Devonshire had come through and the talk was it would be me or him to go to Spain. The game that swung it for me was Holland at Wembley. Alan started and I was the sub and he'd be the first to admit he didn't have a very good night, nothing went right for him. At half-time there was a straight swap, me for him, and I had one of those nights when everything went right. It was 0–0 at half-time, I was involved in both goals and we won 2–0. That was probably my best 45 minutes for England. At the end as I walked off, Ron Greenwood came on the pitch, put his arm round me and said, "Do you realize what you've just done? You've just booked your ticket for Spain." I couldn't tell anybody, but I was absolutely delighted.'

Just before the final squad was announced, the preliminary party of thirty players was split in two, half going to Iceland, the other half off to Finland. Phil Neal remembered, 'Ron made it clear that the lads in Finland had booked their tickets. That left just six places to fill and those would be going to the players in Iceland . . . most of us were frightened of our own shadows.' Regis was in the Iceland party and still thinks that 'I'd had a great year, I played very well and I think I would have gone to Spain. The last game of the season at the Hawthorns we played Leeds to stay up – they smashed the stadium up afterwards – and I pulled a hamstring. I tried to get fit and went out to Iceland with half of the squad, got twenty minutes and pulled it again and that finished my chances.'

Another sweating it out in Iceland was Viv Anderson: 'I got done for the goal, they played the ball inside me, which is the cardinal sin, and I thought my chance had gone. I found out I was in in the middle of Nottingham. I was in the town centre and the squad was in the papers, so it was a fantastic thrill to know I was going to Spain.' In a very significant move by the FA, a recognition of changing times, that party was put on £1000 per man, per match, in win bonuses. In 1966, each member of the squad had received a total bonus of £1000 for winning the whole thing.

Preparations for the World Cup were played out to a backdrop of the Falklands conflict, causing real concern as to what would happen if Argentina and England had to meet at any stage, with suggestions that the government would withdraw the team if necessary. As Graham Rix says, 'As a player, you have to assume you'll be going and prepare properly, but uncertainty like that doesn't help. Overall we were together for about two months. We had a couple of preparation games, then a weekend off, then we joined up and went to Spain a week or so before the tournament started. It was very professional, the facilities were great.' As Viv Anderson says, 'We were lucky in Bilbao, we had an ideal hotel on the beach, we had everything we could want: videos, we had a games room, plenty to do, but it is a long time away. You do get on each other's nerves.'

England had a tricky group, featuring the early incarnation of the wonderful French side of the 1980s, an uncompromising Czech side and Kuwait. Since qualification, England had put together a run of decent results, winning all three Home Internationals, beating Holland and winning well in Finland – in the seven games since the Norwegian defeat, they'd won 6 and drawn 1, scored 14 goals and conceded only 2. Was a side coming together at just the right time? Graham Rix recalls, 'We were in Santander, in the north, and it rained, slung it down for about four days, then the day of the first game against France, it was 40 degrees in the stadium! We'd trained all week on heavy pitches in the rain, then we were suddenly pitched into the baking heat. In the summer, England does become more like a club side simply because you're stuck away together, and especially coming into a World Cup.

'Kevin Keegan and Trevor Brooking were injured, but at the time I don't think the rest of the players realized how serious it was, we fully expected them to play the first game. It soon became apparent a couple of days before that neither was going to be fit and that provided an opportunity for Trevor Francis and either me or Hoddle in the starting line-up. I got the nod, I suppose because of my left foot, to give us a bit of balance. I didn't sleep very well before the game, I knew what was at stake, how much was expected and I was very nervous. But we got off to that great start, with Robbo scoring after 27 seconds. I've watched that tape many times and though it wasn't a classic, we played well, especially second half. We got into them, we passed the ball around well, thoroughly deserved the win. And they were a brilliant side – Tigana was only a sub. I actually swapped shorts with Platini after the game and my little lad put them on the other day. He asked me, "Are these really Platini's shorts?" He was the top man.

'First half we wanted to play with a three of Coppell, Wilkins and Robson and I was supposed to be floating behind the strikers, which didn't work great, I must admit. They kept switching the ball out to their right and they had lots of space and got level, so at half-time we switched to a four, and I played wide on the left. That stopped them playing but it also meant me and Kenny Sansom could play together as we did for Arsenal. We overpowered them second half, as much by luck from that change as by judgement.'

England completed a highly satisfactory 3–1 win, the more so since it was achieved without their two senior players, in whom so many hopes were invested. Keegan and Brooking both realized their only chance of playing in a World Cup could be passing them by. Rix says that the two were nothing but supportive, but in his book, Tony Adams mentions that in preparing for the 1998 World Cup, Hoddle reminded his squad that, 'In 1982 in Spain ... two members of the party had diverted the focus of the campaign. Everyone assumed he meant the injured Kevin Keegan and Trevor Brooking.' Hoddle himself had plenty of reason to feel disgruntled, because he simply could not get in the side. Rix had reason to rue that first game too, though for more diverting reasons: 'I got pulled for the dope test after the game. I was never a heavy lad, I was 10½ at the time, and they weighed me and I'd lost 7 lbs during the game because it was so hot, which is a helluva lot of body weight for someone my size. It took me three and a half hours to produce a specimen ... drinking water, Coke, beer. Everybody else had left, so I got back to the hotel late, and a bit pissed, actually! The heat does take it out of you, but I was a young lad, playing in the World Cup, I was buzzing and I'd have played the next day if we'd had to. We were well looked after on the medical side, so two days later I was really ready.'

The Czechs were next in line and, understandably, Greenwood named an unchanged team for another tough game. Rix recalls, 'The Czechs were dour, negative. We had to get something out of the game and knew that if we won, we were through. We were just pounding away. That was the one and only rollocking I got from Ron. At half-time, he steamed into me and Kenny and said, "You're playing like a couple of farts on the left." For Ron to say that ... they were harsh words! It had the necessary effect, because as a team we were more progressive and we won comfortably, 2–0. Went in after the game and by now we'd been together four or five weeks, so Ron said, "Well done boys, we've qualified, go and do what you want." Basically go and have a few beers and unwind a bit was what he meant. I don't think that would happen now. If one of the lads goes out for a drink now, he'll get hammered. The World Cup was big, but if you look at what goes with it now, it's the biggest thing on earth, it's changed so much in just sixteen years. The game has got bigger, it's a news story now, not just a sport, people want to know what's going on, what players are doing. So today, drinking during the World Cup wouldn't be looked upon as representing England properly, but it didn't do any harm. Ron was just making the point that we'd been in a pressure-cooker situation, we'd done the job, it was time for a break before we got back down to work. Nobody was going to get blotto, it was just to have a couple of hours away from it.'

Ironically, the injury to Keegan didn't only affect his World Cup. With the captain injured, Greenwood turned to Mick Mills to wear the armband – without that, Mills might not have got on the team sheet. In playing Mills, it meant there was no place for Phil Neal or Viv Anderson, either of whom might have otherwise expected to play at right-back. But, as Anderson says, 'Mick was a "steady eddie", we called him "the old pro", and obviously the boss went for experience. And with Kevin injured, Mick was the obvious captain, with Kenny Sansom on the left.' For the Kuwait game, Greenwood drafted in Neal, Hoddle and Steve Foster, in a match Rix remembers as 'the worst international I played in. They were playing offside all the time, it was frustrating, and I was pleased to see the back of them.' England won 1–0, thanks to Trevor Francis' goal.

This was one of the high spots in Francis' rather curious England career. Having come to prominence as the 16-year-old boy wonder at Birmingham City a decade earlier, he never seemed to establish himself as a fixture in the national team, yet still won 52 caps over nine years. He was perceived as being too similar to Keegan in many ways in the first half of his England career, and there was little chance of him ousting such an icon. Like Hoddle, coaches often wanted to find room for a man of his talent, and with his great ability on the ball and range of tricks, it was always tempting for an England coach to stick him out on the wing, just to get him in the side. It was a role that didn't really suit him and he often disappointed. In Spain, with Keegan out injured, Francis enjoyed his role as one of the two main strikers and played some excellent football. Thereafter, his contribution to the side was limited by the bane of his career, regular injuries.

With the World Cup expanded to twenty-four teams for the first time, the successful countries did not progress into a straight knockout format, but instead were placed in four groups of three, the group winners going into the semi-finals. Having done as well as any side thus far, England might well have expected an easy group as reward. They didn't get it. As Rix points out, 'We were unlucky to have won our group and then get stuck with West Germany and Spain when France, who came second to us, got Northern Ireland and Austria in the second phase. But we got through and then I think we got it wrong. West Germany was the first game and they were a very good side, full of world-class players. We'd watched videos, had talks about what we were going to do. I was up against Manny Kaltz, who was one of the best crossers of the ball in the world, so we all knew the little individual battles we wanted to win. The whistle went at the end of the game and it was 0–0 and, walking off the pitch, I was delighted: England had held the European Champions to a draw; great result. By the time I got to the dressing room, I was disappointed because if we had been a bit more adventurous, they were there for the taking. If we'd won that, the whole situation would have been different. They played Spain and won 2–1, which meant we had to beat Spain, the hosts, by two clear goals, which was always going to be a tall order. That was such a bad result for us because it left them trying to salvage something from the last game, because they were out but needed some pride back.'

Again, the roots of England's ultimate failure were to be found in a negative approach that stifled the qualities of our better players. The national side still operated in a suffocating climate of fear, though our press and we, the supporters, must take a share of the blame for treating every international as though it were a war. How can players and managers express themselves under such circumstances, knowing they'll be savaged if things go wrong?

Keegan and Brooking were both improving and were fit for the game with Spain, though they were not match fit. Both started on the bench. Rix remembers; 'For Kevin and Trevor it was the last chance. They were pleased the way the lads were playing. We had good team spirit and they were part of it. While I didn't give the team things that Trevor could, I think I offered things he couldn't do. They were so disappointed not to be part of it, but the longer we stayed in, the more chance they had of playing a part later. It was disappointing for the rest of us too that all the focus was on whether they'd be fit or not. I knew that however well I played, or however well Trevor Francis or Tony Woodcock played, if they got fit, we weren't going to be in the side, no doubt about that. I suppose if we'd battled through to the Final and they'd been fit they'd have come in, which would have been a kick in the teeth, but it didn't affect the way we played, we wanted to win, obviously. And eventually in that game against Spain, with twenty odd minutes to go, me and Tony Woodcock got pulled off for those two. Me and Tony were mates and as we jogged off, he said to me, "That was always going to happen." No matter how well me and him had been playing, they were always going to be the last throw of the dice. We bombarded them, we threw everything at them, but once they got to half-time, we were never going to score, one of those days. So it was 0–0 and that was it. France got to the semis and were very unlucky to lose, and we'd beaten them. The Germans got to the Final and we'd drawn with them, should have beaten them. And Italy won it even though they'd lost a game earlier on. We went out undefeated, which was very disappointing.

'Personally, if I was to analyse my England career, I'd say that certainly the time in Spain was when I played well for England, I really did. Important matches in a good side. After that, I don't think I did myself justice again. After the game Ron told us that was the end for him, and we went back to where we were staying, had a bit of a party, some of the wives and girlfriends had come over by then, and then next day, flew home. So it was really intense for six or seven weeks and then suddenly it was switched off. You feel empty. You don't want to watch the rest of the tournament, you lose interest. We had a good side at that time and I think we were unfortunate. We could have done more with that side.'

Viv Anderson agrees that, 'We were unfortunate against the Germans and then Spain too, had some chances, Kevin and Trevor came on and almost turned things. It was disappointing to go out the way we did, having never lost. We had some good players – Shilton, Robbo, Woodcock, Mariner – we were always hard to beat, and if Kevin had been fit, he might have made the difference. That was probably the best England side I played in.' But with respect to those concerned, England had missed the point. Championship-winning sides aren't those that avoid defeat. They're the ones that go out and win. And England weren't set up to be sufficiently positive. Ultimately, Greenwood was beaten by the same negativity that had destroyed Alf Ramsey and Don Revie. Although Greenwood was well liked and respected, when he went, it was to no great public mourning. Rather than somebody who just wanted to avoid embarrassment, could we have a manager that might actually try to win something now, please?

....

12

You Need Hands

Picking a new England manager was becoming a regular feature of the landscape, as the incumbents dropped like flies. After surviving from 1945 through to 1974 with only one change at the top, in the subsequent eight years the FA had lost three full-time managers and flirted with a caretaker; misfortune bordering upon carelessness. Such promiscuity was doing little for consistency or for developing a cohesive policy at the summit of the game, so when Ron Greenwood's replacement came to be selected, the FA needed to look at the long-term for a change. It's astonishing just how few Englishmen make successful football managers. If you look at the current picture, the top coaches in the Premiership in recent years have been Alex Ferguson, Arsene Wenger, Ruud Gullit, Gianluca Vialli and George Graham. Little wonder the Hoddle succession was so troublesome.

Back in the early 1980s, the picture was little better. Given that Clough was ruled out in perpetuity and that Bob Paisley was of Greenwood's vintage and wasn't interested in the role anyway, the FA were left with a choice between Bobby Robson and Ron Atkinson, though other contenders such as John Lyall were unenthusiastically touted. Atkinson had only been at the top for five years, building on an impressive West Bromwich Albion team bequeathed him by Johnny Giles and Ronnie Allen, but never managing to win anything before moving on to Manchester United, where again he would flatter to deceive. And having walked out on Albion, he was never popular with FA Chairman Sir Bert Millichip, who was still president of the club. That aside, Atkinson didn't have the experience, nor the international pedigree, for the job.

Bobby Robson, on the other hand, had excellent credentials and had even had some involvement with the England squad, taking the side to Australia prior to the 1980 European Championships, and the second string side to Iceland before the 1982 World Cup. Like Alf Ramsey before him, he had turned Ipswich Town into a power in the land, sustaining their achievements over the best part of a decade. They came very close to winning the Championship on a couple of occasions, and really should have done so in 1980–81 when a fixture pile-up and an accompanying late-season slump in form cost them dear. That season was hardly a write-off, though, for Ipswich won the UEFA Cup to add to the FA Cup they'd collected three years earlier. And Robson didn't only have trophies to show for his work. He had proven himself to be one of the most imaginative managers in the country, particularly in his use of Arnold Muhren and Frans Thijssen, the two Dutch midfielders who added such grace and fluidity to his side. Clearly well versed in the subtleties of European football, Robson looked by far the best candidate for the job and was duly appointed to general acclaim from the footballing public. Having had a successful career as an England player – 20 caps, four goals, a squad member at two World Cups – he had all the credentials the public were looking for.

And allied to his undoubted ability as a manager was his very obvious passion for the country and for the game of football: 'It's hard to separate the honour you get by putting the shirt on and that that you feel when you become England manager. To get the manager's job, it's such a prestigious thing. I had a great contract at Ipswich, loved working there, it was an ideal place for me and had I not got the offer to manage England, I might never have left there. I chose to accept the job not just because it was the most prestigious job, but because it was the most important, and I just felt that I had to do it. It's a great feeling, the country has chosen you, like becoming the Prime Minister of football! I understand why people have turned it down because of the pressure from the media, but it is a great job, there's no question about that. I felt it was such a privilege to be asked that I couldn't turn it down. And perhaps after thirteen years at Ipswich, it was the right time to move on.'

It's instructive that Robson should mention the media pressures, because he was the first England manager to fall victim to the sustained, vicious, personalized attacks that so disfigure our press, built upon the spurious idea that savage and cruel journalism is better value than a considered critique. Robson had to suffer the kind of rubbish that eventually led to Graham Taylor being morphed into a turnip and to the vile ACHTUNG SURRENDER headlines before the Euro '96 semi-final. Dehumanize your prey and then you can be as vicious as you like, appears to be the rule. Fine, if you're sending soldiers out to fight the Nazis. But since when was football a war?

The players were generally happy with the appointment and pleased that there would at last be some continuity of management. Viv Anderson sums up the mood of the time: 'Bobby and Ron were similar in many ways, quietly spoken, not ranting and raving. Bobby was more a man's man than Ron, more interested in the collective thing. Bobby knew his players, wasn't perhaps as good a tactician or as much of a connoisseur of the game as Ron, but knew what he wanted his team to do and made it clear.' Phil Neal was a little less enthusiastic, writing that, 'Bobby Robson's approach was based on fear, not of him, but of the opposition. A typical team talk would go on for hours ... he called the squad together for ten minutes one evening before dinner and three hours later, with most of us starving, the head waiter knocked on the door, gave the boss the keys and asked us to lock up the restaurant when we'd finished.'

Even so, most players viewed the manager with affection, as Gary Lineker, a later recruit, makes clear: 'Bobby's enthusiasm was infectious. He waffled a lot, his meetings would go on for ever at times, he'd get muddled up and forget people's names, which I think added to people's fondness for him, because there was a certain fallibility there. He'd look at you sometimes and you'd know he'd forgotten your name, then you'd be talking to him and he'd drift off and you'd see him staring over your shoulder thinking about his next team. I wouldn't class him as a great instructional coach in the Terry Venables mould, who would tactically wind things together, but he was fiercely loyal. He knew a good player as soon as he saw one – terrific eye for a player – and he stuck with his ideas of how the team should play and the kind of players he wanted. He generally always stuck by the best technical players that were around – Barnes, Beardsley, Waddle, Gascoigne – because he knew that at that level you needed players with that bit extra to unlock the door. They were his greatest strengths, added to the fact that players wanted to do well for him because they liked him.'

For all that, Robson's reign began amid huge controversy over the treatment of English football's favourite son – Kevin Keegan. It's in the nature of international football that it be built around the World Cup, planning taking place in four-year blocks. Naturally, some players who have figured in one World Cup squad are simply going to be too old to play in the next one. The coach then has to make the delicate decision as to whether they should be jettisoned immediately to make way for a replacement, or whether their experience can see them through further fixtures and so benefit the squad. After Spain '82, it was apparent that players like Mick Mills, Trevor Brooking and Kevin Keegan weren't going to Mexico in 1986, and might not even make the European Championships in 1984. Robson's judgement was that they should be left out of the squad and that rebuilding should begin at once. As a football decision, it had merit. But Keegan in particular did not take kindly to the end of his career, or at least, to the manner of its termination. Keegan had dropped down to the old Second Division to play with Newcastle, hardly the platform for an England career at his age, and in fact, he retired two years later, so Robson's judgement that he was running out of time was vindicated. What really rankled, though, was that he was dropped from the squad without being told. Robson has since accepted that 'I was wrong ... a telephone call or a letter to him before the announcement of the squad would have been in order.' Keegan then attacked Robson in the *Sun*, effectively ending his England career.

Ironically, though, Keegan might well have forced his way back into the reckoning, because Robson was clearly unsure where the replacements lay. Not only were there the retirements to contend with, there were injuries aplenty too, such as to Graham Rix: 'I carried on having trouble with my Achilles. I wasn't training and was just playing games. So because of that, come international time, Arsenal didn't want me to go away and I had to pull out of a lot of squads, which was frustrating. Don knew the problems and could tell Bobby that he shouldn't pick me. I had three operations in three or four years and I couldn't shake it off.'

Robson was unfortunate enough to be thrown straight into a competitive game for his first test, playing Denmark in a European Championship qualifier (the rest of the group comprised Greece, Hungary and Luxembourg, with only one to go through). No longer the whipping boys of Europe, Denmark had an excellent side, capable of providing a stern examination, and although England were twice ahead, the Danes came back to get a draw. Robson then had a friendly with which to experiment, but West Germany seldom make the most accommodating of opponents.

With imaginative selections, the new manager made it clear that he was not going to be sucked into rigid thinking about his side, and drew upon those players who had excelled in the recent Under-21 game in Denmark, such as Cyrille Regis: 'Bobby Robson came in and I went back to the Under-21s as an over-age player, and captained them. To be in the Under-21s was disappointing, in that it was a backwards step, but you have to look at it positively: I was still in the set-up, I was captain, I still had a chance to show what I could do. We won 4–1 in Denmark, in John Barnes' first game. And that was an occasion where racism reared its ugly head again, because John came on and the England fans started giving him stick. And you wonder what's going on with these people. It is the minority, a very foolish tiny percentage that are against you. The majority are on your side. As a black person, I grew up with it, it was nothing new, this is a country where you're going to get a racist element and you just have to deal with it. Garth Crooks played that game as well, got a hat-trick, but never got a full cap, which is amazing. I got back in against West Germany, who'd done well in the World Cup, and I played 80 minutes and thought I'd done well enough to be included in the next squad. My biggest fan and critic was Ron Atkinson and he was at the game and thought I'd done enough too, but I didn't get another cap after that for years. And that's down to the coach's opinion and the players he thinks will do the job he wants – Alan Shearer didn't score for ages but Venables decided he was what he wanted and kept faith with him. At the same time Ian Wright was scoring left, right and centre but was always in and out of the team. Just opinions.'

The two years leading into the European Championships were rather inconsistent, but looking at team selections, it's apparent that England were in transition. While there were some very good club players, those players were not of true international class – Luther Blissett, Sammy Lee, Graham Roberts, Peter Withe, John Gregory and a number of others came and went without making much impact. For Robson, it was a case of mix and match, with the inevitable consequences, though his use of Glenn Hoddle did leave much to be desired, there being no room for him to take on the central role he craved while Wilkins and Robson dominated. Bryan Robson's qualities have been well documented, but Wilkins' position in the England side was always open to greater questioning. Characterized as negative for his habit of playing the ball square across midfield rather than forward, Wilkins was never as glamorous, nor as popular as Hoddle. Wilkins was in some senses a more Continental style of footballer, ideally suited to the Italian game, where he was to make a living for several successful years. Wilkins' game was based on the principle that possession was all, not a bad starting point in the international game where, once you'd lost the ball, you could spend an age chasing it. Wilkins was never an especially adventurous player, but alongside Bryan

Robson, one of the greatest midfield goalscorers of all time, he didn't need to be.

Although England scored 13 goals in 2 games against Luxembourg and beat Hungary home and away, they lost 1–0 at home to a Danish side inspired by Simonsen and Michael Laudrup, when Phil Neal gave away a penalty. That result was the difference between success and failure, for Denmark topped the group from England by one point. The reaction to this failure was predictably crass, with large sections of the press demanding Robson's head, none taking note of the fact that Denmark could call on better players (they went on to reach the semi-finals of the competition in France, only to go out to Spain on penalties). As Ramsey, Revie and Greenwood had discovered in recent years, no manager can succeed at international level without sufficient quality footballers to do the job. So, in the summer of 1984, instead of looking forward to a few weeks in France, England's diary contained just a brief tour of South America. For a while, it looked as though that would be Bobby Robson's swansong. With Brazil awaiting England at the Maracanã, a bad defeat there would surely finish him.

The omens weren't great, either, as Mark Hateley, a new recruit to the side, recalls: 'It was a bad period for the side, everybody was looking for young blood and people like myself, Mark Chamberlain, John Barnes, Mick Duxbury, Terry Fenwick, Clive Allen, we were all pushed forward. We were going to South America when the Liverpool lads were off to play a European Cup Final, Paul Mariner and Trevor Francis were injured, there were probably a dozen players missing. So from my point of view, circumstances helped me get in the side, but you have to take the chances as they come along. I'd only been at Portsmouth a year in the old First Division, so it was an achievement in itself to get in the squad from there. But I'd had two or three good years in the Under-21s. You know then the manager's looking at you and it does enable you to springboard faster than you would otherwise.'

The game at the Maracanã looked set to be a disaster waiting to happen. History shows that instead, it turned into one of English football's greatest hours, with Mark Hateley and John

Barnes sealing a 2–0 win, Barnes scoring the wonder goal that saw him glide past half the Brazilian team before depositing the ball in the back of the net. In hindsight, perhaps that unrepeatable moment of genius wasn't a wise career move for Barnes, for it became a millstone around his neck. But it certainly launched his England career and saved Bobby Robson's job.

Mark Hateley points to an odd coincidence: 'John and I were born on the same day and our England careers, our football careers, took off on the same day as well at the Maracanã. It's nice to play in those sorts of settings and we played very well, we could have scored more goals that day. Touring is totally different. The secret to a good England side is the harmony in the camp and you have to keep that in mind, work hard at it, because you are away for long periods at World Cups or European Championships. You play, train, play golf, socialize together, which is part and parcel of playing for England – at a tournament, off the field is as important as on it.

'That tour changed my life, absolutely. Ray Wilkins had signed for Milan at Easter. The morning after that Brazil game, Milan phoned Ray and asked him if I'd like to play for them. He came to see me, I thought it was a wind-up, thought he was joking! Being a naïve 21-year-old, I told him I was in the middle of a contract at Portsmouth! But Milan came up with the money Portsmouth wanted, so the deal was done and dusted. There were never any doubts. I've always tried to be a better player all the time, tried to set higher standards all the while. For me, going to Italy was the place where I could do that, learn another side of the game. Italy had the best league, all the top players were there, and it was just an ideal situation. It was an invaluable learning ground for me, made me a far better player. The commuting was hectic in international weeks, but having Ray there too made it easier. It's better to have someone to travel with, and it was comforting to know that our families were together back in Milan, which was very important. It was always a dash catching planes because we played on a Sunday in Italy, which wasn't ideal, because we missed a day of the get-together.'

England proceeded to lose 2–0 in Uruguay and draw 0–0 in Chile, but these comparative disappointments couldn't put a damper on things. England had beaten the mighty Brazil, in their own back yard, for the first time ever, and achieved our first win against them since 1956. Not only that, it had been achieved with a makeshift team, consisting of youngsters who had largely been dismissed before jetting out of London. Though nothing could make up for missing out on France, this was a pretty decent substitute.

More important than the result in Brazil, it had shown the public that England had a future. Not only had they discovered Hateley and Barnes, just before the tour they had unearthed another young and exciting forward, by the name of Gary Lineker: 'I came on for a nice gentle start as sub at Hampden, but it was a massive buzz, a very proud moment. I got a few touches, did OK, but the thing I thought about most was that whatever happened it would be "Leicester City & England" after that! I was lucky, rather than now where there's a lot of talent in one position, I came when it was the end of Woodcock, Francis and Mariner, and Keegan had gone, so there was an opening then and there was really myself, Mark Hateley, then latterly Peter Beardsley who might fill it. It was about another eighteen months before I really got into the side and there were pairings with Blissett, Francis, Dixon. At that stage you don't care who you play with, it's just about making the most of the opportunity.'

That tour of South America seemed to have blown away the threatening clouds. The 1984–85 season started like a runaway train, with five straight wins against East Germany (1–0), Finland (5–0), Turkey (8–0), Northern Ireland (1–0) and Ireland (2–1); the middle three all World Cup qualifiers. The momentum was halted slightly when Romania got a 0–0 draw in Bucharest, but with seven points out of eight and two to go through, qualification was already a virtual certainty. Both Hateley and Barnes were building on their excellent summer, Chris Waddle, Peter Reid and Trevor Steven had come into the reckoning, while Wilkins, Robson and Hoddle were still there, Lineker was starting to break through and a solid back four of Anderson, Kenny Sansom, Mark Wright and Terry Butcher in front of Peter Shilton meant that England didn't give much away. It was suddenly a powerful-looking nucleus on which Bobby Robson could build.

There was a minor setback with a draw in Finland and then a 1–0 defeat at Hampden Park, but England could set out for a series of summer fixtures in Mexico City and then in Los Angeles, confident that this time, it was a worthwhile piece of reconnaissance, a useful learning process prior to the 1986 World Cup. For Lineker, in particular, it was a tour as crucial as the previous year had been for Hateley and Barnes: 'I really got my chance with the tour of Mexico and the United States. I played all right against the Germans, then played in LA against the USA and got two goals, one of them was quite a good one: Glenn knocked it on to my chest and I turned and volleyed it in. They weren't great opposition, but having played reasonably well on tour without scoring, it was important to score, and that set me up for the next season.'

Again, the Liverpool players were missing from the squad, otherwise engaged in a European Cup Final against Juventus. In their absence, England were set to play a friendly against Italy, similarly weakened. A couple of days prior to that fixture, the necessary arrangements were made to allow the players to watch the European game and see Liverpool sweep to yet another triumph. The players filed into the TV room to watch the game, only to find it wasn't on. Slowly they discovered the awful, unfolding reality of the Heysel disaster. Lineker recalls, 'After that, we went to a memorial service with the Italians, and it was very haunting affair, even though we were thousands of miles away, the sense of importance and relevance of it all was crushingly obvious to both sets of players. I suppose it was a strange thing to have hanging over the game and it put things into perspective. It made players behave responsibly, that was the fundamental thing; we knew what we had to do. It was the worst period of English football, really, in many ways. We weren't especially strong football-wise, but the far bigger issue was the hooliganism that followed the game, particularly the national side when travelling. It was embarrassing to be part of it when you went abroad, there was many a time we'd be in a hotel and looking out and seeing it going on. It made you totally embarrassed for your country because the frustrating thing was you knew, by and large, that the great percentage of the population wasn't like that, but the way they portrayed themselves was showing the country up. For all the times you say "it's only a tiny minority" the people in those countries only tend to see that tiny minority and it gives you a sense of being a thug nation. It was cringingly embarrassing at times.'

The only consolation came in the realization that sport can be a healing force as well as a divisive one, as Mark Hateley, who was, of course, earning his living in Italy at the time, testifies: 'The game against them was difficult, a terrible, sad time. It was ironic timing, but it was probably good that we could play Italy so soon afterwards. It was played in the right spirit and I think that helped ease things between the countries.' The game ended 2–1 to Italy and, frankly, there couldn't have been a better result. It was not a game for national pride, but for national humility.

Everton's Paul Bracewell went on that trip and remembers, 'It was a very experienced squad, which helped in the circumstances, and Bobby Robson was keen to get a settled party together, and to get the blend right; so he had his eye on a few younger players, like myself. It turned out that the party that went out in 1985 was pretty much the same squad that went back the following year, except for me and Mark Wright, who broke his leg. Everton had a lot of players in the squad – Peter Reid, Trevor Steven, Gary Stevens, Gary Lineker – so that puts you in line because you know the manager will be watching your club. Don Howe spent a bit of time with the Everton lads because we were doing so well, picking our brains to see what we were doing! And when I got in, and went out on the tour to Mexico, I roomed with Peter Reid, so that helped settle me in. My first game was against West Germany in Mexico City and I came on for Bryan Robson in a 3–0 win, and I thought it was a great opportunity to learn from him.' Much of that trip was an exercise in acclimatization, for, as Bracewell says,

'The altitude was very hard to deal with, you have to experience it to believe it. It was definitely an advantage to the South American sides because as a European you can adapt, but you're never really comfortable with it.'

Yet England showed commendable quality in coming back to thump the West Germans, having lost to Italy and then 1–0 to the Mexicans. When the trip was completed with a relaxed jaunt to Los Angeles and a 5–0 win over the USA, the mission was largely accomplished successfully.

Deftly avoiding any banana skins in drawing with Romania and then beating Turkey 5–0, England wrapped up their campaign in a controversial game with Northern Ireland at Wembley. The Irish needed a point to book their place in the finals and, given the close ties between the players of both countries, when the game meandered to a tedious 0–0 draw, there were those who cried 'fix'. Paul Bracewell remembers, 'It was never going to be a classic! There was certainly no fix and you still have your pride to play for, but if neither side has to win, it changes the whole atmosphere of the game.'

For England, the game had become little more than a friendly, an opportunity for Robson to experiment further, because there were few games left before the World Cup. Defensively, England were taking a reasonable shape. Shilton was the best goalkeeper in the world, Gary Stevens and Viv Anderson were highly capable on the right, Sansom a fixture on the left. Centrally, Butcher and Wright looked the best pairing, but there was a lack of depth there, apparent when Terry Fenwick was first reserve. The loss of Wright to a broken leg was a savage blow, not just to the player but to English hopes in Mexico.

Elsewhere, Robson was striving to find a balance. In midfield, there was an embarrassment of riches. Like most managers, when confronted by players of real top class, he wanted to find a space for each of them, but in doing so he lost the balance of the team. The manager wanted to find room for Bryan Robson, Ray Wilkins and Glenn Hoddle, an impossibility when all three wanted to dominate centrally. Hoddle often found himself stuck out wide as

238

England played an unconvincing 4–3–3. Peter Reid, filling in for Wilkins, writing after the draw with Romania, made the point that, 'We lacked width because of our system with three in the middle. Because Glenn doesn't want to go wide, going wide isn't really my game and nor is it Robbo's . . . you never knew whether Chris Waddle was going to be on the left, or the right.' Bobby Robson's desire to accommodate all his quality players was understandable, but it never quite worked. But who would you sacrifice? Bryan Robson? Impossible. Glenn Hoddle? Drop him and the press sat sharpening their knives waiting for the chance to tell Robson to build his side round the Spurs man. Drop Wilkins? With his experience as an international and in Europe?

Matters were not helped by an uncertainty about the front positions. Lineker was the obvious striker, but who to partner him with? If Waddle was in the side – and Robson admired his technical ability, seeing him as a man capable of doing the unusual – then it made sense to have a target man, such as Mark Hateley. And Hateley was more than that by this stage of his career: 'I always had the aggression and the "old centre-forward" approach as they call it, and I kept that, but in Milan I added to my awareness: the tricks you need to pick up to beat man-to-man marking. The most important thing was the first touch. In England if you lose the ball, you know you'll get it again in a couple of minutes. In Italy, you wouldn't see it again for ten minutes, so you appreciate you have to defend the ball at all costs. I liked playing with goalscorers like Gary. I never classed myself as a goalscorer, I was more a creator who was happy to take a goal if they came along. At that period coming into the World Cup I was scoring too, and if your two forwards score regularly the whole team looks good.'

But the forward pairing was unhinged by the problems in midfield. As Reid pointed out, with Waddle having a floating role, England were very narrow and it was often hard for the midfielders to find the outlet ball. If Waddle wasn't fed, he was hardly the player to go scavenging. Thus, the play was too often down the middle and the Hateley/Lineker partnership wasn't ideally suited to that. For all that, England had a useful run-in to the finals, winning 4–0 in Egypt, getting attacked for only winning 2–1 in Israel, winning 1–0 in the USSR and finally beating the Scots 2–1.

The Scottish game was an important one for Steve Hodge, his full debut: 'I made my debut against Russia, as a sub for Gordon Cowans. It's exciting as you run on, it is a very special moment, but you've got a job to do, there's no time for thinking about it, so it doesn't really hit you until afterwards, when you get your cap. It was a tough place to go to: it took us two hours to get through passport control, every bag was checked, the security was very tight. The hotel was very basic, but I wasn't too interested, I was just thinking about getting a chance in the team. But to make my full debut was exciting, because obviously if you're on the bench, you don't know if you'll get on. For it to be against Scotland, and then with the prize of the World Cup beckoning, it was a massive occasion. Bobby Robson had said in the press that it was between me, Paul Bracewell and Stewart Robson for a place in the squad for Mexico, so I knew I was in the frame. I was so thrilled to play at Wembley for the first time, so within a month I'd achieved the two great ambitions, to play for England and to play at Wembley, so that was a great period for me. You can't slot in straight away, it does take a game or two to really know what they're doing. I was a raw youngster at the time, but I roomed with Peter Reid and he's the kind of character who gets you settled in right away, brings you into things, even if you're quiet and shy. The manager told me to play my normal game, as I did at Villa, so it was left to me to impress him. It was nerve-racking, Scotland had a good team, with Souness in the middle, they were off to the World Cup too, so they had a lot of lads playing for their places too.'

Hodge had jumped ahead of Bracewell in the queue, partly because of his own good form and partly because of an injury to the luckless Evertonian, which cost him dear: 'I got injured in January '86 and knew that I was going to struggle to get in the squad. I was in the twenty-eight and then missed out on the twenty-two, so I was disappointed, but I'd expected it. Bobby Robson phoned me at home to tell me and go through his reasons, and to say the important thing was to get properly fit, that I was still in his mind. But that was the start for me of two years out of the game, which was a huge blow. He kept in contact with me while I was out, he was always concerned about the players and that's why he got such a good response.' Steve Hodge is similarly enthusiastic about the manager: 'Bobby Robson was a very popular man: a bubbly, happy personality, not one to hammer people too much. He was an encouraging manager, he liked the way I played, always looked to help you improve.'

While Bracewell was coming to terms with being dropped, the squad was thinking about the challenges ahead. Again, acclimatization was crucial and well before they flew out to the World Cup, England's players were being medically advised and monitored, as Peter Reid wrote in his diary of the season: 'Seb Coe's doctor gave us a talk on eating and drinking, which was fascinating. He said you should eat carbohydrates before a game – mashed potatoes, bread, all the things you would think you shouldn't. And he said in Mexico we should drink as much as we want, that not drinking before a game was a fallacy ... last year in Mexico we had been given salt tablets, and we asked him about that, but he said they would do you more harm than good.' One day, cigarettes are going to be good for you ...

England set up camp at the Broadmoor Hotel (promising name) in the Rockies in Colorado on 10 May, doing a little early training at the American Air Force Academy. For all the medical advice, as Mark Hateley says, 'All you can do is train away as you would at sea level. Obviously, it's tiring initially for ten days, but then you come through it.' Viv Anderson adds, 'The preparation was more thorough than in Spain, with regular blood tests, monitoring of your diet, lots of fluids. We were away about six weeks and because of the time in Colorado, when we arrived in Mexico we were ready for it.' For Steve Hodge, on his first England trip, it was a worrying as well as exciting period: 'It was a beautiful setting in the Rockies, and it did help adjust your lungs. We had regular saunas, going in the sweat rooms to simulate what we'd be going through in Mexico. And being away from everything for that period did help the camaraderie. I'd caught my ankle in the Scotland game and it hadn't bedded down, so I had a test in Colorado a couple of days before we went on to Mexico and I wasn't even sure of going then. The gaffer had said, "Sorry, son, but if it isn't right, you'll have to go back." That was a really worrying period. I went out with Fred Street and it had actually snowed that morning, and I had a decent run-out with Fred and he passed me fit, so I was mightily relieved. To have got that close and then not gone would have been a disaster. Thirteen years on, I can still remember that run vividly!'

The first friendly was against the Mexicans, who had beaten England in Mexico City the previous summer. This time, the game took place in Los Angeles and England romped home 3–0, Hateley scoring twice, Beardsley adding the other. It was a refreshing start, but not without its price. Bryan Robson had been carrying a nasty shoulder injury for most of the second half of the season, an injury that really required an operation after it had been dislocated. Manchester United were still in the running for the Championship at the time and kept patching him up and sending him out. His fitness was a worry to the England camp as so much seemed to hinge on him. In the Mexico game, his shoulder popped out again. Fortunately the medical staff were able to put it back in again, and nobody outside the camp was alerted to the dangers of persisting with him, but clearly it was a major worry.

England then flew to Vancouver for another warm-up game with Canada. With Robson struggling, they could ill afford further injuries, but that was what they got. Gary Lineker injured his wrist and it looked for a moment like his World Cup might be over before it had started, though the damage turned out to be not as serious as originally thought. Steve Hodge admits, 'Those games are a nightmare, because you want to do well but you don't want to get injured so close to the finals. But I was on the fringes so I couldn't think about that, and you can't really play to avoid injuries. There are times when you see a dodgy tackle coming your way and you keep out of it, but having had the ankle problem, I just wanted to get on and do well, and to be honest that was one of my best games with England. It didn't force me into the team, but I knew I'd done enough to get on the bench.'

Within the camp, it wasn't just injuries that were causing concern, Peter Reid again writing after the Canada game, 'I must say I had a few drinks on the sly (and had a chat with Bryan Robson and Terry Butcher). Interestingly, they both think we should play 4–4–2 as well. And I think the majority of the lads think that.' But the manager doggedly continued to try and accommodate all his most lavishly gifted players. It was a laudable policy in many ways and perhaps the players deserve rather more criticism for failing to make the system work than Robson got for employing it. Against Portugal in the opening game, the 4–3–3 formation took to the field. Lineker recalls, 'There's so much tension at a World Cup that it's hard to get going, and that first game against Portugal it was 110 degrees, terrible pitch, we should have won and ended up losing 1–0. If we'd scored early, we'd have won comfortably, I think. And if you've been sitting around waiting and get off to a bad start, it's very difficult then. You do get on each other's nerves at times, it can be very boring and players do different things to cope. There's the never-ending card game, I read a lot, others listened to music, others constantly talking. You might get the odd game of golf, but it's training, talking, eat together, sleep together – not literally! I suppose the worst part is the couple of weeks leading up to a tournament when you're cocooned in this unexciting environment. Once the tournament starts, at least there's the games to watch, Shilton and myself were the bookies, the players would bet, you want to see how teams go, so it passes much quicker. There's always media around, people wanting to do interviews, which I used to enjoy. It's getting increasingly difficult now to get to talk to players, probably because they get paid lots of money to do things for newspapers, which didn't happen so much then.'

Watching the Portugal game from the bench, Steve Hodge admits, 'We were awful. On paper we had a top-class team, even though Glenn was out on the right, which wasn't really his position. The way systems have changed, now you would sit three in the middle and Glenn would be the spare man, but then we had four strung across the pitch and Robson and Wilkins took the central positions with Chris Waddle on the left, a bit further forward. I can't say why we did so badly – things didn't gel – but it was disappointing not to get at least a draw, because losing the first match puts you on the back foot. And players aren't daft, they know the media will be out to hammer you, quite rightly, if you come home early.' Hodge came on for the ailing Robson and says, 'it was a thankless task to be seen as Bryan Robson's understudy, but at that stage I'd only played for two or three seasons, so to be in the frame was as much as I'd hoped for. I wouldn't compare myself with Bryan, he's one of the all-time greats.'

The game with Morocco, who had drawn 0–0 with Poland, now took on epic proportions. At least because the other game had ended with the points shared, England weren't too far in arrears. But another defeat would end their interest in the World Cup. As usual, English chauvinism decreed that this bunch of African journeymen would give us no trouble and that after the blip against Portugal, we would surge back to form with a rousing victory. This conveniently ignored the fact that against the Poles, Morocco had shown themselves to be well organized and had controlled the majority of the game and, on balance, perhaps deserved to win it. They would not be a pushover by any means. Bobby Robson kept faith with the same side and in the opening exchanges England looked composed but impotent against a Moroccan outfit that seemed to be suffering from an inferiority complex. Coming towards half-time, English frustration began to mount – they showed such a paucity of imagination they could have been commissioned to write an ITV sit-com. With 7 minutes of the half remaining, Ray Wilkins was booked. A minute later, Bryan Robson went down under a challenge and his shoulder popped out again. England's captain was helped from the field and out of the World Cup, to be replaced again by Steve Hodge.

Ray Wilkins took the captain's armband and within a minute had thrown the ball away in petulant frustration. As Mark Hateley says, 'It was out of character, a crazy accident, really, because as

Ray was throwing the ball away, it slipped out of his hand and hit the referee. But that was the way things were running at the time, we were all getting frustrated, we couldn't score, looked dodgy at the back. In the heat of battle – and it was very, very hot – things do boil over.' Hitting the referee with the match ball isn't advisable at the best of times, but if you've already been booked and just lost your main inspiration, then your timing is a little askew. Wilkins buried his face in his shirt as the inevitable red card was flourished. England had their third captain in as many minutes – Peter Shilton – and had to regroup for what promised to be a taxing second half. Fortunately, as Gary Lineker says, 'Ray's sending off ultimately didn't cost us. Beckham's sending off was over the top, but Ray's was even worse, it was absolutely nothing. Those things can turn competitions, but in 1986 with it being one of the qualifiers rather than a knockout game, we had time to turn things round.' Morocco came out totally devoid of ambition, and England were able to negotiate the remaining 45 minutes with surprising ease, coming out of the game with a 0–0 draw and their first point of the series.

Because of the bizarre nature of the qualification process, requiring only eight of twenty-four teams to go home early, England could get through to the second round by drawing with Poland in the final game. But with Wilkins suspended and Bryan Robson apparently out for the tournament, even that seemed a tall order. As Lineker recalls, much of Bobby Robson's strategy revolved around his namesake: 'Bobby's admiration for Bryan was patently obvious. I had the same admiration as well, but sometimes ... I don't say it went too far, but it was embarrassing for Bryan at times, there was an almost worshipping nature towards him. We'd have team meetings and take the piss out of Bryan: "He's only mentioned you five times!" It was Captain Fantastic this and Captain Marvel that. He wouldn't have a word said against Bryan, he was fiercely loyal to him, would do anything to keep him fit and in the side and understandably so, because he was a brilliant player when he was fit. At the same time, the problem for a manager who is so pro a player is if he does suffer an injury and he's not there, it's hard to pick somebody else and say, "You can do exactly what

Bryan does"! It was worth persevering with him because he was so good, but he was obviously struggling and when the shoulder popped out against Morocco, that was it. And we had the Ray Wilkins sending off too, so we were down to ten men and it was an important result to get a draw, even though it was much maligned at the time. Then you get new blood coming in and it can go either way: either you don't gel, or the change lifts the team, which it did. The first goal against Poland was fundamental and once that went in, everyone grew in confidence.'

As Steve Hodge says, for all the work a coach puts into it, team building isn't always an exact science: 'In mid-season internationals, because of injuries, there are a lot of changes. You can't get to know the people you're playing with, so summer tours are better in that respect, because you have the squad together for a period of time. Then again, the team in '86 was thrown together after injury and suspension and took off, so there's no set pattern for it.'

In training, Peter Reid wrote that Bobby Robson was persisting with the 4–3–3 format until Chris Waddle got a knock, forcing him into a more conventional 4–4–2. There is a suggestion that Robson gave the players what they wanted in doing so, but, frankly, he had little choice given the personnel available to him. With Robson and Wilkins gone, the obvious move was to bring Hoddle into the centre to allow him to play his natural game. That was certainly to Lineker's taste: 'I loved playing with Glenn, he was a striker's dream, especially for someone like me. We talked about playing together at club level – I nearly went to Spurs and Monaco to play alongside him, making the runs I made that were never seen by most people, but were always seen by him. But even with England we didn't play together as often as we could.'

The fact that Hoddle was now the key midfielder had the added effect of making Lineker's place secure. He'd certainly not felt that way prior to the Poland game: 'I got a hat-trick against Turkey in October, but then I went a few games where I didn't score before the World Cup. But I had a fantastic season at Everton and scored loads of goals, so it didn't worry me too much. By the time we started, and I didn't get any in the first two games in Mexico, it

We won the Cup. Wembley, 30 July 1966 *(Hulton Getty)*

Banks saves from Pelé, 1970 *(Allsport)*

Peter Shilton, coming to a boutique near you, 1971 (Hulton Getty)

In the presence of horses, Mick Channon practises ball juggling, 1975 (Hulton Getty)

Viv Anderson making headway
against Sweden, 1979 *(Empics)*

The greatest player in the world
swaps shirts with Kevin Keegan,
England v Argentina, 1980
(Allsport)

David Platt in action against Brazil, 1995 *(Allsport)*

Blood on the shirt, Paul Ince inspires England against Italy, Rome 1997 *(Empics)*

Refuelling session for Gazza, courtesy of McManaman, Shearer and Redknapp, England v Scotland, Euro '96 *(Allsport)*

Paul Merson resurrects his England career, England 'B' v Chile 'B', The Hawthorns, 1998 *(Allsport)*

From hero to villain and back again – David Beckham, England's future? *(Allsport)*

Michael Owen, 10 seconds away from immortality, England v Argentina, 1998 *(Allsport)*

was six without a goal and I was one of the prime candidates to lose my place. But he took a chance with me and Beardsley because we'd played well together against Russia. It could easily have been me rather than Hateley who got dropped, and that was pretty much the end of Mark's international career. So I was fortunate to get the chance.' It was cruel luck for Hateley that because of the structural changes in the middle, his place was undermined: 'When Bryan got injured and Ray was suspended, that changed the shape of the team and it meant I was left out. To say I was disappointed would be an understatement, because things had gone well for me. We'd played Mexico in a friendly and I got two in a 3–0 win, then we went to Canada and I scored in a 1–0. I'd scored a few in qualifying to get us there, so to be left out after two games without a goal was bitterly disappointing. But so were the other ten lads who missed out. I understood why, even though I didn't agree with it, but because of the injuries and suspensions the shape had to change.'

With Hoddle largely left to his own devices, there was a need for a ball winner, a slot Peter Reid filled admirably. Rather than wingers, England now employed wide midfielders, Hodge coming in on the left, Trevor Steven on the right. Almost immediately, the side was transformed. According to Lineker: 'Because of the way the team played I got three good chances and took them. Peter and I just hit it off, and playing together – my record was almost a goal a game – we just complemented each other and we were the catalyst for the team. The new players that came in did really well, but it was as much a confidence thing as anything else, and from looking at one of the worst World Cups since we lost to America in 1950, we were flying, playing well.'

England were 3–0 up in 34 minutes, all scored by Lineker, and the job was done. Peter Reid wrote, 'At half-time you go in, throw your shirt off, and put a towel soaked in cold water over you ... Viv Anderson threw this towel over my shoulders and I said, "This towel's hot, that's hot water it's been in," but it was my body heat which had warmed the water up, I was so hot.' In the circumstances, it was little wonder England took their foot off the gas in the second half, coasting through. Nor were the Poles over-inclined to press, having already qualified for the next round. England were a team transformed, and all for the loss of two of their most illustrious players. As Steve Hodge notes, 'There's no way you can say Robson and Wilkins weren't world-class players, but it was ironic that when they dropped out of the side, we suddenly started to play better. For some reason the changing of the side started things off. Obviously Glenn was happier in the middle, Peter Reid came in and played really well, and myself and Trevor Steven were in the up and down roles. Whether things would have gone so well if we hadn't got the early goal against Poland, who knows, but then confidence flooded back, which is as important as anything. Maybe it would have been the same story if Robson and Wilkins had played, we'll never know. I didn't actually play in the Robson role, because the formation changed to make it a more normal four in midfield – Chris Waddle had played further forward, so I came in to take his place on the left. I never felt bedded down in the side because I was more a central midfielder and we had Barnes and Waddle ready to come in on the left if necessary, dying to get on.'

For the second-round game against Paraguay – who had beaten Iraq and drawn with Mexico and Belgium – England had to move from Monterrey to Mexico City. Their new hotel, the Valle de Mexico, wasn't to Reid's liking: 'I must have got two hours' sleep – there's no double-glazing, and I could hear the trucks thundering past all night ... most of the lads had had similar problems ... going into your bedroom is like going into a prison cell – a prison cell with noise ... the food is not good, but the biggest complaint I have is about the uncleanliness. Gary Bailey found a ladybird in his soup.' Two days later they moved to the Holiday Inn. England trained at the Reforma Club, where the 1970 squad had worked out, giving them a sense of the occasion and the continuous thread that passes through the England team regardless of personnel. That was underlined when Stanley Matthews paid a visit to the dressing room before the game. As a morale booster, it must have worked, for England went serenely on their way, Lineker getting two more and Beardsley the other in a second successive 3–0 win. Everything in the garden was suddenly rosy. All, that was, except for the identity of their next opponents: Argentina and Diego Maradona.

Maradona had already begun to make this *his* World Cup, giving a true captain's display in the second-round game with Uruguay. He was the main threat. Knowing it was one thing, stopping him was entirely another. And to add to the tension, there was the strained political atmosphere between the two nations, as Steve Hodge explains: 'You couldn't forget the fact that we'd had the Falklands war just four years before. It was still fresh in the mind, there wasn't the depth of feeling there as there had been in '82 or '83, but there was still an anti-Argentine feeling around, and probably the same from their side. We tried to defuse the situation, we didn't want to get involved in the political side of things, it didn't affect our outlook. In the middle of a World Cup, it's just two sets of players trying to win the biggest prize. We were happy with the way the previous two games had gone and we stuck with the way we were playing. In hindsight you wonder if we should have stuck somebody on Maradona, because he was special, in the company of Cruyff and Pelé, but then that might have taken away from our potential, so it's swings and roundabouts, really. Looking back, he was so much of a threat, perhaps we should have gone man-to-man, but it's easy to say now!' Although England detailed nobody in particular to mark Maradona out of the game, Reid still felt, 'We gave them too much respect . . . I thought if we had been more confident in our own ability. we could have beaten them. I thought we played it wrong . . . our back-four had just settled for doing the defensive side of their job . . . tactically, we are a bit behind. And technically, at least among our back players.' It's perhaps true that the sheer genius of Maradona blinded England to the fact that Argentina were a pretty ordinary side, that there was no great threat from anywhere but the ox-like number ten. As Hodge says, hindsight is the greatest tactician, but had England snuffed Maradona out, it's hard to see how Argentina could have won. Ironically, Argentina did man-mark Lineker and Beardsley.

England got to half-time on level terms, but had created very little, Hoddle barely in the game, Reid toiling and Hodge and Steven stifled when they did get the ball. Then, six minutes into the second-half, Argentina scored one of the most famous goals England have ever conceded. Steve Hodge played a central role in it: 'Maradona ran towards me, the ball bounced at me. People have always asked if I sliced my kick, but I caught it exactly as I wanted to, because I knew where Peter was, knew where the goal was, so I was looping it back up to him. I'd not seen that in flicking the ball towards me, Maradona had changed direction and was running towards the keeper for some strange reason, because normally he'd have followed the ball. My flick was spot on and I turned around not contemplating any trouble at all, really. Behind the goal was all colour, hats and bright shirts, so I assumed he'd headed it in and I turned away thinking I'd made a bit of a ricket there, I didn't know what he'd done. I hadn't got the foggiest that he'd handled the first goal. Those around him like Terry Fenwick and Peter Shilton saw his hand flick up, but I wasn't aware of it until later. I didn't know until I got back in the changing room, I had no idea. I even exchanged shirts with him in the tunnel!' For those readers who have spent the last thirteen years on Mars, Maradona leapt with Shilton and punched the ball past him, into the empty net. When questioned about the dubious morality of the move, Maradona merely suggested that the goal had been scored by the 'Hand of God'. Peter Reid was altogether more realistic, admitting: 'If one of our lads had done it I'd have said, "Great, son." '

England were indignant at the injustice. And then, four minutes later, another of the most famous goals ever conceded by England was scored. But this time, it was also the most sublime goal England have ever conceded. Again, Hodge was on hand to witness Maradona at work: 'He got the ball and did a little trick in their half then ran off. I was five yards away, but the air is so thin there that after an hour we were flagging a bit, where the South Americans are more used to that kind of heat, and I think that told. I was pretty fit, but I just couldn't take off and get back, so I just jogged back to the halfway line because there was no way I could get back. I was right behind him and I watched him go.

Peter Reid couldn't get at him, then he went past somebody else and I was thinking "It's a hell of a run, he's done well to get that far," but he still had a couple of defenders and Peter to get past. I think Terry Fenwick had been booked in an earlier game and had that on his mind, so he went past him with no trouble, then you had the best keeper in the world and he made mincemeat of him by throwing a dummy and going on the narrow side. I don't think you'll ever see a better goal than that, and to do it in a game like that was incredible. All the way down I thought somebody would get to him or he'd make a mistake with his control, but he ran at such pace with the ball he was impossible to live with.'

Viv Anderson 'wasn't on the bench for the Argentina game and we were given this box to watch the match behind one of the goals. Maradona's second was the best goal I've ever seen, from watching him pick up the ball to scoring it was incredible, we all just stood up and clapped!'

Oddly, that moment of absolute genius woke England from the coma they'd been in after the first goal. In the last 20 minutes Barnes and Waddle were thrown into the fray as conventional wingers, Hodge moving inside in place of Reid. Throwing everything forward, England soon unnerved the decidedly shaky Argentine rearguard and gave a glimpse of what might have been had they shown such ambition from the outset. But, as Hodge accepts, 'We put them under pressure but you can't give teams a two-goal start.' Even so, when Lineker headed in Barnes' cross with 9 minutes to go, there was real hope and with a minute to go, there was one final, excellent chance, as Mark Hateley remembers: 'Barnesy chipped the ball to the far post and Gary almost got there, couldn't quite reach it. As you do on the bench, I looked at that and thought, "If only I'd been there!" But it wasn't to be.'

And so England's World Cup was over at the quarter-final stage, equalling their best ever performance outside England, ended by a piece of malice and another of magic. Gary Lineker admits that, 'I don't think we were as good in 1986 as in 1990, especially defensively, but we went into every game thinking we could win it. We didn't play particularly well against Argentina, and looking back on it I suppose that we weren't quite well enough equipped to win it. It was the "Hand of God" comment that really irritated us, probably more than the actual doing of it. People have punched the ball into the net before and got away with it, you don't expect them to run up to the referee and ask him to disallow it! Your irritation there is with the referee and the linesman for missing it. But he was the best player I ever played with or against by miles. He was head and shoulders above everybody – considering that, he should have headed it in! He didn't win the World Cup on his own but he's probably as close as anyone's ever come to doing it.'

England did gain some small consolation when Lineker picked up the Golden Boot as the competition's top scorer with six goals, and returned home as the nation's greatest sporting hero: 'Things were massively different. I was suddenly overwhelmed by the media attention after the hat-trick, but at least I was 25, I had enough experience to know how to handle it. But the real difference was when I came home. I'd done well at Everton, but there's a massive difference between being top scorer in the First Division and scoring goals for England at the World Cup. I remember stopping for petrol somewhere and everyone in the place coming over to me, and I'd never had that before except a little bit in Leicester and then on Merseyside for a year. I got married and there were a million photographers outside the church, but it was exciting, it was a major watershed in not just my career, but my life.'

As an indicator of just how fortunes can contrast even within a squad of just twenty-two players, compare Lineker's rise with the misfortune that beset Bryan Robson, or Mark Wright who didn't even get there after breaking his leg. Or, for that matter, reflect on Viv Anderson's World Cup experience, not getting on the field for the second consecutive World Cup: 'If you don't play, it's hard to watch, then the next day all those who didn't get a game have to train as usual, but in those situations, the squad has to pull together, you have to gee one another up. You've got to keep fit because you never know when you'll get called on. Peter Reid and Steve Hodge were perfect examples of that, coming in later on, but no full-backs got injured, so I was just watching again. But now looking back from twelve years on, going to two World Cups and not getting a game doesn't matter much to me. At the time it did, not now.'

Once again, England returned home from the World Cup finals haunted by a sense of what might have been. Particularly what might have been if Diego Armando Maradona had had English parents.

13

Falls to Climb

For the first time since the far-off days of Alf Ramsey, England entered a new international cycle with the same manager that had begun the previous one. The game of musical chairs had very nearly started again, because following the harsh criticism aimed at him and his team in the early stages of the World Cup, Bobby Robson had offered his resignation. In a rare burst of common sense, the Football Association rejected the offer and allowed Robson to get on with the job. England had gone out to Mexico with an unconvincing tactical shape, but events had conspired to help Robson and Howe forge a new approach in a matter of days. And if they'd never really threatened to win the World Cup, they had pushed the eventual champions pretty close, suggesting that the years ahead could be productive, especially if much-needed stability were injected into the set-up.

Operating the four-man midfield that had looked so much better in Mexico, Bryan Robson was restored in place of Peter Reid and Chris Waddle took over from Trevor Steven, Hoddle and Hodge retaining their places. The personnel had changed a little, but the format remained the same and it served England well in the qualification phase for Euro '88, in a pretty straightforward group that also included Yugoslavia, Northern Ireland and Turkey, not the toughest group they could have had. Comfortable wins over the first two at home set England up nicely, and they went to Madrid for a friendly in February 1987 in good heart. It was a particularly special game for Gary Lineker. His wonderful World Cup form had sealed a summer move to Barcelona, and he was especially keen to do well in his new home: 'Things were a bit manic back in England after Mexico and I escaped it a bit by going to Barcelona. Although the media attention in Spain is massive, the adulation of the fans is enormous, it's slightly different there. They're more in awe of footballers, they almost treat you like godlike figures at Barcelona, they'll smile and sit outside the ground with the kids, but they leave you alone and respect your space, which made it easier. And I had a good few weeks there: I scored three against Real Madrid when we won 3–2 at home, and the stadium – 120,000 people – just erupted. Then I got four for England in Madrid against four or five of the Barcelona team, but such is the nationalism of Catalonia that the headline the next day was CATALAN PLAYER SCORES FOUR AGAINST SPAIN, so they quite enjoyed that!

'And playing in Spain improved my game. In England, because I was quick, a lot of my goals came from the ball over the top, but you can't do that abroad, because you're marked man to man, there's a sweeper on the edge of the box, they defend deep. So you can't get behind them in the same way and you have to think about how to score goals differently, by creating space and losing markers. Working with Cruyff was difficult because he had a huge ego, he had to keep reminding people how great he was, which he didn't need to do, but his ideas were fascinating. He prized possession, he'd talk about making the pitch as long and as wide as you could when you had the ball and as short and narrow as you could when they had it, so that broadened my view of the game too. My touch improved because it had to, because if there's somebody up your backside all the time, your second touch can't be a header any more! As you get older, it's not that your pace goes, but you get physically more tired, you're never fresh because we play so many games, so what you lose there you need to make up for with experience.'

Ironically one of the few other England players getting Con-tinental experience was Mark Hateley, kept out of the side by the success of the Lineker–Beardsley axis: 'By then I was a completely different player, I wasn't the target man that I was labelled as. I was successful in Italy, playing against the best defenders, but that's irrelevant to the press. They didn't come to see me in Milan, so they just say, "He's tall, good in the air, must be old-fashioned." But that was just a small part of my game. When we went to Mexico in '86 I was a better player than when I'd first come into the side, then after the World Cup I went on to another level, which is what you need to do if you want to play at the top. I started scoring more goals than I ever had before, but I was a fringe player then, with Gary and Peter the first choice. Because England play so few games, if you're not a regular, you don't get a fair crack, but that just makes you more determined to keep going!'

And if Hateley, with a sheaf of England caps to his name, found it tough to break down the door, what chance did figures inhabiting the outer fringes, like Cyrille Regis, who'd been out of the reckoning for nearly four years, have? 'I spent a couple of years where I was playing with injuries, my form dipped, confidence dipped and I was out of the picture. Then Coventry came in with a bid of £250,000 and nobody else wanted me, so that slaughtered my ego, because we're all proud, we all believe in ourselves. I reacted immaturely, said, "Stuff it, I'll show 'em," and went to Coventry, which was fatal. I was a big fish in a small pond, we had a bad team, fighting relegation all the time, and things went from bad to worse. It got so bad I nearly went to Wolves for £40,000. Then things turned round. John Sillett came in, we won the Cup and I was back on an even path. It was a massive learning curve, character building to have been so low and come back, and the reward for that was another England cap against Turkey in 1987, when we won 8–0 at Wembley. I was a better person and maybe more of a team player, because Coventry were a lesser side than Albion and so I had to create my own chances, make things happen. I was now a leader of the line rather than an out and out striker. I came on for Peter Beardsley, got twenty minutes, and then never got another chance, and that is confusing – if you're good enough for one squad and you don't get the chance to do anything wrong, why do you get left out? But now I'm a coach, some of the players are probably saying the same thing about me! You have to look at yourself, were you consistent enough, was your attitude right, were there better players around, were you the right sort of player to fit in with the style of the team? In retrospect, it was great to have 5 caps, but it's also disappointing. Potential is a massive word, I look back and think I could have played more times, if I'd done this or that, had fewer beers, done a bit more training, whatever. If I could have polished it up, what could I have done? But you have to live with your decisions. The most important thing is that I can say I was honoured to play for England and that I enjoyed it.'

There were some spectacular displays on the way through qualification, including a superb 4–1 win in Yugoslavia and the 8–0 demolition of Turkey. In friendly competition, England also excelled, drawing with both Brazil and Holland at Wembley and never being embarrassed by two of the world's strongest sides. Little wonder that Gary Lineker rates that as 'probably the best England team I played in. The team came together, and from 1988 to 1990 we were a very good side.' Bobby Robson had had the good sense to build on the momentum generated in 1986. He'd seen at first hand that technique was a prerequisite for success in the higher echelons of the game and had built accordingly. The basic shape remained 4–4–2 and there was only minor tinkering with the personnel – Tony Adams came in for Terry Fenwick, Mark Wright returned, as did Trevor Steven and John Barnes, while Waddle and Hodge dropped out of the reckoning, to Hodge's natural disappointment: 'I'd lost my place and then we went out to Switzerland with a squad of twenty-four prior to Euro '88. I thought I'd struggle and probably didn't deserve to go. Bobby Robson announced the squad after the game in the dressing room, and me and Mick Harford missed out. That wasn't a great flight home, because twenty-two players were happy and me and Mick weren't, but I didn't have too many complaints. Bobby Robson was similar to Brian Clough in that he announced the team and that was it, there was no fuss, no discussion, so it didn't bother me that he didn't explain it. When we got back to the airport, he said,

"Get yourself back to Nottingham, have a good season and get back in the squad." It wasn't a bad thing to miss those Championships as it turned out!'

While Hodge had been left out, there had been a call in certain sections of the press for a young Geordie midfielder to be added to the squad to gain valuable experience and perhaps add a little sparkle to the side if required. Hodge remembers, 'That Switzerland game was the first time I met Paul Gascoigne. He came and sat by me in the stand and said, "Do you want a bit of me Mars bar?" I was obviously a senior player then, I'd been to the World Cup, played plenty of games, but there was no introduction, no "pleased to meet you", just "Do you want a bit of me Mars bar?"! Nothing fazed him, he was a smashing lad and I got on really well with him, but he was one of those people who wasn't overawed by being in the England set-up.' Euro '88 came just a little too soon for Gazza, but it was obvious that the time would come – nobody could suppress a talent that outrageous for long.

Going into Euro '88, England had more reason for optimism than at any tournament since the 1970 World Cup and were the seeded team in their group. Lineker and Beardsley were scoring regularly, Robson was fully fit, Hoddle looked sharp after a season in France, and, defensively, England were secure. They were grouped with Holland, the USSR and Ireland. There are no pushovers when you reach the last eight in Europe, but England's recent record against the USSR was good, they'd done well against the Dutch earlier that season, and Ireland, though familiar with English methods, certainly didn't pack anything like the quality of Robson's men. It was against Ireland that the campaign opened and, as has so often been the case, England were sluggish, falling behind to a Ray Houghton goal after 5 minutes.

From there on in, it was the 1950 USA game all over again, as Lineker relates: 'Things were against us. We were unlucky against Ireland – we had so many chances, Packie Bonner had a blinder, we hit the post, it was just one of those days when it wouldn't go in, though they made it difficult for us and played very well. They were a good side even though we were vilified for our performance at the time.' England's attack offered little in the way of imagination or invention and made no impression on a side who were resolute in playing the archetypal 'British' game, if the Irish will forgive the expression.

Mark Hateley replaced Beardsley and Hoddle took over from Neil Webb, who had been surprisingly selected ahead of him, but to no effect. Hateley well remembers that game: 'It was very frustrating to be stuck on the bench in Germany. John Barnes was in the side putting crosses in, but Gary and Peter weren't the sort of forwards to take advantage, so it was hard to watch! All managers have people that they want to play in the team and they have a system they want to play, but the two don't always go together and you can overlook players who would fit in better to what you're trying to do. I think that's where European coaches often see that a lot quicker. I'd teamed up with Glenn in France and that was a sensational partnership. The first year we were together I got 18 or 19 goals, was second top scorer in France behind Papin, we won the league, Glenn was player of the year, and I certainly felt that partnership could have worked well for England. As a striker it's about creating understandings, you're only as good as the people that make the chances for you and Glenn and myself were on the same wavelength. We are too insular in England. That was the time of the Heysel ban and our players weren't getting any European football, just myself, Glenn and Gary, so I thought it was odd that I didn't get a few more games, Glenn as well.'

After losing to Ireland, the Dutch were next in line. They'd lost 1–0 to the USSR, so it was a crunch game for both sides. In hindsight, Bobby Robson conceded that he had made an error in just having two defenders to mark Ruud Gullit and Marco Van Basten, giving them the freedom to wreak havoc, the genuinely great Van Basten scoring a hat-trick to win the game 3–1. Yet, as Lineker says, 'It was a terrific match against the Dutch, who were probably the best team in the world at that stage and it could easily have been a draw, but Van Basten was brilliant.' Having fallen behind, England fought back strongly and Robson grabbed an equalizer, at which point England looked the more likely to go on and win the game. But England lacked that special genius that the Dutch had, and, in fairness, they lacked luck too. Within a couple of games, two years' work disappeared down the drain. Robson made changes for the final match, though yet again Viv Anderson was restricted to a watching brief. Against the USSR, it was enough, for as he says, 'They tore us apart.' An England team that later couldn't get home quickly enough gave an atrocious performance, losing 3–1, a scoreline that flattered them.

Lineker points to the fact that, 'We were unfortunate in that it came at the end of a season that had left Barnes and Beardsley jaded. I was suffering from hepatitis, though I didn't know it at that stage, I just knew I wasn't right, especially in the last game, when I couldn't put one foot in front of another. I think Bobby just thought I didn't fancy playing and put me in regardless, and I've never felt like that before or since. But when you're out of the tournament it's hard to get anything going, but it was that defeat against Russia that ruined it and really drew the criticism, even though we were already out. It was hugely disappointing, we were capable of winning it.'

That Russian defeat really did open the floodgates for the media. Had England managed a win, or even an honourable draw, the more balanced assessments would have said that England had some ill fortune, were let down by poor performances from some of their key players, notably Hoddle and Barnes, and that we were just short of the highest class. But to lose so spinelessly and with so little pride in the shirt was simply unacceptable, particularly in the light of the high expectations going into the West German tournament. To some it smacked of the manager losing control of his players and being unable to exert sufficient authority over them. Once more, Robson tried to do what he saw as the honourable thing, and offered his resignation. Once more the FA were quite correct to refuse it, understanding that while Euro '88 had been desperately disappointing, it would be foolish to simply ignore the advances of the previous two years and focus merely on three poor results. It was a brave move by the FA, for it would have been easy to cave in to the papers and give them their ritual sacrifice and take the heat off Lancaster Gate for a while. But if Robson had been the man for the job in May 1988 – as the nation all but unanimously agreed – he was still the right man three months later. For all that, Robson knew he was on borrowed time, and he was reminded of that fact in no uncertain terms when England's first World Cup qualifier, at home to Sweden, ended in a dismal 0–0 draw.

It was time to juggle the pack. Hoddle's England career was over, as was Kenny Sansom's, though Steve Hodge got a recall to the colours: 'I had a good start to the season with Forest. We played at Everton and got a draw and Cloughie said to me after the game that he'd get me back in the England squad eventually. A day or two later I was watching a local game and got a call to say I'd been picked for the game against Denmark, which was September '88! I couldn't believe it when I was actually playing, so it showed Bobby Robson had faith in me. Neil Webb came through about then, but I stayed in the squad without getting games.'

Nottingham Forest had a good representation in the England set-up at the time, with Stuart Pearce coming through, along with Nigel Clough and Des Walker. Other new faces were tried, such as Michael Thomas, David Rocastle and Alan Smith: 'I played in a friendly in Saudi Arabia as a sub and we got knocked because we only got a draw there. There was a lot of pressure then because the newspapers were on the manager's back and that gets through to the players. I got my full debut in Greece and again we didn't play particularly well, there weren't many chances created, so it was a difficult game for me to shine in.' England won another friendly 2–1 at a time when it seemed only the drive of Bryan Robson was keeping them on course. As he aged, some felt Robson should move into the heart of defence, where he had always been a supreme player, but who could replace him in the middle? Viv Anderson 'played a couple of times with Bryan at the back, we kept a clean sheet, which is the main thing. I had to do all his running for him, had to keep getting him out of trouble! He was a very good defender, but when you look at the goals he got for England, he had to play in midfield.' It was Robson's goals that helped keep England on track as Lineker, still seemingly suffering the after effects of hepatitis, dried up. Nor was he playing in his central striking position in Barcelona and he was soon forced to leave Spain 'because Cruyff saw me as a wide man and with the World Cup coming up, that was no good for me, I had to re-establish myself as a striker'.

In March 1989 England flew out to play their second qualifying game in Albania, a sobering journey for Alan Smith: 'We got to Albania and there were people just hanging about, everything was grey and brown, it was a real revelation, it really opened your eyes to see the poverty there. We took our own chef, the hotel was the best they'd got, but it was awful. It was an enjoyable trip in an odd way, because it was so different.' Gary Lineker says, 'Going to Albania was like going back a hundred years in many ways, and I ended up going three years on the bounce, twice with Barcelona, so I had my fill of that. It does open your eyes, you sometimes worry about football but when you see the circumstances the people of Albania lived under, it makes you think. They were tough places to play, the pitches were horrible and the atmosphere was different, very noisy but strange.' England ground out a 2–0 win, then the following month won the return 5–0 at Wembley, Gascoigne scoring a superb goal after coming on as a sub.

Gradually England's fortunes were improving, a 2–0 win at Hampden setting them up nicely for another key game against Poland. England totally dominated the match, but this time made their possession count and won 3–0, their ascendancy allowing Alan Smith to make his first England appearance at home: 'Everybody wants to play for England at Wembley, you have your family and friends there, it's a proud moment when you line up for the national anthem. It was great to come on as a sub for Peter Beardsley, even though it was late on. I didn't have a lot to do, but we won well, it was a nice atmosphere and by the time I got on, the game was won, so there was no pressure, really. Coming on late, it depends on how the game's going. We were on top against Poland, so I saw more of the play, but there are times when it's backs against the wall, and you might not get a touch, but you've got to just work. You're normally on for a specific reason, so you just try to carry out instructions, be they tactical, or just giving extra legs.' Smith had come through into the side partly because of injury to Mark Hateley, who remembers the thoughtfulness of the England manager, even when he was under savage attack: 'Bobby was a smashing man. After that I had an ankle injury and I was out for eighteen months, which covered the rest of his time with England, but he would regularly phone me and see how I was doing.'

England had all but qualified for Italia '90 by now, requiring two points to ensure they were one of the best second-placed sides. They got one of them in Sweden, a dour 0–0 draw that saw Neil Webb's career derailed with a ruptured Achilles tendon, just a couple of months after he'd signed for Manchester United – Alex Ferguson must have seen the funny side of that. Terry Butcher probably didn't have too much to laugh at when he sustained a terrible cut to the head in a collision with Ekstrom, though the pictures of England's stand-in captain with his blood-stained shirt, eyes bulging, fists clenched as England moved a step closer to the World Cup finals are among the most iconic in the game. It was typical Butcher in many ways, redolent of his gung-ho, get-stuck-in patriotism. When he first emerged on the scene at Ipswich alongside Russell Osman, it was Osman who was looked upon as the more likely to manage a glorious England career, Butcher dismissed as the more earthy, workmanlike footballer. But he made the most of his abilities, adding a Jack Charltonesque bloody-mindedness to his game, a 'they shall not pass' attitude that ensured he could cope with all but the very best of opposing forwards. But even Butcher's bloodshed left the side with plenty to do in Kato-wice, the scene of the national disaster in 1973 when England lost 2–0. Lineker remembers it as 'an odd place to play. There was nobody there, so that's another thing that you have to overcome in international football. We ended up with the 0–0 draw we needed. They had their long shooting boots on. They never got anywhere near the goal but they kept peppering us with shots. Shilts had one of his great matches that day and we edged through.'

Shilton remained England's pre-eminent goalkeeper some nineteen years after his England debut, his physical fitness and all-round agility a powerful testimony to his single-minded attitude to training and preparation. Having initially been the preferred replacement for Gordon Banks, he had been able to shrug off the disappointment of his error in the Polish qualifier at Wembley in 1973 and had fought back to literally share the goalkeeping jersey with Ray Clemence, the two alternating for much of Ron Greenwood's reign. Ushering Clemence into international retirement, Shilton's huge presence in the England goal was a genuinely reassuring one, and there is no doubt that a number of the defenders who played in front of him owed him a huge debt, and more than a few of their caps.

Further fresh faces were added to a side that had lacked a spark ever since Euro '88. As Gary Lineker suggests, 'The Heysel ban did work against us, you do miss that experience, but we had plenty of players who'd been around long enough. We were hard to beat, good in defence and with Butcher and Wright we had players who could contribute offensively too. We had a great keeper, and the pace of Des Walker. Then with the likes of Barnes, Waddle, Gascoigne and Beardsley we were very creative too. Stuart Pearce had come in, Platt was coming through, we were improving again at the right time.'

The midfield had looked decidedly pedestrian though, with neither Barnes nor Waddle delivering the quality expected of them. It was blindingly obvious that Gascoigne was going to be a lynchpin of the side, though Bobby Robson kept him in reserve, to shield him, to keep his talents under wraps and to maintain his appetite for the game. But the side needed other attributes that were missing, notably goals from midfield allied to the all-important work ethic. Robson turned to Villa's David Platt to see if he might provide them: 'I hadn't played in any of the qualifiers and I got into the friendly against Italy as a trial, really. I had no thoughts about the World Cup. The concentration level needed to play at international level against such a good side is so high that I didn't have time to think about anything else. Coming on as a sub, it's a double-edged thing. You don't have much time to make an impression but you don't have time to worry about the game either; suddenly you've played 13 minutes against Italy and you've got a cap. A month later I had 25 minutes against Yugoslavia, then I made my full debut against Brazil. In that game, I remember working very, very hard but not wanting to take too much responsibility because you're frightened of doing things wrong. By then, March 1990, I was starting to think I'd got half a chance of going to Italy but I still had to make sure by producing a professional performance, not necessarily a personally glorious performance.'

England's displays going into the World Cup were a decidedly mixed bag, with three good wins against Brazil, the Czechs – a 4–2 win in which Paul Gascoigne confirmed himself as the most exciting young talent England had unearthed in years with a virtuoso performance, having a hand in three goals, then scoring the fourth himself – and Denmark followed by a home defeat at the hands of Uruguay. Then, worst of all, England went out to Tunisia and drew 1–1. Who cares? It was a meaningless friendly. You didn't get medals for beating Tunisia, but as David Platt says, 'Whenever you're coming into tournaments, there's a new venom from the media and if you don't win every preparation game, they rule you out. In Tunisia, it was a training game, just to get you right fitness-wise. The result wasn't important, you don't want to get any injuries, you can't read much into those games.' But the press decided it was the end of the world and told Bobby Robson IN THE NAME OF ALLAH, GO! A cretinous statement at the best of times, one which betrayed a total lack of understanding of international football, it shed no light on the possible gain to be had by changing the coach days before the World Cup finals, nor who would be prepared to take the job in such impossible circumstances. Still, it sells papers. (God knows who to, because anybody who reckons that's an intelligent view of the game probably can't read anyway.)

But in the light of these latest attacks, and following eight years of similarly ill-informed abuse, Bobby Robson gave notice that he would leave the England job at the end of the tournament, saving the journos the job of sticking the knife in. Did Robson's decision have an impact on the players? Not according to Lineker: 'Players don't generally worry about the manager, you live for the day of the game; we're a pretty insular bunch. Within the group the pressures and the focus remained the same even after Bobby said he was leaving.'

There was real concern about England's hooligan following, which for a decade and more had been a thorn in the side of the national team. Where in the 1970s it had been club sides going into Europe that had caused the most problems, from the European Championships in 1980 onwards, the Heysel disaster apart, the national side had become the focus. In part that was because UEFA had imposed serious sanctions on club sides when fans had caused trouble – Manchester United had had to play one home European game in Plymouth; others were held behind closed doors – where national sides seemed to be largely immune to such action. Also, for the far right, the England flag was a far more potent symbol than club colours. As they became increasingly organized they began to infiltrate England's support, knowing that wherever England went, they could attract the eyes of the world. When they were added to an element of English support that was taking advantage of ever cheaper airfares and who were only there for the beer but who couldn't hold it, all the ingredients for violence were on tap. With the TV cameras on hand to film the orgy of violence in loving detail, the thugs got their fifteen minutes of fame and the rest of us were left with a game that was treated like a leper. Ironically, it would be Italia '90 that would herald the rehabilitation of football's reputation in England, but prior to the tournament, the authorities were so worried about our supporters that the team were exiled to Sardinia for their first round of matches. Or maybe the Italians didn't want to let Gazza loose on their country just yet – he'd been fortunate to get in in the first place, having left his passport at home. As Lineker says, 'Gazza was always there to entertain everybody with his non-stop antics. He never really realized where the line was, and he'd cross it occasionally. But he was terrific fun, telling stories, playing practical jokes, there was never a dull moment when he was around. Although you wouldn't want to room with him.'

Team spirit was good, but the draw for their group was not an encouraging one, for in addition to Egypt, they were saddled with Ireland and Holland again, in a worrying echo of Euro '88. On the positive side it offered a chance for revenge and England had certainly learned from those games.

Ireland were first up once more, but this time it was England who struck early, Gary Lineker maintaining his excellent World Cup record, much to his relief: 'Mexico changed things on the field as well as off it, which is why I was almost more satisfied with my performance in 1990 than in 1986. In Mexico, people did their homework but they didn't really know who I was, and there's always an element in your mind as to whether it was a flash in the pan. Obviously, I continued to score goals for England but to do it again in 1990 and score four more when people were looking out for me was very satisfying.' In spite of Lineker's goal, Jack Charlton's team were nothing if not resilient and turned the game into a long-ball, pitched battle which suited them admirably. Eventually, the Irish got the goal they had threatened, Kevin Sheedy lashing a shot past the veteran Shilton. At least England had managed a point more than in Euro '88 and their hopes were not fatally damaged by any means. However, with typically generous spirit and complete grasp of the fundamentals of football, the *Sun* decided Robson should bring the team home to spare them further punishment. Genius. Of course, had England tried to outplay the Irish with sweet, free-flowing football and been beaten on the break, as they had been two years earlier, the headlines would have been yet more vitriolic.

If the previous two tournaments had taught England anything, it was the paramount importance of avoiding defeat in your opening fixture – it had been fatal in 1988, almost so in 1986. This time England had a point on the board and were unlikely to finish behind the Irish. Assuming they could beat Egypt, that made second place at worst a real probability, and with it qualification. Of course, the game against Ireland represented a nadir in terms of aesthetic considerations, but as Ramsey had proved, if you won, few remembered how you won. England's performance against Ireland in 1990 was not significantly worse than that against Uruguay in 1966, and look where that had led.

The reaction to what was a desperate spectacle was savage, and from the purist's standpoint, understandably so. Everybody knew the kind of game Jack Charlton's Ireland would play: plenty of pressure on the opponent in possession, long ball, very physical, lots of effort, not much sophistication. Bobby Robson chose to counter that by playing a not dissimilar style, leaving spectators to sit through the unedifying spectacle of Godzilla and King Kong slugging it out in the middle of the field. In the aftermath, England were dismissed as tactically out of touch, playing a game that should have died forty years before. Too much was read into what was effectively a local derby – and how many of those are worth watching? It certainly wasn't pretty, but after 90 minutes, both sides had got what they'd come for, which, in the modern World Cup, is all that seems to matter.

Next up were the Dutch, not quite the side that had won Euro '88 and riven with internal dispute. And England now had a better idea of how to cope with them. Bobby Robson wrote, 'Tactically, I got it wrong against Holland in the 1988 European Championship when I had two versus two against Ruud Gullit and Marco van Basten. I vowed then that it would never happen again, and that I would in future play a sweeper to cover myself against teams like the Dutch or the Germans . . . [that's] why I picked [Mark Wright] to play against the Dutch in Cagliari, not because I had a deputation of senior players, as some of the press continue to suggest.'

That had been one of the controversies of Italia '90 – just who was it that made England switch to a sweeper – though it was a less a classical sweeper system and more a three centre-backs set-up. Steve Hodge remembers that 'the players went into one of the bedrooms one night to talk about it. We always played 4–4–2, and we were talking about changing it to release the full-backs to give more support further forward. Bryan Robson was the captain and senior pro and I know he and Bobby got together to talk about it some more after that. It did change things for the better, because 4–4–2 was a bit stale at that point.' Gary Lineker's version is that, 'I think Bobby had had the idea of the sweeper in mind, but the players definitely wanted to play that way. But ultimately, he makes the decisions, so whether it's his original idea, Don Howe's original idea, Bryan Robson's or whoever, it doesn't matter. Bobby takes the credit or the blame depending on how it works. It wasn't like he said, "We're definitely not playing a sweeper," and all the lads went to him and said, "Yes we are." That wasn't the case. He was thinking it over, he had a meeting with Bryan Robson on behalf of the players; we thought it was the way to play, especially against Holland. But part of the strength of a good manager is to listen to your experienced players, because he has to have their confidence, and he went with it and takes the credit.' Whatever the genesis of the idea, it worked well. Although the game wasn't a classic, it was a huge improvement on the Irish game and England deserved more than the 0–0 draw, with Gascoigne unveiling the full extent of his talent on the biggest possible stage. The result almost sealed qualification for the second round, but it was achieved at a cost. Bryan Robson's World Cup was over through injury for the second time, his place initially taken by the workmanlike Steve McMahon, though he in turn would be replaced by David Platt, who offered similar industry with greater creativity.

England went on to top the group by beating Egypt with a Mark Wright goal, but it wasn't enough for the press. And as they toiled against Belgium in the first knockout game, the obituaries for the Robson era were being finalized. Belgium seemed faster in thought and movement than England and came close to scoring when Jan Ceulemans and Enzo Scifo both hit the post, though England did have a Barnes goal disallowed by a mistaken offside decision. Scifo, the star of Belgium's midfield, orchestrated much of the play, and brought a late tackle from Gascoigne, for which England's emerging hero received what was to prove a very expensive booking. Having dominated against the Dutch, Gascoigne was a little quieter against their lowland neighbours, but still did enough to mark himself down as England's key man.

With a minute of extra-time to go, England were decidedly lucky to be on terms. Then Gascoigne underlined what a supreme talent England had uncovered. Winning a free-kick just inside the Belgian half on the left side of the field, he steadied himself, then played in a beautifully flighted pass, perfectly directed, which found substitute David Platt deep inside the Belgian box. Platt spun, caught the ball perfectly on the volley and put England into the last eight: 'I was a sub looking to maintain the team's position against Holland and Egypt, to keep the scoreline. Against Belgium, there were 19 minutes left of normal time, but the attitude was different because it was a knockout game. By the time we were into the second period of extra-time, both sides were thinking about penalties, your mind does turn to that. That game was a turning point for everything. We'd qualified and got criticism after just the one win against Egypt, hadn't played particularly well in the first game against Ireland, did quite well against the Dutch and then, quite honestly, the Belgian players did better than us in that game. Perhaps if it had been a boxing match they'd have won on points. But the goal coming in the last minute, the momentum suddenly picked up, we were into the quarter-finals, everybody expected us to beat Cameroon and for the media the path was clear to the Final!'

Platt's goal was arguably the most important scored by England in any international game since Geoff Hurst's extra-time efforts in the 1966 Final. It was that goal which made possible all the drama of the following ten days – Lineker's goals against Cameroon, a nation united in front of the telly, the penalty shoot-out, Gazza's tears – the events which transformed the status and standing of football in this country. Just weeks before England flew out to Italy, the mad woman of Downing Street had been lobbying for the FA to withdraw the side in case of hooliganism. Post-Heysel, Bradford and Hillsborough, football fans were social lepers, the game crumbling, grass-roots interest kept alive by the fanzine movement and little else. After Italia '90, football was reborn, not entirely for the better, but certainly saved from what looked a very uncertain future. Platt believes, 'It's a flimsy argument to say everything started from there, but it didn't do any harm. I don't know whether it did turn things round in terms of Sky, the Premiership, but a successful World Cup augured well for the year after. Attendances went up, that brought in sponsors, brought in TV and it carried on from there.' Gary Lineker is more bullish about the impact it had: 'That World Cup was a watershed for football in this country and its popularity. It didn't necessarily shift it away from the working masses, but it brought in middle-class England, women, theatre-goers, and got lots of different people interested who never had been before. There's no question that that and the Taylor report moved football forward and away from the yob culture and the hooliganism of the 1980s.'

England were now in the last eight and set to face Cameroon, who most English observers dismissed as a bunch of naïve Africans incapable of troubling mighty England. Lineker complains that, 'Our press is so black and white. One minute you're the worst team in the world, next minute you're the best. In the camp itself, it's not like that, you just think about the next game, try to get over the fact that you're shattered mentally and physically, get your legs going for the next game. You let everybody else decide how good you are. You get the papers a few days late, but you hear what they've said about you, but in that environment you are cocooned. Outside people might have thought, "Right, beat Belgium, then it's Cameroon, then we're in the semis," but it doesn't feel like that when you're in the middle of it! World Cups are so demanding, mentally and physically, but we came through the group stage well enough, played very well against Holland, when we changed to the sweeper, did just enough to beat Belgium.' Certainly, the victory had caught the public's imagination and Bryan Robson, who had flown back to England, had to call Bobby Robson to tell him, 'I cannot believe what is happening. The atmosphere is incredible. I have never seen anything like it in my life. The whole country is behind you and the team.'

Prior to the game, Lineker recalls, 'One of the scouts said that playing Cameroon was like having a bye to the semi-final, and nothing could have been further from the truth! They were a terrific side, probably the best African side there's ever been, with some fantastic players.' Platt adds, 'Cameroon were very strong. Tactically, they were naïve, but that created problems in itself because they were unpredictable. We were probably fortunate to beat them, but that's what tournament play is about, winning your games. But then the luck balanced itself out because I thought we were the better side against Germany in the semi-final and we ended up going out.'

England were decidedly fortunate to beat Cameroon. Despite Platt's early goal, with 7 minutes to go, England were 2–1 down and in deep trouble. Gascoigne fed Lineker, who was hauled down for a blatant penalty. Lineker got up to take it, knowing England's future in the competition hinged on it: 'You don't think about missing! It's hard not to sometimes, but ultimately you've got to decide where you're going to hit it and do that. It's important not to change your mind. The scary one for me was the equalizer against Cameroon with only a few minutes to go, 2–1 down, knowing we'd have been vilified if we'd lost to an African nation, due to the ignorance of the journalists and critics, and the public generally, towards African football and how good a side Cameroon were. They were brilliant and outplayed us for most of the game. The line between coming home with your head held high and coming home with it down is a very fine one! So there was so much pressure on that one. I'd been penalty taker for England for four years without getting one, then two come along at once! Things go through your mind, I thought of my brother watching the game at home with his hands over his eyes, because he got very nervous when I played, so I wondered how he was. But I practised penalties, took twenty every day and hit every one in the same place, so I just thought, "Do exactly what you do in training." I hit it perfectly.' In extra-time, England gradually took control, but it took another penalty to seal it – Lineker hacked down again: 'The second one . . . the keeper had moved so early for the first, I just thought I'd hit it straight.'

England were now in the semi-finals for the first time in twenty-four years, and faced with West Germany, their perennial rivals, for another one of the games that has earned almost mythical status down the years. Most of the population managed to see it, and were left in despair as England did everything that could be expected of them but couldn't overcome the Germans in normal play. Andreas Brehme had scored with a deflected free-kick, but when Lineker snatched an equalizer 10 minutes from time with a clinical finish, the tide seemed to be flowing in their favour. The 30 minutes of extra-time were played out like an epic drama on millions of TV screens. Both teams hit the post, Platt had a goal disallowed, and then Gascoigne got booked, a caution that would rule him out of the Final if England made it. Clearly distressed, Lineker asked Bobby Robson to have a word with him and Gascoigne held himself together for the remaining minutes. Neither team could manage a final breakthrough, so the Finalists would be decided by a penalty shoot-out.

Lineker was first up for England: 'I just decided to hit it hard and low to the keeper's right and stuck with that. It is a tense moment, it's nice when you've scored and got it out of the way, but you feel as tense for the others as you do for yourself, because at least with your penalty you can do something about it. It's a bad way to lose, because you feel you're so close yet you're out of the competition; yet at the same time it's a good way to lose because in the circumstances you can hold your head up and come home with an element of pride, you can say, "We weren't really beaten." '
As everyone in the world knows, ultimately Stuart Pearce and Chris Waddle missed their spot kicks and the Germans marched relentlessly on. Steve Hodge 'went over to Stuart after the shoot-out because we were club colleagues. He was distraught, so I just put my arm round him and said, "Come on, let's get off, it's not down to you." But there's nothing much you can say. Stuart's a pretty strong character, he came back after that and had another six or seven years in the team. We were all flat afterwards; to be that near to the World Cup Final is probably a once in a lifetime thing and to get so close was hard to bear, especially after we'd played so well in that game. Everybody was calm afterwards, but

just down and disappointed, obviously, with Pearcey and Waddle the worst, I suppose.' As Lineker says, 'What can you say to the players who miss? You're not going to say anything that suddenly brings them out of that moment; we all feel it, there's no blame attached, you just give them a hug and get on with life and let them recover. People knock shoot-outs, and I've lost one or two, but I think they're great. It's a footballing skill – by and large the team with the better technique wins – it's a great thing to be in, it's a massive test of your bottle, a true test of ability and it's a damn good watch. And, ultimately, football is entertainment. Sometimes.'

The tears that flowed after the game encapsulated everything that was best about the World Cup: the passion, the drama, the commitment. The tears that Gazza shed became a symbol of a month in which English football recaptured the heart of the nation. In hindsight, those tears could just as easily symbolize the realization that a great career had already reached its zenith. Thanks to a lethal cocktail of recklessness, stupidity and bad luck, Paul Gascoigne would never again dominate the world stage with his footballing skills. Fittingly for a tournament held in Italy, this was football as grand opera and it held the nation spellbound. England played the hosts in the pointless third-place play-off, losing 2–1, but it was a meaningless result. England's World Cup had been a triumph. Given the nature of our national psyche, a glorious defeat was probably even more appealing than ultimate victory. Whatever the case, the domestic game was rejuvenated.

After eight years, Bobby Robson left the England job – soon to be known as 'The Impossible Job' – to join PSV in Eindhoven. Gary Lineker was pleased he went out at the top: 'Bobby's time was pretty turbulent, but he left the job pretty much a hero. He's much loved, which is what you'd want for him because he's a fantastic bloke. Robson and Howe were great enthusiasts for the game, loved it, talked about pretty much nothing else.' And as Steve Hodge says, 'Bobby did a great job, he took a lot of flak along the way, he rode all that and could point to reaching a quarter-final and a semi-final in the World Cup, going out to the winners both times. Maybe we weren't good enough, I don't know, but on both occasions we were unlucky to lose, so his record was good.'

For the first time ever, an England manager was leaving the job with the people wanting more. Did we not like that.

14

A Masochistic Lamb
to the Slaughter

It's always easier to replace a failure – what have you got to live up to? Almost anything you do has got to be an improvement. For Bobby Robson's replacement, there wasn't a lot of room for manoeuvre – fail to get to the Final of the European Championship or the World Cup and you were taking England backwards. Yet again, there was a paucity of talent on offer, particularly after Howard Kendall and Terry Venables had ruled themselves out of contention. Graham Taylor was a different kettle of fish, however. He played his football for Grimsby and Lincoln in the lower divisions before injury ended his career at 28. He moved into management and won the Fourth Division with Lincoln, the side scoring 111 goals in the process, before he was lured back to the basement by Elton John and Watford. Within four years, they had gone from Division Four to Division One. Another year on and Watford were runners-up in the League to Liverpool, then in 1984 were beaten FA Cup Finalists against Everton. Having achieved all he could at Vicarage Road, in May 1987 he moved on to Aston Villa, won them promotion back to the top flight at the first attempt, then in 1990 steered them to second place in the Championship and looked set to enjoy a lengthy spell at Villa Park.

Once Bobby Robson had informed the FA of his decision to quit after Italia '90, Taylor's credentials made him a forerunner, and he was appointed to the post while Robson was still in situ.

There were few who questioned the appointment at the time, simply because of his track record. What dissent there was came from those who were worried by Taylor's style of play. His success had been won with traditional English long-ball football and the purists were dismayed by the thought that England would follow that line. This was to create a significant fault line in his relationship with press and public in the future, but, for the moment, the manager-elect had other problems. Although Taylor was, like any other patriotic Englishman, delighted with England's progress, as they got further and further on in Italia '90, he wouldn't have been human if he hadn't reflected on how much harder this would make his job.

Bobby Robson left the manager's office with his reputation enhanced and the England team returned as conquering heroes. On the obligatory open-top bus tour Gascoigne claimed the headlines with his oh-so-hilarious comedy breasts routine, but it was his football that really caught the imagination. He and Platt had arrived from nowhere and moved on to the world stage, as Platt accepts: 'I'd gone on from the Belgium game and got a couple more goals and because people hadn't been talking about myself or Gazza before the tournament, we were probably the two new players for the future who really came out of the World Cup. Obviously certain players would leave that team because of age, there was a new manager coming in, so we were looked at as a new nucleus, and it was something for the public to get their teeth into.'

With these exciting new players coming through, and following on from the drama of the semi-final, public expectations were higher than they had been in twenty years. And Taylor had to satisfy them, however unrealistic they were. And they were. Had Platt not scored in the last seconds of the Belgian game, England could have gone out on penalties in the second round. They could just as easily have fallen to Cameroon in the quarter-finals. Had either of those been lost, the attitude towards the England team would have been wholly different and more balanced. After all, Italia '90 saw the end of Shilton and Butcher, Bryan Robson barely played again, Gary Lineker was entering the latter stages of his career, and the standard of the replacements just wasn't good enough, though Taylor did himself few favours by putting his faith in some bizarre selections.

And then there was Gascoigne. Having Gazza as the fulcrum of your side would be enough to drive any manager to distraction, but Taylor's handling of him was less than sympathetic. Alluding obliquely to his 'refuelling' difficulties, a reference to both his weight and his drinking, did little for a player whose self-confidence is decidedly brittle. Gascoigne, the star of Italia '90, was left on the bench for the Euro '92 qualifier in Dublin, the more down-to-earth skills of Gordon Cowans getting the nod, this after Gazza had been the architect of a 2–0 win over Poland at Wembley which got the campaign off to a flyer. That ended Taylor's all too brief honeymoon with the press.

Dropping Gazza was the cardinal sin, because he was meat and drink to the fourth estate, guaranteeing a story of some kind wherever he went. That decision was a perfect example of the problems that would beset Taylor throughout his reign, as Gary Lineker points out: 'As a tactician, Graham was basic. It was 4–4–2, knock it in the channels. He got the format of how he wanted to play and left the players to it. His problem was he'd played a certain way with Watford and Villa, of getting the ball forward quickly, but he wouldn't totally commit himself to playing that way with England and he fell between two stools in many ways. We ended up playing neither one thing nor the other. He didn't really understand the game in the Continental sense of building it up, and perhaps what he should have done was stick to his way, the Jack Charlton style of playing, and see what happened. That can work to a degree at international level, as Ireland proved, but I don't think you can take it all the way. If he'd played a massive centre-forward with me playing off him, it might have worked. But in the end we didn't quite do that and he paid the price. In many ways I'm glad he didn't do that because I wouldn't have wanted that, but for him to be successful, playing a different style to anything he had before wasn't going to do it for him. Whether he was worried about what people would say, I don't know, but ultimately he probably was.'

Mark Hateley backs up that assertion: 'Taylor had tried to buy me at Watford when I was at Coventry, but when he got to the England job he thought he had to be somebody else, to play like England "should" play football instead of the way he'd played it at Watford or Villa. But that's the Establishment bringing him in without looking at that side of it.' Hateley would have been the ideal centre-forward for Taylor following his Italian experience, combining the aerial power of the traditional target man with the craft of a forward used to slipping away from man markers: 'I'd been injured, so a lot of people jump in front of you in the queue, so you have to be mentally strong and say, "I'm going to get back and I'll be better than I was." I spent a lot of time doing that, I left Monaco to go to Rangers and, again, I thought my game improved. But I got one game under Graham Taylor. I was twice the player I'd ever been. I was fit, playing consistently well, me and Ally McCoist were smashing goals in all over the place, we had two years unbeaten in Europe. I was just flabbergasted that an England manager wouldn't even bring me down to have a look at me in training. But it was his loss, and eventually those kinds of decisions cost him his job.'

Nevertheless, Taylor's early games in charge were successful enough. They beat Hungary and Poland at home, drew in Dublin, beat Cameroon at Wembley, then stuttered to another draw at Wembley against Ireland, again without Gascoigne, but with Tony Adams returning to the side a month after his release from prison. And if Gascoigne was a problem, so was David Platt, albeit in a different fashion: 'The World Cup did change my life and nothing can prepare you for it – it's probably the only time in my career where things happened to me that I wasn't in control of. I had to get my life back in order, it was such a dramatic change that it was very difficult just to take it in your stride. I was recognized wherever I went, and I was the man to stop on the pitch. I went and saw a psychologist, someone who wasn't biased. It was good to pour everything out, it helped enormously.'

Post-Italia '90, the status of the top footballers in this country changed dramatically. Certain players had achieved iconic status in the past, but perhaps only George Best had been accorded the hysteria of pop-star status – even Keegan was not fêted in that fashion. But now football was the hottest property; it was cool, fashionable, vital. Footballers were suddenly male models, were on the front covers of a dozen different magazines, were on TV and radio constantly, something which would intensify with the advent of the Premiership, the influx of foreigners, the coverage from Sky and, to a lesser extent, Radio Five Live. Inevitably Gascoigne and Lineker were on a different plane to everyone else, but even for the less stellar individuals, the change in climate was dramatic. Certainly it was welcome, for it ensured that the likes of Platt would make themselves financially secure for life in the slipstream of football's incredible rise. But, for all the rewards, it was still psychologically and physically tiring to cope with these new demands. Although agents are a reviled part of the game today, their arrival was an inevitable consequence of these changing times. Even so, players like Platt did find their form affected, at least in the short term.

England flew out to Turkey for another qualifier at the start of May 1991. After a shambolic performance, a scrambled goal from Dennis Wise won the game, but it was obvious that England were struggling, in spite of harvesting 6 points from 4 games. With all due respect, players like Geoff Thomas and Wise and, later on, Carlton Palmer, were not adequate replacements for the likes of Robson, Waddle or Steven. Did Taylor have any option but to play what were, at top level, mere journeymen? Given the shape and tactics he wanted to play, perhaps not, but to regularly ignore the talents of Nigel Clough or a resurgent Waddle, for example, was offering hostages to fortune faster than a Chechen terrorist group could take them.

Waddle's was another strange England career. Over seven years, he accumulated 62 caps, yet it was not until the tail-end of his time in the side that he came to be appreciated by the public at large. Indeed, Waddle was never more popular with the fans than in the period when Graham Taylor was ignoring his claims. Like any winger in the modern age, Waddle was enigmatic – blessed with immense natural talent, only occasionally did he really come close to fully realizing it with England. That was not all down to him, for as with any wide man, he was at the mercy of the service he received, and that wasn't uniformly good. Equally, because he did stay out wide, either by choice or according to instruction, if an opposing side particularly feared him, they could often cut out the supply, rendering him impotent. That said, a man of his talent should have made a greater impact and it was only once he left Spurs for Olympique de Marseille in the summer of 1989 that he began to make his mark as an international, foreign football improving his game as it had done with Kevin Keegan, Gary Lineker and Ray Wilkins.

It was richly ironic and rather sad that the most sustained spell of excellent form that Waddle was to manage in England colours came in the 1989–90 season and on into Italia '90 and culminated in his penalty miss against the West Germans. After the side returned home, he managed just three games under Graham Taylor at a time when he was the toast of Europe. The press and public call for Waddle became a little embarrassing after a while and was ultimately counter-productive, for how could England's manager be seen to bow so obviously to external pressure? It seems that there must always be some player who cannot get in the side who is the people's choice to right every known ill in a team. Of course, every player seems that much better when he isn't playing, for he can't be to blame for anything that goes wrong, but down the years we have misused or underplayed many fine footballers – Matthew Le Tissier took on Waddle's mantle through the second half of the 1990s, for example.

Another irony was that while Waddle could not get in the side, John Barnes was, injury permitting, one of the first names on Taylor's team sheet. Yet Barnes was every bit as frustrating as Waddle. As influential as any player in the Liverpool side that dominated the late 1980s, Barnes did suffer from the astonishing start he'd made in England colours with that fabulous goal in Rio.

How could anybody – Maradona or Pelé apart – follow that? What was unfortunate, unfair and extremely distasteful, was the way in which Barnes was subsequently treated as a scapegoat for every England failing, real or perceived – little wonder he often played as if intimidated by the deliberately intimidating, and often overtly racist, atmosphere that disfigured Wembley. When Barnes was selected, the question was rarely 'What will he give us?' but 'Why is he in the team and not Waddle/Gazza/the current flavour of the month?' There were many occasions when Barnes did not play at his best with England, but, as with so many other gifted footballers, he often found himself shoehorned into a side in a position he did not favour, simply to get his talent on the field. And again, the compromise often failed.

As Lineker suggests, 'Graham left out one or two flair players, he jettisoned Beardsley and Waddle, which left Gazza and Barnes, and they both suffered from injuries, so then we were totally redundant of flair and created nothing. Bobby Robson knew that at international level, even if you had to abandon a little bit of your team structure, you needed players who could do that bit extra. We couldn't do that under Graham.'

In fairness to Taylor, he had wretched luck with injuries. Worst of all, at Wembley in May 1991, Taylor's chances of making a success of the England job plummeted when Paul Gascoigne decided to play the FA Cup Final like a kamikaze pilot on speed. Within a few minutes, Gazza had been stretchered off the pitch following a tackle on Forest's Gary Charles that was so horrendous he could have been arrested for violent assault. Gascoigne has never consistently been the same player again and Taylor lost the one man who could regularly dig him out of a hole.

Gary Lineker was in the Spurs side that day, and was a colleague of Gascoigne's for a couple of years: 'I think Gazza's always had something within him that means he'll self-destruct, because every now and again he'll take it too far. In many ways he's like a schoolboy and he's not totally equipped to deal with all the attention, he's very hyped up, emotional, so you always feared for his future in that sense. It's not surprising that he's had his problems, he probably wasn't really equipped to deal with things after the World Cup, not mentally strong enough. You have to question whether he was particularly well advised, but he's a difficult bloke to advise anyway, because it tends to go in one ear and out the other, as I know all too well! It's hard to have everything, everyone has a weakness, some fallibility, and his is generally off the field. But when he was fit he was a really great player. Injuries were the sad thing. He was always going to do things that were deplorable, on one or two occasions he's completely let himself down in his personal life, but by and large the thing that perhaps caused most of those things was his self-destruction injurywise, which he's paid a massive price for. I don't think we ever saw how good he could have been.'

Had Gascoigne remained fit, then Taylor's attempt to marry the long-ball tactics with a slightly more sophisticated style might have worked. Without Gazza, he was forced to try new faces and, frankly, none fitted. England played the USSR at Wembley and flattered to deceive with a 3-1 win, which Alan Smith remembers fondly: 'Graham had different ideas, he wanted to play a bit more direct, more like we were used to in the Premiership, getting the ball forward quicker, which suited me. I'd come back to play against Turkey and enjoyed that game and then I played up front with Ian Wright against Russia, I felt sharp, I was very pleased to get my first goal; again, it was at Wembley, my family were there. In the next match against Argentina I played with Gary and it was one of my best games. I got good press for our partnership and at that moment it looked like I'd staked a claim.'

England then flew out for a thoroughly pointless trip to Australia, New Zealand and Malaysia, whose only significance was to present Gary Lineker with five more goals towards his assault on Bobby Charlton's all-time scoring record. Lineker had just one season left in English football, so to overhaul Charlton's record would need some special finishing, but there was no sign that he was slowing up, nor that the captaincy, immediately bestowed on him by Taylor, was having an adverse effect on his game: 'On the pitch, I've always thought it doesn't make a jot of difference who the captain is.

Pearce or Butcher or Adams would behave no differently whether they were captain or not. It's not like being captain in cricket, or even rugby, it's just a question of tossing the coin and wearing the armband. You're more a link man between players and manager and players and press, and you do have something of an ambassadorial role, so it's on that basis that you choose the captain.'

The 1991–92 international season opened with a narrow 1–0 defeat in Germany that was a reasonably encouraging preparation for the final two Euro '92 qualifiers. At home to Turkey, England were desperate, but as the scorer of the solitary goal, Alan Smith says at that point in the campaign 'a win is what counts. To score was a great plus for me, personally, even though we got booed off! At home, the crowd expects you to beat most teams very well and they do get disappointed quickly if you don't, which adds to the pressure.' Serious questions were now being asked of Taylor's methods, with England lacking any sense of imagination and teetering on the brink in their group. As Steve Hodge notes, 'I think with a manager who hasn't played at the top level, if things are going badly, people can always say they haven't got the respect of the players because they haven't been there and done it themselves. I used to subscribe to that theory, that players would always dig out a manager's past, but you can look at some of the coaches from abroad, like Sacchi or Wenger, who have been very successful. They couldn't do it on the pitch but they're good tacticians and psychologists and can get the best out of players, so things have moved on, you have to keep an open mind.'

England had to go out to Poland and get a point to make sure they would be off to Sweden in the summer. The inevitable nerves were compounded by a degree of confusion over tactics. According to Alan Smith; 'Graham wasn't sure about what formation to play and in the end he decided to play defensively, with Gary up front on his own, which was disappointing for me. We didn't play well in the first half, it didn't suit Gary, so I knew that I'd get on in the second half. It looked like we were out until Gary got that goal late on, so that was a good night afterwards, having qualified!' Poland took the lead after 32 minutes and thereafter England pounded away at a locked defence with all the wit of Jim Davidson. The Poles let England off the hook on a number of occasions, but England looked dead and buried until, with 13 minutes remaining, Lineker pounced: 'It was a great moment to get that goal in Poland because it looked like we weren't going to make it. It was also one of my better goals, I struck it sweetly, so that was very satisfying.' Had Lineker not hooked that shot into the roof of the net, Graham Taylor's brief tenure would surely have been over. Instead, he could look ahead to six fixtures in which he needed to find some spark of life for an ailing side.

Southampton's young Alan Shearer was given the chance to stake a claim and duly scored against France, Lineker doing likewise when he came on as a sub, though the 2–0 win is best remembered for poor Geoff Thomas's long-range shot that hit the corner flag. End of one England career. Another one started in the 2–2 draw in Czechoslovakia when Taylor tried the nearest thing he could find to Gazza, Arsenal's Paul Merson: 'To score in any game is a bonus, but to get a goal on your full debut, away in Czechoslovakia, which isn't an easy game to play in, was great. I didn't hit it too well, but a goal's a goal! That got me in the papers, for a change! You do become more noticed when you get to England level, but, to be honest, I had my head in other things then, so I took it for granted, really, didn't pay much attention.'

Taylor's desperate search for players continued, but to little avail – how he must have envied Venables and Hoddle the crop of excellent youngsters who suddenly emerged after his time. Instead he was asked to make do with Palmer, Keith Curle, Tony Daley, Andy Sinton and Paul Stewart, honest players every one, but not good enough for England. Allied to Taylor's odd reluctance to use England's more inventive talent like Clough, Merson and Ian Wright, it meant England just couldn't compete. Lineker says, 'He did like the workmanlike player and we played that way. We were hard to break down, but not creative and that showed. I didn't dislike him, he spoke a lot of sense on the game, but he was a bit schoolteacherish in his manner, he wasn't open to much discussion – we had it, but you felt like he didn't want to hear it. But you could see why he was such a good club manager: his planning, his approach, his methods were all very meticulous, he had lots of strengths. But once he got to the real top level, he did find it difficult.'

A draw against the CIS and a 1–0 win in Hungary improved morale a little, as did a 1–1 draw at home to Brazil, a game in which Gary Lineker actually missed a penalty, a failure which, in hindsight, meant he missed out on Bobby Charlton's record, ending stranded on 48 goals, one behind: 'The goal record didn't bother me, I think it became more of a fascination for the media, maybe even the manager. It didn't prey on my mind: when you're on the field you don't think about it. If I was going to be susceptible to pressure, I think it would have shown before then! With the exception of the penalty against Brazil, I don't remember missing a chance. Perhaps I was trying to be too clever, but I'd done my homework, practised it the day before, I'd seen that the keeper laid down for everything and I got a couple for Spurs like that, so I thought I'd float it in. But the Wembley grass is thick and my studs caught and I ended up fluffing it and it ended up being pathetic – that's the problem with a penalty like that, if you do miss you tend to look stupid! But then the team collapsed, we had no creativity, and that was pretty much the last opportunity I got for England. People say, "You must be gutted about not getting the record," but, to be honest, if somebody had told me in 1984 that I'd finish up one goal behind Bobby Charlton, I'd have been thrilled with it. At least now when Michael Owen starts getting goals they'll call Bobby and not me to ask if he's worried about his record! It didn't matter, it would have been nice but it would have been far better to win the World Cup or the European Championships.' A 2–1 win in Finland was the final preparation game, highlighting all that was wrong with England, the goals having to come from David Platt in midfield. Platt had proved to be an excellent replacement for Bryan Robson as a goalscoring midfielder, but England simply had to start creating opportunities for Lineker and Smith.

England went into the tournament, if not in disarray, then certainly lacking in method. Not only that, but the ravages of a long hard season were, as always, catching up with them, as Smith suggests: 'The length of our season is a disadvantage when you play tournaments in the summer. People say you shouldn't be tired when you play for England, but it doesn't work like that: if you're tired you're tired. You do your best to raise your game and get your rest, but you still have to train, still have to play, so it is difficult. Even then, it didn't look too bad a group in Sweden, with Denmark having just got in at the last minute because of the trouble in Yugoslavia. You're always optimistic going into a tournament. We had a solid team, played OK, but our downfall was we couldn't score goals.'

Denmark were the first opponents, the Danish FA having rounded up a squad from beaches around the world at short notice when UEFA dumped Yugoslavia out of the competition. Most of the Danes may have been on holiday, but they produced a polished, cohesive display that was a contrast to England's difficulties, with Curle having a nightmare, out of position at right-back in a conventional back four. Injuries scuppered Taylor's earlier plan for a sweeper system, and England looked out of sorts as a result. Getting a 0–0 draw was no disaster, but England's discomfort was alarming.

England were pitted against the French next and, as Alan Smith recalls, 'There were a lot of changes for the French game, but Taylor was picking his side according to the opposition, and that sometimes works, sometimes doesn't. Alan Shearer played instead of me against France, and it passed him by a bit. We had a couple of chances, but it ended 0–0 again.'

Taylor's penchant for varying his tactics was a marked change in his typical pattern, and one that did not serve him well. There was little time to inculcate his players with any new system and nor did he have enough players sufficiently gifted to adapt. Both sides chose to defend, gambling that they would be able to book their passage to the semi-finals in their final group games. The major thrills came courtesy of Stuart Pearce who, having been butted by France's Boli (now there's either a very brave man or a complete idiot), cracked a free-kick against the bar, but both sides were deservedly booed off the field after 90 minutes of unremitting tedium.

England were left to face host nation Sweden in the final game, needing victory to go through, while the hosts would progress with just a draw. Forced to be more attack-minded, England produced their best performance of the tournament in the early stages and were well worth their 1–0 lead at half-time, Platt having again done the honours. Paul Merson admits, 'When Platt scored, it looked like it was plain sailing, but it's difficult to play them in their own country; they had the crowd with them, it helped them come back.' In the second half, Sweden recaptured the initiative and were level within six minutes, Eriksson heading past Chris Woods. Although they now had the point they required, the Swedes continued to press and took absolute control of the game. Requiring another goal from somewhere, Taylor then produced a substitution which, for controversial overtones, rivalled Ramsey's removal of Bobby Charlton against West Germany in Mexico in 1970. You need a goal to keep you in the tournament. What do you do? You take off your greatest goalscorer, the one man likely to pinch a goal out of nothing. Taylor dragged off Gary Lineker, to the amazement of everyone, even the man who replaced him, Alan Smith: 'I was surprised that it was Gary who came off for me because we needed a goal and I thought I'd be going to partner him. It was a surprise to replace one striker with another when we needed an extra one.' No Lineker, no hope, though there'd been precious little left even with him. To add insult to injury the pre-Mr Blobby Tomas Brolin put Sweden 2–1 ahead with eight minutes to go, and England were out.

Not only were they out, the career of Gary Lineker was at an end: 'It wasn't until after the Sweden game when the press started asking me about the substitution that I thought about the relevance of it; it hadn't struck me at the time. I was choked about being taken off because we needed a goal and, like always, I fancied my chances. Probably I could have stayed on three years and not scored, but as a striker you always think you'll get the goal to get us through. I didn't sit down and think, "That's my last match," I was shouting for the team to get a goal, nothing else crossed my mind until afterwards. I didn't realize it was over until it was pointed out to me in the press conference! That's how you are in a match, you're so totally focused on it, nothing else comes in. Ultimately, it probably didn't do me any harm, because we were never going to score at that stage and, in many ways, if I'd stayed on and we'd lost I'd have been vilified with everybody else. Instead it almost made a martyr out of me, not that I'd have wanted it that way, but that's how it turned out. Graham got all the stick, and I'm sure he only made the substitution because he thought it was the best way of getting a goal, not to get at me in my last match. But it did him a lot more damage than it did me. I've no malice towards him, we get on perfectly well. Things get blown up because of a decision that probably wouldn't have made any difference – the way that team was playing I don't think I'd have scored in a month of Sundays! It was a disappointing way to go, just as Bobby Charlton had, but maybe that was our fault, for hanging on too long. Leaving the game is a matter of good timing and few of us have the power to get it exactly right.'

Reflecting on one of the all-time great England careers, Lineker has this to say: 'With England, you love playing for your country, but all you really want is for it to be over and to know that you've done well. It's great when you're scoring and that's the thing I miss, the buzz, the ecstatic feeling of scoring a goal, but there is so much else around it. It can ruin your life, playing for England, at least for a while. Look at Beckham after the World Cup, look at the managers. There's such a fine line between getting the ultimate accolades and the ultimate rejection. I didn't think about it while I was playing, luckily, because I think if you did, if you thought how important it was to so many people that England perform well, you'd be too terrified to put your boots on. But it is still the biggest thrill to pull on the white shirt and walk out with the team. I don't miss the playing but the one thing that is irreplaceable is the feeling of scoring or winning a big game.'

Euro '92 was a terrible tournament for England and, in hindsight, the beginning of the end for Taylor. As Paul Merson says, 'The

whole Championships were disappointing because we should have
done a lot better. We should have beaten Denmark, we drew with
France when we could have done more. To be fair, the European
Championships then were nothing compared with what they are
now. It was only all the fuss with Euro '96 and it being held in
England that we started to care about it as much as the World Cup.
But, of course, we wanted to win it and it would have been a big
thing if we'd managed it. That would have made it an important
tournament then! To be out so early was awful.'

As a result England came back to some of the most abusive
headlines ever heaped on a football team. Worst of all was the
treatment dished out to Taylor, led by the infamous SWEDES 2
TURNIPS 1 headline, Taylor's face superimposed on a turnip.
Whether Graham Taylor was the right man for the job, whether
he was good enough or not, the abuse he received was an utter
disgrace – Myra Hindley got a better deal than Taylor did. Sadly,
it wasn't going to get any better as England turned their attention
towards USA '94 and a qualification group comprising Holland,
Norway, the inevitable Poland, Turkey and San Marino, with two
to go through. The Dutch would provide stiff competition, but
there was little else for England to fear, was there?

Encouragingly, there were a few more promising players beginning to show themselves, men such as Shearer, Wright, Les Ferdinand, Paul Ince. And, of course, Gazza was back. His first game
was against Norway and showed both sides of his character –
brilliant playmaking, marred by an outburst of petulance when he
elbowed Nilsen. England thoroughly dominated and deservedly
led through another Platt goal after 55 minutes. Norway were
among the dullest opponents ever to come to Wembley, funnelling
back into defence and using the massed ranks to frustrate England's
constant attacking threat. Once ahead, it seemed England had
pocketed both points, for Norway had apparently no attacking
ideas to contribute. Then, from nowhere, Kjetil Rekdal thrashed
in a shot from 25 yards that on any other night would have sailed
yards over the bar.

Such cosmic misfortune set the tone for the rest of Taylor's reign, though David Platt also points to poor English finishing as a key factor: 'We destroyed Norway, but if you only get one goal in an international, things can quickly turn against you because you are playing against people who can score goals. In the Premiership you can win games 1–0 because you can limit the opposition to a few chances and you know that chances aren't taken so readily. In internationals, the slightest mistake costs you. Against Norway, it wasn't even a mistake, it bounced on the edge of the box, great technique from their player, and he scored from 25 yards.'

Turkey were brushed aside 4–0 at Wembley, Gascoigne revelling in the space left by poor opposition, scoring twice and helping to create another for Shearer. He could well have missed the game with a heavy cold. (He was told to wrap up warm and turned up at training wearing fourteen shirts. Rumours that he was congratulated on his new slim-line figure were quickly discounted.) The next sacrificial lambs were San Marino, slaughtered 6–0 in a game that was especially significant for David Platt, made England captain for the first time: 'Of all the things I've achieved in the game, if I could only keep one of them, it would be captaining England; it's the pinnacle. I've still got my kit from that first game, unwashed, with the armband on, in a frame at home, to keep the memory of it as it was. You get the job by the way you conduct yourself on and off the field around the international scene. People saw I was a bit of a leader and that I did the things you'd expect an England captain to do. I didn't want to do anything different because I'd been given the job because of what I'd been doing before then. There's a lot more media involvement – whatever happens in the world, be it football or current affairs, the England captain is supposed to have a quote for it!'

Platt celebrated by scoring four goals, Palmer scored too, as did debutant Les Ferdinand: 'It was an extraordinary year for me because things took off at QPR so quickly, people started talking about me getting a cap at some time, and then there were a few injuries, Lineker had retired, so fortunately for me I got a chance very quickly. It was nice to get into the squad for the game against

Turkey because I'd played over there and there were four or five players from Besiktas in their squad, so it was good to see them again. Graham had already done his homework, so he didn't need to ask me for any advice! Then there was a lot of speculation about me before the San Marino game; I'd been in good form and the manager told me early on that I'd be in the team. It can work either way, you either get dead nervous or you use the four days to get over that! You want the team to win, it's the same principles as at club level. You get together a week before, they work on how they want the team to play, but obviously you want to give your best. Especially early on, although everyone knows how you play, you're not properly integrated into the team, so you are a bit more concerned about your own performance. It was a big relief to get my first goal against San Marino, but not as much as it should have been, because they'd just been blitzed by Norway 11–0, so we were expected to beat them 21–0. For long periods they just sat behind the ball, threw themselves at everything and although we won 6–0, people still weren't satisfied.' Nor were they when England won in Turkey 2–0, the old firm of Platt and Gascoigne doing the damage.

After four games, England had dropped just one point. Next came one of the key games of the campaign, against Holland at Wembley. It produced one of the finest displays England gave under Taylor, certainly in the first half, until Gascoigne was smacked in the face by Wim Wouters and had to go off with a damaged cheekbone. England had cruised into a 2–0 lead after just 24 minutes. John Barnes clipped in a beautiful free-kick from the edge of the box after 2 minutes, a fitting response to the Wembley boo-boys who were bent on making his life a misery. Platt made it two, knocking home the rebound after Ferdinand had hit the post. But it wasn't simply the size of England's lead that was so pleasing, it was the manner in which they achieved it. They played with style and swagger, total confidence and a remarkable quality – much of the football they produced in that first half was easily the equal of the more famous encounter with the Dutch in Euro '96.

Against the run of play, Dennis Bergkamp pulled a goal back

with an exquisite piece of finishing from a long ball fired over his shoulder, but England refused to panic and kept playing their football. Even when Gazza left the field in the second half, England still held the upper hand and looked set to take a vital win, even reducing the Dutch to pulling off the mighty Ruud Gullit, an impotent figure all evening. One of the most famous terrace chants in England was 'You'll never beat Des Walker', a favourite of Forest fans and testimony to his terrific pace. But this was before we'd seen Marc Overmars, who surged past him with 4 minutes to go. Walker, a shadow of his former self in the middle of a miserable spell in Serie A, could only flail at him, grabbing his shirt. Overmars ran on and on, reached the penalty area and finally succumbed to Des's advances. Van Vossen cracked the penalty past Woods and England had had another crucial point stolen from them. Then it got really serious.

Whoever it was who was responsible for the fixture negotiations and for allowing England to play two away qualifiers in the summer in Poland and Norway should have been sacked on the spot. England's record during the summer months is generally disastrous, so to play two big games then was just asking for trouble, as was allowing a documentary crew to follow the team around. The first, in Poland, went according to type. The Poles could have had the game sewn up by half-time, but instead led by a single goal, scored after another error by Walker. England offered nothing in return, but were saved by a late piece of instinctive finishing by substitute Ian Wright. Taylor later attacked his players for performing like 'headless chickens', an accusation backed up by Tony Adams in his autobiography: '[before the game] Carlton Palmer was going over the top in his attempts to motivate the team. Whereas Terry Butcher had concentrated us, keeping his distance from the Yugoslavs but instilling fear in them in 1987, now Carlton was going up to the Poles and shouting insults in their faces.' Adams' implication is clear enough – Palmer knew he was not international class and mistook being hyped up to the point of hysteria for being focused, otherwise known as 'Vinnie Jones Syndrome'.

A draw in Katowice was again good enough, providing England

could beat the Poles at home. Having only drawn with Norway at Wembley, a draw was the barest minimum they could accept in Oslo. Although England had managed some decent performances by maintaining a degree of continuity in style and selection since Euro '92, Taylor now chose to shuffle his tactics, with the same disastrous consequences he'd suffered in Sweden the summer before. As captain, David Platt was sometimes used as a sounding board by the manager, but shifting emphasis was fraught with danger: 'Going to Italy in 1991 certainly helped my game; it meant I was playing a style of football that was very similar to the way you play at international level, so I was practising it week in, week out. I could sit down and talk with Graham when we got together for England games because my horizons had widened tactically, and he was very open to that. Graham's problem was that any tactical change he might want to try ... he didn't have the games to experiment in, simply because virtually all the games were relevant, all in qualification groups, and you can't experiment in those.'

Now playing Gary Pallister out wide on the left of a three-man defence, employing Lee Sharpe, Lee Dixon, Palmer and Platt in the middle, with Gascoigne just behind Teddy Sheringham and Ferdinand, completely changing the composition of the team, Ian Wright was left to remark, 'Tactically, Taylor muffed everything up. It was a shambles, a débâcle, and we just didn't know what we were doing, which just about sums him up as far as I'm concerned.'

Even then, had they kept their discipline and not made some elementary mistakes, they might have avoided the disastrous 2–0 defeat. Just before the break, Walker committed a foul and, instead of getting into position, stopped to argue with the ref, allowing the Norwegians to take a quick free-kick, Oyvind Leonhardsen scoring from it. Three minutes into the second half, the game was sealed when the unmarked Lars Bohinen drilled home a shot. England had been utterly embarrassed, not just tactically, but technically too. Nor had they shown the heart to dig themselves out of trouble, a sure sign that Taylor had lost the respect of some players. Les Ferdinand was not among them, but he was concerned

by the changing tack: 'Graham didn't exactly go against his principles, but he put out a team that was worried about them, rather
than putting out a team to make them worry about us. I think by
doing that he gave them the initiative, not just by giving them
confidence, but by making us think that we were playing a more
defensive role, and that wasn't the right thing for us to do at the
time. Then, after a result like that, the last thing you want is to go
off for another tournament in America. A few lads got caught in
a nightclub a bit worse for wear, but it was hard to stay focused on
that tournament because we had nothing to gain from it, everything
to lose.'

Paul Merson, on the other hand, loved it: 'A great trip, unbelievable, like an 18–30 holiday! It was very weird for an England trip,
we got beat by America, the football went a bit pear shaped after
that, but it was a good atmosphere, got a good team spirit! If you
asked any of the lads where they wanted to go to play football on
an end of season trip, they'd say America. So it was worth it in
that respect.'

Although a piece of footballing history was made against the
USA when Paul Ince became England's first black captain, a 2–0
defeat was the last thing Taylor needed, and it had football's funeral
directors taking his measurements. As Ferdinand says, 'It was just
a period where things wouldn't go right. We should have beaten
Norway and Holland at home, we went out to the States and got
beaten, some of the lads got caught out having a drink, there was
a lot of bad publicity, the press were having a go at the manager. It
does seep into the performances, you're determined to do well,
but maybe you get too keyed up. If you slate a player or a manager
for how they've performed, that's fair enough. But with Graham
the criticism was personal, it wasn't about football, and that's very
disappointing.'

Ivor Broadis, an England player in the 1954 World Cup and
later a respected journalist, believes that 'TV and the media have
changed everything. The standard of writing has changed, it's
become as if it's the writer's team now, they feel part of it, it's
more partisan and opinionated, and they don't give people a fair

crack. I was in journalism long enough to know the bottom line is how many papers you sell, but I think it goes too far.'

In spite of the American defeat, Taylor was at least able to introduce some players to the rigours of international football, including Tim Flowers, who played in the next game, against Brazil: 'I played at Under-17 and Under-21 for England; it's good grounding, helps you realize a bit of what it's all about. Graham Taylor called me up for the senior squad in summer 1993. We came home from Norway and flew straight out to America and lost to the USA in the first game. By then the press hounding had reached the extent where it was starting to affect him, he was feeling bad, and it all went beyond football; it got very personal. He gave me my debut in Washington in the next game. I'd thought I was out there as kit boy, really, to look and learn, because we had Chris Woods and Nigel Martyn out there. When he named the team for the Brazil game and I was in it, you could have knocked me down with a feather! To have gone from never being in the squad to playing Brazil in front of 70 or 80,000 people . . . the night before I was lying in bed thinking, "What am I in for here? Christ, I'm gonna be a busy man!" It was being chucked in the deep end, though I'd had that throughout my career – I was in the reserves at 14 when I was at Wolves. I suppose I couldn't lose: if I'd had a nightmare, people would have said I was only a kid with plenty of time and they'd have had another go at the manager, and if I played well, then people take notice of you for the future. Fortunately, it went well. After the stinging criticism we got after Norway and the USA, the lads responded well, we dug in, made a scrap of it and were one up for a long while until they equalized late on. I couldn't walk for two days afterwards though, just through the sheer concentration, the 90-degree humidity, the tension.' The tour was wrapped up with a 2–1 defeat at the hands of Germany, but some vestige of pride had been restored.

That was not enough to prolong Chris Woods' career as England keeper, however. For a number of years he'd been the understudy to Peter Shilton, and as Peter Bonetti would agree, playing reserve to the best goalkeeper in the world is a thankless task, especially when you do get pitched in at the deep end. After six years as a travelling reserve, Woods had finally got the number one job after the World Cup in 1990, and had the misfortune to find himself in an English team where the other main bulwark of the defence – Terry Butcher – had also gone. That uncertainty didn't help Woods to settle in, nor did the inevitable comparisons with his predecessor. Even so, he made a decent fist of the task and for three years was as unchallenged as Shilton had been. That summer tour in 1993 was an unhappy one for him personally as well as for the team, and he was left to carry the can. The defeat against the USA was Woods' final game for England, for by the time the 1993–94 season started, David Seaman was ensconced as England's first choice.

With three games to go, England needed three straight wins. The first objective was accomplished easily enough, Poland dismissed 3–0 at Wembley, Gascoigne sparkling, Ferdinand scoring an excellent goal early on, and England generally scaling similar heights to those reached against Norway and Holland. And it was Holland who offered the ultimate test in the next game in Rotterdam. In all likelihood, a draw would be enough to see England through, barring a disaster in San Marino. A victory would send them to the USA with no further worries. Once more, Taylor was beset by misfortune, with the suspended Gascoigne and the injured Pearce both missing. As was Les Ferdinand: 'I felt I was doing well, played against Poland at home and was man of the match, but then I suffered an injury and was out for two or three weeks. For England, they wanted me to have an epidural in my back, but Gerry Francis, the QPR manager, called them and said, "No way," because Gerry had had a lot of back problems as a player and he said there was no way he'd let them do that. And Graham Taylor said for that Dutch game, he wanted eleven fit players on the pitch, he couldn't afford to have anyone 75 per cent fit, so it was his decision.'

As had been the case so often in this series, England played well, weathering an early Dutch storm, gradually clawing their way to parity, before enjoying a huge slice of good fortune when a Frank Rijkaard goal was wrongly disallowed for offside. Had Taylor's luck changed for the better at precisely the right time? No. On the hour, Andy Sinton, on for Palmer, played a clever ball past Ronald Koeman for David Platt to run on to. Platt was through on goal when Koeman cynically chopped him down. The referee had two decisions to make. The first was right – it was a free-kick right on the edge of the box, not the longed for penalty. The second decision was so obvious, it barely classed as a decision. But he got it utterly wrong. Koeman was shown the yellow card when the laws of the game made it crystal clear that he should have been sent off. England squandered the free-kick and the Dutch immediately attacked, winning a free-kick of their own in a similar position. Koeman, who should have been running the bath, stepped up to take it and curled a beautifully placed shot over the wall and into the net. Four minutes later, a strong Merson shot thudded against the inside of a post and came out. A further three minutes on Dennis Bergkamp appeared to use a hand to control the ball, then clipped a shot past Seaman. Within ten minutes, a perfect microcosm of England's 1994 World Cup campaign had been played out before a huge TV audience.

As Platt says, 'In that whole qualifying campaign, you pick holes here and there – we shouldn't have gone abroad to play two games in four days at the end of the season in Poland and Norway, very difficult games. Graham and the team were victims of bad scheduling. And if the referee had made the right decision in Rotterdam that night, that game could have gone a totally different way, and had we beaten Holland we'd have qualified. Or when we were 2–0 up against them at Wembley, we shouldn't have allowed them back into the game – had Paul Gascoigne not been injured and had we held on, they were out. In any qualifying campaign there are a lot of ifs and buts.'

England went to San Marino where the bad luck continued – within 8 seconds, San Marino had scored the fastest goal in the history of international football after Pearce had miskicked a back pass to Seaman. England had needed to win by seven clear goals to have any hope of progressing, and they fought back manfully to win 7–1, Ian Wright getting four. In the end they could have won

17–1 and it wouldn't have helped. Holland won 3–1 in Poland and secured second place behind Norway. Taylor's time was up and, preserving the few shreds of dignity the press had permitted him to keep, he resigned.

Taylor's reputation was not helped by the now legendary TV documentary *The Impossible Job*, which had followed him over the latter stages of the World Cup campaign. Edited to exact the greatest embarrassment and shed the least light, it portrayed Taylor as an incompetent, unable to inspire his team. After the screening some critics implied that in allowing them to film him, Taylor had betrayed his team, though Les Ferdinand refutes that: 'For long periods, we were oblivious to the camera crew – they were off in the distance filming and it was only Graham Taylor that was miked up, so it didn't affect us.' The film is best known for Taylor's admittedly bizarre sentence construction and for bequeathing a new catchphrase to the nation: 'Do I not like that.'

Equally, the spectacle of Taylor trying to cram largely unintelligible tactical advice into Nigel Clough's head as the Forest man – who should have been on from the start anyway – was waiting to replace Des Walker in Norway lingered long in the collective memory and did Taylor no good when he finally relinquished control of the national team. Ian Wright dismissed Taylor's tactics on that occasion as 'gibberish'.

But Taylor was worthy of more than such vicious caricature. He was an honest man who, perhaps, wasn't quite up to the job. But he was not the disaster area the press painted him as. He was dogged by bad luck, inherited a team that was not as good as its semi-final placing in Italia '90 implied, one which was saying goodbye to some of its leading lights, leaving him to preside over a domestic game that was, albeit temporarily, failing to produce players of real class.

Paul Merson says, 'I liked Graham, he gave me my chance and I thought he was a good manager. He had everything sorted out when we met up for games, he kept training interesting, he had things for the lads to do. He made a couple of rickets, but he always gave people their chance, and it was the players who let him down.'

Tim Flowers is also honest enough to accept that players often don't bear as much responsibility as they should: 'The manager picks the team but the players have to do the job. I've got a lot of time for Graham, I learned a lot from him. He was a very nice man, tremendously knowledgeable about the game, but he also understood the stress side too. He was good at helping you relax, he could keep the squad entertained and happy over prolonged periods and I thoroughly enjoyed working for him.' The final defence comes from Taylor's captain, David Platt: 'Graham was unfortunate; we qualified for the European Championships in 1992 but we didn't do well there and then for one reason and another didn't qualify for the World Cup in 1994, which made his position untenable. But if you look at his record in terms of games and wins, it wasn't too bad.'

Finally, it wasn't simply the results that cost Taylor his job. It was the humiliation that had been heaped upon him by an unforgiving press who wouldn't let go of a good story, even if it flew in the face of the facts, the same humiliations that put him and his players under intolerable pressure, thereby ensuring that results continued to be poor. Taylor's face didn't fit, so let's have a new one. It was official. The newspapers hired and fired England's manager. The job description was simple. He not only had to win every game, he also had to be a wisecracking comedian, a game show host, a karaoke expert and a man who could enjoy a drink or two with his pals in the media, preferably at his own west London club. Who could it be?

15

Great Opportunity Blinks

England's stock on the world stage hadn't been so low in twenty years when Graham Taylor finally fell on his sword. In recruiting a new manager, the theme was modernization, much as it was in the Labour Party. So the FA were persuaded to create New England, and the man to fashion it was Terry Venables. Venables had played at the highest level, albeit briefly, and had then experienced Continental coaching with Barcelona and domestic managerial success with Crystal Palace, QPR and latterly Tottenham. Just as important, following his dispute with Alan Sugar, Venables was available and, with his powerbase firmly established in London, the media were keen to advance his case. Almost as soon as Taylor had finished clearing his desk, Venables had moved in, to general acclaim. Gary Lineker reckons, 'Terry was the best coach I worked with, his man management was excellent. The difference between him and the other English coaches I'd worked with was he wouldn't just say this is how the team will play. He'd get someone like me who knew pretty much all there was to know about playing up front by the time I worked with him, and he'd say, "Have you ever thought of trying this run or that run?" Some didn't work, but now and again, he'd come up with something you hadn't considered and he gave that individual input right throughout the side.'

Venables clearly wanted to put his stamp on the team as quickly as possible. The introduction of Darren Anderton and Graeme Le Saux and the return of Rob Jones suggested Venables wanted players with good basic technique who were also tactically fluent and adaptable – thoroughly modern footballers in other words. Within a matter of games – a 1–0 win over Denmark, a 5–0 beating of Greece and a goalless draw with USA-bound Norway – Venables had, according to media folklore, reinvented England and shown that were El Tel leading us across the Atlantic, he would almost certainly be returning with the World Cup in his excess luggage. Palpable nonsense, of course, but such was the breath of fresh air that Venables brought to the job. After what journalist Ken Jones described as 'tutorials rather than press conferences' in the Taylor era, Venables had simple question and answer sessions, feeding perfectly crafted soundbites to an increasingly lazy media. Terry gave them the story up front, removing any need to think them through. The national obsession with the 'Christmas Tree' formation was a case in point. England barely played the system, yet because Venables had offered the press such a neat little catch-phrase at the start of his reign, much of the media decided that was the only way England played. Naturally, not every journalist was onside, with the *Mail On Sunday*'s Patrick Collins a regular and incisive critic of Venables as man and manager. But the players looked relaxed with the appointment. David Platt retained the captaincy and felt that 'within a couple of squads, I think everyone realized that Terry had a very good tactical mind. Working in Barcelona had helped him in the same way that playing in Italy had helped me, and he had lots of ideas. In the two years we evolved a way of playing that proved successful at that level.'

One of the great advantages which Venables enjoyed was the fact that for more than two years in the job, he didn't have to play a single competitive game. England were the hosts for Euro '96, and so automatically qualified. That gave him the opportunity to experiment with his side and, not only that, gave him the freedom to lose games and excuse the result by telling everyone that he had learned things that would be to England's advantage; a perfectly reasonable rationale, but one denied to all his predecessors but Ramsey. David Platt agrees that that period was extremely helpful to the cause: 'You can be a lot bolder when the result isn't the be all and end all because you can come in the dressing room and say, "OK, it didn't work, we'll discard that, but we haven't lost any points." It wasn't just that the competition was in England in 1996 that helped us do well, it was that solid preparation period of two years going into it.'

As Platt implies, where Venables scored was in having the wit to use that freedom to its maximum, switching personnel and tactics with great regularity. Enjoying a full week with the squad before most games, he was able to work on the shape and set-up of the team very effectively and it began to pay dividends. He was definitely helped by the fact that in those two years, England played eighteen internationals, only two of which were away from home – the abandoned game in Dublin and another 0–0 draw in Norway – another game in Germany being cancelled after some genius scheduled it to take place on the anniversary of Hitler's birthday. Understandable, I suppose – who could possibly have predicted that the Fascist element in England's travelling support would want to mark that baleful day? While such a concentration of home fixtures may not have given a totally clear picture of England's abilities, Tim Flowers felt it made sense: 'That's where theimportant games would be in Euro '96. Friendlies are really competitive, but it's never quite the same as games that have points riding on them, so at least we were playing them in the right environment.'

When any new coach comes in, there will be casualties among the players. Les Ferdinand was one who did not benefit from Venables' elevation to the role: 'I was in Terry Venables' first few squads, then I was in and out a bit after that. I'd gone to Newcastle then, I was scoring goals on a regular basis, and I was still left out. The papers were full of it and eventually I got back in, but there was no explanation for any of it.' Ferdinand's surprising absence was commented on by some critics, who pointed to a sudden change in the ethnic balance of the squad. Ferdinand is similarly concerned: 'I don't know if there's a problem in the media, maybe even in the higher echelons of the FA, because only under Graham Taylor was there an abundance of black players getting through to the England side. All of a sudden Terry Venables came in and it was changed straight away, Paul Ince was left out for a long period, I was out, Ian Wright dropped out immediately, Andy Cole couldn't get in, there was a long spell when there were hardly any black players in the squad.' Given the understanding that Alan Shearer received during his lengthy goal drought – a sharp contrast to the vitriol heaped on Ian Wright if he didn't score in every game – Ferdinand has a point. He adds, 'I never really felt a part of things under Terry Venables, always felt I was on the fringes. I always felt I was trying to prove something. It was Terry who felt that me and Alan Shearer couldn't play together, that Alan and Teddy Sheringham would be his first choice, and that was it.' A word to those who see Venables as the great infallible guru – check how many goals Ferdinand and Shearer rattled in in their only season together for Newcastle and then decide whether they could play together or not.

Venables was introducing some exciting new talent though – Steve McManaman, Matt Le Tissier, Stan Collymore, Nick Barmby, Teddy Sheringham (OK, they weren't all exciting). Results weren't fantastic, but good enough, and the performances suggested that the coach knew where he was heading. Having beaten the USA 2–0, Nigeria 1–0 and drawn 1–1 with Romania, Venables faced his first away game in February 1995, though even that only involved the short hop to Dublin. England were out of sorts and went a goal down before the heavy preponderance of morons within the English support began to tear up the seating and hurl it on to the pitch. Rather than a simple, stupid response to Ireland's goal, this was a prearranged attack instigated by the far-right group Combat 18, who saw a game in Dublin as a chance to mount a demonstration against the IRA and anybody else who didn't agree with them. What rigorous intellectualism – one Fascist group attacking the existence of a terrorist organization and then backing up their 'thinking' with violence. Do I see a flaw in the internal logic of that argument somewhere? Once more, England's reputation was in shreds, thanks to people who wouldn't know the right way to sit on a toilet but who believed they were protecting the nation and its flag by turning it into a pariah. As David Platt says, 'We represent the England football team. Who the people think they're representing when they do what they did in Dublin, I don't know; you certainly can't equate it to football.' As a regular target for such odious displays, Les Ferdinand finds them yet more repugnant: 'The idiots in the crowd do make it hard. You're out there to play for your country, the country that has chosen you to play for them; yet you get people who don't want you there because of your colour and it does make it extremely difficult.'

England played out a 0–0 draw with Uruguay, and were then set for the summer tournament that would act as a nice taster for Euro '96, the Umbro Cup. Japan, Sweden and Brazil had been invited to take part in an attractive competition, giving England its first even vaguely competitive football since the game in Rotterdam almost two years before. For Venables it was an opportunity to see if things were progressing as quickly as he'd like, while for the players it was the chance to stake a claim for the following year, particularly as a number of established stars were missing through injury, though one was simply omitted. Les Ferdinand was not enamoured with the way he found out he wasn't going to be playing: 'The first I heard I'd been left out was when I was in Barbados with QPR on an end-of-season trip. Villa were there and Doug Ellis came over and said, 'Sorry to hear the news.' I asked him what news and he told me I'd been left out of the squad!'

But for Tim Flowers, who had long been understudy to David Seaman, the news was better: 'It is difficult to be in the squad as a goalkeeper because you can only play in one position. So once Terry picked David Seaman as his number one, you know that even when you get a chance and do well, unless Dave drops a clanger three or four times in a row, you're not going to replace him. All you can do is take your opportunities when they come, to keep yourself in the coach's mind, because there's always the possibility of injury and you want to be next in line. But it's such a privilege to play for England, you'd wait for ever.

'I got three games pretty quickly under Terry when Dave got injured, against Greece, Nigeria and Uruguay, and I didn't let a goal in. Then I played the three Umbro Cup games and did well against Japan, when we won 2–1. After that I played in the game against Sweden at Elland Road and I had a bad game, I played poorly and then we were beaten by a very good Brazilian side at Wembley. But, personally, that Sweden game cost me dearly, which was perhaps a bit harsh because I'd done well in the games up to then, but that was the one that got remembered. I'd got on a little run there and I actually thought that if I'd had a good Umbro Cup, I felt I had a real chance of maybe cementing a place. I'll always think back to that Sweden game. But you have to accept that. I've had one bad game in eleven for England and that's a pretty decent average. And we did have a pretty experimental back four at the time because of various withdrawals from the squad – Le Saux, Barton, Pallister and Cooper – who'd never played together, so that makes things that bit harder. I learn a lot through it, I think it improved me, but I still wish it hadn't happened, because I was knocking on the door! Then I had to wait a year until we went out to China before I got a game, played 70 minutes and had one save to make.'

The Umbro Cup was a decidedly mixed bag for England. They finally struggled past Japan, 2–1, in a game that could easily have been drawn or even lost. Against Sweden there were defensive lapses by Flowers and the back four and England were 3–1 down going into the last few minutes. A dramatic fightback that grabbed a draw and the headlines hid a multitude of sins, but it was certainly not the performance England craved. That game was played at Leeds' Elland Road, the first time England had played a home fixture away from Wembley since 1966. Although the public seemed delighted with the idea of the national team taking to the road, the players were rather more circumspect. David Platt argues, 'We benefit by playing at Wembley. If you get your pricing right, the timing of the game right, you can fill Wembley and create a great atmosphere; you couldn't have wished for anything better than Euro '96. If you play at Elland Road or Old Trafford, the Manchester United players are happy because they're comfortable with the surroundings, but it's like an away game for the rest. If you play at Wembley, it's a home game for all of us. To have a home ground as an international player, it's beneficial, you get familiar with the surroundings. The Italians swap around the grounds, but to me, you're still playing away from home.'

Returning to the spiritual home of Wembley for the final fixture, with Brazil, England scored the goal of the game through Graeme Le Saux, but it was Brazil who ran the match, winning 3–1 to collect another trophy. The Umbro Cup proved that England still had a way to go to catch up with the best in the world, but a willing populace was able to accept that with a further twelve months to go before the matches that really mattered, Venables would get it right. If all England managers had been given a similar benefit of the doubt down the years, perhaps the national side would have fared rather better.

The tolerance shown to Venables was all the more remarkable given the torrid nature of his business dealings. He was forced to announce his decision to step down from the job after Euro '96 well ahead of the event, because he would have to spend too much time in the law courts fighting assorted libel cases. He felt that would distract him from his England duties and handed in his resignation. Perhaps he was surprised when the FA accepted it with such alacrity, but there were those at Lancaster Gate who were becoming a little twitchy about Venables, and the controversy that seemed to perpetually surround his financial dealings. Would he eventually let the side down? Would he be the first England coach to be selecting his squad at Her Majesty's Pleasure?

On the field, England weren't tremendously convincing either. Defensively they were sound – in the eight games prior to the competition, they let in just two goals. Gary Neville had stepped into the side as though he'd played for England for years, Pearce had returned to add stability, Gareth Southgate and Tony Adams made a good central pairing, combining strength, bloody-mindedness, an ability to read the game and useful covering pace between them. With Ince sitting in front as a further buffer, the defensive shape wasn't unlike that of 1966. The midfield offered plenty of creative options, with Platt when fit, Gascoigne, Steve

McManaman, Anderton and Jamie Redknapp all offering invention, or Steve Stone, a more direct, incisive option out wide. Although England might create opportunities, what began to worry the wider public was: who would score them? Alan Shearer was often left to plough a lone furrow up front, with Sheringham playing a bit deeper, and the common consensus was that that did not suit Shearer, the pundits pointing to his prolific partnership with Chris Sutton at Blackburn as the ideal way to get the best out of him. As a suggestion it had its merits – Shearer went eleven games without a goal as England headed into Euro '96. But Venables kept faith with his striker and made it very clear that he would start as the number one choice.

Prior to getting down to the tournament, England had played well against Hungary to win 3–0 and then set off for a tour of the Far East. Although Venables received some flak for taking the squad halfway round the world so close to such a massive event, the idea was basically sound. The coach felt that it would do the squad good to get away from the razzmatazz and the intensive press scrutiny that would be raging in England – theoretically, a good plan. The opposition was nothing special and England ambled to a comprehensive 3–0 win over China.

While in China, the party took the chance to do a rare bit of sightseeing. According to Tim Flowers: 'The day before the game, we had the chance to see the Great Wall. We went along without the gaffer, and we ended up walking five or six miles along the Wall, all uphill; it was red hot, we were sweating cobs. He'd have hit the roof if he'd found out! Fortunately we played well, because China were a lively team and it was the noisiest crowd I've ever played in front of. I've been lucky. I've played in Europe, in America, in Asia and in Africa for England, so I've done quite well. If they could arrange a game in the Antarctic or on the moon, I'll be there!'

Next, as Flowers recalls, 'We played an exhibition game against a Hong Kong Select XI, which was a non-starter for the lads; you can't really get up for a game like that, you're just flying the flag. The Hong Kong officials organized a meal on a boat in the harbour, one of these ten-course jobs, which took ages. After about five courses a few of the lads must have got bored and they disappeared, then the manager said we could all go out for a drink because we were flying back the next day.'

In the course of that evening and early morning, some of England's players, most notably, and inevitably, Paul Gascoigne, were pictured drinking heavily at the China Jump club. They were clearly enjoying the local attraction, the dentist's chair, where one of the party sat back in a reclining chair and had copious quantities of alcohol poured down his throat. Maybe it wasn't the most edifying spectacle in the world, but nor was it such a production number either. As Flowers says, 'I don't know if some people think the lads can never have a drink, but I cannot believe the way it was reported. Yes, we accept we're representing our country and there's a responsibility that goes with it, but all that happened was the lads had a few drinks.' Les Ferdinand adds, 'The whole Hong Kong thing was disappointing. Yes, we went out and perhaps we didn't behave in a manner you'd expect. But we're normal guys, most of us from working-class backgrounds; we've been brought up a certain way, sometimes we make mistakes, like everybody else. It's disappointing, because everybody there was having a good time. It was no big thing, but somebody there decided to sell a story and there's not a lot you can about that.'

The dentist's chair escapade was simply an irrelevance. No damage was done, maybe a few of the players got drunk, but then the following day they were going to be stuck on a long-haul flight anyway, ample opportunity to sleep any excess off. What was the harm? And if the newspapers were genuinely concerned that the players were ruining the nation's reputation abroad, they could have let the story lie. It's also worth noting that for all the supposed hellraising that went on, nobody broke the 2 a.m. curfew.

Rather more serious were the incidents reported on the flight back, when there was a celebration of Gascoigne's birthday. According to Alan Shearer's autobiography, 'Things got a bit out of hand and a couple of television sets were broken. There was no excuse for that sort of vandalism but immediately the whole squad held their hands up and took the blame.' The party had a whip-round to pay for the damage done, but in this case that wasn't the issue. Where the China Jump club had been a harmless booze-up, this was less defensible. The cost of a couple of TV sets to highly paid England internationals was little more than small change. But paying up didn't make what they'd done right – how is it different to the recurring story of a bunch of rich kids going into a restaurant, making everyone's life a misery, wrecking tables then leaving a huge wad of cash behind to cover the cost? Whisper it now, but money doesn't solve everything, can't always buy you out of your responsibilities.

Tim Flowers accepts that criticism, but adds, 'A lot of people say today's players are only interested in the money. But, honestly, money doesn't come into it. We realize how lucky we are, but you don't go out on the field thinking, "If we win today, we'll get an extra £100." You want to win the match because you're a foot-baller, because football is your life, and you know how bad it is to lose.' In mitigation, he also questions just how rowdy things actually got on the plane: 'I know it sounds as if I'm ducking it, but I didn't see or hear anything on the plane. I started off playing cards and then, bang, I was asleep! I didn't wake up until Heathrow. So I missed all that! The bottom line is that out of all that criticism we got, we got a tremendous spirit, a cast-iron spirit, like a siege mentality. Footballers are a bit like that anyway, if they get any stick from outside they tend to say, "Bollocks to you, we'll stick together in our trench and duck you." Which is what we did; it became a real them and us situation. We got a lot of spirit out of that, so in hindsight it was good it happened.'

Inevitably, when a squad has to be named for a major com-petition, there are those players who will be disappointed. Ian Wright missed out and wrote later, 'It felt like something had died inside of me. I thought I would never get that special buzz ever again. When you find out you're in the squad, no matter how many you've been in, that buzz just grabs you.' Even among the chosen there was upset. David Platt 'went into Euro '96 with the captaincy, but I missed the first game against Switzerland and was injured for the Scotland game, so Tony Adams skippered the side, and then I was on the bench against Holland, so Tony skippered the side again. In that game we got on a roll and Terry said to me that he didn't want to change things too much, just wanted things to keep going, so Tony kept the job. Of course it was disappointing, because you dream of getting the trophy, but by the same token, from a manager's point of view, I could understand it.'

Looking back at the tournament, the scenes of national hysteria, the tumultuous atmospheres created at Wembley Stadium, it's hard to recall just how England had struggled on the opening day. They squeezed a draw out of Switzerland in a thoroughly unimpressive opener to the Championships, and could easily have been beaten. Neither side deserved to win a desperate game, which followed the now familiar first commandment of international tournament football: thou shalt not lose thy first match. Again, all the hoopla of the opening ceremony before the match can have done little to ease the tension, but that was a pretty hollow excuse for such a poor game. The only crumb of comfort came with the knowledge that Alan Shearer had begun scoring goals again. Having taken the lead through Shearer after 22 minutes, a struggling England seemed content to hold what they had, particularly in the second period, when they simply ran out of attacking ideas after Steve McManaman, in one of his most effective games for England, was surprisingly substituted. The Swiss made the most of the territory ceded to them and got a thoroughly deserved equalizer from an admittedly dubious penalty, Turkyilmaz beating Seaman from the spot.

A week later, the old enemy, Scotland, were the opponents and England enjoyed another huge slice of good fortune. Having toiled through the first half, the introduction of Jamie Redknapp brought a new composure to the side, but a 1–0 lead, given them by Shearer early in the second half, was always precarious. With 13 minutes remaining, the Scots won a penalty, which Gary McAllister stepped up to take. Just as he was about to strike it, the ball moved slightly on the spot. Maybe that was enough to disturb his concentration, but his shot wasn't a great one and Seaman saved. Almostimmediately England attacked and the bleached blond Gascoigne, written off in the press as past it, scored a breathtaking goal, flicking the ball over Colin Hendry and then lashing a first-time volleypast Andy Goram, celebrating by allowing his colleagues to pour drinks down his throat in a re-enactment of the Hong Kong dentist's chair escapade. It was hard to tell whether that or the goal won the greatest approval from the Wembley crowd.

And then came the game that set the tournament alight, a performance the like of which England hadn't given in years, maybe since the halcyon days of Ramsey's World Cup winners. Holland were looked upon as a pretty good bet to win the whole competition and could have put England out of the competition if they had won at Wembley. England started well enough, though perhaps Holland shaded the earliest exchanges. Once Ince won a penalty after 22 minutes and Shearer had converted it, the hosts were irresistible. Despite there being just the one-goal lead at the break, England were never troubled. In 11 minutes, they rattled in three goals to put the Dutch on the brink of elimination by the 62nd minute. Sheringham made it 2–0 with a neat header, Shearer smacked in a third after good work by Gascoigne and Sheringham, then Sheringham picked up a rebound to make it four. Kluivert got a late goal that sent the Dutch through on goal difference ahead of the Scots, but it was England's night. Wembley was alive, the feeling of euphoria was such that you could be forgiven for thinking England had already won the tournament. If they could repeat that showing three more times, nothing could stop them. But how tall an order was that?

The real danger was that, returning to play Spain three days later, everything could be anti-climactic and the occasion fall flat. The Spanish had a very good team and as David Platt admits, 'It was very similar to the Belgium game in Italia '90; they played extremely well, should have won the game, I think, but we had the rub of the green.' England had to dig in for long periods and survived the 90 minutes with the assistance of the officials, who disallowed two Spanish goals, one of which was clearly onside.

Entering their first ever period of extra-time that could be decided by the 'golden goal', both sides were cagey and the game had to be decided by a penalty shoot-out. That provided yet more momentous images, few more dramatic than Stuart Pearce's cathartic reaction when he slammed his penalty past Zubizarreta. As Platt recalls, 'It takes a lot of guts to take a penalty in a shoot-out and for Stuart to do it on the back of what happened to him in 1990 was very brave. Everybody was delighted for him.' For Pearce, a chapter in his career had been closed at last, and when David Seaman saved Nadal's kick to win the shoot-out, the same could be said for the sporting nation as a whole. The nightmare of Turin in 1990 had been expunged at last. Or had it?

England met their now traditional nemesis, Germany, in the semi-final. As always, it was a tense, closely fought game, and, as in 1990, England were just the better team. Shearer scored almost immediately, but it was a short-lived advantage, Stefan Kuntz equalizing after a quarter of an hour. England looked the more likely to score, but the Germans know how to get the right result better than any other nation, whatever the standard of their own play (or at least they did then). They took the game into extra-time and watched stoically as Anderton hit the post, reacted phlegmatically when Kuntz had a golden goal disallowed (how would Wembley have reacted had that happened at the other end?), and shrugged off the fact that Gascoigne twice came within an inch of winning the game. Penalties beckoned. Both sides rattled in five each at which point Venables' fabled planning let him down. Who would take number six? It was left to Gareth Southgate, whose record in professional football was taken one, missed one. He missed again, and in doing so immediately qualified for a lucrative career in pizza advertising. Perhaps Andy Möller wasn't so keen on pizzas, because he belted his shot past Seaman and put England out, on the brink of the Final.

For Southgate, that game was a personal disaster. He was candid enough to admit that 'for months afterwards it was all I could think about.' But at least he'd got on the pitch and had had a good series. Others weren't that lucky. Tim Flowers points out that, 'When you're not playing, you feel a part of things, especially with it being at home and the way it panned out, the euphoria, it really snowballed into a massive thing. But even then, you're a bit out of it. The funny thing is, when we were 4–1 up against Holland, if he'd brought me on for just five minutes, then I'd have felt a proper part of it, just because you've put your gloves on and tried to do something in anger. If you're in the squad, you have to help the rest of the lads out, if they want to practise shooting or free-kicks, but you never feel like you've really done much. It's a funny feeling.' Les Ferdinand is of a similar opinion: 'While you're there you always hope you might get in at some time, which is what keeps you going, but it does get boring knowing that you're not in the first team. Had England won Euro '96, had I not played any part in any of the games and been given a medal, I don't think I could have accepted it.'

That was the end of Terry Venables' brief spell as coach. For all the acclaim, he couldn't match Alf Ramsey's success in winning a major competition on home soil. Despite that brilliant 90 minutes against the Dutch, England had simply achieved the minimum expected of them. On the plus side, he left behind him a talented squad, containing a number of youngsters yet to reach their peak, but who knew what was required of them against Continental opposition. Tim Flowers rates Venables as a 'highly qualified coach, one of the best I've ever worked with, along with Roy Hodgson, without a doubt.' To replace Venables, England would appoint another thoroughly modern manager, schooled in the Continental game as much as the English way. And if he could be resolutely non-controversial, have no opinions of any kind and no coaching methods that could be considered outlandish, well that would just suit the FA down to the ground.

16

Instant Karma's Gonna Get You

The fact that Terry Venables had played his hand well in advance of Euro '96 meant that the FA had time to plan the succession, putting the new man in place before the tournament began, in order to ensure a seamless changeover. This time around there were plenty of reasonable candidates, such as Kevin Keegan, Bryan Robson and Howard Wilkinson, though none of these seemed prepared to take on the job. The FA sensibly cast its net a little wider and there were suggestions that Ruud Gullit, then still just a player with Chelsea, might have a role to play. According to his own published diary, Alex Ferguson was actively sounded out for the job, but chose to stay at Manchester United. That exposed one of the key problems for the FA, one which persists – there are few financial benefits to be had in leaving a highly successful club to take on the England role. In addition, the level of public attack you might be exposed to if things go wrong far outweighs any criticism you'd have to field as a domestic manager.

One candidate who was willing was Glenn Hoddle. The great enigma as a player, one who should have been England's Platini yet never really made a place his own, Hoddle had never intended to enter management during his early career as a player. A spell in France under Arsene Wenger awakened his curiosity and he had returned to England to guide Swindon Town into the Premiership, operating as player-manager, prompting and probing as a cultured sweeper with absolute control of the shape of his side. That success took him to Chelsea where, in spite of mid-table finishes, he displayed plenty of imagination, remoulding the side into an outfit run on European principles, reaching an FA Cup Final – Chelsea's first sniff of success since the halcyon days of Osgood and Hudson twenty years before – and then instigating the Stamford Bridge revolution by recruiting Ruud Gullit. With every other potential manager pulling out of the race anyway, Hoddle had a simple path to the job, his footballing credentials enhanced by his reputation as a clean-cut family man of decent religious beliefs. The only embarrassment he seemed likely to cause the FA would come in the event of a re-release of the appalling 'Diamond Lights' single.

Hoddle came into the job under much the same cloud of over-optimism that had afflicted Graham Taylor. The quality of England's performance in Euro '96 had been distorted by memories of the brilliant display against Holland and the final misfortune in going out to Germany on penalties. Yet had the ball not fallen the right way for them, they'd certainly have lost to Spain and might not even have got past the group stage. Venables had improved England's standing, and there were some impressive young players coming through, but we were by no means the world power that some suggested. And having been saddled with Italy and Poland in our World Cup qualifying group, with only the winners sure to go through to France, Hoddle was walking into a potential mine-field. Qualification was no mere formality. Nor did Hoddle have the luxury of a friendly to get to know the squad. He was thrown in at the deep end with a qualifier in Moldova.

Understandably, Hoddle kept broadly to Venables' selections, though he did draft in David Beckham for his first cap. One casualty was Tim Flowers: 'I was the only player from Euro '96 to miss out on Glenn's first squad, which I thought was strange because I hadn't done anything wrong, my League form had been good, so I couldn't fathom it out. But I kept working and then got back in, and I'll never give up on that; I always feel I've got something to offer. Glenn made it fairly plain that Dave was his number one, which is understandable, but it's also hard to take, knowing that you can have a great game when you get a chance but Dave will be straight back in. But you have to perform because otherwise you drop back down the list. I've been part of the senior squad for six or seven years non-stop now and thoroughly enjoyed every part of it. It doesn't last for ever and eventually somebody else will come along and replace you and you have to swallow not being in the squad ever again, so make the most of it while you can.'

David Platt was one player having to wrestle with that particular reality: 'After Euro '96, I looked at my age, I was 30, and wondered if I'd be around in two years' time. That's how an international player has to look at things, I think, and with hindsight, maybe I should have retired from international football at that stage. But you don't because you know how much you'd miss international football and you don't really want to have to make that decision. I was in a couple of squads with Glenn Hoddle but, to be honest, after 1995 the injuries were coming too frequently for me to be able to perform at that level on a regular basis. So the decision was taken away from me. From my point of view, I just felt I deserved more of an explanation, really, and I didn't get one.' This was not the only time that Glenn Hoddle's man management was to be called into question, though in fairness to him, dispensing with top players has proved a problem for almost every England coach through the years.

Hoddle could hardly have wished for a better start to his time in the job when Moldova were beaten 3–0. He then had the kind of good luck Graham Taylor would have paid good money for when England beat Poland 2–1 at Wembley, the revival of the Euro '96 atmosphere costing the side its discipline and very nearly the match. Hoddle complained England had 'just our offensive head on', suggesting that the team got carried away in the search for goals and forgot how to defend. Thanks to some superb finishing from newly appointed captain Alan Shearer, England got out of jail, but were nowhere near as impressive as they'd looked when dropping points against Norway and Holland at Wembley in the previous campaign. But then, as Napoleon said, you're better off with lucky generals. As long as the luck holds.

Things were put back on the rails in Georgia with another accomplished and thoroughly professional display, Ferdinand and Sheringham getting the goals in the absence of the injured Shearer. For Ferdinand, 'When Glenn Hoddle came in it was a fresh start and you hope you can impress the new manager, and things went well to start with. I scored against Georgia when Alan was out, the next game was against Italy, and Teddy was injured, so everyone thought that me and Alan would start because it was coming together for us at Newcastle. But Glenn Hoddle decided to play Matt Le Tissier instead and that was a big disappointment. Since then I've never really regained my place – in the last year I can't complain because I've had injuries, but overall I don't feel I've ever really had the chance of a run of games for England.'

The game with Italy in February 1997 was one of the cornerstones of the campaign. Conventional wisdom had it that both Italy and England would probably compile maximum points against the others in the group, so topping the group would come down to the results they got against one another. For the game at Wembley, England were unfortunate, with Seaman, Adams, Gascoigne and Sheringham all absent, though at least Shearer was fit again. In truth, Shearer might as well have been absent too, so expertly was he marshalled by the Italian defenders. The game was settled by one clever strike by Gianfranco Zola, his fierce shot skimming Sol Campbell's boot and just evading replacement keeper Ian Walker. Walker was savaged for the goal, but Tim Flowers points out that, 'Goalkeepers get remembered for goals that go in rather than those you stop. I felt sorry for Ian Walker after the Italy game, because the criticism was unjustified, he became a scapegoat for no reason. You'd have to face Zola to fully realize what he can do with a football, and then there was a deflection as well, past Ian's hand. At the pace the ball's going, you do well to see it, never mind get a hand to a deflection, but then there's suddenly a "get Ian Walker" campaign and I couldn't go along with that, I thought it was hard to stomach. But when you play for England, if you lose a game, sometimes even if you don't win easily, someone has to carry the can.'

Along with Walker, who never again started a game for Hoddle, Le Tissier was blamed for the failure that many assumed had put automatic qualification beyond England. It was partly his own fault, in that he leaked the team to his family who then broadcast it to the nation via radio, when Hoddle had been especially keen to keep the side close to his chest. The incident was an early component in Hoddle's burgeoning press paranoia and his desire to feed misinformation to the papers whenever possible. Naturally that was a facet of Hoddle's personality to which the fourth estate objected strenuously, but that seemed the least eccentric of his foibles. Why tell the other side your team in advance? Why let them work out a tactical plan to nullify your selection? And why try not to fool them as to our injury position? In the case of the Italy game, few observers expected Le Tissier to get a game, so had the Italians been caught unawares, the Southampton man might have made more of an impact. As it was, he was still England's most threatening player, far more effective than Shearer – with whom he'd played on the south coast – and it was a mystery as to why Hoddle substituted him at a time when he was coming increasingly into the game. Decisions such as this, then later on the Chris Sutton fracas and the ignoring of Le Tissier after a virtuoso display for the England B side, all suggested that Hoddle did not fully agree with the Christian concept of forgiveness.

But if Le Tissier, like Walker, had won his last cap under Hoddle, there was one welcome return to the England side when Paul Merson came on to replace Steve McManaman. Following his well publicized struggles with drink and drugs, Merson had gone through his rehabilitation programme and underlined his return in the best possible manner: 'The FA were very good while I was away from the game, everybody was saying "ban him" but they stuck by me, so when I got back in the England side it was great for them as well. I haven't started many games, but I've been lucky enough to play in the big ones, against Germany, Brazil, Italy, Holland, but it is difficult to come on in games as a sub. It's nice to get on, but if you can do something special in that amount of time, it's a bonus, really. International football isn't like the

Premiership, where you could come on for twenty minutes and get two or three good chances. You can be on that long in an international and not see the ball.'

Good for Merson on a personal level, but the 1–0 defeat looked bad for England. The side got back on track by beating Georgia 2–0 at Wembley, then going to Poland at the end of the season and getting an excellent 2–0 win there, despite Shearer missing a penalty. An impressive first year was rounded off by Le Tournoi, a four-team tournament held in France as preparation for the World Cup, featuring England, Italy, France and Brazil. England played some crisp, intelligent football, to beat Italy 2–0 and the hosts by a single goal. Although they went down to Brazil by a single goal in the final game, England had done enough to win the competition. All over the field there were encouraging signs. Shearer and Sheringham teamed up well, with Ian Wright pushing them hard. In the middle Gascoigne had recaptured some of his influence, though his fitness remained a perennial worry. Real pluses came in the contributions of David Beckham and Paul Scholes, maturing into genuine internationals, with Ince and/or Batty providing the necessary ball-winning bite.

Defensively, England conceded little, in no small part thanks to the powerful midfield axis, for there were doubts as to the way they should play. Were England best served by playing with a four as they had traditionally, and as the most successful sides such as Arsenal and Manchester United did, or was Hoddle right to talk up the idea of playing with a three, allowing him to use wing-backs? There was some sense in Hoddle's assertion that in playing a three, there were far more options in playing out of defence with five midfielders to find. Certainly in a 4–4–2 the ball did tend to travel in easily predictable patterns – right-back to right-midfield, centre-backs to centre-midfield and so on. However, that ignored the fact that a 3–5–2 system required players happy with it. Few English players are. Given that the defence was mostly drawn from Arsenal and Manchester United, disciples of the back four, it was a policy fraught with danger. From a playing point of view, Gary Neville argues, 'I enjoy playing in a four at United, either as right-back or centre-back. But I enjoy playing a three for England – we played a three sometimes under Terry Venables, against Spain and Scotland in Euro '96. As a footballer it's good to try different systems, part of the learning curve.'

He's right that modern day players need to be adaptable in play and in thought, but where the learning curve is concerned, the problem is England get so few games in which to experiment. In international football, mistakes are often irrecoverable. And looking at England's games post-qualification, poor defending often went unpunished, notably in Switzerland and against Portugal. But when there were good teams around – Chile, Romania and Argentina – defensive uncertainties were ruthlessly exploited.

Those doubts aside, Le Tournoi had provided an excellent launching pad for the final two qualification games, though it also signalled the end of the England hopes of Wimbledon's Robbie Earle, who had long been touted as a potential member of Hoddle's squad: 'Joe Kinnear knew Glenn, I knew John Gorman pretty well, and they kept telling me that Glenn was interested in me and in Chris Perry, but it never got further than that. It never progressed and I gave myself a deadline of Le Tournoi, because I just felt that if I wasn't in the squad then, I wasn't going to make it. It wasn't a slap in the face not to make the squad but equally there were one or two players named around that time who I didn't think had had great seasons at clubs that hadn't done much, so I felt that was the end. Being at a club like Wimbledon, it doesn't seem to matter how many goals you get or how well you play, you don't seem to be considered as being on the same plane as players at Arsenal or Manchester United. Yet when one of our players is up for sale, they're highly sought after and often get caps afterwards! It was a big disappointment, I'm English, I wanted to play for the country, but that was quickly tempered by the way Jamaica made me feel wanted, how quickly I was welcomed into the squad and so on.'

By the time England played their next game in September, Italy had dropped points in Georgia, so an emphatic England win at home to Moldova would leave them only needing a draw in Rome to progress, especially encouraging given the long-term absence of the injured Shearer. There was never any doubt England would do just that against a team that was just making up the numbers. Beckham, Gascoigne and Wright were rampant as England won 4–0 and placed one foot firmly in the World Cup finals.

The build-up for the Italian game was immense and it would have been very easy for the England side to succumb to the weight of expectations – Mark Palmer, in *Lost in France*, quotes Paul Ince's memory of the moments before the game: 'You should have seen David Seaman. He is usually unflappable. He never shows any nerves, and then six minutes before the game he said to me, "I feel sick." That's how much it means.'

Hoddle wisely accepted that this was a one-off game and generally looked to pack the side with experience, at the expense of regulars such as Gary Neville: 'With England, you have the best in the country and there are times when the opposition suits different players. I started six of the eight qualifiers but, in Italy, Glenn Hoddle made it clear that it was a game where he thought Gareth Southgate would be better suited than me, and he was proved right.' The side was constructed to take no chances and though that made for a remarkably dull game – only the tension of the occasion, Ince's head injury and, sadly, the trouble off the field, giving it any life at all – England appeared to have finally mastered the lessons of Continental football. They had beaten Italy at their own game, shutting down the match from the first whistle, frustrating them totally and not offering a glimmer of a chance until the final seconds. England were in the World Cup finals without having to go through the lottery of the play-offs, to which Italy were now consigned.

In the aftermath of the game, Gary Neville noted a cultural difference in the attitudes of the two teams: 'They're a lot more relaxed about losing than we are. I went into the dressing room afterwards and they were so relaxed, invited me in, got a shirt signed by Paolo Maldini, having just gone through a bad experience of not qualifying for the World Cup outright: having to go through another qualifying game. I'm not sure we'd have been as gracious or welcoming if we'd lost!'

That draw in Italy was the high watermark of the Hoddle era. When he returned home the following day, it was announced that his marriage was over. Upsetting enough for anyone, but Hoddle's life had, by definition, to be played out in the spotlight of publicity. The newspapers dissected the reasons for the split and TV adverts for Shredded Wheat, depicting the Hoddles as the archetypal happy family unit, were quickly pulled. The England coach had had a pretty easy ride from the papers up to November 1997, but he would never enjoy that luxury again. Professionally, though, things were still ticking over nicely. England beat Cameroon 2–0 in November at Wembley in a game where Hoddle was able to utilize some of his reserve strength, such as Nigel Martyn, Phil Neville, Robbie Fowler and Chris Sutton and to give a debut to 19-year-old Rio Ferdinand. Then, when the draw for the World Cup was made in December, TV pictures found Hoddle finding it hard to conceal his delight when England were grouped with Romania, Colombia and Tunisia, as comfortable a draw as he could have possibly wished for.

Following the draw, the country was alive with talk of just how far we might go in France, with many openly predicting we could win the competition, a perfect illustration of the triumph of hope over experience. England were in a batch of teams, perhaps six or seven who could, possibly, make it through, because at world level any successful team needs at least one inspirational player who could turn a game on his own. Brazil had Ronaldo, France had Zidane, Holland had Bergkamp, Italy had Del Piero, Argentina had Batistuta. England had, it was to be hoped, Alan Shearer. But Shearer had been out injured since the start of the season. Although he was now back in the squad, who could tell what impact the injury would have had on him? Bearing that in mind, surely the time had come to blood a new striker, Michael Owen? Against Chile in February 1998, Owen became England's youngest debutante at 18 years, 59 days, Dion Dublin also making his first appearance at a rather more advanced age. In a game in which England were thoroughly outplayed, Owen impressed with his pace, but it was Chile's Marcelo Salas who showed the kind of brilliance that unlocks international defences. His first goal, a wonderful volley from the edge of the box (having brilliantly controlled a long ball dropping over his shoulder), took the breath away. The 2–0 defeat – Salas also converting a penalty – might not have done any harm, in that it did reduce the burden of expectations. What it also did was to show just how rickety England's defence could be, and how a top-class forward could exploit it.

The day before the first team was beaten, Hoddle had arranged a B international, also against Chile, to allow him to look at some fringe players. That idea was tinged with controversy before it began when Chris Sutton refused to join the squad, feeling it was a waste of time and would prove nothing. But the game, held at the Hawthorns, was anything but a waste for Paul Merson: 'It was an honour to captain the B side at West Brom and it was pleasing to give a good performance, and that kick-started my England career, it got me in the World Cup squad. Chris Sutton turned a B cap down – if he'd played 60 times for England and got 40 goals, then I'd understand, but when you haven't set the international scene alight, I don't see how you can turn it down.'

On the back of that game, Merson was in the England side which gave another dismal showing in Bern, Merson grabbing the goal that got a draw they barely deserved. Hoddle was tight-lipped after the game as it became obvious that the level of criticism was starting to affect him. Not only were the critics pointing to the sudden collapse in England's form with some alarm, they were beginning to ask questions of his use of faith healer Eileen Drewery. As Hoddle became less articulate in his comments, more scrutiny was focused on Drewery and her role in Hoddle's life and her supposed influence on him. The feeding frenzy that went on around it was ludicrous. Maybe there is something in the idea, maybe not – certainly some people report startling results. But everyone is entitled to their own opinion. As Les Ferdinand says: 'She works for some players and not for others. Some players are very sceptical, some accept it and respond to it – I know Ian Wright and Darren Anderton have responded very positively to what she does. I went to see her and I didn't see anything wrong in what she was doing – if she was called a sports psychologist, there'd have been no problem, but because she's called a healer, which hasn't been heard of in football before, it's something to pick at.' And while the results were deteriorating, the press were only too happy to look for reasons why.

What did rankle with the more objective observers however was the suggestion of compulsion in visiting Drewery. One anonymous England player likened the atmosphere in the camp to a religious cult, while there had long been speculation that Ray Parlour was excommunicated from the squad after showing Drewery insufficient reverence, asking for a short back and sides when he went for a healing session. Add to that her assertion that it was she who prevented Ian Wright scoring in the last minute in Rome by erecting a glass wall across the Italian goal, so that there would be no further crowd trouble, and you start to move a little too far from alternative thinking for most people's tastes and into the realms of looney tunes. Hoddle had offered another hostage to fortune, as he was to do with monotonous regularity through the rest of his tenure.

Hoddle returned to his favoured side against Portugal and though England won 3–0, had Salas been Portuguese, the game would have been over by half-time. The three-man defence was again exposed, with none seemingly sure of their positioning against the quick opposition forwards. In the traditional back four, which the likes of Tony Adams, Sol Campbell and Gary Neville inhabited at club level, each player had clearly defined sections of the penalty area for which he was responsible. While they were coming to terms with the three-man set-up, it was often easy for opposition forwards to find gaping holes between the three. The central man tended to stay on the penalty spot and the other two drifted out towards the edge of the box, or even further, particularly as wing-backs such as Le Saux or Beckham were naturally attacking players. If one of the central defenders had to come across to cover on the wing, that left much of the penalty area untended, particularly if the defender on the opposite side stayed out wide. The defensive frailty against Portugal was hidden beneath the avalanche of relieved praise for Shearer's return to the big time with two goals, all the more important given his indifferent club form. But when England then struggled woefully against Saudi Arabia in May, in their final home game before the World Cup, doubts began to surface again. Beyond the opening moments, England rarely threatened to get a goal and, as the game wore on, the Saudis took control, their lack of a striker of any worth finally thwarting them.

An England party comprising thirty players then flew out to La Manga, ready to play two games in the King Hassan II International Cup in Morocco before the squad was pared down to twenty-two names. England struggled early on against Morocco in the first game and almost lost Owen following a nasty collision after he had come on for Ian Wright, whose World Cup aspirations perished with a hamstring injury. Fortunately Owen was fit to carry on and made more history by becoming England's youngest ever goalscorer, to win the game 1–0. England's performance was again derided, but bearing in mind the qualities Morocco were to show in France, the 1–0 win was a good one. Tim Flowers rightly complains that, 'There's a lot of old thinking; people still think countries like Morocco are as far behind as they were in 1970, or something. I don't know how much you can read into FIFA's rankings, but when we played out there, Morocco were above us! There are some very fine African teams. But for the press and a section of the public, when England go on the field, it's not a matter of whether we're going to win, but by how many, and that's naïve nowadays. Some sides would have come to Wembley twenty years ago and got thumped by five or six, but that just doesn't happen now. Look at Paraguay's performance in France; they came within a couple of minutes of taking the French to penalties and might have beaten the team that won the World Cup. But if Paraguay had come to Wembley the month after, the pundits would have expected us to beat them 3–0. These teams are all far more tactically and technically aware now.' Flowers, one of four goalkeepers in the squad, was selected for the game and 'it did help. You have to look at it positively: "Great, I've got a game, I'll play well and cement my place in the squad." And I got a clean sheet in front of a big crowd, and that secured my place, I suppose. Ian was unlucky in that he didn't get a game, but had either Nigel or myself had a bad game, maybe he would have benefited.'

Where Flowers had done his case no harm, Paul Gascoigne was clearly struggling, bereft of form, fitness and confidence. Substituted in the game with Belgium, an insipid 0–0 draw, few seriously doubted that Hoddle would leave him out of the final twenty-two, but would Gazza actually make it into the side? That looked very unlikely. But Hoddle had clearly run out of patience with Gazza. Having backed him very publicly – and undeservedly – when Gascoigne was accused of beating his wife, Hoddle had hoped he would become a reformed character. Instead, in the days before England flew out to La Manga, he'd been pictured out on the town with media celebrities Chris Evans and Danny Baker, considerably the worse for a spot of refuelling. Added to that, he had chosen to start smoking at a time when his fitness was well below par. He was well overweight and his attitude at La Manga apparently left a lot to be desired, indulging in heavy drinking rather than a quiet pint when Hoddle allowed the squad a night off. His performances against Saudi Arabia, Morocco and Belgium had been frankly pathetic and it appeared that, finally, Gascoigne's off-the-field excesses were catching up with his sublime footballing talent. It was painful to watch this genius struggling like a Sunday morning player. He was no longer worthy of selection for the England squad, and there seems no question that, on footballing issues alone, Hoddle's decision was spot on.

Paul Merson, well aware of what turmoil Gascoigne was, and still is, going through, says, 'I did feel for Gazza, he'd worked hard, but it all got on top of him at the wrong time. I don't think he was in the right state to go, and now he's got honest with himself, I think he'd admit it as well. When you're playing that kind of football, you have to be spot on or you can't play.'

Ironically, Gascoigne's decline left a slot open for Merson, who was surprised to have made the squad: 'In La Manga, I didn't think I'd go to France, just from the vibes I was getting, but you just get on with it in training as best you can. Then, to finally get picked, was something you always treasure, maybe more because it hadn't been my priority that year. When I went to Middlesbrough, I wasn't worried about England; I went there because it was a big challenge. My job was to get them up and I said all along that if Middlesbrough didn't go up but I went to the World Cup, it would be a bad season. Managed both, so that wasn't a bad year!'

As Hoddle made clear, his job was to ensure England had the best possible chance of winning the World Cup. In jettisoning Gascoigne, he had improved the odds. It was an undeniably brave decision, not dissimilar to the one made by Ramsey when he left Greaves out of the Final in 1966. If England failed badly, it didn't take much imagination to picture the vicious editorials condemning Hoddle for leaving England's genius at home. At the very least, Gazza would be guaranteed to have a great World Cup by simply not being there. But his absence was bad news for the tabloids because no Gazza meant fewer stories. Which is presumably one of the things Hoddle took into consideration. The sagacity of that view was demonstrated in the furore generated by Gascoigne's omission, a story which filled news bulletins and acres of newsprint for days. Not for the first time, the newspapers paid scant attention to the facts – that Paul Gascoigne was not up to the task – and instead built stories around his personality and the gifts that had illuminated the World Cup in Italy eight years earlier. Any objective viewer of his lethargic, flabby displays in the warm-up games could only have applauded Hoddle, but Gascoigne is not the kind of player that encourages objectivity.

In the storm, it was forgotten that other players had had their hopes dashed too. After Wright and Jamie Redknapp had dropped out through injury, six players had to be omitted, including Andy Hinchcliffe, who was carrying a thigh injury, Nicky Butt, Ian Walker, Dion Dublin and Phil Neville.

Neville had felt he had made the squad, Hoddle's assistant John Gorman having intimated as much to him. To be left out was 'Devastating. It helped on the way home to have a good friend like Nicky, who was in the same boat, to talk to, but not much! I think that because Paul got a lot of the attention, it let me get on with my holiday, let me get over it quicker. I still got asked to do interviews but I declined, and did it the right way, really, I didn't want to start talking about whether it was the right decision or not. It was difficult for everybody, including the coach. Having thought about it afterwards, I tried to think of any other way the twenty-two could have been announced, and there isn't any. For Euro '96 it was the same, we were in the Far East and Terry Venables had to leave five players out – it was probably better this time because we were in Portugal, only two hours from home, rather than thirteen in Hong Kong. If you name the twenty-two before you start preparing but take thirty in case of injury, then the rest might take it easy, or be unhappy. There's no way round it.' Understandably, Phil's omission had an impact on his brother Gary: 'My excitement at getting in was taken away by Philip not getting in. The people around were very good. It was a very difficult day for lots of people, the staff, players, there were five others left out, players whose friends missed out; it wasn't a nice day for anyone. But it was always going to come, so you just have to get on with it.'

One player who some were surprised to see in the squad was Les Ferdinand: 'The press made a lot of it being me or Dion, and people felt Dion would go because he'd had a good season and he offered the option of playing at the back if necessary. I didn't agree with that view. I'd had a bad season with injuries, so that would have been a perfect excuse not to have me in the thirty. Glenn Hoddle could have said, "Les hasn't played enough games, I can't take him." But the fact that he took me to La Manga made me think I had a good opportunity to make the final twenty-two. I thought that I'd come on at some stage in the World Cup, which I hadn't at Euro '96. When he named the squad, the manager took us all into a room individually and he said, "I want you to concentrate all the time on the bench, because if you come on for the last 20 or 30 minutes" – then he slipped in, "I'm not saying you won't start a game," which I suppose he had to! – "but if you come on late in the game, I want you to be ready, I want you to see a way you can influence the game." I felt really positive after he'd said that, but then the next day we saw the papers and he had said that he took me rather than Dion because if anything happened to Michael Owen, he was lacking pace up front and wanted me to provide that, which was a totally different thing to what he'd said to me the previous day. Once I read that, I felt my chances were pretty slim; it was disappointing to read something different.'

It wasn't the only instance of Hoddle seemingly going out of his way to alienate the players he needed to rely on, though it was apparently less out of malice than clumsiness. As Phil Neville explains, 'A club manager has lots of time to keep you involved, even if you're out of the side, and they need to talk to you more. Glenn Hoddle doesn't see you from one week to the next, and he can only pick the best team as he sees it when you do get together. There's no time to talk things through as much.'

The squad flew back from La Manga and took a break for a few days before flying out to France and their base in La Baule. Hoddle gave specific instructions to the players to get plenty of rest and keep their heads down. So Teddy Sheringham flew out to Portugal and was pictured in a bar at 6 a.m., having been there all night. Sheringham claimed the story had been fabricated, and there's some truth in that – Sheringham posing for photos with holidaymakers with an unlit cigarette in his mouth and a drink in front of him, the incriminating photo that was used to portray him as a womanizing drunk resulting from a naïve desire to please the fans in the bar – but as Paul Merson says, 'To be fair to the press, they only report on things that you're doing bad. If you're going out drinking, being silly and smashing up bars like I used to, then you're going to be in the papers. If you sit at home with your wife and family, you don't get on the front page.' Hoddle made it clear he would have liked to drop Sheringham there and then, but having named the twenty-two, accepted he would only be damaging England's chances if he did so. Sheringham was required to issue a contrite apology in an attempt to smooth things over, but with Michael Owen breathing down his neck in the race to partner Alan Shearer, Sheringham did more damage to himself than to the nation's hopes.

England did not get started in the World Cup until almost a week after the opening game. The first fixture was against Tunisia, seemingly the weakest side in the group. By the time the game was played, English followers had once again been involved in outbreaks of violence in Marseille. Paul Merson argues that, 'A lot of the time the England fans get a lot of blame and it's not their fault; a lot is put on them because of their reputation in the past and by bad policing.' There was an element of that in these disturbances, but there were plenty of English thugs involved too, only too willing to go looking for trouble, or start their own if necessary. Understandably, players like Gary Neville refuse to allow the hooliganism to interrupt their concentration on the task in hand: 'When there's trouble, to be honest, players don't get involved in anything away from the playing side. You see it, it's unfortunate, but you can't let it affect your preparation.' Not that Neville was actually playing in the Tunisia game, one of two surprising omissions: 'It was hard to miss that first game, it's a prestigious game, the first ever game for all of us in a World Cup, but the manager picks a team to win, and they won. I got my chance in the next game and obviously enjoyed it more from that point onwards, because you always want to play.'

Even more staggering was the decision to leave out David Beckham, who had played in all the qualifiers. Hoddle had previously moved Beckham into central midfield, in itself an excellent decision, but then against Tunisia chose to play Ince and Batty in midfield holding roles, suggesting that England were determined not to concede anything. With Darren Anderton returning on the right of midfield, that left no place for Beckham. Hoddle wrote in his *1998 World Cup Story*, 'I just felt that his club form had dipped towards the end of the season ... he'd been drifting in and out of too many games ... there had been a vagueness about him, on and off the pitch, and sometimes in training. I'm sure he was missing Victoria [his girlfriend], who's away a great deal. As a result of all this, he was a bit distant around the hotel.' It was a charge that Beckham's club colleague Gary Neville refutes: 'He couldn't wait to play, he wanted to show everybody how good he is.' With

Beckham the one player that Alex Ferguson excuses from his rotation policy, selecting him in virtually every game because, he says, he 'has the best stamina at Manchester United', it's hard to see how Beckham could be tired, and his performances when he got into the side belied that view.

Hoddle's handling of Beckham was very poor. Of course he isn't entitled to special treatment, but as England's most creative footballer, it seemed inevitable he would be among the first names on the team sheet. To be dropped, told he wasn't concentrating on the World Cup but on his girlfriend instead, and then be forced to take a press conference, something Beckham is not much good at anyway, was atrocious man management, the more so since it followed attacks on Beckham's ability during training, when, according to Tony Adams in *Addicted*, Hoddle told him, 'Obviously you're not good enough to do that skill,' when he was struggling with a particular free-kick routine in training. It testified to Hoddle's massive self-belief, but it's a fine line between making a sensible but brave and unpopular decision, as he had with Gazza, and acting dogmatic with almost Messianic certainty. The Beckham decision smelt of the latter, as did his refusal to play Owen instead of Sheringham. And why had it been necessary? Because of Hoddle's dogmatic insistence on the three-man defence. The series of friendlies had given ample evidence that England's defence was far from watertight. Knowing the importance of the first game, knowing he could not afford to lose it, even draw it, and knowing his defence was suspect, Hoddle had to play two out and out ball winners in the centre of midfield in order to give that threesome additional protection. With Scholes playing in an advanced role, Beckham could not be fitted into the side. That it was a needless tactical device was quickly brought home when, though they created a couple of early chances, Tunisia's finishing was so woeful they could have played until the next World Cup and not scored. English caution had been overdone and though it didn't prove to be a fatal error in terms of that one game, the Beckham affair had repercussions that rumbled through the tournament to its ultimate untimely end. With a professional if unenterprising display,

England came through 2–0, Shearer getting the first before half-time and Scholes adding a superb second just before the end to give the scoreline a more comfortable look. England had chances to win more easily, but though they never looked in danger, the press reaction suggesting it was a World Cup-winning performance was way over the top. Scholes had been the major plus, effectively silencing the questions about Gascoigne's omission with his impressive display. But despite the low-key performance, Tim Flowers is right to say, 'The Tunisia game gave us a good start because often in the past England have struggled in the first game. And Marseille's about twelve miles off the coast of north Africa, so they had plenty of support.'

England returned to La Baule to rest and recover, the only real casualty being Gareth Southgate. Tim Flowers recalls, 'We completely took over the hotel, there was nobody else there. They had an underground car park, 40 or 50 feet long, and they filled it with pool tables, table tennis tables, amusement arcade games, a jukebox, and quite a few of the lads liked to spend time there, some went back to their rooms and read, some played cards. There's a wide mix of personalities in there. Sol is very quiet, likes to go off and do his own thing; then you've got Paul Ince, who's very open and very loud, wherever you went you could hear him shouting somewhere. We got on well. It's a helluva long time, so we had to! When you're not playing it's so easy to get disgruntled, to start moaning; you need the lads who aren't playing to keep upbeat. And you know it's great to be there, but it's still difficult at times to keep smiling, when you're sat there for six weeks you want to play. When you're just cannon fodder at shooting practice, when you're working twice as hard as those who're playing because you need to keep your fitness up, and it's baking hot, sometimes your fuse does get short and you have to bite your lip. Somebody can say something, I know it happened to me a couple of times, and I was close to exploding, because you're frustrated, but you don't. Glenn Hoddle wrote us a letter thanking us all for our effort and application and attitude to it all afterwards, and you then know you did the right thing. But in the middle of it, it's a long time to be away, you do sometimes think, "What am I here for?" The manager did warn us that it would happen, that you had to keep your head down, that if you felt that way it was best to get out of the way for an hour and do something. Because he'd been in the same boat when he'd been in the squad in 1982. We got together a week before the Saudi game, had a week in La Manga, came back for three days, then went out to France for about a month. It's a long time to be away from the family, stuck in the middle of a forest, and you basically eat, sleep and drink football, but it's a small price to pay for the chance to be involved in the World Cup.'

The game against Romania was the centrepiece of the group, always likely to be the game that sorted out the placings, and therefore the second-round opponents. Romania had beaten Colombia competently enough and would offer a greater threat than Tunisia, so it was no surprise that Hoddle chose two holding midfielders again, leaving Beckham on the sidelines. More surprising was the continuing refusal to play Owen in what looked like a display of sheer bloody-mindedness directed at the media and the fans who were baying for his introduction. Hoddle did little to placate them by suggesting that Owen wasn't a natural goalscorer. And Teddy Sheringham is? Certainly there were legitimate questions as to whether Shearer and Owen could play together successfully – there still are – but to pretend that Owen is not a goalscorer did little for Hoddle's credibility.

Ironically both Beckham and Owen were to get on the field in the Romanian game, Beckham in the first half when Ince limped off. Immediately he made an impact, proving just how good a user of the ball he is, the best in England by a wide margin. But despite the increase in English creativity, the frailty of the back three persisted. There was some lax marking on Hagi who was able to get in a cross. None of the defenders seemed to know who should be attacking the ball, nobody did, and Moldovan was left free to shoot past Seaman. With 17 minutes left, Owen was belatedly brought into the game. Beckham played a neat ball into the box, Shearer pulled it back, and Owen swept the ball into the net. As Kevin Keegan so rightly said, 'There's only one team gonna win this now,' but it wasn't the one he, or 30 million others, thought it would be. (With insight like that, Keegan has a great future ahead of him.) Further poor defending and confusion between Le Saux – strangely left as last man in the last couple of minutes – and Seaman allowed Petrescu in to give Romania the points. Tim Flowers was left to admit, 'We didn't play well against Romania, though they didn't have many chances. They were technically good, looked good on the ball, and so losing that put us under pressure.'

Needing a draw against an ageing and impotent Colombia, England were never really in any danger of not qualifying, but top place now looked beyond them. Stung into action at last, Hoddle played Beckham and Owen from the start against Colombia and got a vastly improved performance out of the team. As Flowers says, 'Colombia have had some great players over the years, but maybe the likes of Valderrama have been going that bit too long. We were full value for the 2–0 win, could have been more, their keeper made lots of good saves and Dave didn't have anything to do, really.'

Darren Anderton scored early on, hammering in a shot from the right, and then Beckham registered his first England goal with a brilliantly executed free-kick. His delight made it obvious that Beckham was totally focused on the job in hand, determined to make up for lost time and perhaps just a little too committed, surely a reaction to Hoddle's decision to drop him.

As England trooped off, they discovered that Romania had achieved the necessary point against Tunisia to deprive England of top spot. That meant a second-round meeting with Argentina rather than Croatia. With a rapid piece of spin doctoring of which Peter Mandelson would have been proud, Hoddle tried to convince a worried populace that he preferred to play the Argentines, intimating that his master strategy was working out perfectly. Having seen Batistuta, Ortega, Simeone, Veron and Roa look as good as any players in the competition thus far, and remembering that the Argentines had been among the strongest pre-tournament favourites, having beaten Brazil in Rio earlier in the year, the nation found it hard to take Hoddle seriously. Obviously Croatia were a good side too – any team with Boban and Suker in its ranks would always be a threat – but offered the choice, you'd have been pushed to find an England fan who wouldn't have preferred to be playing them. To an extent that was because of the historical connotations of England–Argentina fixtures, and because, as a new nation, Croatia weren't really taken seriously. The difference in quality between the two sides was small and Croatia, as a hard-working European outfit, and very difficult to break down, would have posed different problems, much as Romania had. Even so, to argue that we were now facing the lesser of two evils stretched credulity.

The game with Argentina was another one of those epochal games, with the whole country congregated around the TV. The game started badly for England when Seaman raced off his line and upended Simeone to concede a penalty that Batistuta converted. In truth, England were fortunate that the goal was the only penalty following Seaman's challenge, for as Tim Flowers says, 'When Dave conceded the penalty in the first few minutes, he could have been sent off, because referees' discretion and interpretation varies so much. Neither Nigel nor me knew who was the number two, though from the squad numbering it looked as if it was Nigel, but we didn't actually know. At the time, I didn't really think about it; I was more disappointed that we conceded the penalty.' That in itself is strange given that goalkeepers are sent off with increasing regularity nowadays. Surely Hoddle should have made the position clear to his reserve goalkeepers to aid their concentration in case of emergency? As Tony Adams wrote in *Addicted*, 'I have to be honest and say that a lot of what Glenn was doing and saying did not particularly impress me,' and it's hard to disagree with that assessment. Fortunately, England got back into the game and Michael Owen, now number one choice, way ahead of Teddy Sheringham, won a penalty with his first burst of lightning pace. Shearer put the side level.

The game was then distinguished by an opening half of cut and thrust, of high quality, high excitement and two quite wonderful goals. Surely, there isn't a person in England who hasn't seen Michael Owen's strike, but little attention has been given to the quality of the pass from Beckham which set him off on his run. Perfectly weighted and placed into his stride, it allowed Owen to run at the heart of the Argentine defence, which simply backed away and let him continue. Once in the box, his venomous shot was never going to finish anywhere but in the back of the net. Argentina were thrown into disarray momentarily and England could have snatched another – Scholes had a golden chance to make it 3–1. On the stroke of half-time, Argentina got a free-kick on the edge of the box. Instead of the expected shot from Batistuta, the ball was played along the ground to Zanetti, who peeled away from the defensive wall and, in space, stuck the ball calmly past Seaman: a goal every bit as good as Owen's in its execution, even better in its conception.

Argentine delight at that equalizer made it apparent that England had more than matched the favourites in the first period, so they could approach the second half with some optimism. All that fell apart within a couple of minutes of the restart. Beckham was scythed down by Simeone, in front of the referee, who was clearly ready to book the Argentine. As he walked past, Beckham flicked out his foot, caught Simeone, who fell to the floor. As Flowers says, 'There were players going straight through a tackle with two feet in the same tournament without getting booked, yet Dave flicked out a handbag and got sent off! The inconsistency in interpretation is frustrating but I suppose it's inevitable because there were lots of referees from different cultures. It was disappointing that he was a Danish referee, who must have seen all that kind of thing before. Simeone went down like a sack of spuds after being barely touched; it was a shame and spoilt the game, really.' Simeone has since admitted that he made a meal of things in order to get Beckham booked, but the blame is all Beckham's. He exhibited violent conduct in retaliating, a mandatory sending-off offence, whether damage is done or not. It was a stupid thing to do, but under the pressure of the World Cup, it's inevitable that players will react from time to time. It was a mistake, but hardly a hanging offence, whatever some 'supporters' seemed to think.

With England down to ten men, the game took on a completely different character, with England concentrating almost solely on defence, with Owen and Shearer taking turns to play a lone role up front. They almost snatched the game at the death when Campbell headed in, but Shearer was adjudged to have elbowed the Argentine keeper and it was disallowed, leaving us with the tragic-comic scene of half the England side celebrating while the other half were desperately trying to get back to defend a quickly taken free-kick. The game went into extra-time, and England were unlucky not to get a penalty that would have allowed them to snatch the golden goal. As it was, the match went to penalties. With Seaman making the first save, England looked favourites until Ince's kick was saved.

Roa indulged in some gamesmanship to try to defeat Merson, who had come on as a substitute: 'There were no real instructions other than to go out and play. It was nice to get on, great to score a penalty.' Argentina were 4–3 ahead with David Batty stepping up to take the last of England's five. Roa saved and Argentina were through. Tim Flowers says, 'Argentina was always going to be a hard game. I do think with eleven men on the field, we would have won, but to get into extra-time and then penalties was a magnificent effort by the lads. Sitting on the bench was almost like being a fan: we were up and down, dancing about, cheering the lads on. It was such a shame, I wouldn't want to take a penalty in those situations ever, you're on a hiding to nothing, but the public realize that. I hope they'll be as understanding of the David Beckham thing, those things happen in football. Batts is a very strong character, a very strong personality. And he's very experienced, he's been in the England set-up a long time, played in the Champions League, been in Championship-winning sides, played in the FA Cup Final. He knows as well as anyone that anybody can miss a penalty. He hit the target and the goalie saved it, so you've got to give the keeper some credit. If he'd dived the other way, it would've gone in, that's how simple it is; the goalie guessed right. He was all right pretty quickly. I know Batts and he wouldn't dwell on it for long!' Paul Merson is equally philosophical: 'It was upsetting to lose that way but worse things happen than that. Beckham was gutted, he'll always have to live with it, but it's not like he's 33 and it was his last game for England. He'll have another chance to make amends.'

Popular legend now has it that if Beckham had stayed on England would have won, but is that necessarily true? We've all been to games where one side has been reduced to ten men and then simply falls back on blanket defence to frustrate the opposition. If your only ambition is to keep the other team out, ten well organized men are very capable of that. That takes nothing away from the performance of the England side at all, because Argentina had some highly imaginative footballers, though they weren't always as well employed as they could have been. To keep them out required a high degree of skill, discipline and concentration, but it wasn't the impossible task some commentators suggested. Ironically, Beckham's dismissal possibly made the draw in normal and extra-time more likely. Had the game progressed as an eleven a side, England would have been more adventurous, seeking the winner. Naturally, that would increase their chances of winning the game, but equally it would have given Argentina a greater chance of hitting them on the counter. Argentina were particularly well equipped to do just that, rather less set up to take a game by the scruff of the neck. So Beckham, while acting childishly, did not cost England the game, that's too simplistic a reading of the situation.

What of Hoddle's role, though? The most criticism was drawn when it was revealed that David Batty had never taken a penalty in a senior game and that the squad had not practised taking them. Hoddle's view was that practising penalties does not replicate the pressure of taking them in a big game. Of course it doesn't, but surely if you regularly slot them in in training, you're going to feel a lot more confident of scoring in a match situation? The logical extension of Hoddle's argument is that it's pointless practising anything, because it's never really like that in a game. If taking penalties in training was so pointless, why did Gary Lineker keep doing so for years? When it came to shoot-outs, or really crucial penalties for England, he was never found wanting. Some connection perhaps?

If Hoddle's statement on penalties was hard to understand, so was his attitude towards Beckham, who has since admitted that the coach did not speak to him after the game. It was left to the likes of Tony Adams to try to bring Beckham out of his depression, hardly the actions of a great man manager. Once again, there was an almost evangelical zeal about Hoddle and his crusade to win the World Cup. It could be that he'd been so convinced he was going to come home in triumph that he could not bring himself to talk to Beckham, making it very clear that he regarded him as the scapegoat for the defeat. Given that Beckham was clearly going to be part of the England side for years to come and that Hoddle would have to work with him in future, this was a strange way to deal with him. Never mind anyone else, Hoddle's dreams had been dashed, so he was the man who should be most upset. Of course, he was desperately disappointed have worked long and hard towards France '98, but a coach has to rise above personal emotions and take care of his whole squad. Hoddle did not seem willing to do so and possibly began to lose the respect of the players at that point.

The players were a fairly miserable bunch after the game, as Tim Flowers remembers: 'When you get beat, even at League level in a fairly meaningless game, the dressing room is a pretty depressing place. Sometimes somebody will have a go at another player and there'll be a row, or they'll throw a boot at someone; I've seen all that happen. But after Argentina, everybody came in, heads were down and there was a lot of just gazing into nowhere, there were people crying. But after an hour the lads started talking again, there was a bit of patter on the bus, then we flew back to La Baule. We got there about 1.30 and the manager said we could have a beer, so the lads were sat up to about 5 in the morning just talking it through. It was a strange feeling because we were geared to going all the way, to playing another three games. The manager had taken great pains through qualifying to gear us up to win the Cup, it wasn't, "We'll give it our best shot," I honestly think he believed we would win it and had us thinking the same way. Then when we got knocked out, and to lose that way, everything disappears, it's very deflating.'

Given the circumstances of their defeat, England returned home to a very warm reception – all except David Beckham – with few questions asked. But there were many that needed answers. Why leave Beckham out at the start of the tournament, then treat him so poorly, not offering an explanation, castigating him in training, forcing him into a press conference? Wouldn't all of this have fired the young man up, to a point where it must have had a bearing on his state of mind and the consequent sending off? How did it take Hoddle so long to bring Michael Owen into the side? Had Owen been on from the start, or even from the start of the second half against Romania, England's chances of grabbing a draw would surely have improved given the havoc he wrought in the Romania defence, and England would have thus avoided Argentina. Why did Hoddle order Paul Ince, of all people, to approach the referee in the Argentine game and ask why there were no bookings when England were awarded their penalty; Ince, inevitably, picking up a yellow card himself? Why not practise penalties and why only decide at the last moment who the five spot kickers would be in the shoot-out? Why persist with three at the back when England were palpably uncomfortable with it on many occasions? Why not tell Flowers and Martyn who the reserve goalkeeper was in order to put their minds at ease? But the biggest question of all was yet to be asked. Why did the England coach write a diary during the World Cup, which revealed full details of private thoughts and private conversations held with members of the team? Apart from making Hoddle a lot of money, what good did it do? The book was full of comments on players whom he would have to work with again in qualifying for Euro 2000. Would it help their respect for the coach if he attacked them in print? Paul Merson reckons, 'Everybody knew Glenn was writing the book, everything he put in the book was true, so I can't see the problem with it. That's my point of view. If you write a book, it's there to tell the truth. If people start lying, then you get the hump. But I can't see what the problem is with telling the truth.' There's plenty to sympathize with in that view, but equally you can point to the greatest managers – Shankly, Busby, Stein, Paisley, Ferguson – who hardly ever criticized a player in public. Their players knew they could rely implicitly on their boss' loyalty towards them in public. If there was any arguing to be done, it was done behind closed doors. Again, though none of the players would say so in public, it must have harmed their trust in their coach. Once players lose respect for a manager, it's very difficult to get it back.

That became readily apparent when England began their assault on Euro 2000 with a game in Sweden, who had failed to reach the World Cup. After getting off to a great start with an early goal, England inexplicably fell apart as Sweden took absolute control of the game, their slick passing making England look decidedly second rate. As Paul Merson points out, 'None of the teams that played in France have done much since because none of them have had a break. Sweden aren't a bad team, they didn't make it to the World Cup, but they beat Italy and Russia recently; they were fresh, at home, with something to prove.'

Even so, the way in which England capitulated so rapidly suggested there was something amiss within the squad. Paul Ince's sending off simply put the cap on a miserable day at the office. The Ince affair was not allowed to end there, however, the FA ordering an enquiry into the dismissal and gestures he subsequently made as he left the field. Les Ferdinand makes the valid point that, 'For all that Paul Ince is, and the things he does sometimes, all he wants to do is play football and he's happiest when he's playing football, although it doesn't look like it at times! He was disappointed about the length of ban he got, and especially that the FA were thinking of banning him as well. You look at the support Alan Shearer got at the end of last season over that tackle at Leicester when he might have been sent off, and then the way Paul has been treated, and it does make you wonder.'

Failure in Sweden wasn't the end of the world, though with the controversy about the Hoddle diaries rumbling away in the background, the coach was not having an easy time. Nor did he make life easier for himself with further comments about Eileen Drewery, to the effect that not taking her out to France earlier was his biggest mistake. Really? Would she have slotted home a penalty in the shoot-out, even without practising them? Hoddle suggested that she would have helped avoid Beckham's sending off by getting him in a better frame of mind. There's no reason to dispute that, or that she can get good results as a sports psychologist, as Les Ferdinand described her. But to apportion her such a key role was alarming. And if Beckham was in such a poor frame of mind, you have to ask just who did most to put him there. Yet as every manager knows, there's no amount of bad publicity that can't be washed away with a couple of convincing performances. England had the chance to do just that, with a home fixture against Bulgaria – who had had a dismal World Cup, getting caned by Spain – and then an away game in Luxembourg in the space of five days.

After the Bulgaria match, it was hard to recall the last time England had given such an uninspiring performance at Wembley. The goalless draw was, according to Merson, 'The biggest disappointment ... not making a chance.' Briefly, things looked like they might get worse in Luxembourg when the home side got an early penalty and there were sudden shades of San Marino in the dog days of Taylor's reign. Luxembourg missed and England gradually asserted some measure of superiority, winning 3–0, but convincing nobody in the process.

By now the whispering campaign against Hoddle had reached a crescendo, and it was backed up by an alleged conversation that took place between Hoddle and his captain Alan Shearer. Supposedly, while Hoddle was castigating his players for another lacklustre showing, Shearer turned to the manager and asked if it had ever occurred to him that he might be the problem. Tapes of the conversation were said to exist, though they never surfaced and the two principal characters had to face the media to deny the story. Others were dragged into the fray, such as Gareth Southgate, who spoke to the Internet daily *Football 365*: 'Judging by all the criticism that has been aimed at Glenn recently, I cannot see why anybody would like to take the England job when he finally decides

343

to call it a day. I don't know him personally, but I can't imagine Tony Blair's job being any easier than Glenn's at the moment. The thing that worries me is the lies that seem to be coming from the dressing room. The supposed row Glenn had with Alan Shearer was total nonsense, but where did the story come from? I would be alarmed to find out that someone was leaking stories to the press from the England dressing room.' At the same time, Paul Merson argued that, 'The morale has been very good, we talk about the games, the boss wants us to have our say, but it's not like we have rows. It gets carried away in the press, sells papers, that's all!'

The media came to bury Hoddle at the friendly with the Czech Republic in November, but a much improved performance helped calm the situation. With no further European qualifiers due until the end of March, it looked as if Hoddle had weathered the storm, until he put his foot neatly in his mouth once more with his comments on the disabled. Attempting to explain his belief in the concept of reincarnation and the importance of karma in that, he managed to suggest to a journalist that the disabled were paying for crimes in a previous lifetime. The comments came across especially harshly, though it's hard to imagine that Hoddle meant them that way, rather that this was yet another example of his inability to communicate precisely what he meant to say. When he followed that up with a stumbling performance on TV, where he failed to retract or apologize adequately for any offence caused, he was in serious trouble. Over the following few days what little support he had left after the publication of the diaries fell away, notably that of new sponsors Nationwide, who moved quickly to disassociate themselves from Hoddle's views. With a friendly against France to follow a week later, it seemed likely that Wembley would be empty, or that it would contain only those who wanted to hurl abuse at Hoddle. His days were numbered and he resigned before he was pushed. For all that Hoddle might not have been the right man for the job any longer following his catalogue of misjudgements since the qualifier in Rome just over a year earlier, for him to be ousted on a matter like this was disturbing. If we were going to start persecuting people for their personal beliefs, what next? A public burning of Hoddle's diary in Wembley Stadium? Not that far removed from stoking up racism again, is it? If football is going to be responsible for starting ludicrous philosophical witch-hunts of this nature, then the sport is getting too serious.

With a friendly against France in the offing, the FA Technical Director Howard Wilkinson was put in charge of the side, with the suggestion being that he would take the team on through the Euro 2000 competition, especially as all the forerunners were busily putting themselves out of contention. After 90 minutes of Zinedine Zidane, Howard Wilkinson's hopes were finished. France toyed with England and dished out as comprehensive a beating as those administered by Hungary in 1953, West Germany in 1972 or Holland in 1977. If it wasn't for the fact that watching the French side was such a delight, no Englishman could have beared to watch such a débâcle. Exit Howard Wilkinson.

As had been the case in 1996 when Hoddle took the job, the public were united behind Kevin Keegan. Then he was at Newcastle and would not leave; this time he was at Fulham, with similar loyalties to his employer Mohammed Al-Fayed. With the FA in their traditional post-manager torment, they thrashed out a peculiar agreement with Keegan whereby he would manage the England side on a part-time basis through three Euro 2000 qualifiers. Keegan certainly had the best credentials for the job, but the idea of a part-time manager seemed faintly ridiculous.

He got off to a great start with a 3–0 win over Poland at Wembley and it was clear that actually taking the job had kindled his interest to a far greater extent than he had ever imagined it would. Working with the top players in the country and for the national side about which he was always so passionate clearly thrills him. He told *Football 365*, 'I'm very proud to have the chance to manage England and to work with the best players in the country. I'm just like anyone else – I want the best for England and I'm doing my best to make sure they get it. I've been delighted with the way that the managers of the top clubs have responded. I speak to Arsene

Wenger and Alex Ferguson a lot. They've been very helpful with letting me have their players, as well as with advice and support. Gerard Houllier at Liverpool, too. He understands the needs that I have as well, having been manager of a national side himself. He's been very useful to me.'

Clearly the tide was turning against Fulham, and following the 1–1 draw in a friendly in Hungary, Keegan confirmed he wanted to extend his contract beyond the original four games and go on to cover the 2002 World Cup. Apart from the lure of the job, perhaps he also sees it as a chance to redress the balance, after having his England playing career end in such anti-climax. The 1982 World Cup proved to be his swansong, when he managed just 27 minutes of football following injury. Perhaps he sees coaching England as offering him the irresistible opportunity of rewriting history and signing off in the positive manner that is normally associated with Kevin Keegan.

His enthusiasm for the job is understand, for as one of England's most impressive performers of recent times, Sol Campbell, has said, 'I think some of the young players are gaining in experience from the strength of the League – which is better than it's ever been. The younger players tend to come in packs, like David Beckham, Paul Scholes and me, for example . . . things are looking good.' With Keegan at the helm, England will always be a good-looking side, entertaining crowds all over the world. Whether he can deliver the success the nation demands and withstand the inevitable attacks from the media at the slightest provocation is another matter. But Keegan has the job that has looked destined to be his from the day he walked into football management at St James' Park in 1992. And if he wins England the World Cup, we'd love it. Just love it.

7

....

Pride

As the first full century of international football comes towards its close, England can look back on its role in the development of the sport with some satisfaction. In the early days of the century the national side played a pioneering role, taking Association Football around the world. Once established, it was to our shame that we refused to grasp the importance of the World Cup, but having caught up, it has become central to our game. Few nations generate the passion that the sight of the three lions can ignite in England supporters and though there are downsides to that, notably media xenophobia and sporadic outbursts of crowd violence, for the most part, England still manage to adorn tournaments with their presence. Even in France, where things started so unpromisingly off the field, the English support in the fixtures against Colombia and Argentina was magnificent, and the team rose to the occasion, participating in perhaps the most exciting single match of the competition. And while we often denigrate the quality of our team – sometimes fairly – we also underestimate the importance of an English presence to give a degree of legitimacy to tournaments. Much as we would miss the Italians, the Brazilians or, whisper it, the Germans, if they weren't at a World Cup, so the rest of the world feels that England should always be competing, if only because of its historic position in the development of the world game.

Ironically, after the hugely successful France '98 competition, the long-term future of international football has rarely looked so precarious. As European club football in particular falls into the hands of big business, and as the oxymoron that is the Champions League expands to take in as many clubs as it can, the already congested calendar is filled with yet more futile fixtures that leave less and less time for international games. As great a luminary as Franz Beckenbauer has said that time will be called on the World Cup before long, and that national prestige will be fought for solely by club sides, each of which will be a multinational. Much as I hate to contradict the Kaiser, if that day comes, it will be a terrible day for football. Can you see England uniting in its entirety behind Arsenal or Manchester United? And if one of them wins the ultimate prize, this World Club Cup he envisages, could we claim it as an English prize if the triumph were masterminded by Bergkamp, Petit, Anelka, Stam, Yorke or Giggs? The greatness of the World Cup lies in the very fact that, just for a few hours, a whole country is behind one team – though the Manchester United players who have been stupidly vicitimized at Wembley of late might think otherwise. When England play a major international, they can pull in 30 million viewers. Even mighty Manchester United can only attract a fraction of that figure, and a goodly proportion of those are only watching to see them lose. Club football, by its very nature, divides. International football unites.

The England team has played many memorable matches, shared epochal moments with the population, brought us together as fans and as people. How many conversations were struck up between strangers on buses, trains, in pubs and clubs the day after the semi-final in Turin in 1990, the game against Holland in Euro '96 or the Argentina game at France '98? How much of football's history emanates from England games – Banks' save from Pelé, Hurst's hat-trick, Puskas' goal at Wembley in 1953, Gazza's tears in 1990, Owen's goal against Argentina, Maradona's performance in 1986, Moore in Mexico? Those men and those images form an enduring part of football's lexicon, making it obvious that the international scene is a vibrant, even essential part of football's future.

And what of those who are the lucky few, the men who actually get to take part, the men who wear the three lions on the shirt? While we revere a select few – the 1966 immortals, Finney, Matthews, Lineker, Edwards, Wright – a lot of internationals have had a pretty rough ride, drawing grudging praise when they succeed and stinging criticism if they do not produce world-class displays time and again. As football has become a bigger and bigger business and as its most successful exponents have become richer and richer, so the attacks have become more and more vituperative. Maybe that's part of the trade-off. You earn wages beyond the wildest dreams of the ordinary person, so the other side of the Faustian pact is to take your place in the freak show, to have your public and personal life laid bare for scrutiny, to be put under intense pressure to perform at your peak day in, day out. While accepting that they are fallible human beings just as we all are, that they are susceptible to pressures most of us don't understand and that they are often victims of media fabrications, it's hard to have sympathy with, for example, some of the behaviour of the likes of Paul Gascoigne and Teddy Sheringham in the last couple of years. There have been times when they, and others, have let themselves down and have let England down. Those are valid criticisms. But there is one criticism that crops up time and again, one to which we all seem to subscribe after a poor result. It is the suggestion that England players from any era, particularly those from the current day, have no pride in the shirt they are wearing, that they won't run themselves into the ground for their country, that an international is just another game and another way to further their own image, that playing for England means nothing to them. It is an argument that seems to me to be wholly groundless. No one who has contributed to this book was less than thrilled to have represented England. 'It's the ultimate, it has to be,' according to Sir Tom Finney. Of course players have poor games. Some just aren't good enough. But to say that they do not try, or that they do not care, seems to me to be just plain wrong.

But why listen to me? Try Bobby Robson's verdict, the thoughts of a man who was in the England set-up for more than four years as a player, then managed his country for a further eight years, a key figure involved in 115 international matches in two very different eras: 'I was lucky enough to play with people like Tom Finney, Duncan Edwards, Bobby Charlton, Jimmy Greaves – great, great footballers who loved playing for England. Then, over the years, the players I selected, guys like Gary Lineker, Peter Beardsley, Bryan Robson, Paul Gascoigne, Ray Wilkins, Gary Mabbutt, they all felt the same way that we did. There is a great passion about the English players, and in all the eight years that I was in charge, which is a long time, I never met a player who wasn't just absolutely captivated and thrilled by their selection. You do get a lot of rubbish written in the papers about players not caring when they play for England, and I know that upsets the public. The supporters would cut off their arm to get a chance to play for England, but the truth is that the players have that same attitude. It isn't easy to play for England in the spotlight, but they all want that chance. Some are nervous about it, and it takes some four or five internationals under their belt before they feel comfortable, before they can put on the white shirt, stand on the pitch at Wembley and be themselves. Some, like Gascoigne, just take to it. He played his first game as though he'd played fifty times, but others, you know they've got the talent and the character, but the occasion gets to them. But I never found a player who wasn't captivated by it, and that's as it should be.' Amen to that.

Appendix

....

England Fixtures

Date	Opponent	Venue	Score
30 Nov 1872	Scotland	Glasgow	0-0
8 Mar 1873	Scotland	Kennington	4-2
7 Mar 1874	Scotland	Glasgow	1-2
6 Mar 1875	Scotland	Kennington	2-2
4 Mar 1876	Scotland	Glasgow	0-3
3 Mar 1877	Scotland	Kennington	1-3
2 Mar 1878	Scotland	Glasgow	2-7
18 Jan 1879	Wales	Kennington	2-1
5 Apr 1879	Scotland	Kennington	5-4
13 Mar 1880	Scotland	Glasgow	4-5
15 Mar 1880	Wales	Wrexham	3-2
26 Feb 1881	Wales	Blackburn	0-1
12 Mar 1881	Scotland	Kennington	1-6
18 Feb 1882	Ireland	Belfast	13-0
11 Mar 1882	Scotland	Glasgow	1-5
13 Mar 1882	Wales	Wrexham	3-5
3 Feb 1883	Wales	Kennington	5-0
24 Feb 1883	Ireland	Liverpool	7-0
10 Mar 1883	Scotland	Sheffield	2-3
25 Feb 1884	Ireland	Belfast	8-1
15 Mar 1884	Scotland	Glasgow	0-1
17 Mar 1884	Wales	Wrexham	4-0
28 Feb 1885	Ireland	Manchester	4-0
14 Mar 1885	Wales	Blackburn	1-1
21 Mar 1885	Scotland	Kennington	1-1
13 Mar 1886	Ireland	Belfast	6-1
29 Mar 1886	Wales	Wrexham	3-1
31 Mar 1886	Scotland	Glasgow	1-1
5 Feb 1887	Ireland	Sheffield	7-0
26 Feb 1887	Wales	Kennington	4-0
19 Mar 1887	Scotland	Blackburn	2-3
4 Feb 1888	Wales	Crewe	5-1
17 Mar 1888	Scotland	Glasgow	5-0
31 Mar 1888	Ireland	Belfast	5-1
23 Feb 1889	Wales	Stoke	4-1
2 Mar 1889	Ireland	Everton	6-1
13 Apr 1889	Scotland	Kennington	2-3
15 Mar 1890	Ireland	Belfast	9-1
15 Mar 1890	Wales	Wrexham	3-1
5 Apr 1890	Scotland	Glasgow	1-1
7 Mar 1891	Wales	Sunderland	4-1
7 Mar 1891	Ireland	Wolverham'n	6-1
6 Apr 1891	Scotland	Blackburn	2-1
5 Mar 1892	Wales	Wrexham	2-0
5 Mar 1892	Ireland	Belfast	2-0
2 Apr 1892	Scotland	Glasgow	4-1
25 Feb 1893	Ireland	Birmingham	6-1
13 Mar 1893	Wales	Stoke	6-0
1 Apr 1893	Scotland	Richmond	5-2
3 Mar 1894	Ireland	Belfast	2-2
12 Mar 1894	Wales	Wrexham	5-1
7 Apr 1894	Scotland	Glasgow	2-2
9 Mar 1895	Ireland	Derby	9-0
18 Mar 1895	Wales	Kennington	1-1
6 Apr 1895	Scotland	Everton	3-0
7 Mar 1896	Ireland	Belfast	2-0
16 Mar 1896	Wales	Cardiff	9-1
4 Apr 1896	Scotland	Glasgow	1-2

Day	Month	Year	Opponent	Venue	Score
20	Feb	1897	Ireland	Nottingham	6-0
29	Mar	1897	Wales	Sheffield	4-0
3	Apr	1897	Scotland	Crystal Pal.	1-2
5	Mar	1898	Ireland	Belfast	3-2
28	Mar	1898	Wales	Wrexham	3-0
2	Apr	1898	Scotland	Glasgow	3-1
18	Feb	1899	Ireland	Sunderland	13-2
20	Mar	1899	Wales	Bristol	4-0
8	Apr	1899	Scotland	Birmingham	2-1
17	Mar	1900	Ireland	Dublin	2-0
26	Mar	1900	Wales	Cardiff	1-1
7	Apr	1900	Scotland	Glasgow	1-4
9	Mar	1901	Ireland	Southampton	3-0
18	Mar	1901	Wales	Newcastle	6-0
30	Mar	1901	Scotland	Crystal Pal.	2-2
3	Mar	1902	Wales	Wrexham	0-0
22	Mar	1902	Ireland	Belfast	1-0
5	Apr	1902	Scotland	Glasgow	1-1
3	May	1902	Scotland	Birmingham	2-2
14	Feb	1903	Ireland	Wolverham'n	4-0
2	Mar	1903	Wales	Portsmouth	2-0
4	Apr	1903	Scotland	Sheffield	1-2
29	Feb	1904	Wales	Wrexham	2-2
12	Mar	1904	Ireland	Belfast	3-1
9	Apr	1904	Scotland	Glasgow	1-0
25	Feb	1905	Ireland	Middlesbro.	1-1
27	Mar	1905	Wales	Liverpool	3-1
1	Apr	1905	Scotland	Crystal Pal.	1-0
17	Feb	1906	Ireland	Belfast	5-0
19	Mar	1906	Wales	Cardiff	1-0
7	Apr	1906	Scotland	Glasgow	1-2
16	Feb	1907	Ireland	Everton	1-0
18	Mar	1907	Wales	Fulham	1-1
6	Apr	1907	Scotland	Newcastle	1-1
15	Feb	1908	Ireland	Belfast	3-1
16	Mar	1908	Wales	Wrexham	7-1
4	Apr	1908	Scotland	Glasgow	1-1
6	Jun	1908	Austria	Vienna	6-1
8	Jun	1908	Austria	Vienna	11-1
10	Jun	1908	Hungary	Budapest	7-0
13	Jun	1908	Bohemia	Prague	4-0
13	Feb	1909	Ireland	Bradford	4-0
15	Mar	1909	Wales	Nottingham	2-0
3	Apr	1909	Scotland	Crystal Pal.	2-0
29	May	1909	Hungary	Budapest	4-2
31	May	1909	Hungary	Budapest	8-2
1	Jun	1909	Austria	Vienna	8-1
12	Feb	1910	Ireland	Belfast	1-1
14	Mar	1910	Wales	Cardiff	1-0
2	Apr	1910	Scotland	Glasgow	0-2
11	Feb	1911	Ireland	Derby	2-1
13	Mar	1911	Wales	Millwall	3-0
1	Apr	1911	Scotland	Everton	1-1
10	Feb	1912	Ireland	Dublin	6-1
11	Mar	1912	Wales	Wrexham	2-0
23	Mar	1912	Scotland	Glasgow	1-1
15	Feb	1913	Ireland	Belfast	1-2
17	Mar	1913	Wales	Bristol	4-3
5	Apr	1913	Scotland	Chelsea	1-0
14	Feb	1914	Ireland	Middlesbro.	0-3
16	Mar	1914	Wales	Cardiff	2-0
4	Apr	1914	Scotland	Glasgow	1-3
25	Oct	1919	Ireland	Belfast	1-1
15	Mar	1920	Wales	Highbury	1-2
10	Apr	1920	Scotland	Sheffield	5-4
23	Oct	1920	Ireland	Sunderland	2-0
14	Mar	1921	Wales	Cardiff	0-0
9	Apr	1921	Scotland	Glasgow	0-3
21	May	1921	Belgium	Brussels	2-0
22	Oct	1921	N. Ireland	Belfast	1-1
13	Mar	1922	Wales	Liverpool	1-0
8	Apr	1922	Scotland	Villa Park	0-1
21	Oct	1922	N. Ireland	West Brom.	2-0
5	Mar	1922	Wales	Cardiff	2-2
19	Mar	1923	Belgium	Arsenal	6-1
14	Apr	1923	Scotland	Glasgow	2-2
10	May	1923	France	Paris	4-1
21	May	1923	Sweden	Stockholm	4-2
24	May	1923	Sweden	Stockholm	3-1
20	Oct	1923	N. Ireland	Belfast	1-2
1	Nov	1923	Belgium	Antwerp	2-2
3	Mar	1924	Wales	Blackburn	1-2
12	Apr	1924	Scotland	Wembley	1-1
17	May	1924	France	Paris	3-1
22	Oct	1924	N. Ireland	Everton	3-1
8	Dec	1924	Belgium	West Brom.	4-0
28	Feb	1925	Wales	Swansea	2-1

Date	Opponent	Venue	Score
4 Apr 1925	Scotland	Glasgow	0-2
21 May 1925	France	Paris	3-2
24 Oct 1925	N. Ireland	Belfast	0-0
1 Mar 1926	Wales	Crystal Pal.	1-3
17 Apr 1926	Scotland	Manchester	0-1
24 May 1926	Belgium	Antwerp	5-3
20 Oct 1926	N. Ireland	Liverpool	3-3
12 Feb 1927	Wales	Wrexham	3-3
2 Apr 1927	Scotland	Glasgow	2-1
11 May 1927	Belgium	Brussels	9-1
21 May 1927	Luxemb.	Luxemb.	5-2
26 May 1927	France	Paris	6-0
22 Oct 1927	N. Ireland	Belfast	0-2
28 Nov 1927	Wales	Burnley	1-2
31 Mar 1928	Scotland	Wembley	1-5
17 May 1928	France	Paris	5-1
19 May 1928	Belgium	Antwerp	3-1
22 Oct 1928	N. Ireland	Everton	2-1
17 Nov 1928	Wales	Swansea	3-2
13 April 1929	Scotland	Glasgow	0-1
9 May 1929	France	Paris	4-1
11 May 1929	Belgium	Brussels	5-1
15 May 1929	Spain	Madrid	3-4
19 Oct 1929	N. Ireland	Belfast	3-0
9 Nov 1929	Wales	Chelsea	6-0
5 Apr 1930	Scotland	Wembley	5-2
10 May 1930	Germany	Berlin	3-3
14 May 1930	Austria	Vienna	0-0
20 Oct 1930	N. Ireland	Vienna	5-1
22 Nov 1930	Wales	Wrexham	4-0
5 Apr 1931	Scotland	Glasgow	0-2
14 May 1931	France	Paris	2-5
16 May 1931	Belgium	Brussels	4-1
17 Oct 1931	N. Ireland	Belfast	6-2
18 Nov 1931	Wales	Liverpool	3-1
9 Dec 1931	Spain	Highbury	7-1
9 Apr 1932	Scotland	Wembley	3-0
17 Oct 1932	N. Ireland	Blackpool	1-0
16 Nov 1932	Wales	Wrexham	0-0
7 Dec 1932	Austria	Chelsea	4-3
1 Apr 1933	Scotland	Glasgow	1-2
13 May 1933	Italy	Rome	1-1
20 May 1933	Switz.	Bern	4-0
14 Oct 1933	N. Ireland	Belfast	3-0
15 Nov 1933	Wales	Newcastle	1-2
6 Dec 1933	France	Tottenham	4-1
14 Apr 1934	Scotland	Wembley	3-0
10 May 1934	Hungary	Budapest	1-2
16 May 1934	Czechos.	Prague	1-2
29 Sep 1934	Wales	Cardiff	4-0
14 Nov 1934	Italy	Arsenal	3-2
6 Feb 1935	N. Ireland	Everton	2-1
6 Apr 1935	Scotland	Glasgow	0-2
18 May 1935	Holland	Amsterdam	1-0
19 Oct 1935	N. Ireland	Belfast	3-1
4 Dec 1935	Germany	Tottenham	3-0
5 Feb 1936	Wales	Wolverham'n	1-2
4 Apr 1936	Scotland	Wembley	1-1
6 May 1936	Austria	Vienna	1-2
9 May 1936	Belgium	Brussels	2-3
17 Oct 1936	Wales	Cardiff	1-2
18 Nov 1936	N. Ireland	Stoke	3-1
2 Dec 1936	Hungary	Arsenal	6-2
17 Apr 1937	Scotland	Glasgow	1-3
14 May 1937	Norway	Oslo	6-0
17 May 1937	Sweden	Stockholm	4-0
20 May 1937	Finland	Helsinki	8-0
23 Oct 1937	N. Ireland	Belfast	5-1
17 Nov 1937	Wales	Middlesbro.	2-1
1 Dec 1937	Czechos.	Tottenham	5-4
9 Apr 1938	Scotland	Wembley	0-1
14 May 1938	Germany	Berlin	6-3
21 May 1938	Switz.	Zurich	1-2
26 May 1938	France	Paris	4-2
22 Oct 1938	Wales	Cardiff	2-4
9 Nov 1938	Norway	Newcastle	4-0
16 Nov 1938	N. Ireland	Manchester	7-0
15 Apr 1939	Scotland	Glasgow	2-1
13 May 1939	Italy	Milan	2-2
18 May 1939	Yugoslav.	Belgrade	1-2
24 May 1939	Romania	Bucharest	2-0
28 Sep 1946	N. Ireland	Belfast	7-2
30 Sep 1946	Eire	Dublin	1-0
13 Nov 1946	Wales	Manchester	3-0
27 Nov 1946	Holland	Huddersfield	8-2
12 Apr 1947	Scotland	Wembley	1-1
3 May 1947	France	Arsenal	3-0

Date	Opponent	Venue	Score
18 May 1947	Switz.	Zurich	0-1
25 May 1947	Portugal	Lisbon	10-0
21 Sep 1947	Belgium	Brussels	5-2
18 Oct 1947	Wales	Cardiff	3-0
5 Nov 1947	N. Ireland	Everton	2-2
19 Nov 1947	Sweden	Arsenal	4-2
10 Apr 1948	Scotland	Glasgow	2-0
16 May 1948	Italy	Turin	4-0
26 Sep 1948	Denmark	Copenhagen	0-0
9 Oct 1948	N. Ireland	Belfast	6-2
10 Nov 1948	Wales	Villa Park	1-0
2 Dec 1948	Switz.	Arsenal	6-0
9 Apr 1949	Scotland	Wembley	1-3
13 May 1949	Sweden	Stockholm	1-3
18 May 1949	Norway	Oslo	4-1
22 May 1949	France	Paris	3-1
21 Sep 1949	Eire	Everton	0-2
15 Oct 1949	Wales	Cardiff	4-1
16 Nov 1949	N. Ireland	Manchester	9-2
30 Nov 1949	Italy	Tottenham	2-0
15 Apr 1950	Scotland	Glasgow	1-0
14 May 1950	Portugal	Lisbon	5-3
18 May 1950	Belgium	Brussels	4-1
25 Jun 1950	Chile	Rio	2-0
29 Jun 1950	USA	Belo Horiz.	0-1
2 Jul 1950	Spain	Rio	0-1
7 Oct 1950	N. Ireland	Belfast	4-1
15 Nov 1950	Wales	Sunderland	4-2
22 Nov 1950	Yugoslav.	Arsenal	2-2
14 Apr 1951	Scotland	Wembley	2-3
9 May 1951	Argentina	Wembley	2-1
19 May 1951	Portugal	Everton	5-3
3 Oct 1951	France	Arsenal	2-2
20 Oct 1951	Wales	Cardiff	1-1
14 Nov 1951	N. Ireland	Villa Park	2-0
28 Nov 1951	Austria	Wembley	2-2
5 Apr 1952	Scotland	Glasgow	2-1
18 May 1952	Italy	Florence	1-1
25 May 1952	Austria	Vienna	3-2
28 May 1952	Switz.	Zurich	3-0
4 Oct 1952	N. Ireland	Belfast	2-2
12 Nov 1952	Wales	Wembley	5-2
26 Nov 1952	Belgium	Wembley	5-0
18 Apr 1953	Scotland	Wembley	2-2
17 May 1953	Argentina	Buenos Aires	0-0
	(abandoned after 23 minutes)		
24 May 1953	Chile	Santiago	2-1
31 May 1953	Uruguay	Montevideo	1-2
8 Jun 1953	USA	New York	6-3
10 Oct 1953	Wales	Cardiff	4-1
11 Nov 1953	N. Ireland	Everton	3-1
25 Nov 1953	Hungary	Wembley	3-6
3 Apr 1954	Scotland	Glasgow	4-2
16 May 1954	Yugoslav.	Belgrade	0-1
23 May 1954	Hungary	Budapest	1-7
17 Jun 1954	Belgium	Basle	4-4
20 Jun 1954	Switz.	Bern	2-0
26 Jun 1954	Uruguay	Basle	2-4
2 Oct 1954	N. Ireland	Belfast	2-0
10 Nov 1954	Wales	Wembley	3-2
1 Dec 1954	W. Germ.	Wembley	3-1
2 Apr 1955	Scotland	Wembley	7-2
15 May 1955	France	Paris	0-1
18 May 1955	Spain	Madrid	1-1
22 May 1955	Portugal	Oporto	1-3
2 Oct 1955	Denmark	Copenhagen	5-1
22 Oct 1955	Wales	Cardiff	1-2
2 Nov 1955	N. Ireland	Wembley	3-0
30 Nov 1955	Spain	Wembley	4-1
14 Apr 1956	Scotland	Glasgow	1-1
9 May 1956	Brazil	Wembley	4-2
16 May 1956	Sweden	Stockholm	0-0
20 May 1956	Finland	Helsinki	5-1
26 May 1956	W. Germ.	Berlin	3-1
6 Oct 1956	N. Ireland	Belfast	1-1
14 Nov 1956	Wales	Wembley	3-1
28 Nov 1956	Yugoslav.	Belgrade	0-5
5 Dec 1956	Denmark	Wolverham'n	5-2
16 Apr 1957	Scotland	Wembley	2-1
8 May 1957	Eire	Wembley	5-1
15 May 1957	Denmark	Copenhagen	4-1
19 May 1957	Eire	Dublin	1-1
19 Oct 1957	Wales	Cardiff	4-0
6 Nov 1957	N. Ireland	Wembley	2-3
27 Nov 1957	France	Wembley	4-0
19 Apr 1958	Scotland	Glasgow	4-0
7 May 1958	Portugal	Wembley	2-1

Date	Opponent	Venue	Score
11 May 1958	Yugoslav.	Belgrade	0-5
18 May 1958	USSR	Moscow	1-1
8 Jun 1958	**USSR**	**Gothenburg**	**2-2**
11 Jun 1958	**Brazil**	**Gothenburg**	**0-0**
15 Jun 1958	**Austria**	**Boras**	**2-2**
17 Jun 1958	**USSR**	**Gothenburg**	**0-1**
4 Oct 1958	N. Ireland	Belfast	3-3
22 Oct 1958	USSR	Wembley	5-0
26 Nov 1958	Wales	Villa Park	2-2
11 Apr 1959	Scotland	Wembley	1-0
6 May 1959	Italy	Wembley	2-2
13 May 1959	Brazil	Rio	0-2
17 May 1959	Peru	Lima	1-4
24 May 1959	Mexico	Mexico City	1-2
28 May 1959	USA	Los Angeles	8-1
17 Oct 1959	Wales	Cardiff	1-1
28 Oct 1959	Sweden	Wembley	2-3
18 Nov 1959	N. Ireland	Wembley	2-1
19 Apr 1960	Scotland	Glasgow	1-1
11 May 1960	Yugoslav.	Wembley	3-3
15 May 1960	Spain	Madrid	0-3
22 May 1960	Hungary	Budapest	0-2
8 Oct 1960	N. Ireland	Belfast	5-2
19 Oct 1960	**Luxemb.**	**Luxemb.**	**9-0**
26 Oct 1960	Spain	Wembley	4-2
23 Nov 1960	Wales	Wembley	5-1
15 Apr 1961	Scotland	Wembley	9-3
10 May 1961	Mexico	Wembley	8-0
21 May 1961	**Portugal**	**Lisbon**	**1-1**
24 May 1961	Italy	Rome	3-2
27 May 1961	Austria	Vienna	1-3
28 Sep 1961	**Luxemb.**	**Highbury**	**4-1**
14 Oct 1961	Wales	Cardiff	1-1
25 Oct 1961	**Portugal**	**Wembley**	**2-0**
22 Nov 1961	N. Ireland	Wembley	1-1
4 Apr 1962	Austria	Wembley	3-1
14 Apr 1962	Scotland	Glasgow	0-2
9 May 1962	Switz.	Wembley	3-1
20 May 1962	Peru	Lima	4-0
31 May 1962	**Hungary**	**Rancagua**	**1-2**
2 Jun 1962	**Argentina**	**Rancagua**	**3-1**
7 Jun 1962	**Bulgaria**	**Rancagua**	**0-0**
10 Jun 1962	**Brazil**	**Viña del Mar**	**1-3**
3 Oct 1962	France	Hillsborough	1-1
20 Oct 1962	N. Ireland	Belfast	3-1
21 Nov 1962	Wales	Wembley	4-0
27 Feb 1963	France	Paris	2-5
6 Apr 1963	Scotland	Wembley	1-2
8 May 1963	Brazil	Wembley	1-1
29 May 1963	Czechos.	Bratislava	4-2
2 Jun 1963	E. Germ.	Leipzig	2-1
5 Jun 1963	Switz.	Basle	8-1
12 Oct 1963	Wales	Cardiff	4-0
20 Nov 1963	N. Ireland	Wembley	8-3
11 Apr 1964	Scotland	Glasgow	0-1
6 May 1964	Uruguay	Wembley	2-1
17 May 1964	Portugal	Lisbon	4-3
24 May 1964	Eire	Dublin	3-1
27 May 1964	USA	New York	10-0
30 May 1964	Brazil	Rio	1-5
4 Jun 1964	Portugal	São Paolo	1-1
6 Jun 1964	Argentina	Rio	0-1
3 Oct 1964	N. Ireland	Belfast	4-3
21 Oct 1964	Belgium	Wembley	2-2
18 Nov 1964	Wales	Wembley	2-1
9 Dec 1964	Holland	Amsterdam	1-1
10 Apr 1965	Scotland	Wembley	2-2
5 May 1965	Hungary	Wembley	1-0
9 May 1965	Yugoslav.	Belgrade	1-1
12 May 1965	W. Germ.	Nuremberg	1-0
16 May 1965	Sweden	Gothenburg	2-1
2 Oct 1965	Wales	Cardiff	0-0
20 Oct 1965	Austria	Wembley	2-3
10 Nov 1965	N. Ireland	Wembley	2-1
8 Dec 1965	Spain	Madrid	2-0
5 Jan 1966	Poland	Everton	1-1
23 Feb 1966	W. Germ.	Wembley	1-0
2 Apr 1966	Scotland	Glasgow	4-3
4 May 1966	Yugoslav.	Wembley	2-0
26 Jun 1966	Finland	Helsinki	3-0
29 Jun 1966	Norway	Oslo	6-1
3 Jul 1966	Denmark	Copenhagen	2-0
5 Jul 1966	Poland	Chorzow	1-0
11 Jul 1966	**Uruguay**	**Wembley**	**0-0**
16 Jul 1966	**Mexico**	**Wembley**	**2-0**
20 Jul 1966	**France**	**Wembley**	**2-0**
23 Jul 1966	**Argentina**	**Wembley**	**1-0**

Date	Opponent	Venue	Score
26 Jul 1966	Portugal	Wembley	2-1
30 Jul 1966	W. Germ.	Wembley	4-2
20 Oct 1966	N. Ireland	Belfast	2-0
2 Nov 1966	Czechos.	Wembley	0-0
16 Nov 1966	Wales	Wembley	5-1
15 Apr 1967	Scotland	Wembley	2-3
24 May 1967	Spain	Wembley	2-0
27 May 1967	Austria	Vienna	1-0
21 Oct 1967	Wales	Cardiff	3-0
22 Nov 1967	N. Ireland	Wembley	2-0
6 Dec 1967	USSR	Wembley	2-2
24 Feb 1968	Scotland	Glasgow	1-1
3 Apr 1968	Spain	Wembley	1-0
8 May 1968	Spain	Madrid	2-1
22 May 1968	Sweden	Wembley	3-1
1 Jun 1968	W. Germ.	Hanover	0-1
5 Jun 1968	Yugoslav.	Florence	0-1
8 Jun 1968	USSR	Rome	2-0
6 Nov 1968	Romania	Bucharest	0-0
11 Dec 1968	Bulgaria	Wembley	1-1
15 Jan 1969	Romania	Wembley	1-1
12 Mar 1969	France	Wembley	5-0
3 May 1969	N. Ireland	Belfast	3-1
7 May 1969	Wales	Wembley	2-1
10 May 1969	Scotland	Wembley	4-1
1 Jun 1969	Mexico	Mexico City	0-0
8 Jun 1969	Uruguay	Montevideo	2-1
12 Jun 1969	Brazil	Rio	1-2
5 Nov 1969	Holland	Amsterdam	1-0
10 Dec 1969	Portugal	Wembley	1-0
14 Jan 1970	Holland	Wembley	0-0
25 Feb 1970	Belgium	Brussels	3-1
8 Apr 1970	Wales	Cardiff	1-1
21 Apr 1970	N. Ireland	Wembley	3-1
25 Apr 1970	Scotland	Glasgow	0-0
20 May 1970	Colombia	Bogotá	4-0
24 May 1970	Ecuador	Quito	2-0
2 Jun 1970	Romania	Guadalajara	1-0
7 Jun 1970	Brazil	Guadalajara	0-1
11 Jun 1970	Czechos.	Guadalajara	1-0
14 Jun 1970	W. Germ.	Leon	2-3
25 Nov 1970	E. Germ.	Wembley	3-1
3 Feb 1971	Malta	Valletta	1-0
21 Apr 1971	Greece	Wembley	3-0
12 May 1971	Malta	Wembley	5-0
15 May 1971	N. Ireland	Belfast	1-0
19 May 1971	Wales	Wembley	0-0
22 May 1971	Scotland	Wembley	3-1
13 Oct 1971	Switz.	Basle	3-2
10 Nov 1971	Switz.	Wembley	1-1
1 Dec 1971	Greece	Athens	2-0
29 Apr 1972	W. Germ.	Wembley	1-3
13 May 1972	W. Germ.	Berlin	0-0
20 May 1972	Wales	Cardiff	0-0
23 May 1972	N. Ireland	Wembley	0-1
27 May 1972	Scotland	Glasgow	1-0
1 Oct 1972	Yugoslav.	Wembley	1-1
15 Nov 1972	Wales	Cardiff	1-0
24 Jan 1973	Wales	Wembley	1-1
14 Feb 1973	Scotland	Glasgow	5-0
12 May 1973	N. Ireland	Everton	2-1
15 May 1973	Wales	Wembley	3-0
19 May 1973	Scotland	Wembley	1-0
27 May 1973	Czechos.	Prague	1-1
6 Jun 1973	Poland	Chorzow	0-2
10 Jun 1973	USSR	Moscow	2-1
14 Jun 1973	Italy	Turin	0-2
26 Sep 1973	Austria	Wembley	7-0
17 Oct 1973	Poland	Wembley	1-1
14 Nov 1973	Italy	Wembley	0-1
3 Apr 1974	Portugal	Lisbon	0-0
11 May 1974	Wales	Cardiff	2-0
15 May 1974	N. Ireland	Wembley	1-0
18 May 1974	Scotland	Glasgow	0-2
22 May 1974	Argentina	Wembley	2-2
29 May 1974	E. Germ.	Leipzig	1-1
1 Jun 1974	Bulgaria	Sofia	1-0
5 Jun 1974	Yugoslav.	Belgrade	2-2
30 Oct 1974	Czechos.	Wembley	3-0
20 Nov 1974	Portugal	Wembley	0-0
12 Mar 1975	W. Germ.	Wembley	2-0
16 Apr 1975	Cyprus	Wembley	5-0
11 May 1975	Cyprus	Limassol	1-0
17 May 1975	N. Ireland	Belfast	0-0
21 May 1975	Wales	Wembley	2-2
24 May 1975	Scotland	Wembley	5-1
3 Sep 1975	Switz.	Basle	2-1

Date	Opponent	Venue	Score
30 Oct 1975	Czechos.	Bratislava	1-2
19 Nov 1975	Portugal	Lisbon	1-1
24 Mar 1976	Wales	Wrexham	2-1
8 May 1976	Wales	Cardiff	1-0
11 May 1976	N. Ireland	Wembley	4-0
15 May 1976	Scotland	Glasgow	1-2
23 May 1976	Brazil	Los Angeles	0-1
28 May 1976	Italy	New York	3-2
13 Jun 1976	Finland	Helsinki	4-1
8 Sep 1976	Eire	Wembley	1-1
13 Oct 1976	Finland	Wembley	2-1
17 Nov 1976	Italy	Rome	0-2
9 Feb 1977	Holland	Wembley	0-2
30 Mar 1977	Luxemb.	Wembley	5-0
28 May 1977	N. Ireland	Belfast	2-1
31 May 1977	Wales	Wembley	0-1
4 Jun 1977	Scotland	Wembley	1-2
8 Jun 1977	Brazil	Rio	0-0
12 Jun 1977	Argentina	Buenos Aires	1-1
15 Jun 1977	Uruguay	Montevideo	0-0
7 Sep 1977	Switz.	Wembley	0-0
12 Oct 1977	Luxemb.	Luxemb.	2-0
16 Nov 1977	Italy	Wembley	2-0
22 Feb 1978	W. Germ.	Munich	1-2
19 Apr 1978	Brazil	Wembley	1-1
3 May 1978	Wales	Cardiff	3-1
16 May 1978	N. Ireland	Wembley	1-0
20 May 1978	Scotland	Glasgow	1-0
24 May 1978	Hungary	Wembley	4-1
20 Sep 1978	Denmark	Copenhagen	4-3
25 Oct 1978	Eire	Dublin	1-1
29 Nov 1978	Czechos.	Wembley	1-0
7 Feb 1979	N. Ireland	Wembley	4-0
19 May 1979	N. Ireland	Belfast	2-0
23 May 1979	Wales	Wembley	0-0
26 May 1979	Scotland	Wembley	3-1
6 Jun 1979	Bulgaria	Sofia	3-0
10 Jun 1979	Sweden	Stockholm	0-0
13 Jun 1979	Austria	Vienna	3-4
12 Sep 1979	Denmark	Wembley	1-0
17 Oct 1979	N. Ireland	Belfast	5-1
22 Nov 1979	Bulgaria	Wembley	2-0
6 Feb 1980	Eire	Wembley	2-0
26 Mar 1980	Spain	Barcelona	2-0
13 May 1980	Argentina	Wembley	3-1
17 May 1980	Wales	Wrexham	1-4
20 May 1980	N. Ireland	Wembley	1-1
24 May 1980	Scotland	Glasgow	2-0
31 May 1980	Australia	Sydney	2-1
12 Jun 1980	Belgium	Turin	1-1
15 Jun 1980	Italy	Turin	0-1
18 Jun 1980	Spain	Naples	2-1
10 Sep 1980	Norway	Wembley	4-0
15 Oct 1980	Romania	Bucharest	1-2
19 Nov 1980	Switz.	Wembley	2-1
25 Mar 1981	Spain	Wembley	1-2
29 Apr 1981	Romania	Wembley	0-0
12 May 1981	Brazil	Wembley	0-1
20 May 1981	Wales	Wembley	0-0
23 May 1981	Scotland	Wembley	0-1
30 May 1981	Switz.	Basle	1-2
6 Jun 1981	Hungary	Budapest	3-1
9 Sep 1981	Norway	Oslo	1-2
18 Nov 1981	Hungary	Wembley	1-0
23 Feb 1982	N. Ireland	Wembley	4-0
27 Apr 1982	Wales	Cardiff	1-0
25 May 1982	Holland	Wembley	2-0
29 May 1982	Scotland	Glasgow	1-0
2 Jun 1982	Iceland	Reykjavik	2-0
3 Jun 1982	Finland	Helsinki	1-0
16 Jun 1982	France	Bilbao	3-1
20 Jun 1982	Czechos.	Bilbao	2-0
25 Jun 1982	Kuwait	Bilbao	1-0
29 Jun 1982	W. Germ.	Madrid	0-0
5 Jul 1982	Spain	Madrid	0-0
22 Sep 1982	Denmark	Copenhagen	2-2
13 Oct 1982	W. Germ.	Wembley	1-2
17 Nov 1982	Greece	Salonika	3-0
15 Dec 1982	Luxemb.	Wembley	9-0
23 Feb 1983	Wales	Wembley	2-1
30 Mar 1983	Greece	Wembley	0-0
27 Apr 1983	Hungary	Wembley	2-0
28 May 1983	N. Ireland	Belfast	0-0
1 Jun 1983	Scotland	Wembley	2-0
12 Jun 1983	Australia	Sydney	0-0
15 Jun 1983	Australia	Brisbane	1-0
19 Jun 1983	Australia	Melbourne	1-1

Date	Opponent	Venue	Score
21 Sep 1983	Denmark	Wembley	0-1
12 Oct 1983	Hungary	Budapest	3-0
16 Nov 1983	Luxemb.	Luxemb.	4-0
29 Feb 1984	France	Paris	0-2
4 Apr 1984	N. Ireland	Wembley	1-0
2 May 1984	Wales	Wrexham	0-1
26 May 1984	Scotland	Glasgow	1-1
2 Jun 1984	USSR	Wembley	0-2
10 Jun 1984	Brazil	Rio	2-0
13 Jun 1984	Uruguay	Montevideo	0-2
17 Jun 1984	Chile	Santiago	0-0
12 Sep 1984	E. Germ.	Wembley	1-0
17 Oct 1984	Finland	Wembley	5-0
14 Nov 1984	Turkey	Istanbul	8-0
27 Feb 1985	N. Ireland	Belfast	1-0
26 Mar 1985	Eire	Wembley	2-1
1 May 1985	Romania	Bucharest	0-0
22 May 1985	Finland	Helsinki	1-1
25 May 1985	Scotland	Glasgow	0-1
6 Jun 1985	Italy	Mexico City	1-2
9 Jun 1985	Mexico	Mexico City	0-1
12 Jun 1985	W. Germ.	Mexico City	3-0
16 Jun 1985	USA	Los Angeles	5-0
11 Sep 1985	Romania	Wembley	1-1
16 Oct 1985	Turkey	Wembley	5-0
13 Nov 1985	N. Ireland	Wembley	0-0
29 Jan 1986	Egypt	Cairo	4-0
26 Feb 1986	Israel	Tel Aviv	2-1
26 Mar 1986	USSR	Tbilisi	1-0
23 Apr 1986	Scotland	Wembley	2-1
17 May 1986	Mexico	Los Angeles	3-0
24 May 1986	Canada	Vancouver	1-0
3 Jun 1986	Portugal	Monterrey	0-1
6 Jun 1986	Morocco	Monterrey	0-0
11 Jun 1986	Poland	Monterrey	3-0
18 Jun 1986	Paraguay	Monterrey	3-0
22 Jun 1986	Argentina	Mexico City	1-2
10 Sep 1986	Sweden	Stockholm	0-1
15 Oct 1986	N. Ireland	Wembley	3-0
12 Nov 1986	Yugoslav.	Wembley	2-0
18 Feb 1987	Spain	Madrid	4-2
1 Apr 1987	N. Ireland	Belfast	2-0
29 Apr 1987	Turkey	Izmir	0-0
19 May 1987	Brazil	Wembley	1-1
23 May 1987	Scotland	Glasgow	0-0
9 Sep 1987	W. Germ.	Dusseldorf	1-3
14 Oct 1987	Turkey	Wembley	8-0
11 Nov 1987	Yugoslav.	Belgrade	4-1
17 Feb 1988	Israel	Tel Aviv	0-0
23 Mar 1988	Holland	Wembley	2-2
27 Apr 1988	Hungary	Budapest	0-0
21 May 1988	Scotland	Wembley	1-0
24 May 1988	Colombia	Wembley	1-1
28 May 1988	Switz.	Lausanne	1-0
12 Jun 1988	Eire	Stuttgart	0-1
15 Jun 1988	Holland	Dusseldorf	1-3
18 Jun 1988	USSR	Frankfurt	1-3
14 Sep 1988	Denmark	Wembley	1-0
19 Oct 1988	Sweden	Wembley	0-0
16 Nov 1988	Saudi A.	Riyadh	1-1
8 Feb 1989	Greece	Athens	2-1
8 Mar 1989	Albania	Tirana	2-0
26 Apr 1989	Albania	Wembley	5-0
23 May 1989	Chile	Wembley	0-0
27 May 1989	Scotland	Glasgow	2-0
3 Jun 1989	Poland	Wembley	3-0
7 Jun 1989	Denmark	Copenhagen	1-1
6 Sep 1989	Sweden	Stockholm	0-0
11 Oct 1989	Poland	Katowice	0-0
15 Nov 1989	Italy	Wembley	0-0
13 Dec 1989	Yugoslav.	Wembley	2-1
28 Mar 1990	Brazil	Wembley	1-0
25 Apr 1990	Czechos.	Wembley	4-2
15 May 1990	Denmark	Wembley	1-0
22 May 1990	Uruguay	Wembley	1-2
2 Jun 1990	Tunisia	Tunis	1-1
11 Jun 1990	Eire	Cagliari	1-1
16 Jun 1990	Holland	Cagliari	0-0
21 Jun 1990	Egypt	Cagliari	1-0
26 Jun 1990	Belgium	Bologna	1-0
1 Jul 1990	Cameroon	Naples	3-2
4 Jul 1990	W. Germ.	Turin	1-1
	(England lost 4-3 on penalties)		
7 Jul 1990	Italy	Bari	1-2
12 Sep 1990	Hungary	Wembley	1-0
17 Oct 1990	Poland	Wembley	2-0
14 Nov 1990	Eire	Dublin	1-1

Date	Opponent	Venue	Score
6 Feb 1991	Cameroon	Wembley	2-0
27 Mar 1991	Eire	Wembley	1-1
1 May 1991	Turkey	Izmir	1-0
21 May 1991	USSR	Wembley	3-1
25 May 1991	Argentina	Wembley	2-2
1 Jun 1991	Australia	Sydney	1-0
3 Jun 1991	N. Zealand	Auckland	1-0
8 Jun 1991	N. Zealand	Wellington	2-0
12 Jun 1991	Malaysia	Kuala Lump.	4-2
11 Sep 1991	Germany	Wembley	0-1
16 Oct 1991	Turkey	Wembley	1-0
13 Nov 1991	Poland	Poznan	1-1
19 Feb 1992	France	Wembley	2-0
25 Mar 1992	Czechos.	Prague	2-2
29 Apr 1992	CIS	Moscow	2-2
12 May 1992	Hungary	Budapest	1-0
17 May 1992	Brazil	Wembley	1-1
3 Jun 1992	Finland	Helsinki	2-1
11 Jun 1992	Denmark	Malmo	0-0
14 Jun 1992	France	Malmo	0-0
17 Jun 1992	Sweden	Stockholm	1-2
9 Sep 1992	Spain	Santander	0-1
14 Oct 1992	Norway	Wembley	1-1
18 Nov 1992	Turkey	Wembley	4-0
17 Feb 1993	S. Marino	Wembley	6-0
31 Mar 1993	Turkey	Izmir	2-0
28 Apr 1993	Holland	Wembley	2-2
29 May 1993	Poland	Katowice	1-1
2 Jun 1993	Norway	Oslo	0-2
9 Jun 1993	USA	Boston	0-2
13 Jun 1993	Brazil	Washington	1-1
19 Jun 1993	Germany	Detroit	1-2
8 Sep 1993	Poland	Wembley	3-0
13 Oct 1993	Holland	Rotterdam	0-2
17 Nov 1993	S. Marino	Bologna	7-1
9 Mar 1994	Denmark	Wembley	1-0
17 May 1994	Greece	Wembley	5-0
22 May 1994	Norway	Wembley	0-0
7 Sep 1994	USA	Wembley	2-0
12 Oct 1994	Romania	Wembley	1-1
16 Nov 1994	Nigeria	Wembley	1-0
15 Feb 1995	Eire	Dublin	0-1
	(abandoned after 27 minutes)		
29 Mar 1995	Uruguay	Wembley	0-0
3 Jun 1995	Japan	Wembley	2-1
8 Jun 1995	Sweden	Leeds	3-3
11 Jun 1995	Brazil	Wembley	1-3
6 Sep 1995	Colombia	Wembley	0-0
11 Oct 1995	Norway	Oslo	0-0
15 Nov 1995	Switz.	Wembley	3-1
12 Dec 1995	Portugal	Wembley	1-1
27 Mar 1996	Bulgaria	Wembley	1-0
24 Apr 1996	Croatia	Wembley	0-0
18 May 1996	Hungary	Wembley	3-0
23 May 1996	China	Beijing	3-0
8 Jun 1996	Switz.	Wembley	1-1
15 Jun 1996	Scotland	Wembley	2-0
18 Jun 1996	Holland	Wembley	4-1
22 Jun 1996	Spain	Wembley	0-0
	(England won 4-2 on penalties)		
26 Jun 1996	Germany	Wembley	1-1
	(England lost 6-5 on penalties)		
1 Sep 1996	Moldova	Chisnau	3-0
9 Oct 1996	Poland	Wembley	2-1
9 Nov 1996	Georgia	Tblisi	2-0
12 Feb 1997	Italy	Wembley	0-1
29 Mar 1997	Mexico	Wembley	2-0
30 Apr 1997	Georgia	Wembley	2-0
24 May 1997	S. Africa	Old Trafford	2-1
31 May 1997	Poland	Katowice	2-0
4 Jun 1997	Italy	Nantes	2-0
7 Jun 1997	France	Montpellier	1-0
10 Jun 1997	Brazil	Paris	0-1
10 Sep 1997	Moldova	Wembley	4-0
11 Oct 1997	Italy	Rome	0-0
15 Nov 1997	Cameroon	Wembley	2-0
11 Feb 1998	Chile	Wembley	0-2
25 Mar 1998	Switz.	Bern	1-1
22 Apr 1998	Portugal	Wembley	3-0
23 May 1998	Saudi A.	Wembley	0-0
27 May 1998	Morocco	Casablanca	1-0
29 May 1998	Belgium	Casablanca	0-0
	(England lost 4-3 on penalties)		
15 Jun 1998	Tunisia	Marseille	2-0
22 Jun 1998	Romania	Toulouse	1-2
26 Jun 1998	Colombia	Lens	2-0

30 Jun	1998	Argentina	St Etienne	2-2
		(England lost 4-3 on penalties)		
5 Sep	1998	*Sweden*	*Stockholm*	*1-2*
10 Oct	1998	*Bulgaria*	*Wembley*	*0-0*
14 Oct	1998	*Luxemb.*	*Luxemb.*	*3-0*
18 Nov	1998	*Czech Rp.*	*Wembley*	*2-0*
10 Feb	1999	*France*	*Wembley*	*0-2*
27 Mar	1999	*Poland*	*Wembley*	*3-0*
28 Apr	1999	*Hungary*	*Budapest*	*1-1*
5 Jun	1999	*Sweden*	*Wembley*	*0-0*
9 Jun	1999	*Bulgaria*	*Sofia*	*1-1*

Italics – European Championship
Bold – World Cup

Bibliography

BOOKS

Adams, Tony with Ian Ridley, *Addicted* (Collins Willow, 1998)

Agnew, Paul, *Tom Finney: Football Legend* (Carnegie Press, 1989)

Allen, Ronnie, *It's Goals That Count* (Stanley Paul, 1955)

Bastin, Cliff with Brian Glanville, *Cliff Bastin Remembers* (Ettrick Press, 1950)

Bowler, Dave, *Shanks: The Authorised Biography Of Bill Shankly* (Orion, 1996)

Bowler, Dave, *Danny Blanchflower: A Biography Of A Visionary* (Victor Gollancz, 1997)

Bowler, Dave, *Winning Isn't Everything. . . : A Biography of Alf Ramsey* (Victor Gollancz, 1998)

Brooking, Trevor, *Trevor Brooking* (Pelham, 1981)

Buchan, Charles, *A Lifetime in Football* (Phoenix House, 1955)

Carr, Steve, *The Old Uns: Wednesbury Old Athletic* (1994)

Croker, Ted, *The First Voice You Will Hear Is . . .* (Willow, 1987)

Cullis, Stan, *All For the Wolves* (Hart-Davis, 1960)

Edworthy, Niall, *England: The Official FA History* (Virgin, 1997)

Finn, Ralph, *World Cup 1970* (Robert Hale, 1970)

Fry, C.B., *Life Worth Living* (Pavilion, 1986)

Fynn, Alex and Lynton Guest, *For Love or Money?* (Boxtree, 1998)

Gibson, John, *Wor Jackie: The Jackie Milburn Story* (Sportsprint, 1990)

Glanville, Brian, *The Story of The World Cup* (Faber, 1997)

Hapgood, Eddie, *Football Ambassador* (Sporting Handbooks, 1944)

Jackson, Nicholas Lane, *Sporting Days & Sporting Ways* (Hurst & Blackett, 1932)

James, Brian, *England V Scotland* (Pelham, 1969)

Keegan, Kevin with John Roberts, *Kevin Keegan* (Arthur Barker, 1977)

Kirkup, Mike, *Jackie Milburn in Black and White* (Stanley Paul, 1990)

Leatherdale, Clive, *England: The Quest for the World Cup* (Two Heads Publishing, 1994)

Lees, Dr Alan and Ray Kennedy, *Ray of Hope: The Ray Kennedy Story* (Pelham Books, 1993)

Longmore, Andrew, *Viv Anderson* (Heinemann, 1988)

Matthews, Stanley and Mila Matthews, *Back in Touch* (Arthur Barker, 1981)

Miller, David, *Stanley Matthews, The Authorized Biography* (Pavilion, 1989)

Moore, Bobby, *England! England!* (Stanley Paul, 1970)

Mullery, Alan, *Autobiography* (Pelham, 1985)

Murrant, Andrew, *Don Revie: Portrait of a Footballing Enigma* (Mainstream, 1990)

Neal, Phil, *Life at the Kop* (Queen Anne Press, 1986)

Palmer, Mark, *Lost in France* (Fourth Estate, 1998)

Perryman, Steve, *A Man For All Seasons* (Arthur Barker, 1985)

Ramsey, Alf, *Talking Football* (Stanley Paul, 1952)

Reid, Peter with Peter Ball, *Everton Winter, Mexican Summer* (MacDonald Queen Anne Press, 1987)

Robinson, John, *The European Championships 1958–1996* (Soccer Book Publishing, 1996)

Robson, Bobby with Bob Harris, *An Englishman Abroad: My Autobiography* (Macmillan, 1998)

Rollin, Jack (editor), *Rothman's Football Yearbook* (various editions)

Sharpe, Ivan, *Forty Years in Football* (Hutchinson, 1952)

Shearer, Alan with Dave Harrison, *My Story So Far* (Hodder & Stoughton, 1988)

Sheringham, Teddy with Mel Webb, *My Autobiography* (Little, Brown, 1998)

Taylor, Rogan and Andrew Taylor, *Kicking & Screaming* (Robson, 1995)

Venables, Terry, *The Autobiography* (Michael Joseph, 1994)

Wall, Sir Frederick, *Fifty Years of Football* (Cassell, 1935)

Watt, Tom and Kevin Palmer, *Wembley: The Greatest Stage* (Simon & Schuster, 1998)

Wheeler, Kenneth, *Champions of Soccer* (Pelham, 1969)

Wright, Billy, *The World's My Football Pitch* (Arrow, 1956)

Wright, Billy, *Football is My Passport* (Stanley Paul, 1957)

Wright, Ian, *Mr Wright* (Collins Willow, 1996)

AUDIO TAPES

Matthews to Moore 1948–1966: The Golden Age Of Football (BBC)

INTERNET PUBLICATIONS

Matchday Magazine (*www.matchdayusa.com*)
Football 365 (*www.football365.co.uk*)

MAGAZINES

Charles Buchan's Football Monthly
The Footballer
FourFourTwo

Soccer Monthly
Shoot!
Total Football
Total Sport
When Saturday Comes

Index

370